Craft, Industry and Everyday Life: Finds from Anglo-Scandinavian York

By A.J. Mainman and N.S.H. Rogers

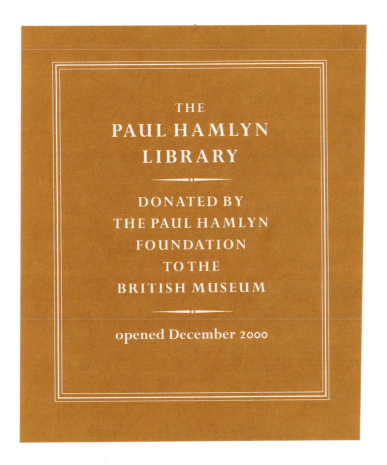

Published for the York Archaeological Trust by the
Council for British Archaeology

2000

Contents

List of Figures

List of Tables

Volume 17 Fascicule 14

Craft, Industry and Everyday Life: Finds from Anglo-Scandinavian York

By A.J. Mainman and N.S.H. Rogers

With contributions by J. Bayley, R. Doonan, G.D. Gaunt, R.A. Hall, M. Hutchinson,
I. Panter, J. Spriggs, M. Stiff and P. Walton Rogers

Keywords: amber, Anglo-Scandinavian, art-styles, craft, dress accessories, glass, industry, jet, jewellery, non-ferrous metalwork, stone, trade, York

Introduction

The vibrant urban centre and focus of population which York became in the Anglo-Scandinavian period provided a fertile ground for the development of a diverse range of crafts. Much of the evidence which underpins this assertion has come from in and around the streets of Coppergate, Piccadilly and High Ousegate, in the area south of the site of the Roman fortress. This focus of Viking Age York has been identified on the basis of discoveries made by antiquaries, collectors and archaeologists for over a century, but has been underlined by excavations undertaken at Coppergate and adjacent streets since 1976. The majority of the evidence presented here is from excavations carried out between 1976 and 1981 at 16–22 Coppergate (Fig.1187, **11**), but much smaller groups of material from the subsequent watching brief on the site (carried out in 1982), and at the adjacent site of 22 Piccadilly (excavated in 1987), are included (Fig.1187, **12**), as well as a few finds from levels below the site of the College of the Vicars Choral at the Bedern (excavated in 1973–80) (Fig.1187, **1**). In addition, an important collection of amber found in the late 19th century near Coppergate, at the Friends' Meeting House, Clifford Street (Waterman 1959), is published here for comparison with the amber from the other sites (Fig.1187, **14**).

The first three published reports on the Coppergate artefacts were presented on a material-by-material basis, and cover the textiles (*AY* 17/5), the pottery (*AY* 16/5) and the iron and ironworking evidence (*AY* 17/6). The next two reports brought together artefacts related to non-ferrous metalworking (*AY* 17/7) and textile production (*AY* 17/11). Changes in English Heritage funding and publication strategy, however, have resulted in the remaining reports, which include bone, antler, ivory and horn (*AY* 17/12), wood and woodworking (*AY* 17/13), leather and leatherworking (*AY* 17/–), medieval finds (*AY* 17/–) and this fascicule, being organised on a different basis. In these five fascicules an attempt is made to divide the evidence into that which relates to craft and industry, and that which illustrates aspects of everyday life. In the case of the larger corpora of evidence such as bone and antler, wood or leather, this is done in reports dealing with a single type or related types of material. This fascicule, however, brings together the smaller groups of material and includes stone, jet, amber, glass, fired clay and non-ferrous metalwork. The materials are presented here thematically according to the evidence for craft and industry, and everyday life.

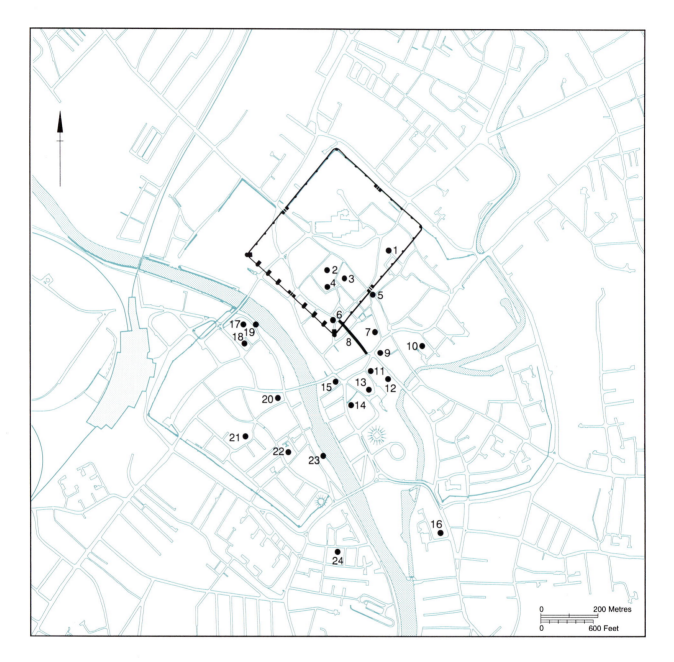

Fig.1187 *Sites in York mentioned in the text*

Key to sites

1	The Bedern	9	6–8 Pavement	17	Wellington Row
2	Coffee Yard	10	Hungate	18	Rougier Street
3	12–18 Swinegate	11	16–22 Coppergate	19	North Street
4	Little Stonegate	12	22 Piccadilly	20	Queen's Hotel, 1–9 Micklegate
5	King's Square	13	St Mary Castlegate	21	St Mary Bishophill Junior
6	1–3 Parliament Street	14	Friends' Meeting House, Clifford Street	22	St Mary Bishophill Senior
7	34 Shambles	15	Nessgate	23	City Mills, Skeldergate
8	Parliament Street sewer trench	16	46–54 Fishergate	24	Clementhorpe

Inevitably there is some overlapping of evidence between these two sections and in some cases it is debatable where the evidence would be best presented. Textile production equipment, for example, is included in the first section as representing a domestic *craft*, while recognising that textile production at this period was essentially an aspect of *everyday life*. The fossils found on the site were presumably gathered for their amuletic properties and curiosity value rather than for use in any production process, and appear, therefore, in the second section. There are other groups within the material types which sit uncomfortably astride this division but an attempt has been made to use cross-referencing to minimise potential confusion.

Thus, in broad outline, the first half of this fascicule deals with evidence related to a range of crafts and industries. Some of the new evidence presented includes artefact groups which were used in industries which have already been discussed in earlier reports. Some of the stone artefacts are, for example, associated with metalworking and these have been grouped together as 'relating to metalworking' with cross-references to the fascicules on the iron and ironworking (*AY* 17/6), and the non-ferrous metalworking (*AY* 17/7). Similarly, other finds relate to textile working, and these sections cross-refer to publications on the textiles (*AY* 17/5) and the textile working evidence (*AY* 17/11). Artefacts published in earlier *AY* 17 fascicules have catalogue numbers lower than *9247*, the first in the sequence of finds to be newly published in this report. Previously published artefacts are included in the catalogue at the end of this report, appearing at the beginning of the relevant material and object type categories. The first section of text also presents new evidence relating to other crafts which have not been described elsewhere. These include the manufacture of personal ornaments, beads, finger-rings, pendants etc. from glass, amber, jet, fired clay and stone.

The second half of this book discusses how the products of these industries were used in everyday life. There is evidence for household equipment, for structures and structural fittings and furnishings, as well as items relating to commerce, games and pastimes, dress accessories and personal ornaments. Reference is made throughout to comparable items made from other materials which are published elsewhere in the series, as well as items from elsewhere in Britain and Europe (Figs.1299–300, pp.2606, 2608).

Some of the copper alloy dress accessories from 16–22 Coppergate have previously been published as possibly Anglian, though Tweddle states (*AY* 7/2, 259) 'some may testify to a conservative artistic streak in the craftsmen of the Viking Age city, rather than to production in the Anglian epoch'.

Other published groups of artefacts and ecofacts from 16–22 Coppergate include the animal bones (*AY* 15/3), biological evidence (*AY* 14/7), the Anglian helmet (*AY* 17/8), and the post-Roman coins (*AY* 18/1). The structures and strata recorded in the Coppergate excavations will be published in *AY* 6, 7, 8 and 10. The Anglo-Scandinavian pottery has been published in *AY* 16/5. Once all the Anglo-Scandinavian structures, artefacts and environmental data have been studied and published, a synthesis of the entire assemblage will be produced.

The report begins with an introduction to the sites from which the material was recovered. This is followed by two small methodological sections; the first describes the conservation treatments carried out on the material, and the second describes the results of a project on the identification of jet and amber.

Several specialists have been involved in the preparation of this report. Except where otherwise stated, sections which deal with glass and non-ferrous items have been written by Nicola Rogers; those dealing with stone, jet and amber have been written by Ailsa Mainman, who also wrote the general introduction and summary.

The material discussed in this report, together with copies of all appropriate records, will be deposited at the Yorkshire Museum, York, under the Museum and YAT accession codes 1976–81.7 (16–22 Coppergate), 1982.22 (Coppergate watching brief), 1987.21 (22 Piccadilly), 1978–80.14.II/IV (Bedern north-east) and 1974–5.13.III/IV (Bedern south-west, long trench). The amber from Clifford Street is part of the Yorkshire Museum's collection, kindly loaned to YAT for comparative research.

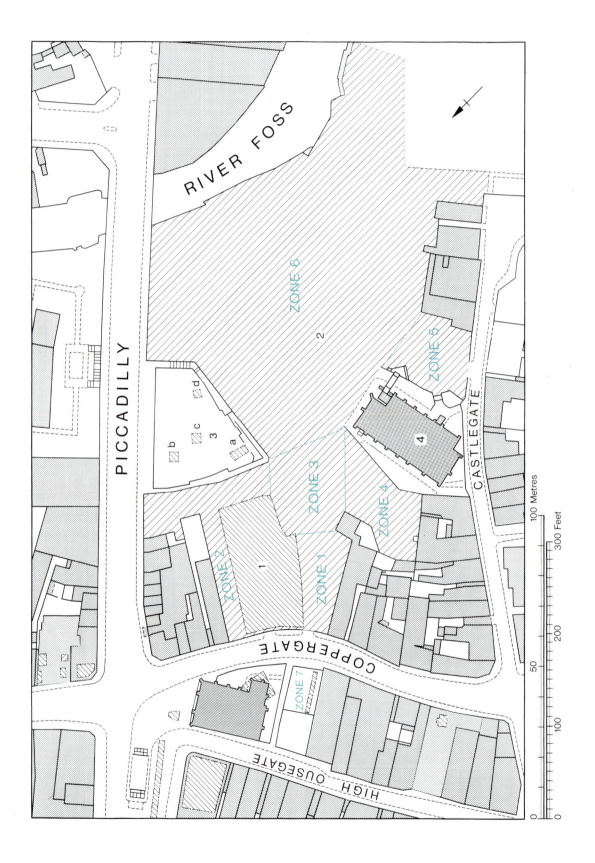

Fig.1188 *Plan showing position of (1) 16–22 Coppergate; (2) area of Watching Brief, zones 1–7 (shown in green); (3) 22 Piccadilly, a–d correspond to Trenches 1–4; and (4) St Mary, Castlegate. (Based on the 1982 Ordnance Survey 1:1250 National Grid Plans. Reproduced from Ordnance Survey mapping on behalf of The Controller of Her Majesty's Stationery Office © Crown Copyright. MC 012225) Scale 1:1250*

Archaeological Introductions to the Sites

Excavation at 16–22 Coppergate

By R.A. Hall

The site and the recovery of evidence

The site of 16–22 Coppergate lies on the spur of land between the Rivers Ouse and Foss. It is bounded to the west by Coppergate, a street leading towards the only bridge across the Ouse in the medieval period, and to the east by the banks of the Foss (Figs.1187, **11**; 1188, **1**).

The excavation took the form of a continuous archaeological campaign of five years and four months during 1976–81. Resources were provided principally by the Ancient Monuments Inspectorate of the Department of the Environment (now English Heritage), the Manpower Services Commission, the British Academy and a host of private individuals and corporations.

The data recovered have been attributed to six broad periods; the evidence presented here relates to the Roman and post-Roman centuries, and in particular the 9th–11th centuries. During this time the site was subdivided into four tenement plots which, in general, were more densely occupied as time passed.

The characteristics of the demolition site that was handed over for investigation, notably the varying extent of modern intrusions, coupled with the logistics of excavation and the continual financial uncertainties, dictated the strategy and tactics employed throughout the excavation process. Anglo-Scandinavian deposits were revealed below modern cellars within a few days of excavation commencing, yet elsewhere on the site later medieval deposits were still being investigated two years later.

During the redevelopment of 1981–3 a continuous watching brief over an extended area, running down to the present edge of the River Foss (Fig.1188, **2**), was maintained under the direction of N.F. Pearson. The results of this exercise are incorporated in the summary given below (pp.2461–2).

Mid 10th century to late medieval deposits were investigated over the entire excavated area, which comprised c.1000m². Owing to a shortage of funding, the earliest levels, dating from the Roman period to the early/mid 10th century (i.e. up to and including what is described below as Period 4A), were not examined right across the c.1000m² open in the subsequent levels. Instead, a strip measuring approximately 20 × 7·5m across the Coppergate street-frontage and a contiguous strip up to 12m wide and 37m long, running down the southern half of the site towards the River Foss, were excavated to natural soils (Fig.1189).

Layers attributable to Periods 1 and 3 were recorded throughout these strips. A well-defined Period 2 horizon existed only in the street-frontage strip; elsewhere, because of stratigraphic interruptions and an overall thinning of these earlier layers as they ran eastwards from the street-frontage, Period 2 contexts could not be isolated with certainty. Therefore, although some deposition of soil must have taken place throughout Period 2, remains of this period are shown as of limited extent. Similarly, the Period 4A horizon, while extending right across the frontage, could not be traced convincingly down the southern strip beyond a point where diagnostic features petered out. It is thus conceivable that a small amount of soil build-up which took place during Period 4A on that part of the southern strip to the east of the limit of identifiable 4A features has been subsumed into Period 4B, which was investigated over the entire excavated area.

For reasons outlined below (p.2460), the deposits designated as Period 5A were limited in extent to the front part of the site. Deposits of Period 5B were traced across the entire area excavated. Deposits of Period 5Cf and 5Cr were limited to the front- and rear-most portions of the excavation respectively, and no contemporary levels could be isolated stratigraphically in the central part of the excavation. Layers of Period 6, a designation that encompasses all deposits of the Anglo-Norman to post-medieval/early modern eras, covered the entire excavated area except where removed by more recent disturbances. Structures which could be attributed to Period 6 were

Table 223 Summary of archaeological development at 16–22 Coppergate

Period	Date	Characteristics
1	late 1st–late 4th century or later	Roman timber and stone buildings; late Roman cemetery. Limited survival of organic materials
2	5th–mid 9th century	Apparent desertion. Homogeneous loamy deposits which did not preserve organic materials
3	mid 9th–late 9th/early 10th century	Rubbish disposal, suggesting occupation close by. Post/stake and wattle alignments, possibly boundaries. Organic materials preserved only in pit cuts
4A	late 9th/early 10th century–c.930/5	Realignment of boundaries, suggesting that Coppergate was laid out by this period. Possible buildings at Coppergate frontage. Organic materials preserved mainly in pit cuts
4B	c.930/5–c.975	Four tenements distinguishable, with post and wattle buildings at Coppergate frontage. Evidence for iron-working and other trades on a commercial scale. Organic-rich deposits nearer to Coppergate; organic content thinning to zero towards River Foss
5A	c.975	Near Coppergate frontage only. Layers between structures of Periods 4B and 5B; probably mixture of occupation deposits, dump deposits and soil from 5B semi-basements
5B	c.975–early/mid 11th century	Perpetuation of boundaries. Introduction of sunken-featured structures in double row at street frontage. Organic-rich deposits as in Period 4B
5Cf	mid–later 11th century	Organic-rich deposits at street frontage, associated with buildings which survive only in Tenement D
5Cr	mid–later 11th century	Post-built structure closest to River Foss sealed by earliest in a succession of dump deposits. Little organic material surviving
6	later 11th–16th century	No remains surviving at street frontage, but area to rear increasingly built up above later dump deposits. New methods of building and rubbish disposal, leading to reduction in organic content of deposits

not in evidence at the modern street-frontage, but structures were found across the rest of the excavated area. Survival of these remains was affected in places by modern (19th and 20th century) disturbances, particularly those related to the occupancy of part of the site by Cravens, the Victorian and later sweet factory.

These variations in the size of area excavated must be borne in mind in any chronological or quantitative analysis of the artefactual evidence.

Site history and a summary (Fig.1189)

The earliest occupation on the site, designated Period 1 (Table 223) was in the Roman era. At that time the legionary fortress lay 160m to the north-west; the immediate vicinity was certainly occupied by temples, and it probably also contained a variety of commercial establishments. Evidence for Roman buildings constructed of both timber and stone was recovered, but the functions of these structures could not be deduced. The site also contained a small late

Roman cemetery. The admixtures of silt, clay and loam which characterised soil conditions associated with Period 1 did not permit the survival of any organic-based artefacts except the very fragmentary remains of some wooden coffins and items made of osseous material.

At the present stage of research there seems no reason to suppose that Romano-British activity continued here beyond the conventional date of c.400 or shortly after, and from then until the mid 9th century the site seems to have been unoccupied (Period 2). This period was marked stratigraphically by the accumulation of up to 1m of grey silty clay loam soils; there was no evidence for structures, domestic or otherwise. All of the pottery in these layers was Roman with the exception of a small quantity of Anglo-Scandinavian sherds which are believed to be intrusive; the contexts from which they were recovered were adjacent either to upstanding baulks incorporating later material, or to later, down-cutting features which may have been the source of obviously later sherds. Although, once again, soil conditions would not have preserved organic-based artefacts other than those made of osseous material, the dearth of other, more durable, artefactual evidence for contemporary activity indicated that this absence reflects accurately the site's apparent desertion at this time. A later 8th century helmet, found only 9m beyond the excavation's perimeter during construction work in 1982, lay within a wood-lined shaft. This was, perhaps, a mid–late Anglian well, and may possibly relate to a contemporary settlement nucleus, either on the ridge now represented by Nessgate/Castlegate, and/or around what may be an early ecclesiastical foundation at St Mary, Castlegate (Fig.1188, 4). The final backfilling of the shaft is dated to the Anglo-Scandinavian period on the basis of a characteristic suite of accompanying palaeobiological remains (AY 17/8, 870–81).

Above the clean grey loams which mark the four and a half centuries interpreted as Anglian desertion of the site, a band of dirtier grey silty clay loams was recognised, and into this was cut a series of features. One of the earliest of these features was a sequence of hearth/oven/kiln bases represented by a horizontal setting of re-used Roman tiles, perhaps used in glassworking. An archaeomagnetic determination of 860 ± 20 was obtained from these features. This is the single most precise indication of the date when renewed use of the site (Period 3) began, although it allows no more than the approximation of mid/late 9th century. It is not possible to determine whether a date of c.840, c.860 or c.880 is more likely, and therefore impossible to relate the inception of the period with conviction to either a definitely pre-Viking (i.e. pre-866) or post-Viking date. It does seem, however, that the assemblage of Anglian pottery from the site (just under 200 sherds) is best seen as in a direct typological and thus chronological succession with that from the Anglian occupation site at 46–54 Fishergate (Fig.1187, 16; AY 7/1; AY 16/6, 650–1) where occupation is thought to have ceased in the mid 9th century.

Apart from one porcupine sceat of c.720–40, found in an 11th century layer at the river end of the site, all nine of the other identifiable Anglian coins from the site are of 9th century date (four of Eanred c.810–41; five of Æthelred II 841–4, 844–8: AY 18/1, 51–3). All were found in contexts stratigraphically later than that with the archaeomagnetic determination of 860 ± 20. Such coins were certainly available for hoarding in the reign of Osberht, the last pre-Viking king of Northumbria, and they occur in coin hoards found in York which may be interpreted as a response to the Viking attack of 866. Such coins might even have continued in use in York until Viking kings began minting coins c.895.

The writer interprets this evidence as indicating that activity and settlement in this area, on anything but an occasional and sporadic basis, recommenced in the middle of the 9th century. There is no stratigraphic or artefactual evidence such as the stratified 8th century sceattas from 46–54 Fishergate (AY 7/1, 17) to indicate that there was protracted Anglian activity before that time.

Other features in this period included several pits containing domestic debris, and some pits also contained human skeletal remains. The latest features of this period were a series of post-holes, some apparently forming alignments at an angle to the later tenement lines, and an accompanying cobble spread at the south-west of the area. It is conceivable that these features represent the remains of a building, although this is not certain. This entire horizon, Period 3, is tentatively dated c.850–900 on the basis of a combination of archaeomagnetic and numismatic

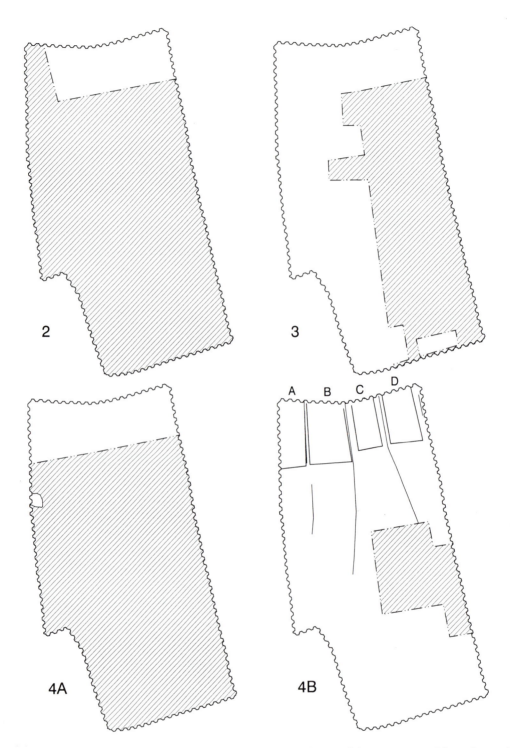

Fig.1189 *(above and facing) Plans of the site at 16–22 Coppergate showing the area of deposits excavated for each period (Periods 2–5). The variation is due either to restricted excavation or to the limited occurrence or survival of the relevant deposit. Scale 1:500*

evidence; in later periods, dendrochronological data provide a greater level of chronological precision.

Sealing the post-holes, cobble spread and other features of Period 3 were deposits into which wattle alignments were inserted. These anticipated the alignment of the subsequent tenements and structures, but do not themselves form obviously coherent structures. The alignments and both their underlying and associated layers and features are

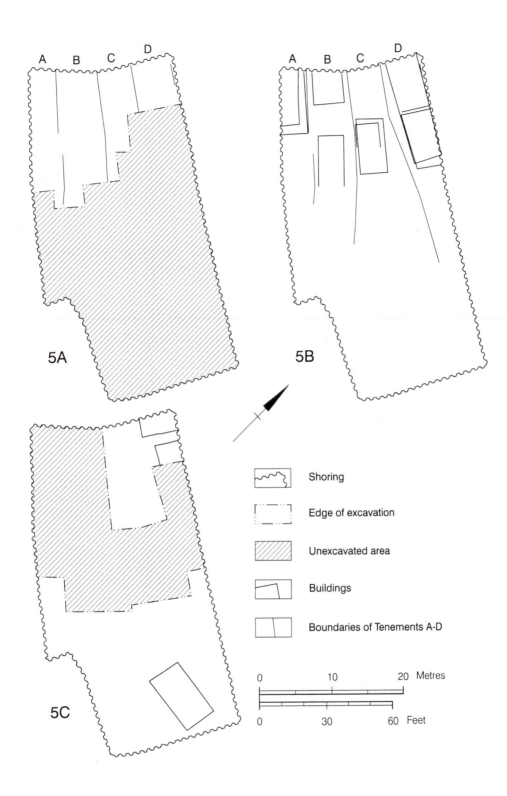

5A

5B

5C

Shoring

Edge of excavation

Unexcavated area

Buildings

Boundaries of Tenements A-D

0   10   20   Metres

0   30   60   Feet

assigned to Period 4A and dated c.900–930/5. Dark grey, silty clay loams, very similar to those of Period 3, were characteristic of the layers of this period but differentiated by the inclusion of patches of grey clay, brown ash, scatters of charcoal and occasional very small fragments and slivers of wood. These conditions, like those of Period 3, were not particularly conducive to the survival of organic artefacts.

The next phase on the site, Period 4B, is marked by the division of the area into four tenements, designated A–D (Fig.1189), and if the street Coppergate was not in being before it must have been laid out at this time. The tenements were defined by wattle fences, whose lines fluctuated only very slightly over the succeeding millennium; towards the River Foss end of the site, however, there was no trace of any continuation of the fences discovered nearer to Coppergate. Whether this should be attributed to the nature of the soil conditions in this area, or whether tenement divisions never extended this far, is not clear. Each tenement contained buildings of post-and-wattle construction, positioned with their gable-ends facing the street. All had been truncated towards their front by the subsequent widening of Coppergate; the greatest surviving length was 6·8m, and they averaged 4·4m in width. The buildings on Tenements A and B had been substantially disturbed by the digging of semi-basements for the Period 5B buildings, but those on Tenements C and D were very largely intact. The buildings had to be repaired or replaced frequently, for they were vulnerable to fire as well as to natural decay, but successive refurbishments varied little in their dimensions and position. Hearths were found on the long axes of the buildings in Tenements B, C and D; any trace in A was destroyed by later intrusion, and even in B only vestiges remained. In C and D the hearths measured up to 2·4 × 1·3m and consisted of a clay base, sometimes resting on a stone slab underpinning, and surrounded by a revetment of horizontal timbers, limestone rubble or re-used Roman tiles. Discolouration of the clay base by burning was quite restricted, and the large size of the hearth appears to reflect a desire for a margin of safety for embers rather than the size of the fire itself.

Only one rank of buildings stood in each tenement and their lengthy backyards were not built up but used for rubbish disposal and other ancillary functions. Although sometimes difficult to differentiate, a sequence of superimposed floor levels built up by gradual accumulation within each building. Their accompanying artefacts allow the activities within each tenement to be followed with varying degrees of assurance. Metalworking seems to have been the predominant activity, with the manufacture of items in iron, copper alloy, lead alloy, silver and gold. A notable feature was the quantity of crucibles recovered, with their important corroborative evidence for the range and variety of metalworking techniques (AY 17/6; AY 17/7). Occupation was evidently intensive, generating organic-rich occupation deposits which accumulated rapidly, in particular in and around the buildings, and which accounted for a continual rise in ground level. Deposits which were rich in organic remains extended to approximately half-way down the excavated area in the direction of the River Foss. From this point their organic component lessened until, in the south-eastern quarter of the excavation, furthest from the Coppergate street-frontage, organic materials other than bone and antler did not survive except in the fills of pits and other cuts.

In the later 10th century the remains of the latest phase of post-and-wattle structures at the street-frontage were covered to a depth of up to 1m. This horizon, which was not traced in the yard areas behind the buildings, is interpreted partly as occupation deposits, partly the upcast from digging out the sunken structures of Period 5B, and partly as a deliberate dump of make-up or levelling material. Some of it thus accumulated very quickly, probably within a period of weeks or months, and contained a mixture of material of c.975 and before.

The dating of Period 5A is assisted by the dendrochronological analysis of timbers from the immediately succeeding plank-built semi-basement structures of Period 5B. These were erected at the Coppergate end of each tenement, sometimes in two closely spaced ranks; as in Period 4B, organic-rich deposits were concentrated in the vicinity of these buildings, and the organic content of the deposits decreased towards the river. As in the buildings of Period 4B, successive layers and lenses of silty loam usually characterised the superimposed floors. Manufacturing continued at this period, although new trades were practised. On Tenement D sufficient overlying stratification remained undisturbed to show that the latest of the Period 5B sunken buildings was eventually replaced by structures built at ground level. The chronology of these subsequent buildings is imprecise: they can be assigned only approximately to the mid 11th century. They and their associated stratification are designated as belonging to Period 5Cf. A series of approximately contemporary mid 11th century levels was also identified at the rear of the site, associated with and sealing a post-built structure, the latest timber of which has been dated through dendrochronology to 1018–58 (*AY* 8/4 in prep.). These levels, which did not preserve their organic component, are designated Period 5Cr. They were themselves covered by a series of dumps of very dark grey silty clay loam interleaved with evidence for sporadic activity, and dated to the Norman period.

Within the Anglo-Scandinavian stratification there is clear evidence from coins and pottery for the displacement of objects from the context in which they were originally deposited and their redeposition in later, often appreciably later, layers. The principal mechanism of this movement was the cutting of pits, wells and the like, and, more particularly, the digging out of the sunken element in the Period 5B buildings, which penetrated earlier levels and redistributed the soil removed from them. In the case of the precisely dated coins it can be seen that, in the Anglo-Scandinavian levels, coins sometimes occur in contexts dated 75–100 years later than their striking (*AY* 18/1, 24), although their wear patterns do not suggest circulation for this length of time and there is no evidence that they were hoarded. Less precisely, but none the less clearly, study of the pottery from Anglo-Scandinavian levels has shown, for example, that sherds both of Roman wares and also of handmade middle Saxon type which are unlikely to have been produced after c.850–900 are found residually throughout the era, another testimony to the redistribution of earlier material (*AY* 16/5, fig.144).

Period 6 incorporates all later activity on the site, most of it datable to c.1100–1500.

The Watching Brief

By N.F. Pearson

The Coppergate watching brief embraced the whole of the 2·02 ha area of the Coppergate Shopping Centre redevelopment from the Castlegate frontage in the west to Piccadilly at the east. Observations were also made in the areas of 16–22 Coppergate not explored during the main excavation campaign, that is, strips to the west, east, and south of the open area (Fig.1188, **2**). A watch was also kept at 14 Coppergate, where the rear of the property was redeveloped in 1984 only after the construction of the rest of the shopping centre had been completed. Recording also took place to the rear of the former Market Tavern,

24 Coppergate, where a medieval building on the Coppergate street-frontage was refurbished as part of the development.

Observation and recording was carried out in often adverse conditions during ground preparation and building works undertaken by Wimpey Construction plc. The ground preparation works were undertaken largely by machine, under archaeological supervision. Where significant archaeological deposits were disturbed, work was suspended to allow recording, or, where appropriate, small-scale excavation. To facilitate recording the redevelopment area was split into discrete zones.

The main archaeological discoveries for the watching brief can be summarised as follows.

The principal Roman features encountered included the fragmentary remains of a largely robbed-out stone building recorded between the Coppergate excavation and 14 Coppergate (Zone 1). This has tentatively been interpreted as a warehouse, on the basis of its proximity to the River Foss. In the helmet pit area (Zone 3), four pits were excavated in addition to a linear feature. In the Fossbank area (Zone 6), a red gritstone wall was observed briefly during machine clearance. It was well constructed with individual blocks measuring 0·8 × 0·6 × 0·4m. No other associated material was seen and although it was clearly structural in nature its north-east/south-west alignment precludes it from being interpreted as a river wall. The only feature from the site which may be attributable to the Anglian period is the pit containing the Coppergate helmet.

From the Anglo-Scandinavian period, the west wall of Structure 5/1 (Period 5B), which had already been excavated during the main excavation, was uncovered in the area between the Coppergate excavation and 14 Coppergate (Zone 1). Associated tenement boundaries and pits were also recorded. Between the Coppergate excavation and the Market Tavern public house (Zone 2), further well-preserved timber buildings and associated features, attributed to Periods 4B and 5B, were recorded.

The recorded medieval Period 6 features included structural remains, fence lines, riverside reclamation, the outer defences of York castle, and parts of the cemetery of All Saints, Pavement. From the post-medieval and early modern periods the most significant discoveries were part of the cemetery of St Mary, Castlegate (Fig.1188, **4**), traces of the canalisation of the River Foss, and part of the footings for the Victorian prison in the Castle Yard.

Excavation at 22 Piccadilly

By R. Finlayson

When the site of the ABC Cinema at 22 Piccadilly was to be developed an excavation was carried out in 1987 to examine, in four trenches, some of the material which would be destroyed by the new development (Fig.1188, **3**). The excavation lay to the south-east of the tenements excavated on Coppergate, in an area between them and the River Foss. From these limited areas of excavation some interpretation of the changes in topography and depositional regimes relating to the River Foss could be made. Trench 4 was within the course of the River Foss prior to its canalisation in or after 1793. A steeply sloping bank of natural sandy clay in Trench 3 is likely to have been a part of the riverbank. Trenches 1 and 2 were located to the west of this bank and demonstrated intensive occupation of the area from the 1st century to the 16th century; later deposits had been truncated by the foundation of the ABC Cinema (Table 224). Many of the deposits were dumps and build-up material containing domestic and industrial waste which provided important information about craft activities, the utilisation of resources, diet and living conditions.

Roman activity comprised what was probably a drainage ditch, aligned at right-angles to the modern day River Foss. The cut silted up and filled with a variety of material c.AD 280 (*AY* 16/8).

Table 224 Summary of archaeological development at 22 Piccadilly

Period	Date	Description
Natural		Sandy clay
1	Roman	Riverine deposition, drainage ditch at right angles to the Foss, silting of ditch and dumping
2	9th century	Small pit and fill, riverine deposition, fence parallel to the Foss, dump and build-up material, two fence lines at right angles to each other, peaty and silty clay build-up and dump
3	10th century	Riverine deposition, silty clay, organic build-up and dump, timber revetment of river bank, silty clay, organic build-up and dump
4.1	975–early/mid 11th century	U-shaped timber revetment and wattle fence on river bank, silty clay and organic build-up and dump, fence
4.2	later 11th century	Renewal of intersecting fences, organic build-up and dumped large sawn timbers, timber revetment of river bank, silty clay build-up and dump
4.3	mid–late 12th century	Riverine deposition, compact peat build-up, small pit cuts, river bank timber revetment, silty clay build-up and dump, clay levelling on river bank
5.1	13th century	Pit cut with organic fill, drainage channel, soak-away?, peaty build-up, levelling
5.2	early–mid 14th century	Clay and peaty build-up and dump, rubbish pits
6	15th–early 16th century	Drainage? cut, organic build-up and dump, pit cut, barrel-lined well
7	15th century–modern	Levelling, concrete

During the 9th–12th centuries there were a series of attempts to make the area close to the Foss usable. Periods when the area was in use and timber features were built were interspersed with periods when activity declined. Flood deposition, the decay of vegetation and the dumping of domestic and industrial waste material all resulted in an accumulation of deposits. Particular evidence was found of the glass industry, small pelt preparation, horn and antler-working, and butchery on a commercial as well as a domestic scale.

The first timber feature in Trench 1 was a fence parallel to the present course of the River Foss. This fence was no longer in use when a dump and build-up of organic material (1058) covered the whole area. Environmental evidence suggests the area was wet grassland, and associated pottery is consonant with a 9th century date.

A further series of fences (1040 and 1059) was constructed with two elements aligned parallel to the River Foss, and an alignment intersecting them at right-angles. Pottery in associated dump and build-up deposits also dates from the first half of the 9th century.

In Trench 3 there were indications of an attempt at revetment to try to prevent soils slumping towards the sloping bank in the second half of the 10th century. A second phase of constructional activity in Trench 3 is represented by wattle which broadly followed the contour of the land, forming an open U shape. A similar U-shaped construction was found on the south-west bank of the River Ouse at North Street (YAT 1993.1; Fig.1187, 19), and also dated to the 11th century.

In Trench 2 timber fences and revetments indicate that some land management and manipulation of the course of the River Foss is likely to have taken place during the late 10th–early 11th century. There was evidence for the natural accumulation of material, for a deliberate raising of the ground surface, for fences and for possible revetments, but there was evidently continued periodic waterlogging of the area. Dumped material included concentrations of smashed crucibles with glass making waste, a number of glass beads and antler waste (3079).

A broadly similar series of activities and structures was continued into the later 11th century.

Glass beads, numerous worked goat horncores, antler waste, two bone skates, an increased amount of crucible waste, and a dump of large sawn timbers were recovered from this material and reflect the continuation and range of craft activity. A series of revetment timbers found closer to the river in Trench 3, and a fence line in Trench 1, both dated to the same period.

In the 12th century the area continued to be used for the disposal of rubbish and debris although glass industry waste ceases to appear. However, the soil now included a higher proportion of inorganic material, including demolition debris, although peaty deposits also continued to accumulate.

The area continued to be used for the disposal of domestic and industrial waste throughout the medieval period, with some evidence for drainage in the form of cuts and a large soakaway. The latest significant feature found on the site was a cask-lined well dating to the 15th or 16th century. Later deposits had been truncated by the foundations of the ABC Cinema.

Excavations at the College of the Vicars Choral at The Bedern

By R.A. Hall

The Bedern, an area of notorious slums in the 19th century, lies c.105m south-east of York Minster (Fig.1187, 1). The name survived into the 1970s as that of a minor street, formerly a cul-de-sac, approached through a medieval gatehouse fronting on to Goodramgate, and giving access to the obvious remains of Bedern Chapel and the considerably less obvious traces of a medieval stone and timber hall. These three structures were the only survivals from the College of the Vicars Choral of York Minster. The college was established in 1252. The office of Vicar Choral derived from the obligation upon absentee canons to appoint personal deputies to take their place in the choir of York Minster. Throughout the 14th century the college housed 36 vicars but it began to decline from the end of the 15th century. In 1574 the vicars ceased to dine in common, although the college was not formally dissolved until 1936.

In 1968 Lord Esher, in his study, recommended that the existing light industrial usage of the area be

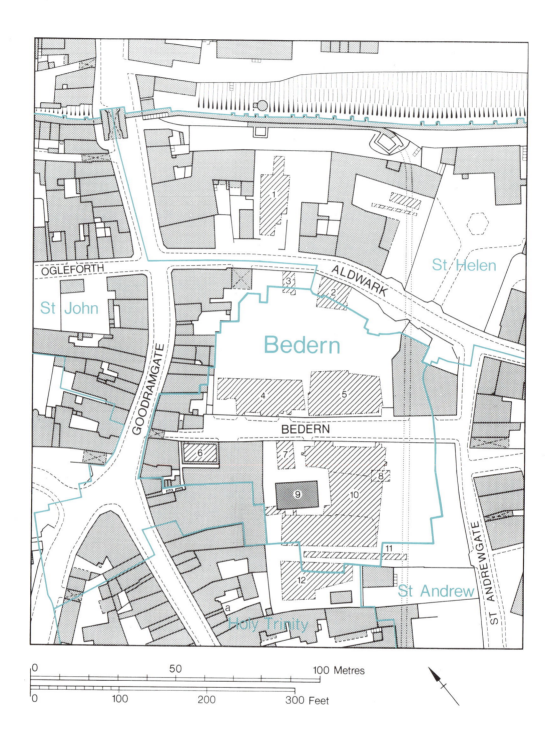

Fig.1190 *Plan showing the location of excavations, and building recording, in the Bedern area. The outline of the parish boundaries (in green) defining the precinct of the College of the Vicars Choral is based on the 1852 Ordnance Survey map. (1) 1–5 Aldwark, 1976–7.15; (2) 2 Aldwark, 1978–80.14.III; (3) Cellar, 1976.14.I; (4) Bedern north-east, 1978–9.14.II; (5) Bedern north-east, 1979–80.14.IV; (6) Bedern chapel, 1980.20.I/II/III; (7) Cellar, 1976.13.V; (8) Cellar, 1976.13.VI; (9) Bedern hall, 1980.13.XV; (10) Bedern south-west, 1976–9.13.X; (11) Bedern long trench, 1973–5.13.III/IV; (12) Bedern foundry, 1973–6.13.I/II. (Based upon the 1982 Ordnance Survey 1:1250 National Grid Plans. Reproduced from Ordnance Survey mapping on behalf of The Controller of Her Majesty's Stationery Office © Crown Copyright. MC 012225)*

replaced by housing. York City Council subsequently purchased land in The Bedern and promulgated redevelopment of the vicinity. It was this which prompted the initiation by York Archaeological Trust of a campaign of excavations which eventually lasted from 1973 to 1980.

The largest portion of available resources and effort was devoted to the precinct of the College of the Vicars Choral, as defined on the 1852 Ordnance Survey map of York (Fig.1190). In total, an area of 2,500m² was investigated, representing about 30% of the estimated college precinct at its maximum extent. Modern deposits were usually machined off; excavation by hand then continued to a fairly uniform depth of 1·5m below the modern ground surface. This self-imposed limit was designed to allow the recording of all deposits which would be destroyed by the redevelopment campaign. Fortuitously, this depth of strata encompassed all archaeological remains from the 13th century onwards and thus included the entire span of the archaeological record for the structures and deposits associated with the College of the Vicars Choral. Quantities of earlier, residual material brought to the later medieval or post-medieval ground surface by pit-digging and other intrusions included a small number of Anglo-Scandinavian artefacts which are reported here. Virtually all material was recovered by hand, the excavation pre-dating the introduction of routine riddling/sieving on York sites.

The total depth of stratification hereabouts, and the nature of Roman–early Norman occupation and activity, was tested in excavations of a long trench, and beneath some modern cellars (*AY* 3/3; *AY* 14/5). The upper levels of the long trench contained a sequence of deposits and structures which can often be firmly linked either with those in the area to the north-east occupied by the Vicars Choral or those to the south-west in the area occupied by a foundry (*AY* 10/3). Clay-loam layers dating to the 11th and 12th centuries were seen, however, only in the long trench.

Table 225 Summary of phasing at sites within the College of the Vicars Choral at the Bedern (including Bedern long trench, Bedern south-west and Bedern north-east)

Note: Periods 6–8 have been sub-divided into phases as follows: Period 6, Phases 1–3; Period 7, Phases 1–4; Period 8, Phases 1–3

Period	Date
Period 0	Roman
Period 1A	11th–12th century (applies only to the long trench)
Period 1	early–mid 13th century
Period 2	mid–late 13th century
Period 3	mid–late 13th century
Period 4	late 13th century
Period 5	early 14th century
Period 6	mid–late 14th century
Period 7	late 14th–early 15th century
Period 8	mid 15th–early 17th century
Period 9	mid 17th century onwards

Here too was evidence for the robbing of the Roman fortress wall in the 12th century, and for a series of pits, clay floors and other features indicating 12th century occupation (Period 1A) (see Table 225).

Bedern Foundry has been published in *AY* 10/3. Roman occupation in The Bedern has been discussed in *AY* 3/3. The coins have been published in *AY* 18/1; the pottery will be published in AY 16. The structural report for the site will be published in *AY* 10/5 in prep. The considerable number of re-used architectural fragments recovered from the exavations have been published in *AY* 10/4. Historical research on the tenemental history of the Bedern area will be published in *AY* 20.

The Conservation and Identification of the Finds

By J. A. Spriggs

The aims of the conservation work undertaken on these collections of finds were, firstly, to ensure the preservation of the finds from site, through to storage, study and beyond, and, secondly, to reveal, analyse and record information relevant to the manufacture and use of the objects. The bulk of the work was carried out between 1976 (the commencement of the Coppergate excavation) and the end of 1989, with small groups being returned for further investigative work after an assessment of the whole collection in 1995. The non-ferrous metal objects from 22 Piccadilly, although excavated in 1987, received no active conservation until 1996. Credit for the work of conserving these collections is due to the York Archaeological Trust conservation team, and to the many students and volunteers who have assisted in the conservation laboratories over the years.

Burial conditions and preservation

The waterlogged deposits at the Coppergate and 22 Piccadilly sites are typified by a high water content, low oxygen levels, a neutral pH and attenuated micro-organism activity. The highly organic nature of the deposits, the result of centuries of domestic and industrial waste and refuse, created conditions in which artefacts survive burial remarkably well, though they display an unusual variety of corrosion products and other symptoms of deterioration. Commonly occurring oxides and carbonates are replaced by sulphides and phosphates, and damage caused by micro-organisms, oxygen (in its various forms) and salts is greatly reduced. These deeply buried anoxic conditions tend to be very stable, with little annual or seasonal change, which also favours preservation. The effects of high chloride levels at a neutral to mildly alkaline pH in the Coppergate deposits were not apparent in the corrosion products observed on the copper alloy objects (Hunter 1980).

The method of recovery, and the approach and care used for storage, are crucial for long-term survival, even of these well-preserved finds. Regimes were quickly established to cope with the large influx of finds from Coppergate (Spriggs 1980; Clarke 1976),

and the excellent condition of the finds reported on in this volume is proof of the level of care these collections have received since the date of excavation.

Copper alloy

This group of almost 200 pieces (177 from Coppergate; eleven from 22 Piccadilly; three from Bedern) are mainly small decorative items which, from the elemental analyses which have been undertaken, are either brass (copper and zinc) or bronze (copper and tin), both of which may contain lead. The corrosion found is typified by voluminous corrosion crusts, which often become powdery on drying, and fall away to reveal a shiny, often brassy, metal surface beneath. The corrosion products formed are usually the brown-black to black-coloured copper sulphides, such as chalcocite (Cu_2S), or the gold-coloured copper/iron sulphides, such as chalcopyrite ($CuFeS_2$) and bornite (Cu_2FeS_4) (Duncan and Ganiaris 1987). These form directly over the metal surface, which normally appears shiny and metallic when revealed, but is often quite heavily etched. Most of the sulphides of copper and iron, and their admixtures, are visually indistinguishable and are of varying stability in the above-ground environment. Some of the copper alloy objects from waterlogged deposits, particularly those from 22 Piccadilly, which were not cleaned of their superficial corrosion until many years after excavation, were found to be partially covered by the more oxidised green forms of copper corrosion products (mainly carbonates). One cannot be certain that these formed during post-excavation storage as opposed to during burial.

Another commonly observed form of corrosion on these finds was redeposited copper, found either as reddish-gold flakes or as a quasi-continuous red metallic layer on top of, within or below the sulphide crust. This redeposited copper is believed to be caused by the reduction of more highly oxidised forms of copper corrosion product under anoxic conditions. This suggests that these objects were already corroded when they became included in the waterlogged deposits. In several cases, the copper was botryoidal ('bobbly') in form, but it is unclear what causes this characteristic, although it did sometimes accompany small deposits of red cuprous oxide and green carbonates.

It was also observed that a number of objects had a grey-white powdery corrosion product, often located immediately over the surviving metal surface, e.g. a dress pin, *10443*. Analysis of these items by X-ray fluorescence (XRF) at the Ancient Monuments Laboratories indicated that the white deposits are tin and/or lead, and that the objects were made from lead and tin alloys of copper.

The surviving metal surface was often revealed as the corrosion crust dried and fell away, or was deliberately removed. The surface often had a bright, brassy appearance, occasionally mistaken for gilding. The appearance was often granular, as though one phase of the bronze or brass had been leached out, and occasionally presented the bright pink surface of fresh copper. Those objects that had only a thin powdering of sulphide corrosion presented a virtually pristine surface, preserving fine detail (e.g. disc brooches *10429–30*). In other cases, where the corrosion crust was thicker, the original surface was missing altogether and the surviving metal was often severely etched and pitted. Because of the voluminous nature of the corrosion and the ease with which it fell away from the metal surface, there was little option but to remove the whole crust. Little sign of decoration remained on the metal surface beneath, which, although metallic in appearance, was severely etched. The potential loss of original surface detail incorporated in these crusts was of some concern, but there seemed little that could be done to avoid this at the time. In the case of pendant *10525*, the surface decoration of runic-style marks had become replicated in the undersurface of the relatively compact corrosion crust. It proved possible through careful handling, cleaning and consolidation to allow the decoration to be recorded, although little remained on the surviving metal surface (Fig.1283, p.2589).

One or two items had unusual surfaces which were later identified as being either gilding or other special decorative finishes: a ring *10396* (mercury gilding), strap distributor *10402* (red enamel) and scale pan *10409* (lead/tin solder). A cross brooch, *10431*, was observed to have a smooth blackish-grey corrosion layer, suggestive of the original presence of silver plating.

Conservation

Most of the corrosion layers were powdery crusts, which could readily be removed using simple mechanical cleaning techniques under a low-power binocular microscope. In most instances the crust was brittle, yet soft enough to cleave away from the metal surface using probes and scalpels. The 'airbrasive' technique was employed in a few instances, as was chemical cleaning, with either formic acid or alkaline glycerol, where the corrosion was more adherent.

Two of the three disc brooches with backward-looking animal motifs were particularly difficult to investigate and clean for recording, owing to their extreme fragility. *10429* and *10430* were composed of very thin *repoussé* copper alloy foils, mounted onto iron discs and fastened by folding the edges over. The presence of some type of packing material between the iron disc and the decorated foil must be assumed, although no such material was observed at the time of preliminary investigation. Through the use of radiographs, it was possible to make out the remains of pin fastenings, though these and the rest of the iron discs were completely corroded, making it necessary to consolidate the iron corrosion with a synthetic resin before it was safe to handle the objects with any confidence. Both of the decorated foils were observed, under magnification, to have series of fine parallel striations across their surfaces, which were disrupted by the decoration. These striations are therefore assumed to have been produced at some stage during the manufacture of the foil.

Only one item was observed to be actively corroding soon after excavation, a strip fitting, *10373*. One of the principal causes of the active form of corrosion, often referred to as 'bronze disease', is the presence of chlorides in the burial environment. Although identified as being present (Hunter 1980), high chloride levels were not evident from the types of corrosion products observed on copper alloy objects. The ironwork from the same levels was, however, liable to chloritic attack during storage (p.470, *AY* 17/6). There was therefore a potential problem with the future stability of the copper alloy objects, which prompted a policy of mass treatment with benzotriazole at a time when dry storage of copper alloys was not a normal procedure. This approach is no longer practised on health and safety grounds, benzotriazole being a suspected carcinogen.

However, individual objects found to be actively corroding have continued to receive this treatment.

Lead, lead alloys and tin

Of the 94 items in this category (84 lead alloy and four tin from Coppergate; six from 22 Piccadilly), a large number appeared virtually unaffected by burial, and were covered by only a thin layer of dirt. This was removed by washing or light brushing, to reveal pristine surfaces with a grey/black shiny patina of galena (PbS). With the exception of those noted below, the few items that have been analysed have been found to be pewter. Some pieces had suffered severe corrosion (e.g. brooch *10600*; penannular ring *10610*; pendant *4148*). These had pale-coloured corrosion products and their pitted metal surfaces, once cleaned of the white product, were a dull grey in colour, with a granular texture. On analysis, these badly corroded items were found to be pewter with a high tin content and, as with the copper alloys, it seems the tin was being preferentially leached out, causing damage to the surface. On analysis at the Ancient Monuments Laboratory, a number of items were identified as being almost pure tin (twisted wire ring *10617*; arm-ring *10618*; ring *10619*; pendant *10620*). These could not be differentiated from the other lead or lead alloy objects by appearance, but were all in fine condition, requiring only a little light cleaning to remove dirt encrustations.

Amongst the objects made of pure lead, the Period 4 spindle whorls stand out as a group (*6635–6, 6638–9, 10544–50*). On the removal of surface dirt there was little evidence of any corrosion, the surfaces having a shiny light grey appearance with many signs of manufacture and wear being clearly visible. One of the more unusual objects amongst the lead alloys is decorated disc brooch *10601* (Fig.1191). The face was found covered with a layer of grey horn silver (AgCl), a corrosion product not normally encountered on objects buried in anoxic conditions. This contained flakes of gold-coloured copper, overlying a thin layer of black silver sulphide. The rear of the brooch was covered with a layer of golden-coloured copper, but incorporating two lumps of iron corrosion (vivianite), representing the remains of the iron pin loop and hinge. Mechanical cleaning of both surfaces revealed enough silver to permit chemical cleaning with a proprietary chemical cleaner to produce a shine for the purposes of display.

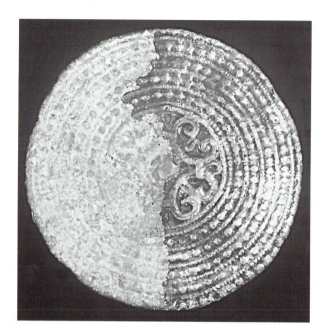

Fig.1191 *Lead alloy disc brooch* (10601) *in the process of conservation. Actual diameter 70mm*

Gold

Only one item was composed entirely of gold, a stud, *10536*. Two other items were composed of gold alloy, containing 20–30% silver and a trace of copper, kite brooch fragment *10535* and ring *10537*. In each case, the gold required only superficial cleaning for the removal of dirt.

Silver

Under the reducing conditions of burial on the sites in question, silver tends to corrode to black sulphide, a compact and very adherent material, which is often difficult to remove. Neither is sulphide removal always desirable, since any decoration and other surface features will have been replaced by the sulphide. In the case of the six silver items from Coppergate, four had thin enough sulphide patinae to permit complete removal by mechanical means, presenting a bright silver surface which could be enhanced by polishing for display. One, a silver-gilt stud with a glass setting (*10541*), was cleaned using a proprietary silver cleaning reagent; the others, three finger-rings (*10539–40, 10543*), a mount (*10542*) and a wire fragment (*10538*), were brought to brightness using gentle mechanical cleaning.

Glass

The collection of 342 glass beads and fragments (289 from Coppergate; 44 from 22 Piccadilly; nine from Bedern) represents a wide variety of colours, shapes and sizes (pp.2591–6). Most were found to be virtually unaffected by burial. Each item was carefully washed clean and allowed to dry naturally, resulting in only a slight dulling of the surfaces.

About six started to develop opalescent layers, caused by devitrification, and these were consolidated using a synthetic resin emulsion. These were segmented beads (clear and coloured), which had formed an opalescent layer of hydration on their surfaces (e.g. *10302, 10319*), and which are probably made of soda alkali glass. A number of dark brown and black opaque beads cracked and fragmented, when allowed to dry (e.g. *10323*). It is suspected that the glass used in these darker beads was based on potash alkali, although no analyses have been carried out to substantiate this. Potash glass is known to be unstable in almost all burial environments, due to the rapid leaching of the potash and the precipitation of dark-coloured manganese and iron salts into the silica lattice structure (Newton and Davidson 1989, 154). A few of these black beads were 'eyed' with blobs of coloured glass applied to the surface (e.g. *10346, 10352*). These applied eyes are of a different type and colour of glass, as they have survived intact despite the degradation of the black glass matrix beneath.

One black bead, *10240*, was in particularly fine condition, with a metallic sheen to the surface. On analysis, this proved to be a high-lead glass. Other beads, mainly yellow in colour, also had a high-lead content on analysis and were amongst the best preserved of the collection (see report by Bayley and Doonan, pp.2519–28).

The glass slick-stones form another group of objects that, because of their generally poor state of preservation, required consolidation after discovery, and some are assumed to be composed of potash glass. Analysis at the Ancient Monuments Laboratory showed that the better preserved examples had a high-lead content. However, the type of analysis employed (XRF) was not able to distinguish between an alkali-lead glass and a true lead glass (Mortimer 1995).

The condition and treatment of the 62 glass vessel finds (56 from Coppergate; six from 22 Piccadilly) was very similar to the beads, most requiring no special treatment, as preservation was good. However, as with the beads, a few pieces were black in colour, and unstable, and assumed to be deteriorated potash glass, though further analysis is required to substantiate this. A number of the more devitrified pieces (e.g. vessel fragments *10007–8)* were consolidated whilst still damp with poly-vinyl acetate emulsion, and have held together well. Other pieces, such as vessel fragments *10012* and *10015*, which did not receive consolidation whilst still damp, have since partially disintegrated.

Stone and fired clay

Virtually none of the artefact types in these material classes required any type of conservation intervention beyond careful cleaning, drying under observation and the piecing together of fragmented objects, such as ceramic vessels and cresset lamps. One gaming counter, *9756*, is of white chalk covered with a red pigment which required more attention, including consolidation, and two pieces of the same steatite bowl fixed with iron staples, *9671*, required extra attention, mainly on account of the iron fittings.

Jet and amber

By I. Panter

The jet and amber from Coppergate was uniformly well preserved, whereas artefacts made of these materials would be in poor condition if recovered from normal oxygenated sites. Careful cleaning with de-ionised water and slow drying under observation was all that was necessary. Although some pieces appeared dull on drying, they were structurally sound and show no further sign of deterioration in the post-excavation period. The temptation to consolidate these materials was resisted, as this would have interfered with the later provenancing using infra-red spectroscopy and XRF techniques (pp.2470–4).

There is always the concern that amber, in particular those worked pieces presenting a fresh surface, will slowly oxidise in the air (as does fresh amber). Early finds of amber from waterlogged sites close to Coppergate, held at the Yorkshire Museum, now appear dull and crazed (J. Spriggs, pers. comm.).

Conclusion

During the conservation process, many of the priorities for further analysis and research were identified, particularly where anomalies in condition or corrosion products indicated the presence of residues or other associated material. The conservation of these collections has provided the finds researcher with well documented, well packaged, clean and stable objects for study and illustration.

Jet and amber identification and provenancing

By I. Panter

Identification

Correct identification of jet, as opposed to other black shiny materials, can prove difficult. A number of materials such as cannel coal, lignite and shale, to name a few, resemble jet when worked and polished.

With the exception of shale, all of these materials have been formed as a result of the action of pressure on decaying organic material millions of years ago. Jet resulted from the compressive action of decaying animal and plant material settling on top of tree trunks which had sunk to the sea bed. Cannel coal and lignite are soft brown coals produced from decayed plant materials in swamps.

Shale is a sedimentary rock, principally composed of clay minerals. Although there are a number of varieties of shale, the principal one used in antiquity appears to be the oil-rich shale, which had a high concentration of hydrocarbons, which allowed it to be highly polished.

The proposed approach to identification was based on the methodology suggested by Hunter et al. (1993), and the following techniques were used.

Microscopic examination

The artefacts were examined under the binocular microscope for evidence of manufacturing technology, and to record diagnostic features such as fracture type, crack type and surface appearance (Davis 1993). Some of these features can be used with ease to identify the different types of materials. Jet,

for example, has a typical conchoidal fracture, whereas shale is non-conchoidal. Unfortunately, if the object is complete, or has no fractures or cracks, identification by this method is difficult. As all the materials can take a high polish, it is easy to make mistakes using visual examination techniques. In some instances, though, identification by this method alone was sufficient. For example, shale will often lose its polish during burial, and its surface takes on a stony appearance. Jet and the other materials tend to retain their polish much longer. For a more objective and scientific approach, the following two methods proved invaluable.

X-radiography

Earlier work by both Hunter (1993) and Davis (1993) had shown that because of the compositional variances exhibited by these materials, different images were produced during X-radiography. The objects were exposed at 20 KVp for 90 seconds using Kodak D4 film. This was found to produce the most contrasting results. Reference samples of Whitby jet, shale, cannel coal and lignite (all obtained from the Yorkshire Museum) were also X-rayed.

Shale, having a much higher iron content, produced a very solid dense image under these conditions, whilst jet, with a much lower iron concentration, produced a more translucent image, containing numerous inclusions. The images produced for lignite and cannel coal appeared to be in between those for shale and jet. A very thick piece of jet could produce as dense an image as a thinner piece of shale, so relative thickness had to be taken into account.

X-ray fluorescence spectroscopy (XRF)

This technique can be used to investigate the elemental composition of a material. The equipment used was the X-ray fluorescence spectrometer at the Ancient Monuments Laboratory. During this process, the item under investigation is bombarded with X-rays, causing an excitation of some of its atoms. When these atoms lose energy, a fluorescence is emitted. A spectrum is recorded, which is used to identify the elements present. Typical spectra for jet, shale and lignite are shown in Figs.1192–4. Unfortunately, the sample of cannel coal from the Yorkshire Museum did not produce the expected spectrum, and further work is required.

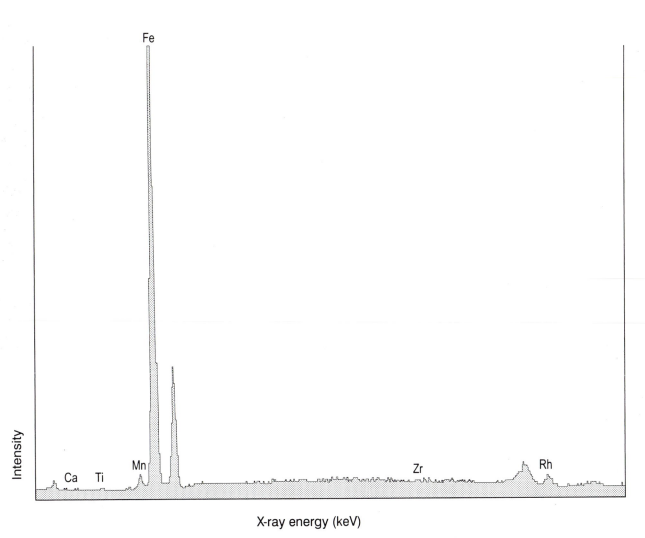

Fe

Ca　Ti　Mn　　　　　　　　　　　　　　　　Zr　　Rh

Intensity

X-ray energy (keV)

Fig.1192　Typical XRF spectrum for shale

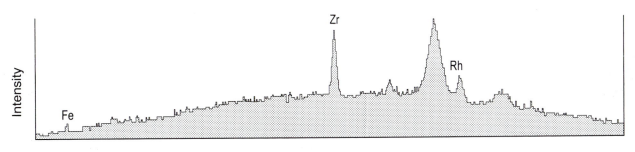

Zr

Rh

Fe

Intensity

X-ray energy (keV)

Fig.1193　Typical XRF spectrum for Whitby jet

For each object, an area was cleaned using cotton-wool swabs, moistened with alcohol. This removed surface dirt. In the case of lumps of raw jet, care was taken to avoid analysing the 'spar' or crust of shale usually found on jet. If a non-jet reading was produced, then another area of the object was analysed to give a second confirmation of the result. The equipment was operated at 30keV at 100mA. Again, the amount of iron recorded is the main distinguishing feature. Jet has a very low iron concentration, compared with the tube Kα Compton peak, whereas shale has an extremely high iron level.

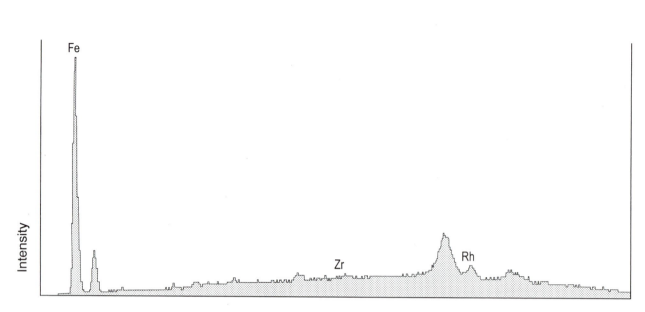

Fig.1194 *Typical XRF spectrum for lignite*

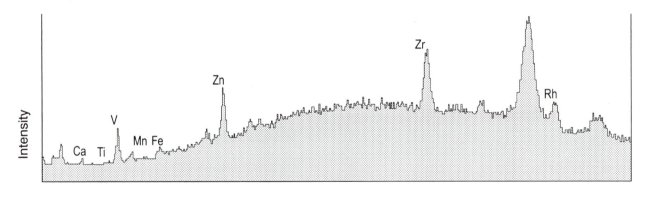

Fig.1195 *XRF spectrum for jet ring fragment from 16–22 Coppergate, 9851*

Fig.1195 shows a typical spectrum for a jet object. This is a ring fragment (*9851*). Note the other characteristic elements that are often present in Whitby jet — zirconium (Zr), vanadium (V), titanium (Ti) and zinc (Zn).

The spectra for other materials, such as cannel coal and lignite, tend to exhibit an iron level higher than jet, but lower than shale. Because of concern over the true identity of some of the reference samples, it has not yet been possible to identify positively cannel coal, lignite or other fossil coal substances. This is an area for further research, beyond the scope of the current project.

Conclusions

As a result of the analyses carried out, it has been possible to classify the material into three groups: jet, non-jet and shale. This should be sufficient for the purposes of this project but, as and when more definitive samples become available, it should be possible to define further the non-jet group.

Table 226   Jet and jet-like material from 16–22 Coppergate

Period	Jet	Non-Jet	Shale	Total
3	10	2	3	15
4A	1	3	1	5
4B	12	8	1	21
5A	2	2	2	6
5B	9	1	4	14
5Cr	1	–	–	1
Total	**35**	**16**	**11**	**62**

As a result of the above work, approximately 40% of the objects had their material identification changed. A further 10% were discarded from the project, having been identified as either black glass, stone or bone. The results are presented in Table 226.

Amber provenancing

Ambers are fossilised tree resins, formed almost 135 million years ago, and are found throughout the world. The main European variety is termed Baltic amber, as its primary source is the Baltic Sea region. Another important variety is Etruscan amber, and there is evidence for its use in antiquity from the 6th century BC (Fraquet 1987).

Although the chemistry of these resins is very complex, and little is known about the composition of many of them, it is fortunate that Baltic amber has been studied quite extensively. This amber is composed of a polyester, formed from communol and communic and succinic acids. This is used as the distinguishing feature of Baltic amber.

A number of techniques have been suggested for typifying amber, one of which is infra-red spectroscopy. In this process, the adsorption of infra-red light by a sample is recorded as a series of peaks and troughs on a chart. These peaks represent the presence of functional groups within the sample, and these diagnostic groups can be used to identify the material.

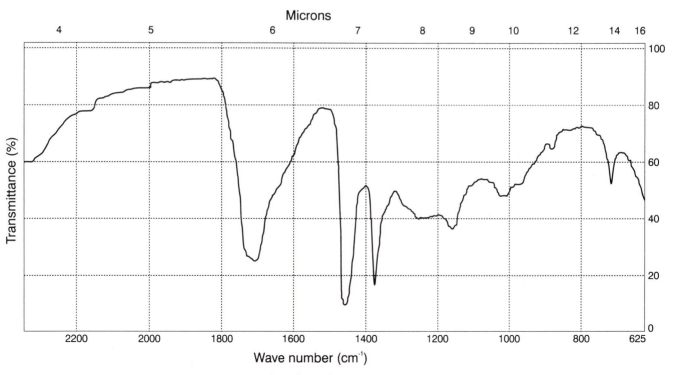

Fig.1196   *Typical infra-red spectroscopy spectrum for Baltic amber*

Table 227 Identification of raw amber from Anglo-Scandinavian York

sf number	Catalogue number	Period	Identification
6982	–	3	Baltic
6989	–	3	Baltic
13398	–	3	Baltic
14515	–	3	Baltic
4669	–	4B	Baltic
6614	–	4B	Baltic
8006	–	4B	?
8007	–	4B	Baltic
8135	*9882*	4B	Baltic
12412	–	4B	Baltic
12981	*9940*	4B	?
13109	–	4B	Baltic
2343	*9944*	5B	?
2710	–	5B	Baltic
3614	–	5B	Baltic
3656	–	5B	Baltic
4388	–	5B	?
4585	–	5B	Baltic
6826	–	5B	Baltic
10768	–	5B	Baltic

A typical spectrum for Baltic amber is shown in Fig.1196. The diagnostic region is between 1100 and 1250cm^{-1}; a shoulder is visible between 1175 and 1250cm^{-1}, with a peak close to 1150cm^{-1}. The near horizontal line between 1175 and 1250cm^{-1} is due to the presence of the succinyl ester group. This profile characterises Baltic amber, although there may be minor variations depending upon the extent of decay, the sampling procedure and the methodology used.

The method requires approximately 2mg of powdered resin, and therefore the technique is con-sidered destructive. For this reason, the initial decision was taken to sample the assemblage, investigating examples of raw amber, working debris and also finished but broken objects from Periods 3, 4B and 5B, the main amber working periods on the Coppergate site. Examination of the raw material and the actual working debris would indicate whether the source of the amber was Baltic. Investigation of the broken objects was considered because of the possibility that some of it may have been manufactured from non-Baltic ambers. After careful discussion, however, it was decided to exclude this group of material from the study because even filing the broken edges of the objects to obtain a sample of the amber was considered too destructive.

Initially twenty objects were selected (representing about 5% of the assemblage). This consisted of two samples each of raw and waste amber from Period 3, and four samples each of raw and waste amber from Periods 4B and 5B. The results of the infra-red spectroscopy are shown in Table 227.

Conclusions

Although all the objects produced spectra exhibiting an adsorption maximum at or close to 1150cm^{-1}, indicating Baltic amber, four samples of working debris (*9940, 9944* and sfs4388 and 8006) did not show the shoulder between 1175 and 1250cm^{-1}, characteristic of Baltic amber. Studies have shown that for Baltic amber in progressive states of oxidation and decay, this shoulder tends towards a negative slope until it reaches the adsorption maximum, then the slope becomes positive (Beck and Shennan 1991). In each of the four samples mentioned, the shoulder did not conform to this pattern.

Because of the scarcity of information pertaining to the composition of other fossil resins, it is impossible to take the identification any further, other than stating that four of the waste samples would appear to be from non-Baltic amber. This material may be indigenous, or may have been imported into York from abroad. Unfortunately, it is impossible to state which is the case.

Craft and Industry

Evidence Relating to Metalworking

Ferrous and non-ferrous metalworking was focused on two tenements (Tenements C and D) at 16–22 Coppergate during the late 9th to 11th century, and there was additional evidence from 22 Piccadilly and the Coppergate watching brief. These processes and the range of products made have been discussed elsewhere in the series (*AY* 17/6 and *AY* 17/7). The following sections describe other artefactual evidence which is related to these activities but, although referred to, is sometimes not fully described in these earlier reports. Where previous descriptions are adequate there is a simple cross-reference to either *AY* 17/6 or *AY* 17/7.

Non-ferrous metalworking evidence

In summary, the non-ferrous metalworking evidence from 16–22 Coppergate described in *AY* 17/7 includes large numbers of crucibles, ingot moulds, scrap metal and tools as well as evidence for precious metal refining, both cupellation and parting. Silver-working was the major non-ferrous metal industry and was at its peak in the mid 10th century; some of this activity may have been related to coin production. There is evidence for tinning objects of other metals in the mid 10th century, but most casting of small lead/tin objects took place later. Both gold and copper alloy working became more important in the 11th century. The concentration of working debris, especially in the form of crucibles, suggests that these activities were focused on Tenement D and, to a lesser extent, on Tenement C (Figs.324, 329, 354, 355, 358, *AY* 17/7).

Failed castings (Fig.1197)

This wide range of evidence includes a number of failed lead alloy and pewter castings, indicating that jewellery and other dress accessories may have been produced there. These objects (*4147–9, 4277–8*) have been described in *AY* 17/7 (p.780) but a fuller discussion of them is presented here. The catalogue entries for these objects are reproduced in this fascicule at the beginning of the lead alloy section in the catalogue.

An unfinished lead alloy bow brooch (*4147*) was recovered from a Period 4B build-up deposit on Tenement C. It has an incomplete rectangular head and foot, of the same width as the slightly bowed central field, a beaded edge and an axial row of three bosses. In this instance, the metal appears to have incompletely filled the mould, and the brooch also retains some casting flashes. A close parallel for this brooch comes from a Viking Age hoard or grave group in Lerchenborg, Denmark (Roesdahl et al. 1981, YD18).

Both *4148* and *4149* are circular pendants with suspension loops at the top, and both were found in Period 4B deposits, the former in the floor level of the wattle building on Tenement B, the latter in build-up on Tenement A. *4148* is of pewter, decorated with an untranslatable runic inscription around a central boss; the suspension loop is unperforated, and the sprue has not been removed. On *4149*, which is lead, the central motif has been punctuated by unintentional perforations; both pendants retain casting splashes. Pendants similar to these, many with a central boss as on *4148*, were found in some numbers at Birka, Sweden (Arbman 1940, taf.96–7) (Fig.1300, **1**, p.2608), and another has been recovered from Quidenham, Norfolk (H. Geake, pers. comm.).

Of particular interest are two rare examples of lead openwork badges (*4277–8*), on both of which the metal failed to fill the moulds; both retain U-shaped loops, possibly to enable the badges to be sewn onto clothing, as both lack any evidence of catch plates. Wherever these badges were made, probably in a local workshop, perhaps at Coppergate or nearby, it is likely that a third very similar example found in Beverley derives from the same workshop (Tweddle 1991, 156, *708*) (Fig.1299, **5**; p.2606). All three badges have been decorated with a cross superimposed upon concentric circles, with triangular animal masks at the cardinal points of the cross. These masks appear to be related to the gripping beasts motif typical of Borre-style ornament (ibid.). The possibility that these badges were made in York is enhanced by the recovery of a lead alloy matrix for making moulds for the casting of pendants also decorated in the Borre style (Roesdahl et al. 1981, YMW13). The Borre-style ornament on the York and Beverley badges dates them to the late 9th–early 10th centuries, although

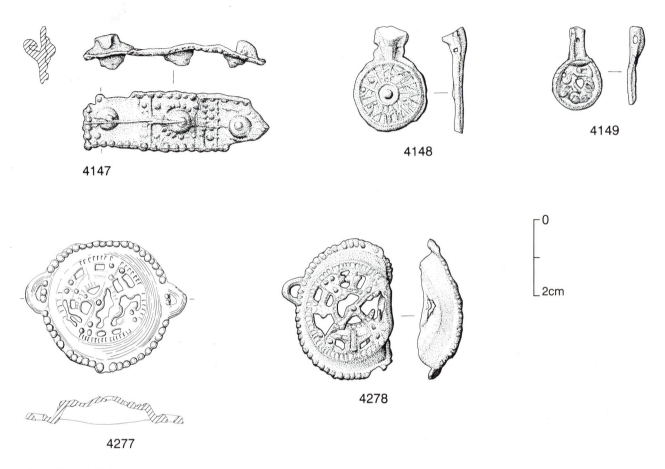

Fig. 1197 Failed castings from 16–22 Coppergate. Scale 1:1

all three were found in 12th–13th century levels; another very similar brooch with attachment loops and decoration comparable to the York brooches was found at Wharram Percy in a late 15th–early 16th century context (Andrews and Milne 1979, 114–15, fig.59, 1).

Lead matrix (Fig.1198)

Matrix 10544, made of pure lead, was found in a Period 5B build-up deposit. One of only two Ringerike-style decorated metal objects found at Coppergate, the other being a hooked tag 10437 (see p.2567), the U-shaped decoration between the arms of the cross echoes the spirals which typically form part of the foliate patterns of tendrils of the Ringerike style, which dates to the first half of the 11th century (Graham-Campbell 1980b, 147–9). A finished piece found in Kielby (Lincs.) suggests that 10544 could have been used to create a mould for casting a mount of some kind. The Kielby cross has been cast in copper alloy and is slightly concave, with perforations at the cardinal points, three of which contain copper alloy

wire; as on 10544, it has the U-shaped decoration between the cross arms (K. Leahy, pers. comm.).

Several pieces of lead alloy scrap and spillages were found at 22 Piccadilly (10692–7) and may be added to the already comprehensive picture of non-ferrous metalworking in the Coppergate/Piccadilly area (see AY 17/7).

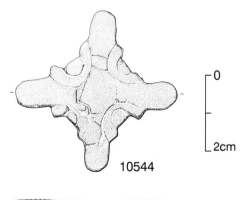

10544

Fig.1198 Lead matrix from 16–22 Coppergate. Scale 1:1

3990

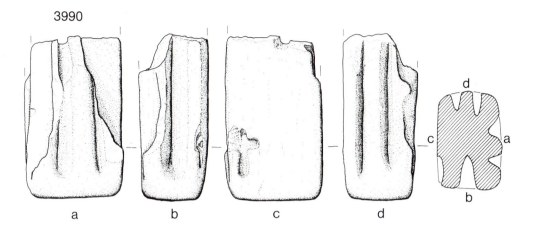

a   b   c   d

3998

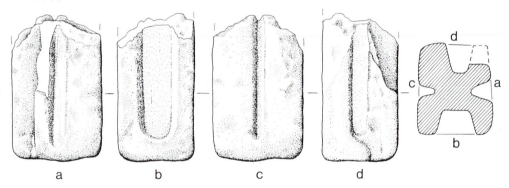

a   b   c   d

4000   4001

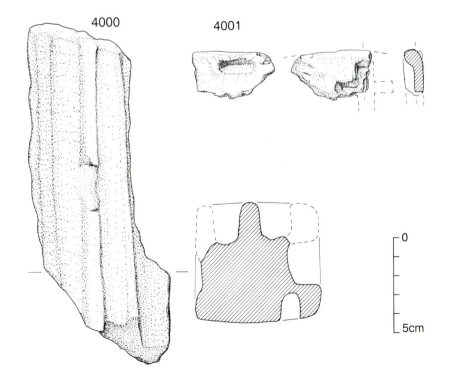

0

5cm

Fig.1199   *Ingot moulds of steatite. The letters a–d relate to the four faces of the sections of 3990 and 3998. Scale 1:2*

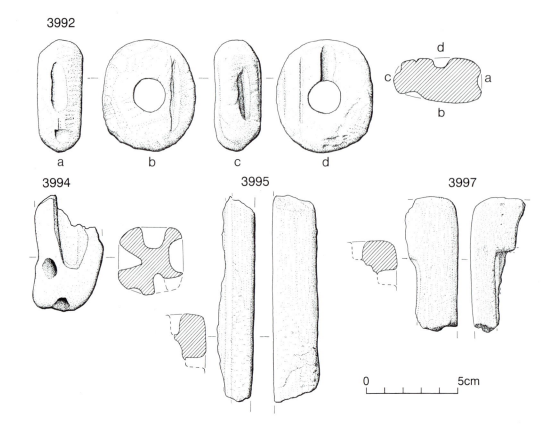

Fig.1200 *Ingot moulds of talc schist. The letters a–d relate to the four faces of the sections of 3992. Scale 1:2*

Stone moulds (Figs.1199–1200)

There are ten stone ingot moulds from 16–22 Coppergate, all identified by Dr G.D. Gaunt as being made of steatite and talc schist. Eight are from Anglo-Scandinavian levels, and there are two from Period 6 which are believed to be residual and are included here. These were clearly used in metalworking processes and have traces of copper and silver on them. With the exception of *9247* and *9248*, the latter being one of the Period 6 examples, the moulds are described in *AY* 17/7 (pp.767–78), and catalogued as *3990, 3992, 3994–5, 3997–4001*. The catalogue entries for these finds are reproduced in this fascicule at the start of the stone section of the catalogue. *9247* is a possible mould made from a pebble, *9248* is a fragment of talc schist which came to light after the publication of *AY* 17/7 and might also have been used as an ingot mould.

There is also a possible mould fragment (*10630*) from Period 4 and a fragment of haematite (*10636*) from Period 5 at 22 Piccadilly.

The manufacture of lead alloy dress accessories in the Coppergate area

Analysis of metalworking debris from 16–22 Coppergate, published in *AY* 17/7, noted that a wide range of metals were being worked during Anglo-Scandinavian occupation of the site, including lead (pp.814–15). Evidence of leadworking included a sprue (*4215*) and runners (*4280–1*) as well as spillages, showing the use of moulds for casting, although no moulds for lead objects were recovered (p.814, *AY* 17/7). The unfinished objects discussed above point to the casting of decorative lead and pewter accessories, possibly from as early as Period 4A (late 9th/early 10th century) when the Borre-style badges (*4277–8*) were made, and certainly during Period 4B (c.930–975) with the bow brooch (*4147*) and two pendants (*4148–9*). A poorly cast 10th century pewter disc brooch (*10604*) (see pp.2571–2) is another possible product of the site.

The 9th and 10th centuries saw a growing demand for decorative fittings and accessories in cheaper base metals such as lead (Richards 1991, 81), a demand which may have extended into the 11th century as indicated by the pewter brooches, rings and beads, many unfinished, found in the Cheapside Hoard, London (Murdoch 1991, 155–6, no.408). It appears that by the later 9th century metalworkers at Coppergate had begun to produce such objects in response to this demand. In addition to the incomplete products, finished lead and lead alloy fittings and accessories have been recovered, including a strap-end, five pewter or lead alloy disc brooches, and a brooch pin, arm-rings, finger-rings and pendants (*10599–605, 10608–9, 10611–16*). While some of the other crafts and industries at Coppergate, such as ironworking, appear to have been concentrated on particular tenements the lead and lead alloy metal-working debris was scattered across the tenements (p.814, Fig.358, *AY* 17/7), and cannot be attributed to any one area of working. This may indicate that lead, and other non-ferrous metals, were worked by craftsmen who also worked ferrous metals, or that groups of more specialised craftsmen shared workshop facilities (p.816, *AY* 17/7).

Ferrous metalworking evidence

AY 17/6 describes evidence recovered from 16–22 Coppergate for every aspect of the production of iron artefacts, although some of the smelting slags recovered are unlikely to derive from processes undertaken on the site itself. The large quantity of smithing slag suggests that the manufacture of iron objects took place on, or adjacent to, the site from the late 9th to the late 10th century (Periods 3–4B). This is confirmed by the abundance of iron blanks and other scrap. There is a particular concentration of this material in and around the Period 4B buildings at the front of Tenements C and D which probably indicates that they were, amongst other things, ironworking workshops. A number of smithing tools were found. Among the iron objects probably manufactured here were needles and tin-plated dress fittings. The wide range of ironwork found includes a large collection of knives and tools for other crafts as well as a range of domestic fittings, dress fittings and weapons.

The following two sections describe artefacts which are likely to be associated with the ferrous metalworking industry. These include a range of stone grinding, sharpening and polishing implements which must have been used both in the final stages of production and in the maintenance of edged tools.

Rotary grindstones (Figs.1201–2)

Twenty-nine cylindrical rotary grindstones were recovered from 16–22 Coppergate, all but three from Anglo-Scandinavian contexts; these three are considered to be residual Anglo-Scandinavian examples as they fall within the same range of size and shape as the rest of the group. There is only one example, *9610*, from Period 3 and this is one of the largest in terms of diameter and thickness. Period 4B produced the most examples and these eleven fragments are distributed across the fronts of Tenements B, C and D where the buildings would have been situated. The remaining examples are more widely scattered across the site, showing no marked concentrations.

The grindstones were all identified by Dr G.D. Gaunt as being almost certainly of Upper Carboniferous sandstones with likely provenances in the eastern Pennine Millstone Grit and the Coal Measures of the Yorkshire Coalfield, although he comments that it is conceivable that a few of those attributed to the Coal Measures could be lithologically comparable with Middle Jurassic sandstones from eastern Yorkshire. There is blackening on the surfaces of some of them, e.g. *9611, 9616, 9618* and *9636*, but this is believed to be secondary sooting.

Previous examples are known from York. These include a large example, 540mm diameter, recovered from 6–8 Pavement (*378*, p.76, Fig.38, *AY* 17/3) and another large example, 265mm diameter, from Barclays Bank, 1–3 Parliament Street (Radley 1971, 42, 49) (Fig.1187, **6, 9**, p.2452). A further example was recovered from the Parliament Street sewer trench (*683*, p.184, Fig.86, *AY* 17/4) which measures 91·4mm diameter (Fig.1187, **8**).

The grindstones would have been mounted on a horizontal axle and used for sharpening blades and other cutting edges. Amongst the Coppergate examples the smallest has a diameter of 50mm and the largest 440mm. The majority have diameters under 100mm. The diameters of the central perforations range between 15mm (*9627*) and 140mm (*9610*) but sixteen examples have perforations with diameters of 20mm. The perforations are usually centred or slightly off-centre. The length of the cylinders ranges between 20mm (*9617*) and 111mm (*9631*).

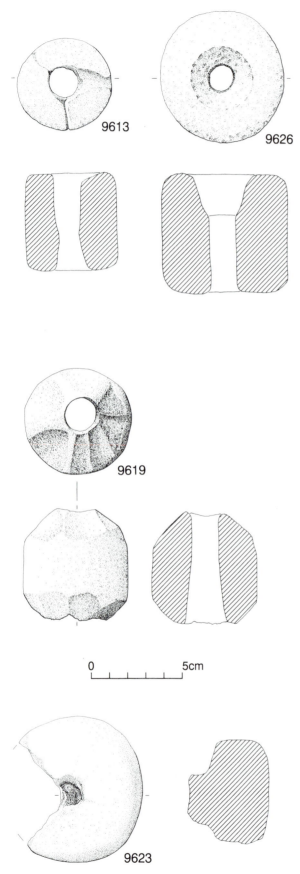

Fig.1201 *Rotary grindstones from 16–22 Coppergate. Scale 1:2*

There appear to be two distinct groups and a number of miscellaneous others. Eight (*9613–14, 9616, 9618–19, 9621, 9627, 9634*) have small diameters (i.e. 50–60mm) with the length of cylinder varying between 35 and 65mm. All of these, except *9627* and *9634*, are from Period 4B contexts; these are from Period 5A and Period 5B respectively. All examples are worn on the grinding surface (the edges) and in most cases the faces are roughly finished and show no signs of having been used for grinding. *9619* is unusual as the faces have been roughly faceted to form slightly tapering ends which may have something to do with the methods of mounting the grindstone. *9613* has a worn groove next to the central hole on one end which might also relate to its positioning or to its function.

The second group (*9611–12, 9617, 9623, 9625–6, 9628, 9636–7*) occupies a wider chronological span as there are examples from Period 4B to Period 6. They are distinguished by having a larger diameter which is fairly consistent at around 70–80mm. Again there is a wider range of cylinder lengths from flat examples such as *9617* (20mm) to much longer examples such as *9612* (90mm). *9623* seems to be unfinished and gives some insight into how the grindstones were produced; the shape was formed, possibly on a lathe as it is quite regular, the perforation was then drilled from one side to a depth of about 20mm and then begun on the other side. At this point the grindstone split and the unfinished object was discarded. *9626* is also slightly unusual as the perforation at one end is cone shaped to just above the central point and then straight through the second half. The holes in the other examples are straight tubes. One or two examples have slightly smoothed surfaces, most marked in *9625*, which might suggest friction against an adjacent surface at the ends.

The remaining examples are all larger and cannot be grouped convincingly. *9635* (Period 5Cr) is less than half complete and has a worn grinding edge and one worn surface suggesting that it had a secondary use once the grindstone had broken. Only half of *9622* (Period 5A) survives but in this case there is no evidence of secondary use. One quarter of *9638* (Period 6) survives and the grinding surface is not as smooth as on other examples. *9630* and *9631* (Period 5B) are both from the same context and are similar in

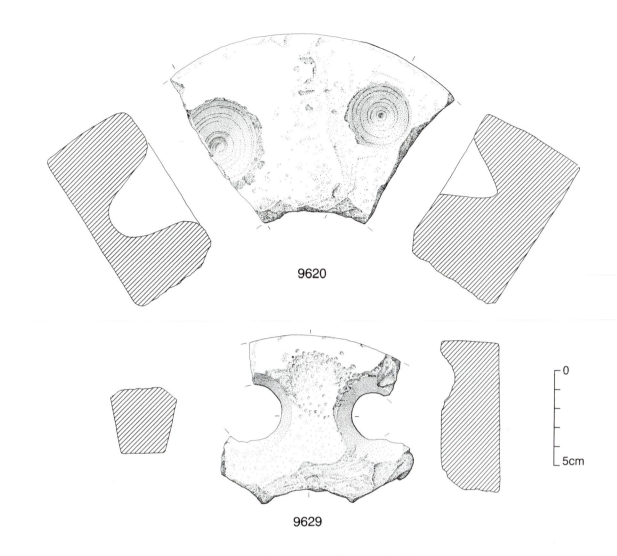

Fig.1202 *Rotary grindstones from 16–22 Coppergate with cone-shaped holes. Scale 1:2*

size and shape, although *9631* is slightly longer and narrower than *9630*. Their recovery together might imply they had once been set side-by-side. *9615* is very fragmentary but it has a worn edge and is believed to be a grindstone. *9624* is also fragmentary and only a small area of the grinding surface survives. *9633* is almost as large as the example recovered from 6–8 Pavement and is the largest in this assemblage in terms of diameter (440mm).

Two unusual fragments, *9620* (Period 4B) and *9629* (Period 5B), are parts of two different objects which are likely to belong to this category. The earlier of the two (*9620*) is also the thicker (56mm, *9629* is 32mm) and has the slightly greater diameter (*9620* is 240mm as opposed to *9629* which is 224mm). In both

cases only about one-quarter of the stone survives so it is not possible to reconstruct the rest. Both are much better finished than the other examples discussed above. The surfaces are very smooth and they have a very smooth grinding edge. What is unusual is that both have two regular cone-shaped holes ground into one flat surface, one deeper and wider than the other in both examples. In the case of *9629* these holes go right through the thickness of the stone, although it is possible that the original surface has been lost, and that they too originally only penetrated into the surface as is the case with *9620*. Although these holes may be for secondary use it seems likely that they were part of the original object and probably served some purpose in securing or rotating the stone in use.

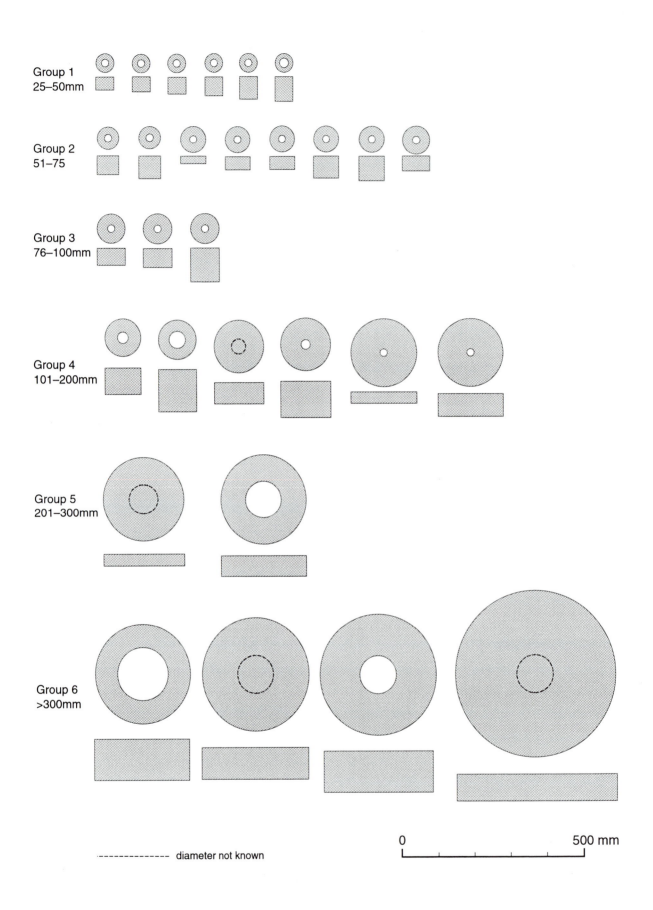

Group 1
25–50mm

Group 2
51–75

Group 3
76–100mm

Group 4
101–200mm

Group 5
201–300mm

Group 6
>300mm

-------------- diameter not known

0   500 mm

Fig.1203 *Range of sizes of rotary grindstones from 16–22 Coppergate*

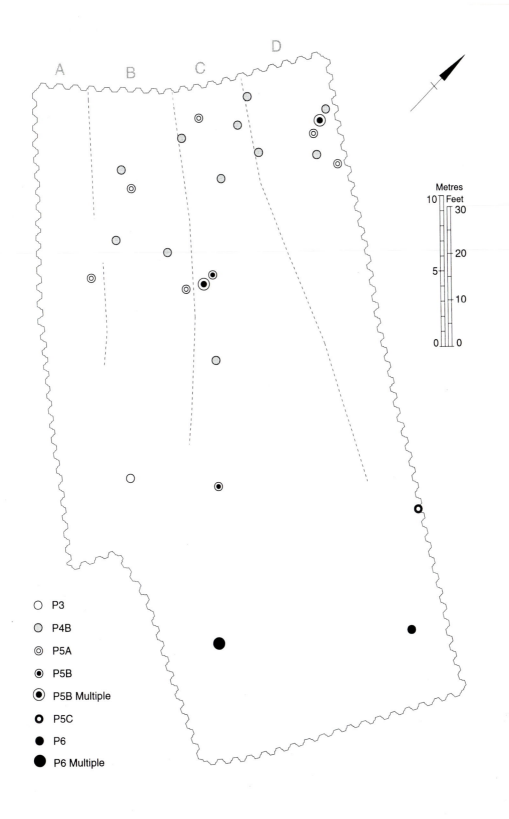

Fig.1204 *Distribution of rotary grindstones at 16–22 Coppergate in all periods*
(tenement divisions A–D relate only to Periods 4B, 5A and 5B)

Table 228 Rotary grindstones according to period at 16–22 Coppergate

Period	3	4B	5A	5B	5C
	1	11	6	7	1

The purpose of these grindstones must have been for sharpening edged tools including a range of blades. Their distribution in Tenements C and D (Fig.1204) where the metalworking industries were focused suggests that they might have had a role in the original manufacture of these objects as well as a continuing function in household contexts for maintaining a sharp edge on a range of implements. There is, however, no correlation between the distribution pattern of particular sizes with their position within tenements on site. Given that these are very simple functional objects made from raw materials available within the region, it is surprising that there are not more parallels published from contemporary sites. They do not appear in pre-Anglo-Scandinavian sites in York and there is only one from post-Norman Conquest deposits at 46–54 Fishergate (Ottaway and Rogers, *AY* 17/– in prep.) to add to those recorded from medieval deposits at Coppergate which are described above (Fig.1187, **16**). Few parallels can be cited in areas where the influence of the Scandinavians is most marked; none were found at Lurk Lane, Beverley (Armstrong et al. 1991), nor at Flaxengate, Lincoln (Mann 1982) (Fig.1299, **9**, p.2606), nor at any of the East Anglian urban sites. Even the large assemblages recovered from outside the Danelaw at Winchester (Biddle 1990a) and London do not include examples (Fig.1299, **13**, **14**). For the time being these seem to be a York phenomenon, with most examples coming from the Anglo-Scandinavian period.

Hones (Figs.1205–9)

Hones or sharpening stones played an important role in the final stages of the production of blades, as well as in the continuing maintenance of a sharp edge. The hones have been included in this section because their distribution suggests that, like the rotary grindstones, some were associated with the ferrous metalworking which was taking place in

Tenements C and D. There is also some evidence that a number of the hones might themselves have been produced at Coppergate.

Dr G.D. Gaunt writes:

Almost all the hones are referable to one or other of three lithological categories — sandstones, schists and phyllites — with only three exceptions.

A majority of the sandstone hones are from Upper Carboniferous (i.e. Millstone Grit and Coal Measures) sources in the eastern Pennines, although several of those from the Coal Measures, with an Elland Flags-type lithology, may have been made from old Roman roofing-stones found in situ in York. Most of the other sandstone hones have sufficient degrees of compaction and content of dark minerals and/or rock fragments to suggest provenances either in more northerly Pennine Carboniferous outcrops or in the Lower Palaeozoic outcrops of southern Scotland or Cumbria, and two more hones are undoubtedly from these Lower Palaeozoic outcrops. The remaining five sandstone hones have calcareous matrices. Two of these are from Middle and Upper Jurassic sources, almost certainly in north-eastern Yorkshire. The other three are probably also from these sources but, alternatively, two of them could be from northern Pennine Carboniferous outcrops and the third may, just conceivably, be from the Lower Cretaceous of south-eastern England.

The schist hones, which form the largest lithological category, consist of quartz-muscovite schist with only minor variations in mineralogy, grain size and, with a few exceptions, texture. On lithological grounds most of them are classifiable as schist hones of Norwegian Ragstone type, for which a sources in the Eidsborg area of central southern Norway is suggested by thin-section petrological and archaeological evidence (Ellis 1969, 149–50; Moore 1978, 65–8). This suggestion is enhanced by potassium-argon radiometric dating of rock from the Eidsborg quarries and from Norwegian Ragstone-type hones from north-western Europe and England (including 9469 from Anglo-Scandinavian Coppergate), which gave a metamorphic age range of c.860–1000 million years (Ellis 1969, 149; Mitchell et al. 1984; Crosby and Mitchell 1987). Metamorphism of this age indicates the Grenvillian Orogeny, well represented in Canada, Greenland and Scandinavia but virtually absent elsewhere in Europe. Until recently it was thought to be absent in Britain but traces of it have now been found in the Scottish highlands (Johnstone and Mykura 1989, 74–7; Craig 1991, 47, 55 97–100, 233). As yet, however, these Scottish Grenvillian traces have only been found in rocks petrologically distinct from Norwegian Ragstone schist, so the combination of archaeological, petrological and radiometric-dating evidence for the Eidsborg source remains valid.

A few of the schist hones have a textural variation which suggests that they may not necessarily be of Norwegian Ragstone type, and for which, without radiometric dating, sources in the Scottish highlands and islands are conceivable. Five hones (9425, 9454, 9468, 9503, 9514), although otherwise lithologically comparable to those of Norwegian Ragstone type, have a banded appearance. Possible Scottish provenances include the Strath Fionan Banded Formation (formerly the Honestone Series of Barrow et al. 1913, 17–21) and its lithostratigraphical correlatives in the Dalradian Supergroup of the southern and eastern Grampians. Several other schist hones (9370 and its analogues) are finer grained than the normal Norwegian Ragstone type, being almost phyllite in granuality. Finally, two hones (9477, 9500) consist partly of schist comparable to Norwegian Ragstone types and partly of phyllite similar to purple-phyllite (see below), the boundary between the two being sharp along the schistosity, and possibly dislocational in origin. They cannot be attributed to either lithological type with any confidence.

The phyllite hones have, with few exceptions, a consistent lithology that equates them with the hones of purple-phyllite type as described by Ellis (1969, 144–7), and referred to by Moore (1978, 68) as blue-phyllite. Examples of this type of hone from north-western Europe and England have yielded K-Ar radiometric metamorphic ages of c.395–470 million years, indicating the Caledonian Orogeny, well represented in northern and western parts of the British Isles and the western half of Norway (Mitchell et al. 1984, who referred to them as 'dark-grey schist'; Crosby and Mitchell 1987). Archaeological distributions suggest a source in the Norwegian Caledonide outcrops according to Crosby and Mitchell, but provenance in the Scottish highlands or Shetland Islands cannot be precluded. Five phyllite hones have textural variations which cast doubt on their identification as purple-phyllite type. Three of these (9582, 9595 and 9598) are slightly coarser (although still very fine- to fine-grained in absolute terms), being almost schist in granularity. Another (9563) is appreciably darker than normal and the fifth (9571) has a brownish tinge and a quartz-rich layer, both features unusual in purple-phyllite hones. The remaining phyllite hone (9577) has a marked platy cleavage and laminated appearance, and is not considered to be of purple-phyllite type; Crosby and Mitchell (1987, tables 5 and 7) also excluded it from their purple-phyllite type.

Three hones (9606–8; see Fig.1210, p.2419) are not sandstones, schists or phyllites. They are all too dark coloured and too fine grained to reveal any diagnostic mineralogy or textures, even with a hand lens, so their lithology and provenance are uncertain. They have variously a cherty or basaltic appearance, but these rock types appear to be unknown as hones, at least in north-western Europe. The most likely lithologies are tuffs, indurated quartzitic siltstones and silty mudstones which, if from Britain, would probably be from Lower Palaeozoic sources. However, the dark colour and fine granularity are suggestive of touchstones, and if so they may have been imported, with implications for a wide range of provenances (Moore 1983).

Hones were a very common find and occur in a range of sizes from small personal hones, which would have been suspended from a belt by a thong, to larger, less portable, examples. The three earliest hones are from contexts which cannot easily be phased (Period 1/3). All three are fragmentary, two are of sandstone and one of schist. As they fit both in terms of the range of form and lithology with the rest of the group, they are likely to belong to Period 3. Nineteen hones were recovered from Period 3, the majority (twelve) of which are sandstone (e.g. 9310, 9312, 9317–18) but there are also a few examples of schist (four) and phyllite (three). These early hones were recovered from two zones, one group from the front of the site, where they are almost exclusively sandstone, and the second group at the rear of the site where they are of all three lithologies (Fig.1212, p.2493). In Period 4A, the pattern is much the same with four of the eight examples being of sandstone and the others phyllite (two) and schist (two). They are distributed in what were to become Tenements B, C and D at the front of the site, predominantly in the north-east corner.

Table 229 Distribution of hones at 16–22 Coppergate according to tenement and stone type in Period 4B

Tenement Geology	A	B	C	D	Total
Sandstone	0	5	3	9	17
Schist	2	17	26	22	67
Phyllite	0	12	22	4	38
Uncertain	0	4	0	0	4
Total	2	38	51	35	126

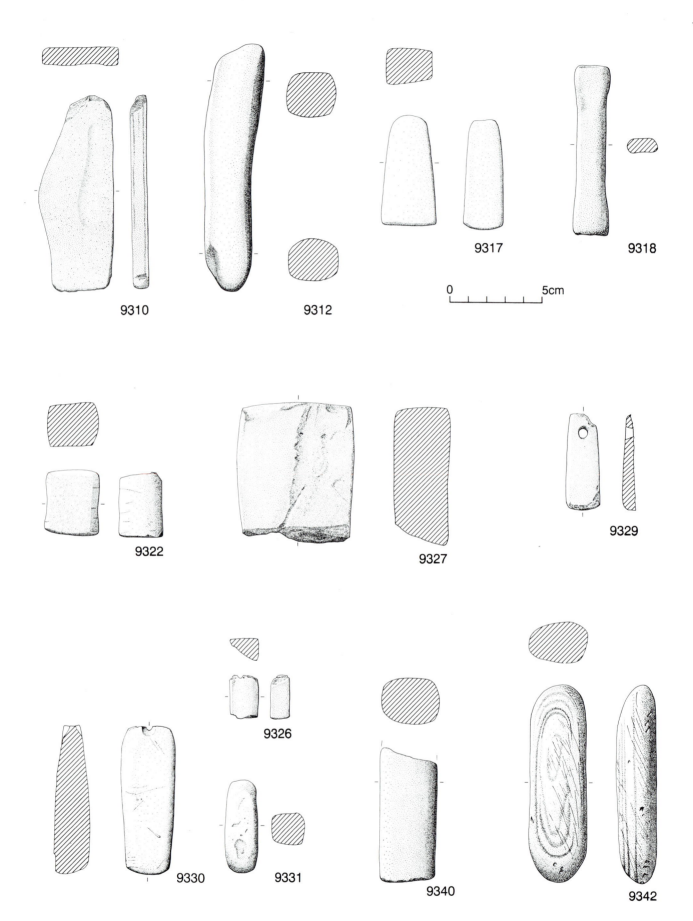

Fig.1205 *Sandstone hones from 16–22 Coppergate. Scale 1:2*

9310

9312

9317

9318

0   5cm

9322

9327

9329

9326

9330

9331

9340

9342

Many more hones were recovered from Period 4B, the period during which most of the ferrous metal-working took place. There is also a shift away from the preference for sandstone to schist, which comprises 50% of this group. Table 229 and Fig.1213 (p.2494) show the differing distribution across the site of hones made from sandstone, phyllite and schist.

The paucity of evidence from Tenement A must be accounted for by the poor survival of deposits in

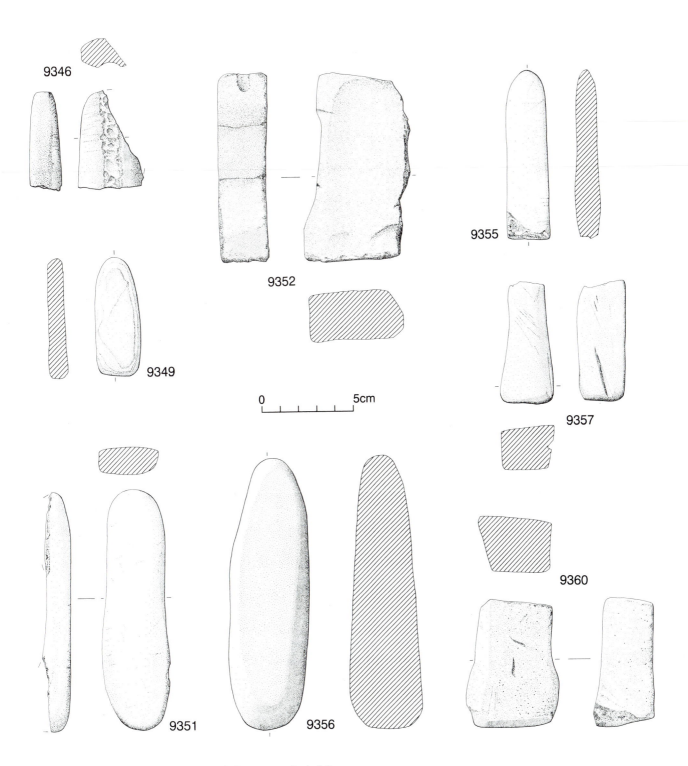

Fig.1206 *Sandstone hones from 16–22 Coppergate. Scale 1:2*

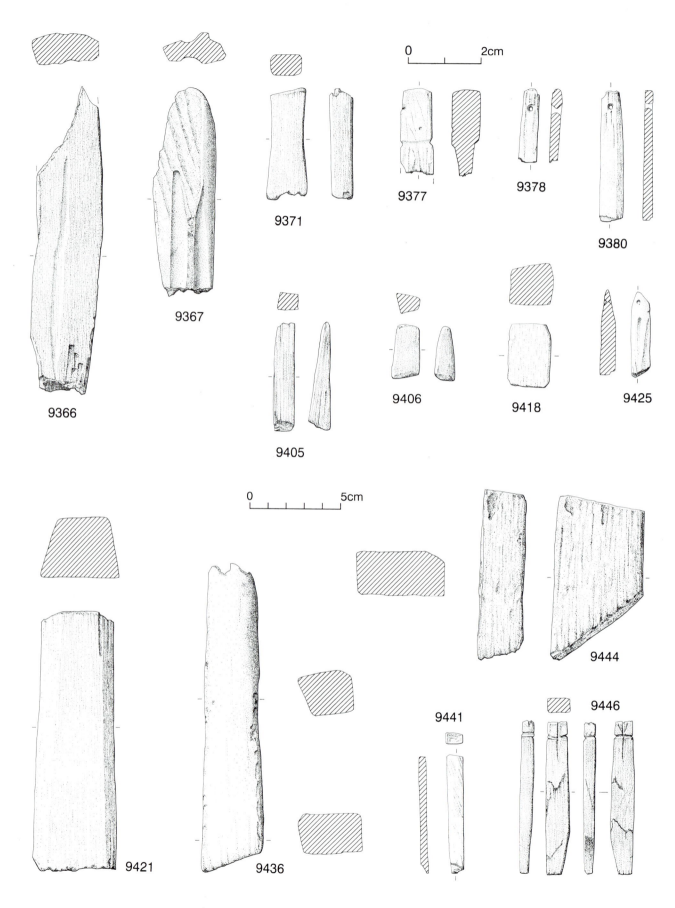

0   2cm

9371

9377

9378

9367

9380

9366

9405

9406

9418

9425

0   5cm

9421

9436

9441

9444

9446

Fig.1207 *Schist hones from 16–22 Coppergate. Scale 1:2, 9377 scale 1:1*

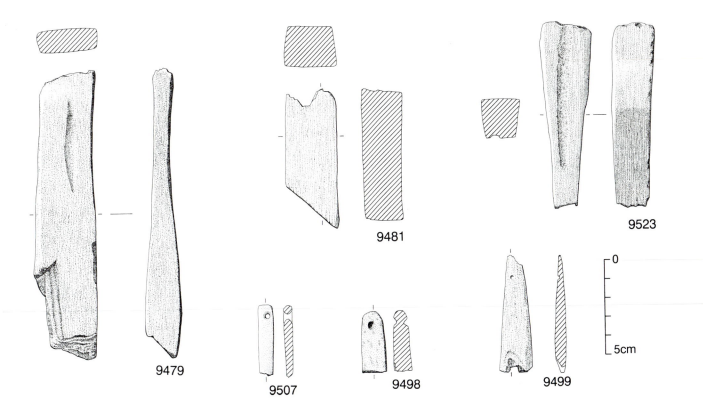

Fig.1208 *Schist hones from 16–22 Coppergate. Scale 1:2*

that area (see p.2460). In Tenement B the hones are distributed more or less evenly down the first two-thirds of the property, tailing off noticeably in the rear of the tenement. Hones made from schist predominate, with those made from phyllite a close second.

In Tenements C and D the pattern of hone distribution is rather different. Tenement C has the greatest number of hones (51 examples which represent 39% of the Period 4B total) consisting of schist and phyllite in almost equal proportions (26 and 22 respectively), with only three sandstone examples. On Tenement D fewer hones (35) were recovered but a higher proportion of these (22 or 62%) were made from schist with smaller numbers of sandstone (nine) and phyllite (four).

Of the Tenement D hones seventeen schist, six sandstone and three phyllite hones came from a single context (25934) which is a floor level in the wattle building. These are all small flakes and fragments many of which (*9335–7, 9411, 9413–15, 9419, 9554*) show little sign of wear. They could result

from the production of hones or the shattering of hones in the course of use. The latter explanation is more likely for a second group (*9407–9, 9412, 9420*), which is also made up of small slivers or fragments which have at least one worn surface. *9406, 9418, 9553* and two sandstone examples *9332* and *9338* are all distinctive short stubby hones which might have been the sawn off ends of larger hones or shaped for particular usage.

The hones from Tenement C present a similar picture. Forty-four of these hones or hone fragments were recovered from deposits in and around the wattle building at the front of the tenement. Sixteen were recovered from floor levels and a further 28 from build-ups and dumps in and around the building. Again there is a group of long narrow thin slivers which show no sign of having been worked (e.g. *9384–5, 9387–9, 9390, 9395*) but might have shattered in the course of production or use. *9383* and *9392* are slivers but have one worn surface. *9381* is a roughly triangular form which has one sawn end and is angled at the other end. This appears to be an

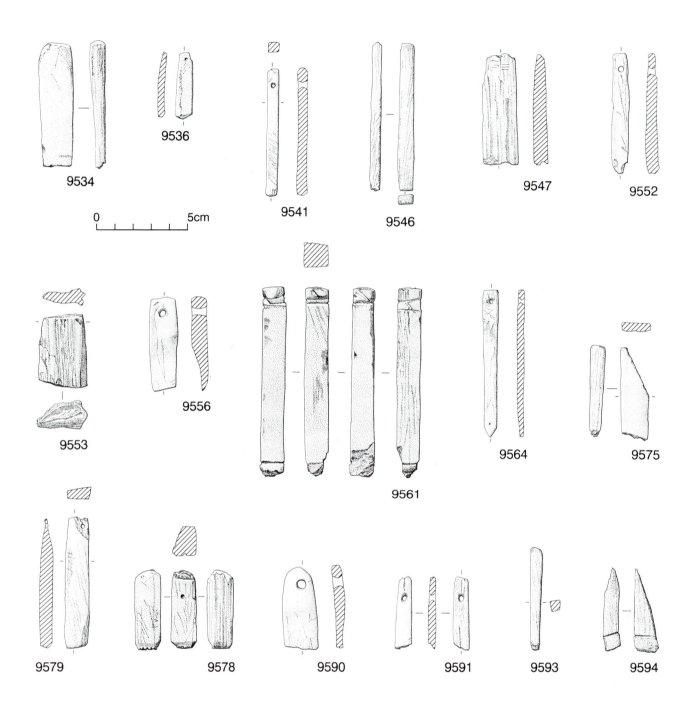

Fig.1209 *Phyllite hones from 16–22 Coppergate. Scale 1:2*

incomplete hone which has been shaped but the surfaces not ground down smooth prior to use. There are a number of short stubby examples as were seen in Tenement D, including *9391* and *9437*.

It is tempting to equate these different spatial distributions with different activities in the various tenements. Over much of the site the distribution may be the normal pattern of loss or discard, but in Tenements C and D the pattern argues for some specific activity taking place in and around the wattle buildings. This might have been the production or finishing of the hones themselves or their use in some other craft. These tenements provide the best evidence for metalworking at this period which includes the manufacture of objects needing to be sharpened, such as blades and needles or pins. Ottaway has shown that there was a concentration

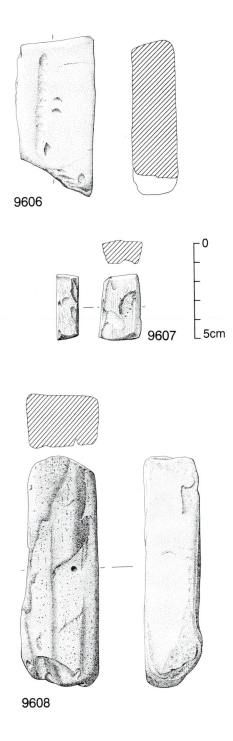

9606

9607

0

5cm

9608

Fig.1210 *Possible touchstones from 16–22 Coppergate. Scale 1:2*

In Period 5A only 39 hones were recovered, of which 24 are schist, nine are sandstone, five are phyllite and one (*9607*) was of uncertain lithology. There is no marked pattern to their distribution and these are probably largely residual from Period 4B.

Eighty-six hones were recovered from Period 5B deposits (Table 230), with schist still the most popular choice of raw material, followed by phyllite and sandstone.

The distribution across the tenements in Period 5B shows that there is still a concentration of hones, especially schist, in Tenements C and D. The concentration, however, is no longer along the street-frontage but is associated with the structures behind them (Structures 5/5 and 5/6 on Tenement C and, to a lesser extent, Structures 5/7 and 5/8 on Tenement D) and with the deposits around and behind the structures. This echoes the distribution of knife blades noted by Ottaway (Fig.242, *AY* 17/6) and, perhaps, the distribution of needles towards the back of Tenement C (Fig.218, *AY* 17/6), but in neither case is there the marked concentration seen in Period 4B.

In Period 5Cf only three hones were recovered in the western corner of the site whereas in Period 5Cr eighteen were found distributed fairly generally across the back of the site. Schist and phyllite are of almost equal frequency and a single sandstone hone was found.

There are also four hones from 22 Piccadilly which can be compared with the Coppergate examples. These are *10631–4* and all show signs of wear,

of needles (p.547, Fig.218, *AY* 17/6) in Tenement C where, in addition, a small anvil was found which he suggests might have been used in needle-making (p.547, *AY* 17/6). Several hones have worn grooves or cavities which might result from the sharpening of their points (e.g. *9310, 9327, 9346, 9357, 9366–7, 9425, 9479, 9523*).

Table 230 Distribution of hones at 16–22 Coppergate according to tenement and stone type in Period 5B

Tenement Geology	A	B	C	D	Rear	Total
Schist	1	8	26	12	2	49
Phyllite	2	2	9	3	7	23
Sandstone	1	2	2	4	1	10
Other	2	0	1	1	0	4
Total	6	12	38	20	10	86

Fig.1211   Unfinished stone hones from 16–22 Coppergate: (from left) 9464, 9504, 9508 and 9510. Actual length of 9510 100mm

especially in the case of *10633* which is the worn out end of a small perforated hone. All were found in Anglo-Scandinavian contexts (Period 4) and all are phyllite, with the exception of *10634* which is schist.

Hones would have had a variety of uses in sharpening and polishing blades and points of all kinds. Some of these uses may have required particular shapes and sizes of hones and there is a wide range amongst the hone assemblage from Coppergate. Size and shape also sometimes correlates with the choice of raw material from which the hones were produced.

The largest hones appear to be made from sandstone (with the exception of *9488* which is schist). Amongst the earliest examples (Period 3) there are broad flat hones (*9310, 9313, 9319*), long thin hones (*9318*) with rounded (*9316*) or square (*9311*) cross-sections. The largest examples in Period 4A are also sandstone, some of which are neat and square (*9322*) while others are more irregular (*9321*). In Period 4B there is a greater variation in size and form among the sandstone examples: *9327* is part of a very large example with squared edges, *9342* is another very large example but has well-rounded edges. There are also examples of small sandstone hones (*9337*), flat

ones (*9324, 9327*) and rounded ones (*9340*), as well as hones which have been perforated for suspension (e.g. *9329*). *9330* has broken across the perforation as it seems the weight was too great to be sustained. *9331* is a good example of a small complete well-worn sandstone hone; *9326* has been cut down from a larger original. This variety in size of sandstone hones continues through Periods 5A, 5B and 5C.

The schist and the phyllite hones show a range of sizes but there are many more smaller, finer examples made from these materials. In Period 4B, where a larger sample is available, there are large schist examples such as *9421, 9435* and *9436* but the majority are smaller. The trapezoidal form of *9444* (Period 5A) appears to be its original shape. Large but still portable examples were recovered from Period 5B deposits, e.g. *9480, 9509*, while other examples, which would have been too heavy to carry about, include *9462, 9464, 9471, 9488* and *9493*. The schist has a tendency to laminate and split which gives an uneven surface and flaking edges. There are many examples of broken hones some of which have been reworked as smaller hones e.g. *9481, 9486, 9496, 9505*; the results can be very small square examples such as *9418*. Many schist and phyllite hones have

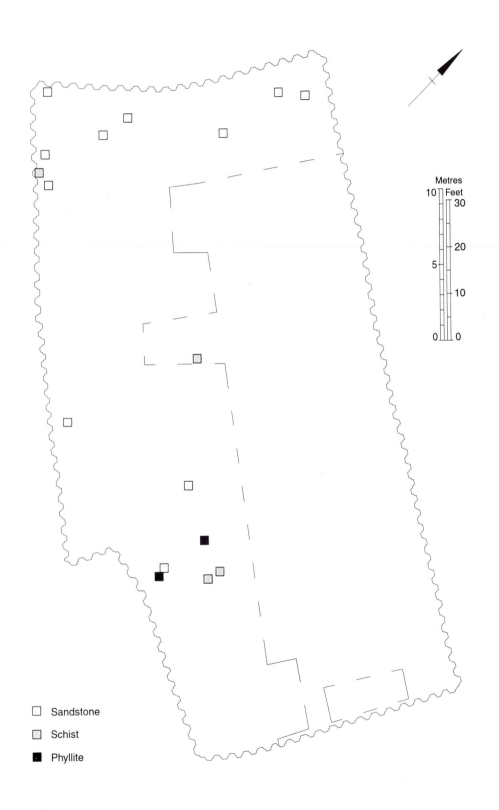

Fig.1212 *Distribution of hones at 16–22 Coppergate in Period 3*

□ Sandstone

▨ Schist

■ Phyllite

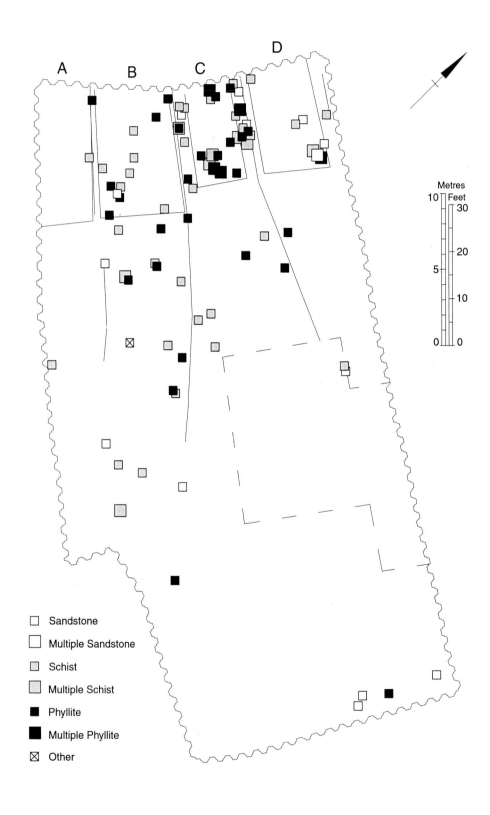

Sandstone

Multiple Sandstone

Schist

Multiple Schist

Phyllite

Multiple Phyllite

Other

Fig.1213 *Distribution of hones at 16–22 Coppergate in Period 4B*

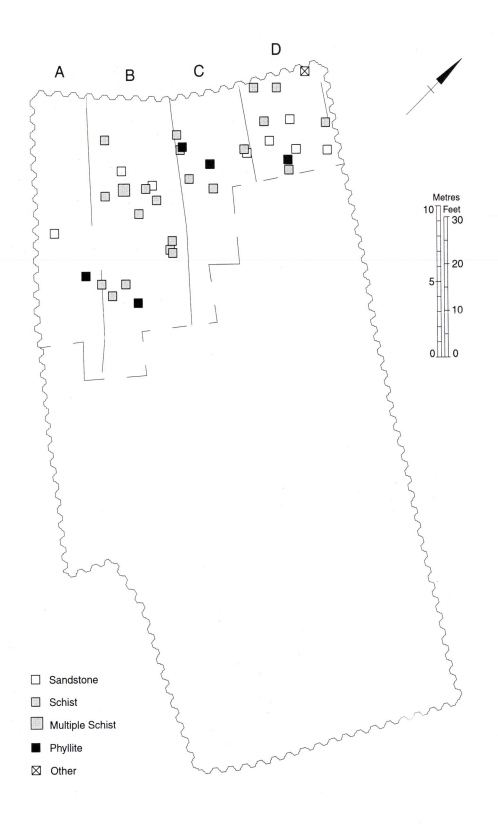

A   B   C   D

Metres
Feet

☐ Sandstone

▨ Schist

▨ Multiple Schist

■ Phyllite

⊠ Other

Fig.1214   *Distribution of hones at 16–22 Coppergate in Period 5A*

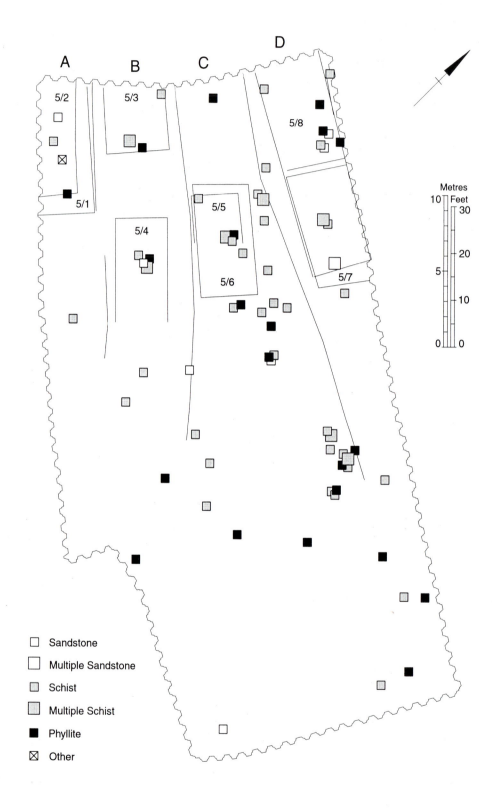

Fig.1215 *Distribution of hones at 16–22 Coppergate in Period 5B*

perforations drilled near one end through which a thong could be threaded to fasten to a belt (*9378, 9380, 9507, 9542, 9552, 9556, 9564, 9579, 9590–1*). Others have a horizontal groove cut around one end into which a thong could be fitted and tied (*9377, 9561, 9594*). *9446* is an elaboration of this idea with a cross sawn into the top of the hone, presumably to knot the thong more securely (Fig.1207). *9563* and *9529* have a number of notches cut into the four corners of the square top, also to secure a thong or thread.

Phyllite was also used mainly to produce small fine hones but again there is a range of sizes. *9551* is amongst the broadest and *9537* at 100mm is the longest. There is a number of very fine examples, such as *9541* which is perforated for suspension, and *9546* which is not (Fig.1209). Phyllite personal hones, those designed to be suspended and carried on a belt, were first recovered in Period 4B (e.g. *9539, 9541, 9552, 9556*) but continue through Period 5A (e.g. *9568, 9572*) and Period 5B (e.g. *9573*). Other small hones in both schist and phyllite, such as *9405, 9534, 9547* and *9575*, exhibit no evidence of having been suspended and must have been carried in small pouches of which there are examples known from this period (P. Walton Rogers, pers. comm.).

The choices between coarseness and size may also have been influenced by differences in function. It has been suggested by MacGregor (p.79, *AY* 17/3), with reference to finds from 6–8 Pavement, that the coarser-grained more local sandstone might have been used for the initial sharpening, and the final honing done with the finer-grained hones. It is worth noting in this regard that the assemblages from the postulated ferrous metalworking tenements (C and D) include the full range of stone types in Period 4B, although there is a marked preference for schist and phyllite as opposed to sandstone. There are, however, large sandstone examples (*9327, 9342, 9351–2* and *9356*) which might be examples of tools used for initial sharpening by the metalworkers.

The question remains as to whether the hones were traded as finished or part-made objects, or as raw material. The evidence from the 12th–13th century Klåstad (near Kaupang, Norway) ship (Christensen 1970) suggests that complete hones were exported, but this one later example may not reflect common practice. There is some evidence from Coppergate that the stone was imported as raw

material or part-made objects and worked into finished hones upon arrival. *9464, 9504, 9508* and *9510* are amongst the best examples of what might be termed roughouts where the shape has been formed but remains unfinished (Fig.1211, p.2492). The techniques of making the hones involved splitting the stone, presumably with some sort of wedge and hammer, then sawing the piece to the required size. There are many examples of hones being sawn halfway through then being crudely broken, leaving a rough end. The ends and the surfaces could then be smoothed and used, though again there are many examples where there are one, two or three worn surfaces and the other surfaces or ends remain unfinished. There are also several examples of a part-drilled perforation, for instance, *9499, 9536* and *9572*. The perforation, however, need not have been part of the original hone as there are examples of part-drilled but incomplete perforations on the ends of hones which are well worn on several surfaces (e.g. *9425, 9572*) or even broken (e.g. *9498*). These may have been hones which have broken across existing perforations, such as *9593*, and a second, or in this particular case, a third perforation is made; or they may be fragments of larger hones which have been reworked; or simply that a perforation was subsequently seen as desirable. In the case of many of the part-drilled perforations (e.g. *9425, 9429, 9498, 9536, 9539, 9572*) it is not clear why the perforation was not finished as the hone has not broken and remained serviceable. Even hones which had fractured across this weak point could still be used (e.g. *9436, 9441, 9499*). There are several unusual examples: a very fine hone *9564* has a worn perforation at the top and a deliberately pointed end which has the beginnings of another hole drilled into it. Broken hone *9377* has a groove for a suspension thong but also the beginnings of a perforation hole drilled into it.

In addition to the five hones discussed above by Dr Gaunt (*9563, 9571, 9582, 9595, 9598*), as being doubtfully equated with purple-phyllite types, there are three objects which may be touchstones (*9606–8*, Fig.1210, p.2491). There is a further example, *9609*, which has the appearance of a hone but which would have been unsuitable for that purpose. Dr Gaunt remarks: 'If the stone is of British origin, then it probably comes from a Lower Palaeozoic source in northern or western Britain. One such possible source suggested by Jack Hartley, formerly Reader in

Geology at the University of Leeds (pers. comm.), is that part of the Silurian Austwick Formation, exposed in Crummock Dale north-west of Settle, formerly called the Moughton Whetstones (Arthurton et al. 1988, 15)'. It is pierced for suspension and still has a copper alloy hoop in place. It has been published elsewhere as a hone or whetstone (Roesdahl et al. 1981, YTC18, 127), but its attractive appearance suggests it may have been used as a pendant.

The shift in preference from sandstone to schist and phyllite has been noted in previous studies in York. At Fishergate hones were made exclusively from sandstone in the Anglian period, but a wider range of imported raw materials was introduced in the Anglo-Scandinavian period (p.1315, *AY* 17/9). This move away from local stones to imported stones is noted again at Flaxengate, Lincoln (Mann 1982), where the range of hones is similar to that from Coppergate and at Lurk Lane, Beverley (Foreman 1991b, 105–6), and is part of a consistent pattern throughout the Viking world. A fall-off in popularity of purple-phyllite during the 11th century has been noted at many of these sites, something which will be taken up in the study of the hones from the post-Conquest period (Ottaway and Rogers, *AY* 17/– in prep.).

Evidence for Manufacture Using Materials other than Metal

Personal ornament and dress accessories

As well as non-ferrous jewellery, personal ornaments in the form of finger-rings, beads, bracelets and pendants were made in York in a variety of other materials including jet, shale, amber and glass.

Evidence for jet and shale working

There is a small amount of evidence that jet, shale and jet-like material were made into personal ornaments at 16–22 Coppergate. This evidence includes raw material, roughouts and both fragmentary and complete objects. There is a larger group of finished objects which are, on typological grounds, certainly Roman in date and, therefore, residual in these post-Roman deposits; this group is not included here. Other classes of object are less diagnostic and while some may also be of Roman origin, there remains the possibility that they are correctly stratified in Anglo-Scandinavian levels. This latter group of material is described in the second half of this fascicule, but the questions surrounding its dating must be emphasised.

The evidence for the working of jet and jet-like material from Anglo-Scandinavian levels includes four pieces of raw material, three from Period 4B levels (*9833, 9835, 9836*) and one from Period 5B (*9837*). These show no spatial clustering and are widely distributed across the site from the front of the street-frontage to the rear of the backyards (Fig.1216). There is a worked fragment from Period 4A (*9832*) and two disc-shaped roughouts, from Period 3 (*9831*) and from Period 4B (*9834*; Fig.1217).

The worked fragment (*9832*) is roughly rectangular in shape and may have been intended for a pendant. The two roughouts (*9831, 9834*) are both disc-shaped and have central V-shaped indentations, presumably in preparation for securing on a lathe. They are likely to have been intended for finger-rings, although the possibility that they were intended as spindle whorls has been raised (Roesdahl et al. 1981, YAJG6, 137). This has been challenged, however, as they would have been too light to have served this function (P. Walton Rogers, pers. comm.), and jet would have been too highly prized to have been used for so humble a task. These three objects are all from the street-frontage area.

Whether this material represents the working of jet and jet-like material during the early Anglo-Scandinavian period or is also residual Roman evidence cannot be determined. Although there is only one fragment of raw jet (sf13924) and no rough-outs from preceding Roman levels on the site, the jet industry thrived in Roman York (Allason-Jones 1996). There are far fewer finds of jet and jet-like material

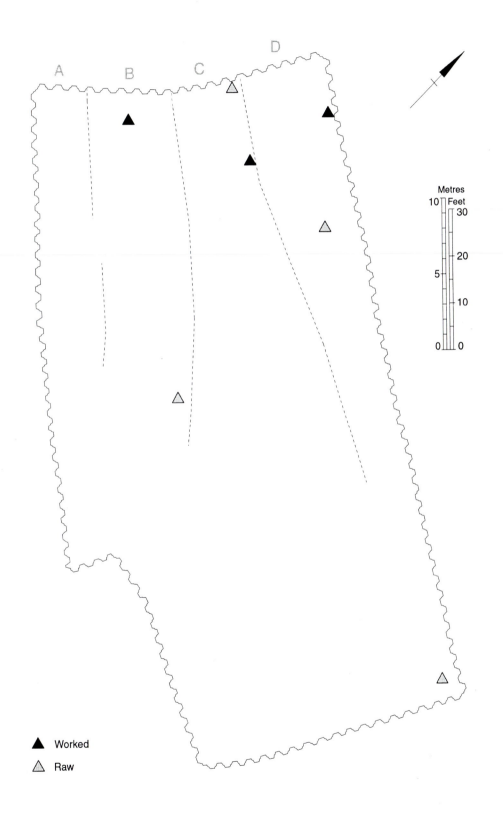

A B C D

Metres
10 Feet
30

20

5
10

0 0

▲ Worked
△ Raw

Fig.1216 *Distribution of evidence for jet working for all periods at 16–22 Coppergate (the tenement divisions A–D relate only to Periods 4B, 5A and 5B)*

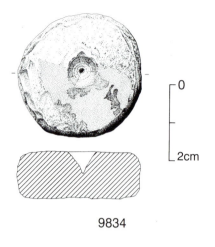

9834

Fig.1217 Evidence for jet working from 16–22 Coppergate: a roughout for a finger-ring. Scale 1:1

from post-Roman contexts in the city. Three pieces of jet or shale were recovered from Anglian contexts at 46–54 Fishergate (*4570–2, AY* 17/9). These include a roughout and two beads, one of which (*4571*) might itself be Roman. A roughout, probably for a ring or perhaps for a large bead was found, unstratified, at 6–8 Pavement where quantities of Anglo-Scandinavian material were also found (*392, AY* 17/3). A roughly worked fragment of uncertain date was also found in the Parliament Street sewer trench (*692, AY* 17/4).

The Clifford Street assemblage produced only a single oval perforated jet disc (Waterman 1959, fig.21.2, 94). Waterman's report, however, includes an exceptional jet pendant in the form of a coiled serpent which is believed to be of 'Norse workmanship' (ibid., fig.21.3). It is believed to have come from the area of the Railway Station.

In addition to the objects described above there are further items made from jet and jet-like material which, although found in medieval contexts, have appeared previously in discussions of Anglo-Scandinavian evidence from this site. Many of these publications appeared soon after excavation had finished and before stratigraphic analysis was complete (Roesdahl et al. 1981, YAJG7, 137–8). This material may well be Anglo-Scandinavian in date; the cross roughout (sf3406) in particular should be seen in the context of two other crosses which are

believed, on typological grounds, to be Anglo-Scandinavian in date and which are discussed on pp.2590–1. They include a small equal-armed pendant cross (*9862*) and a larger more elaborate cross (*9863*) both of which come from Period 6 deposits (Figs.1283–4). A *hnefatafl* piece (*9840*) from post-Norman Conquest deposits is also believed to be residual, but the two jet dice (sfs3696, 4954) are probably medieval in date (Ottaway and Rogers, AY 17/– in prep.).

The extent to which jet was worked and used elsewhere in the Anglo-Scandinavian period is uncertain. There is evidence for working from Flaxengate in Lincoln from mid to late 11th century contexts (Mann 1982, 39, 45), suggesting that rings and possibly pendants were produced there. The quantity, although small, is greater than that recovered from York, and Mann has suggested that this jet constitutes part of a small hoard of Roman date. Evidence of jet working from Lurk Lane, Beverley, appears to be post-Conquest in date (Foreman 1991, 122), with the exception of a triangular pendant (ibid., 210) which is described as being from Period 4 (early 9th–early 10th) and elsewhere as being from Period 5 or 6 (930–1070 or 1070–1188). This, apart from an unworked lump (ibid., 200), is the only pre-Conquest jet from the site. Outside England there is a limited amount of jet working evidence from Dublin (P.F. Wallace, pers. comm.).

Amber working

Two sites, situated about 50 metres apart, provide a range of evidence for Anglo-Scandinavian amber working which is unparalleled in this country. The first collection was recovered in 1884 when building work took place at the Quaker Meeting House on Clifford Street, and it is now part of the Yorkshire Museum collection; the second was recovered almost a hundred years later at 16–22 Coppergate. A few fragments were subsequently found at 22 Piccadilly and the Coppergate watching brief. Although the Coppergate material was recovered from a controlled modern excavation, the assemblage which survives from the Victorian building site gives a fuller picture of the processes involved in the production of beads, finger-rings and pendants. What is missing from the Clifford Street assemblage are the small waste flakes found at Coppergate; these were either not seen during building work or not considered interesting enough to collect. Also missing is a physical and a temporal context for this collection. It is believed to be 11th century in date (Waterman 1959), which is broadly contemporary with the Coppergate evidence, but any evidence for associated structures or features was not recorded. There is, in contrast, some evidence for a focus of activity, if not an actual workshop, at 16–22 Coppergate. Seen together, therefore, these two collections provide much new and complementary evidence for amber working in the 10th and 11th centuries in York.

Amber working tools and techniques

By I. Panter

Acquisition and selection

The raw material was imported into York from Scandinavia and other Baltic regions (pp.2473–4). The absence of an oxidised weathered crust on both raw and working waste suggests that the amber was collected, either from the beach or from shallow inshore waters, rather than being mined.

Baltic amber can be collected from beaches around eastern England (amber is light and floats in sea water), particularly in the aftermath of violent storms. However, the amounts recovered would be insufficient to satisfy the demands of the flourishing trade that the assemblage suggests.

Nevertheless, it is feasible that local sources were used to augment the imported supplies, perhaps being obtained at the same time as quantities of jet and shale were collected from the Whitby region. As the chemical composition of the locally recovered amber is identical to the imported material, it is impossible to distinguish the two by scientific analysis.

Both raw and waste amber from 16–22 Coppergate are generally yellow and orange in colour, with examples ranging from completely transparent through to completely opaque (Fig.1218). Whether the amber is clear or opaque is dependent upon the presence of microscopic air bubbles within the resin, and it is possible to get both transparent and opaque regions within the same lump. These types are known as 'bastard' ambers and are represented in the assemblage, as are the 'osseous' or white opaque types.

The Clifford Street amber tends to be of a much darker variety. The Romans were capable of altering the colour by the use of such substances as kid fat and vegetable matter (Pliny, *Natural History*, Book XXXII), but there is no evidence that this practice was occurring, nor that the technology was understood, during the Anglo-Scandinavian period. The darker colours are more likely to be the result of greater oxidation of the amber caused by the different burial environments found on each site.

Where possible, care would be taken to avoid selecting material which exhibited too many hairline cracks caused by stresses set up as the amber resins solidified and hardened. These are easily seen in transparent ambers, but not in more opaque types. If these flaws were hit during working, then hours of patient skilled work could be undone as the object splits along the natural stress line.

Another internal feature created by such drying stresses are 'stress rings' or 'sun spangles' and their inclusion within an amber lump has usually been highly prized. Pendants *9922* and *10820* exhibit such features; their scarcity indicates that the technology of artificially creating them was not known during this time. There are no examples surviving of either insects or leaves preserved within the material.

Stages in manufacture

A large number of the pendants, rings and beads from both sites retain evidence of the processes and tools used in their manufacture.

For any object, in the first stage the basic shape was roughed out using a knife. Amber cannot be cut into slices, but is soft enough to be carved like ivory or bone, producing a powdery waste. When worked with a knife, a series of characteristic striations which follow the direction of the blade, and ovoid pits, whose long axes are always at right angles to the striations, remain in the surface. These pits result from small chunks of amber being removed by the passage of the knife blade (Egan and Pritchard 1991). A large number of the roughouts and broken pendants still exhibit these features, and *9923* is a good example. The knife was used through all periods.

It is feasible that larger lumps were initially reduced in size, using either a chisel or a saw, although the former is not very controllable and the latter is very slow as the teeth tend to clog up with

Fig.1218   *Amber objects from Clifford Street. Actual length of pendant on far right, 25mm*

the fine amber powder. Pendant *10821*, from Clifford Street, has a series of fine striations within the surface which are not characteristic of a knife blade. Too fine to be caused by a small saw, they may perhaps represent the use of a file, similar to *2248* from Period 5B, which Ottaway (p.522, *AY* 17/6) describes as being used for organic material such as wood and bone, as the teeth are widely spaced to prevent clogging.

Once trimmed to size and shape, the next stage for pendants and beads would be to make the perforation. As with jet, the common practice was to work from both sides, to alleviate the possibility of heat building up and cracking the object, and often the typical hourglass effect created by doing this can still be seen, as in pendant *10821*. Despite the patience

and skill of the person working the amber this way, accidents still occurred as evidenced by the number of objects which fractured at this stage.

Evidence exists which suggests that the perforation was either drilled or an awl was used to force the hole. If drilled, then a series of striations often survive within the amber surrounding the hole, as seen in pendant *9929* (Period 5B) and bead *10773*. Amber is soft enough to enable a hand-held drill to be used, rather than a bow drill, which is usually used on jet. Indeed, the author has successfully perforated amber using small hand-held drills. Although no drill bits themselves have been identified from 16–22 Coppergate, a tool similar to *2267* (Period 5B), described as a twist auger or gimlet (p.535, Fig.208, *AY* 17/6), may have been used.

Pendants *9926* and *9930* have slightly worn surfaces around the perforations which may indicate that an awl was used. As the awl is worked into the amber, the motion used may create a slight flaring similar to wear patterns. As neither of these pendants are completed objects it is likely that such a tool was used. Awls similar to *2707*, described as a leather awl (p.553, Fig.222, *AY 17/6*), or tanged punches, such as *2230* (p.518, Fig.198, *AY 17/6*), may have been used. Bead *9880* appears to have broken when the hole was starting to be pecked out with a similar pointed tool.

Another technique for perforating amber would be to heat up a pointed iron tool and gently push it through to the other side. No evidence for the use of this method has been found in York.

The final stages in the operation would be to remove all traces of the previous work and polish the object, thus improving its colour and lustre. It is known that the translucency of amber will be affected by working, and although no physical evidence survives of the techniques used to improve the quality of the material, it is likely that polishing methods similar to those employed on jet were used (Allason-Jones 1996). The amber powder produced during initial roughing out could be mixed with a suitable oil and applied to the object using a soft cloth or leather. Whether soft polishing stones such as pumice were used is open to debate although there is some evidence for chalk powder being used for this purpose (pp.2517–19).

Lathe turning

A number of rings and beads from both sites have been turned on a lathe, and still retain, within the amber surface, the typical striations made by the tool.

After carving out the rough design, followed by perforating, the object would be attached to the lathe. There is no surviving evidence to suggest whether a pole or bow lathe was used. The object was then worked from both sides, until the desired size and shape were obtained. The outer edges were probably polished whilst still attached to the lathe, then the nearly complete bead or finger-ring was cut off from its central core.

The operation of cutting out the nearly complete bead or finger-ring seems to have been a very risky one, as suggested by the number of broken rejects recovered from Clifford Street. It is interesting to note that when the author carried out a similar operation, an almost identical fracture pattern was obtained.

It is not clear how the roughout was attached to the lathe. Materials such as shale and jet were often attached by either cutting out a square hole from the centre of the roughout and pushing it onto a square peg (Earwood 1993), or by pecking out a series of holes on either side and fastening it to the lathe bed by means of a matching series of iron pins in the lathe spindle (Allason-Jones 1996). These fastening methods were common during the Iron Age and Roman periods, and amber may have been treated in a similar way in the 9th and 10th centuries, particularly as other aspects of jet and amber working were closely connected. The surviving evidence suggests otherwise, however, and a less satisfactory method seems to have been used, possibly contributing to the relatively high number of rejects. From the surviving evidence it would appear that once the central hole had been drilled, the roughout would be pushed onto a circular spindle and worked. As the piece rotated on the lathe, this hole would rapidly wear larger and the amber would become loose and possibly break, if it was not securely fastened. Central cores from Clifford Street have larger and varying diameter holes than the basic roughouts which broke soon after turning commenced. The roughout could have been inserted onto a square or other irregular shaped spindle, but no evidence exists for this.

The best evidence for lathe turning comes from the Clifford Street site, where both beads and finger-rings were produced. Several beads and rings from 16–22 Coppergate, mainly Period 4B, show slight traces of lathe turning. A number of complete beads were probably lathe turned — their almost perfect symmetry suggests this. Most of these artefacts have been turned from opaque ambers, but transparent ambers have been used as well.

Burnt amber

Two pendants, *9928* and *9931,* and a fragment of working debris (sf12712) appear to have been charred or burnt. Although there is evidence to suggest amber was used as a flux during the soldering of gold (Follett 1985) and burnt in oil as a candle (Pliny, *Natural History*, Book XXXII), there is no way of establishing whether the burning was deliberate or accidental. Similar examples were found from Ribe

(Botfeldt and Brinch Madesen 1991) (Fig.1300, **2**, p.2608).

Amber working evidence from Clifford Street

The assemblage comprises 128 pieces of amber which includes evidence for several stages in the manufacture of beads, rings and pendants. These are described below.

Raw amber and preliminary selection of material

There is a collection of fifteen raw amber 'pebbles' which show no sign of having been worked (*10711*). A further group has one possibly cut or flaked surface (*10712–27*), which may be the result of their being discarded as a by-product of initial shaping. The next group includes pieces either shaped in a very preliminary way or retained because their shape was appropriate for a particular item (proto-beads: *10728–9, 10731*; proto-pendants: *10730, 10732*).

Bead making (Fig.1219)

Stage 1: There are two roughly shaped discs, *10733–4*, selected for bead making, which have been discarded before central perforations were begun.

Stage 2: Four examples (*10735–8*) reached the next stage, where the central perforation was begun but not drilled through. In the cases of *10735, 10737* and *10738* this was because the roughout split at this point. The perforation through *10736* was never completed.

Stage 3: Three discs (*10739–41*) have perforations successfully drilled through but they were abandoned at this stage before further shaping or finishing was carried out.

Stage 4: The point at which the perforation has been completed and the bead was being finally shaped, prior to polishing, was clearly a hazardous one. There is a large group of beads of varying thicknesses and diameters which have broken across the perforation at this point (*10742–74*). These include examples with rough surfaces only.

Stage 5: Even at the stage where the surfaces were smoothed and regular but the final polishing had not taken place, the bead could still split across the weak perforation point. Those with surfaces which are finished but unpolished include *10775–9*.

Stage 6: *10780* is an example of an unbroken, but unpolished, bead which was abandoned or lost at this advanced stage. *10781* appears to have had some polishing and may be a completed bead, although there is no sign of wear around the perforation. *10782* has clearly been well polished and is worn around the perforation.

Finger-rings (Fig.1220)

Stage 1: As with the beads, the initial stage was to achieve a flat round disc, of which *10783* is the sole example.

Stage 2: Again, as for beads, the blank was abandoned if it split across a part-drilled perforation (*10784*).

Stage 3: Although the perforation was successfully drilled, the unfinished blank (*10785*) was abandoned at this stage.

The next stages in finger-ring production were more complicated, as they involved cutting out the centre of the blank using a lathe to secure it in place. Several of the rings broke at the stage where the central core was partly cut away. It is clear that polishing was done while the ring was still on the lathe, as several fragments have well-finished surfaces but still retain most of the core. The sequence of tasks is clearly shown by the surviving examples.

Stage 4A: The core was cut away on one side only; no polishing of surfaces was done. Two examples, *10786* and *10787*, broke across the perforation at this stage.

Stage 4B: The core began to be cut away on the other side, some preliminary polishing was done and then in three examples (*10788–90*) they broke, again across the weak point of the perforation.

Stage 4C: The core was deeply cut from both sides and the surfaces were well polished before *10791–2* broke at the same place.

There are two cores (*10793–4*) which have been successfully removed from the blanks. Waterman described them as 'rare barrel-shaped beads' (Waterman 1959, 95), and indeed they could have been used as such, but there is no indication that they have been further worked, finished or polished for this purpose.

Stage 5: There is a single example (*10795*) of a broken finger-ring fragment which shows some signs of wear on the surfaces and represents the finished product.

One unfinished and broken ring (*10796*) which might be a small finger-ring was not produced in this manner. It does not have the regular appearance of being turned on the lathe and seems to have been shaped with a blade from a flat disc. It broke at one point on the circumference before the surfaces were finished, prior to final smoothing and polishing.

Pendants (Fig.1221)

Stage 1: As with the beads and finger-rings, the first stage was to shape an appropriate blank. In the case of *10797*, a flake from a raw pebble was suitably formed and could have provided a tapering pendant blank. *10798* and *10800* were cut to form tapering rectangular blanks and *10801* is a similar smaller example. *10802* is a thin well-shaped blank with cut and bevelled shoulders. None have suspension holes drilled or begun and all could have gone on to the next stage of production.

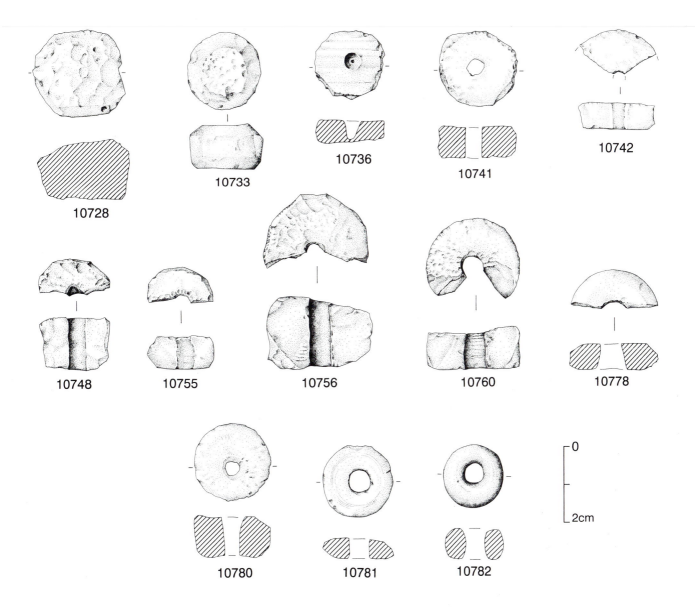

Fig.1219 *Evidence for the manufacture of amber beads from Clifford Street. Scale 1:1*

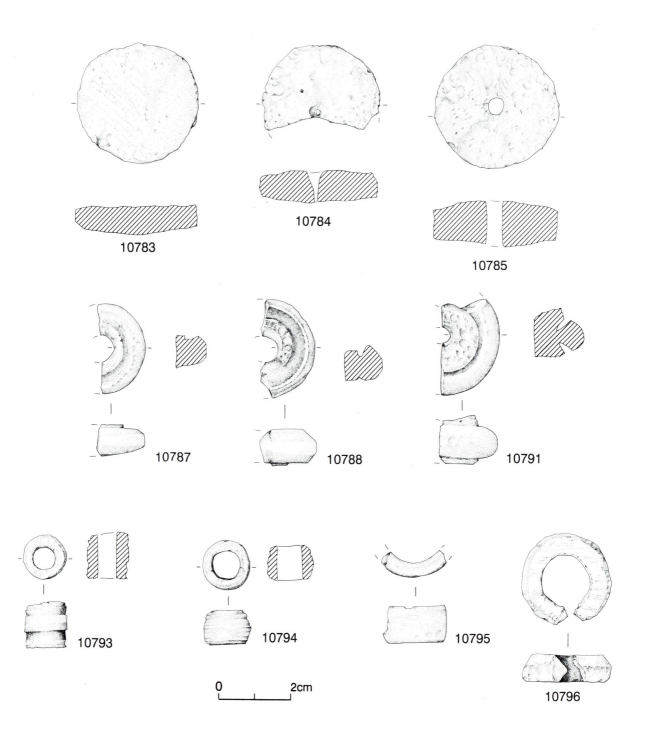

Fig.1220 *Evidence for the manufacture of amber rings from Clifford Street. Scale 1:1*

Stage 2: *10803* and *10804* were abandoned at the stage where a perforation was part-drilled at the top of a pendant roughout.

Stage 3: Drilling suspension perforations was as hazardous with pendants as with rings and beads, and several broke across the part-drilled perforation at this stage: *10805, 10807–8*. In the case of *10811*, it has sheared off at this point although no trace of a part-drilled perforation survives. In other cases the perforation was drilled right through and then broke, before final polishing was done (*10812–14*). *10806* was broken across a natural fissure in the amber.

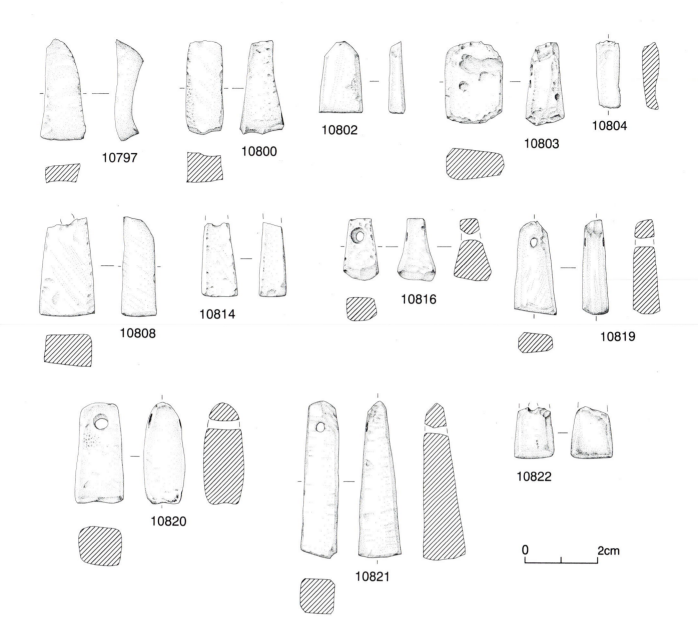

Fig.1221 *Evidence for the manufacture of amber pendants from Clifford Street. Scale 1:1*

Stage 4: Pendants *10815–22* could all have been worn, although some (*10815–17*) have surfaces which are less well finished than others. There has been no attempt to polish these, but some (e.g. *10817*) appear to have some wear around the perforation hole. *10819–21* all appear to be worn around the hole and on the flat surfaces. *10822* has broken across the perforation but in the course of wear, judging by the surfaces, rather than in production.

Two other pendants (*10823–4*, Fig.1283, p.2589) are included for comparison, although they cannot be more closely provenanced than to York. Both are flat wedges with perforations at the narrow end and notches cut into the wide end. One of them, *10823*, broke across the perforation and it can be clearly seen that it was drilled from both sides as it does not meet exactly in the middle.

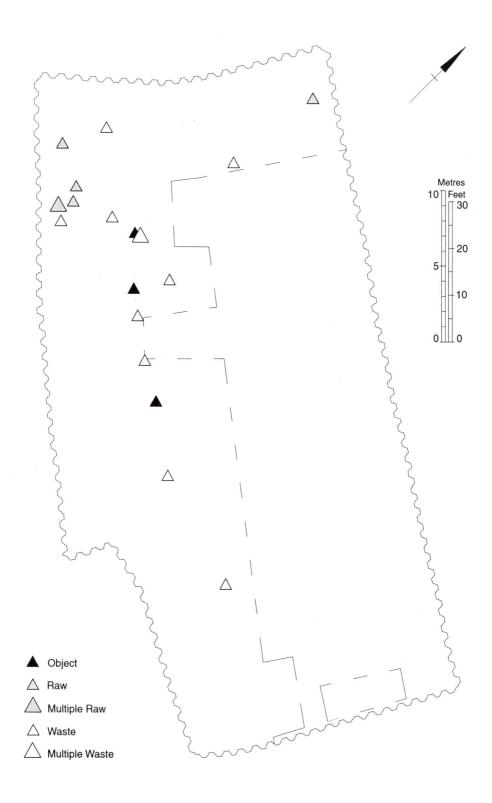

Fig.1222 *Distribution of evidence for amber working in Period 3 at 16–22 Coppergate*

Amber working evidence from 16–22 Coppergate

Raw amber and waste fragments as well as objects roughed-out or broken during production survive from Coppergate, indicating that amber working was taking place there during the Anglo-Scandinavian period. This may have been contemporary with activities at Clifford Street, but there are fewer examples of the different stages of production at Coppergate. This may indicate less activity at Coppergate, although for reasons given above the two assemblages cannot be reliably compared. The material from Coppergate has been grouped into different categories, broadly representing the stages in manufacture seen at Clifford Street, but here they can be given a temporal and spatial context. They appear in the catalogue as raw amber, waste (small flakes which could not be re-used), roughouts and items broken in the course of production.

The number of objects which are complete, or which appear to have been broken and lost during use rather than production, is comparatively small, and their spatial distribution is significantly different from that of the manufacturing evidence. They have been included in the following tables in order to give complete quantifications for each period, but are described in the second half of this fascicule.

Period 3 (c.850–c.900) and Period 1/3

Twenty-one pieces of amber were recovered from Period 3 contexts and one from Period 1/3. Most of this was raw amber and waste material (see Table 231) suggesting that there was some manufacture in the late 9th and early 10th century. The lumps of raw amber were quite small, the largest weighing only 5·18g, and most of the waste material consisted of small chips fractured off larger cores. There are two incomplete objects, a roughout of a bead or ring (*9864*, Fig.1292, p.2597) and a finger-ring (*9903*), which were broken before completion, as the surfaces are unfinished. A further finger-ring (*9904*, Fig.1280, p.2587) shows signs of wear.

Most of the amber was recovered from the strip of land immediately behind the street-frontage and mainly from the south-west corner of the site. This is an area relatively free from pits where a structure might have stood. There is a collection of two finger-

Table 231 Evidence for amber working in Period 3 at 16–22 Coppergate

Raw	Waste	Roughout	Broken in production	Complete	Broken after use
6	12	1	1	1	0

rings and two waste fragments from a dump, a little way back from the street-frontage. The distribution of the amber in the backyards is towards the centre of the site where the build-up of deposits is deepest, and apparently avoids the main area of pits encountered along the south-west boundary.

Only six pieces of amber (including two of the rings) were recovered from pit-fills; the rest are from dumps and built-up material.

Period 4A (c.900–c.930/5)

Twelve pieces of amber were found in Period 4A deposits, and these were distributed fairly generally across the area excavated, though avoiding the south-west corner (Fig.1223). In the south-eastern corner of the site four contexts (25890, 25994, 30039, 30352) produced four pieces of waste and a bead (*9877*) from dumps and material accumulation.

A total of seven pieces of waste were recovered together with a small bead (*9875*) which was broken during production, a bead or possibly a small ring (*9876*) and another broken bead (*9877*). A further bead, *9881*, shows clear signs of wear.

Period 4B (c.930/5–c.975)

In the middle decades of the 10th century, post-and-wattle structures were constructed in each of the four tenements, and in the course of Period 4B they

Table 232 Evidence for amber working in Period 4A at 16–22 Coppergate

Raw	Waste	Roughout	Broken in production	Complete	Broken in use
1	7	0	3	1	0

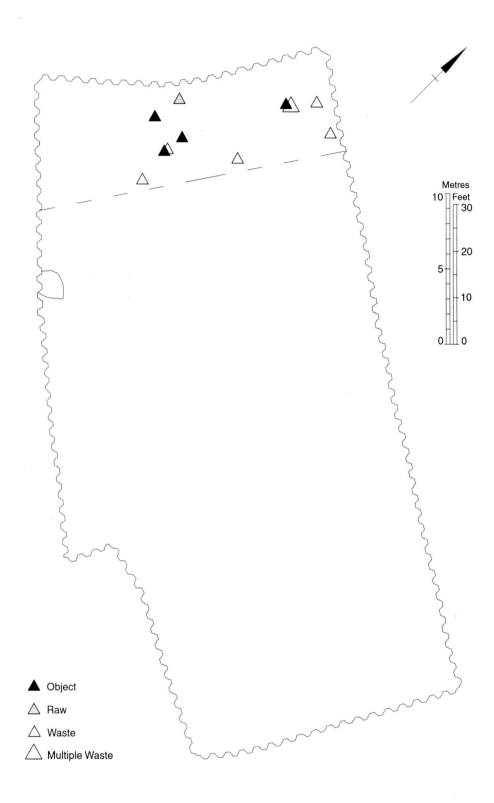

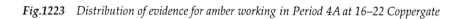

Fig.1223   Distribution of evidence for amber working in Period 4A at 16–22 Coppergate

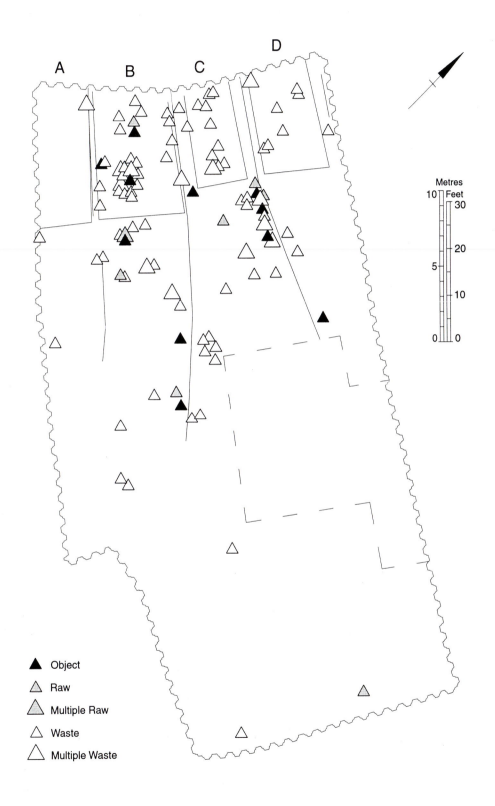

Fig.1224 *Distribution of evidence for amber working in Period 4B at 16–22 Coppergate*

Table 233 Evidence for amber working in Period 4B at 16–22 Coppergate

Raw	Waste	Roughout	Broken in production	Fragment	Broken in use	Complete	Total
8	124	12	7	1	5	4	161

went through several phases of repair and reconstruction.

The first large assemblage of amber is from Period 4B deposits, from which over 160 fragments were recovered (Table 233). Only nine are finished objects, of which only four survive intact. Of the remaining 152, seven objects appear to have been broken during production and twelve are part-made but incomplete (e.g. *9898, 9900*). The rest of the material is raw, unworked amber and manufacturing waste (see Table 233).

The distribution pattern of raw amber and manufacturing debris shows a concentration in the succession of wicker buildings in Tenement B, suggesting some manufacturing took place there. The floor deposits in particular produced almost 60 fragments of amber, much more than the surviving floor levels in the wicker buildings in Tenements A, C and D (see Table 235 and Fig.1224).

The small amount of material which survives from Tenement A must result in part at least from the almost entire destruction of the post-and-wattle building on that site by the succeeding Structure 5/1 in Period 5B. The post-and-wattle structure on Tenement B was also substantially destroyed in Period 5B by the construction of Structure 5/3, and most of the amber from Tenement B comes from a strip of land between the back of the Period 5B Structure 5/3

and the front of Structure 5/4 where Period 4B deposits survived intact. It is reasonable to suppose that there may have been more amber from within the Period 4B building which was removed when Structure 5/3 was constructed. The rest of the material is from the backyard areas.

Although the structures on Tenements C and D survived well, there is less evidence for amber working from their floor levels and interior deposits. This is in marked contrast with the evidence for ferrous and non-ferrous manufacturing evidence in Period 4B which shows a concentration on Tenements C and D, with correspondingly little evidence of activity in Tenement A and B.

The build up of deposits and the dumps behind the post-and-wattle buildings also produced raw amber, waste and half-finished objects. This material may have arrived there as a result of the periodic cleaning of the floors of the structures, with the sweepings being dumped immediately outside. Alternatively, manufacturing may have taken place outdoors, the craftsmen taking advantage of good light to shape objects. There is very little material from further back in the backyard areas and as amber debris would pose no hygienic or obstructive problem, in most cases it would remain where it fell, unless the deposits were subsequently disturbed or larger pieces of waste amber retrieved for reworking.

Table 234 Evidence for amber working in Period 4B at 16–22 Coppergate according to object type

	Rough-out	Broken in production	Broken in use	Complete	Total
Pendant	3	1	2	2	8
Beads	5	2	1	1	9
Rings	4	4	2	1	11

Table 235 Location of evidence for amber working in Period 4B at 16–22 Coppergate

Tenement	A	B	C	D
Floor deposits	5	56	9	10
Dumps and build-up behind the buildings	2	28	30	1
Total	7	84	39	11

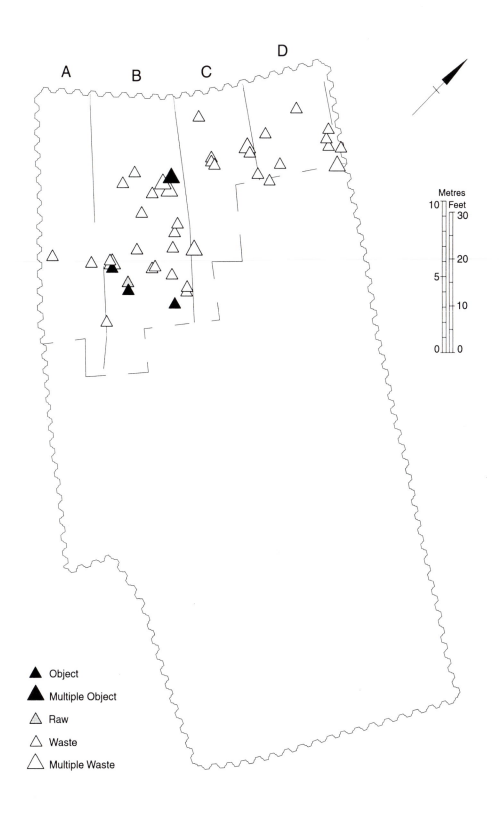

Fig.1225 *Distribution of evidence for amber working in Period 5A at 16–22 Coppergate*

Table 236 Evidence for amber working in Period 5A at 16–22 Coppergate

Raw	Waste	Roughout	Broken in production	Fragment	Broken in use	Complete	Total
2	43	1	8	1	2	1	58

Although little amber was recovered from the floor levels of the post-and-wattle structure on Tenement C, the amount of amber recovered from the dumps and built-up deposits behind the wattle building on this tenement is comparable to the amount found in this area on Tenement B (Table 235). The material is incorporated into dumps, which are concentrated along the northern boundary between Tenements C and D. There may, therefore, have been a short-lived and small-scale episode of amber working on Tenement C which may or may not have been contemporary with the ferrous and non-ferrous metalworking.

The manufacture of beads, rings and pendants seems to have been carried out in almost equal proportions (Table 234), with examples of each being lost or discarded during production.

Period 5A (c.975)

Fifty-eight fragments of amber were recovered from Period 5A (Table 236) and the distribution echoes that of the Period 4B pattern (Table 237). Most of the amber was recovered from Tenement B. This material most probably derives from Period 4B activities as there is no occupation ascribed to Period 5A. It is of some interest that most, although not all, of the amber from Period 5A deposits is from along the northern edges of the property boundaries,

perhaps indicating that that was the direction in which the upcast material from the digging of the basements of the Period 5B buildings was dumped. Bead production predominates in this small collection of identifiable object types (Table 238).

Period 5B (c.975–early/mid 11th century)

During Period 5B the second major phase of building took place along the street-frontage. A number of contemporary and successive plank-built structures with semi-basement features were erected on each tenement (see p.2460).

On Tenement A, two successive structures were erected, 5/1 followed by 5/2. Five pieces of amber were recovered from the backfill of Structure 5/1 and one fragment of waste was recovered from a Structure 5/2 floor level. The rest of the material came from dumps and cut features behind the building. The twelve pieces of amber recovered all represented the various stages in the manufacturing process.

On Tenement B there is evidence for two probably contemporary structures. Structure 5/3 stood on the street-frontage with Structure 5/4 behind it. Only four fragments of amber waste were recovered from floor levels in Structure 5/3; a further eleven pieces were recovered from backfill material. The pottery

Table 237 Evidence for amber working in Period 5A at 16–22 Coppergate by tenement

Tenement			
A	B	C	D
3	33	10	12

Table 238 Evidence for amber objects in Period 5A at 16–22 Coppergate

	Rough-out	Broken in production	Broken in use	Complete	Total
Pendant	0	2	0	1	3
Beads	1	5	1	0	7
Rings	0	1	1	0	2

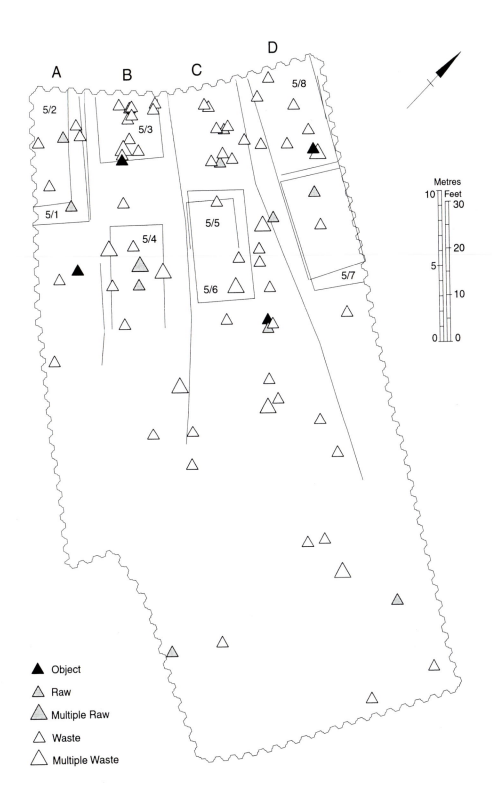

Fig.1226 *Distribution of evidence for amber working in Period 5B at 16–22 Coppergate*

Table 239 Evidence for amber working and objects in Period 5B at 16–22 Coppergate

Tenement	A	B	C	D	Total
Raw	3	7	2	2	14
Roughout	1	1	4	2	8
Broken in production	0	3	2	5	10
Waste	8	26	38	16	88
Total of manufacturing evidence	12	37	46	25	120
Complete	0	0	2	2	4
Broken in use	0	0	0	1	1
Total of finished items	0	0	2	3	5

(*AY* 16/7, fig.222) suggests that the building was out of use by the early/mid 11th century.

Four pieces of amber (two waste and two raw) were recovered from floor levels in Structure 5/4, and another twelve fragments from later dumps and backfills. The other pieces of amber from Tenement B were scattered around and behind the structures, and is representative of the different stages of production (including two roughed-out pendants) and does not include complete items or items broken in use.

No evidence survives of a structure at the front of Tenement C in Period 5B but a sequence of two buildings, Structures 5/5 and 5/6, were excavated 6–7m back from the street-frontage. Few occupation deposits survived in either of these and most amber was recovered from dumps, build-up and from the fills of pits, gullies and other cut features. A high proportion of manufacturing debris of one sort or another was found and only two complete objects, a pendant (*9927*) and a bead (*9891*). Roughed-out but recognisable objects included five further beads, a finger-ring and a pendant. Most of these were found along a strip adjacent to the northern property boundary with Tenement D.

The pattern of structures is different again on Tenement D where two successive structures were excavated. No occupation layers could be identified in either structure. Manufacturing debris and a completed bead and pendant came from the backfill of Structure 5/7 while the rest of the material was recovered from pits, build up and subsequent dumps in Structure 5/8.

In Period 5B there appears to be a slight shift in favour of pendants over beads and rings being manufactured, but the sample is small.

Period 4/5

Contexts ascribed to Period 4/5 produced two pieces of waste (sfs5401 and 14359) and a single piece of raw amber (sf4678).

Period 5Cf and 5Cr

In two areas of the site, deposits were recovered which have been ascribed to the central decades of the 11th century. While the two areas are broadly contemporary they cannot be linked stratigraphically. Apart from a pendant (*9935*), small amounts of raw and waste material were recovered from Period 5C. Both this and the amber from Period 6 deposits is likely to be residual from earlier activities. Only a single fragment of amber was recovered from a dump deposit in the north-east corner of the site in Period 5Cf. In Period 5Cr amber was found in accumulated deposits, dumps and occasionally from pit-fills across the rear of the site.

Discussion

The material from Clifford Street and 16–22 Coppergate represents the first detailed evidence for the manufacture of amber objects in York. There are further small amounts of material from the Coppergate/High Ousegate/Piccadilly area, which suggest that amber working was common practice in the Anglo-Scandinavian period. Three pieces of raw unworked amber were recovered from Period 4 deposits at 22 Piccadilly (*10678–80*); a finger-ring roughout (*10626*) and a polished fragment from a ring or bead (*10627*) were found during the watching brief at Coppergate. Nearby excavations at 6–8 Pavement in 1972 produced four beads and a fragment of a finger-ring (*393–7, AY* 17/3) (Fig.1187, **9**, p.2452); one of the beads (*396*) appears to have been broken during production. Nine fragments of raw amber, one of which is partly worked, were recovered from a sewer trench in Parliament Street together with a finger-ring fragment (*693–4, AY* 17/4), and a further two fragments, one raw and one worked (*989, AY* 17/4), were found at 34 Shambles (Fig.1187, **7, 8**). Excavations in King's Square (YAT 1988.8) produced further evidence in the form of raw amber, waste material, two beads broken in production as well as a broken discoid bead (Fig.1187, **5**). Excavations in the Little Stonegate and Swinegate area (YAT 1990.1) produced further limited evidence of amber working in the form of waste flakes and a decayed bead fragment (Fig.1187, **3, 4**). Across the River Ouse, a fragment of raw amber was recovered at North Street (YAT 1993.1) and further evidence was found at the Queen's Hotel site, 1–9 Micklegate (YAT 1988.17), where twelve minute fragments of amber were recovered, as well as a faceted pin-head of uncertain date (Fig.1187, **19, 20**). A further eight to ten sites in the city have produced one or two pieces of raw or waste amber flakes and isolated objects. The bulk of this evidence comes from Anglo-Scandinavian deposits but it must be noted that medieval amber rosary beads are known from a number of sites in the city and may also have been produced in York.

Outside York, in the rest of the Danelaw, there is no evidence of amber working on anything approaching the same scale. At Lurk Lane, Beverley, there is only one piece of amber, or some other form of resin, which could be classified as working waste, and only one further amber bead (Foreman 1991, 221, fig.99, *215*); both pieces are likely to be post-Conquest. A single piece of weathered, raw amber was recovered from a 10th or early 11th century context at Flaxengate, Lincoln (Mann 1982, 39, *392*). No amber is recorded from Viking Age levels in the East Anglian sites of Thetford or Norwich and the amber working evidence from London is medieval in date (Egan and Pritchard 1991, 305–9) (Fig.1299, **5, 9, 10, 11**, p.2606).

Beyond England there is plentiful evidence from Dublin where excavations at Wood Quay/Fishamble Street produced a range of types comparable with those found at Coppergate (P. Harvey de Terra, pers. comm.) (Fig.1299, **16**). If recent finds to the east of Wood Quay at the West End site, Temple Bar, are taken into account, an even greater quantity, over 4,000 pieces, was found. Over half of the Dublin houses and yards produced amber finger-rings, pen-

dants and beads as well as raw amber, roughouts, broken objects and waste. One building plot (Plot 2) and one house in particular (House FS20) produced a large concentration of amber. The range of bead type appears to be more extensive than in York but methods of production are closely comparable.

Chalk cores or burnishers (Fig.1227)

The Anglo-Scandinavian assemblage includes a group of objects whose purpose is not clear but which might have had a role in amber, and possibly jet, working. These objects are made of chalk and all have evidence of having been used either as a source of powdered chalk or for directly polishing or burnishing some softer material. The nearest sources of chalk are in the Yorkshire Wolds, which extend to within 25km of York.

They can be roughly categorised into three groups on the basis of form. The first group contains eleven examples which are either rod-shaped or cone-shaped, their form resulting from wear on all the outer surfaces, creating a faceted, conical effect. Although three of these examples belong to Period 4A, the bulk of them are from Period 4B, with one or two later examples. Three of them are distinctly cone-shaped; *9648* and *9657* appear to be the bases of cones from which the tips have been broken and *9640* is either a small cone or the tip off a larger one. *9657* is burned and the chalk surface has fractured. All show signs of wear around the outer surfaces as if either a blade has repeatedly scraped chalk off the core or the core has been used as a polisher or burnisher. The others in the group have the same wear patterns but are more rod-shaped than conical. In most cases the objects appear to be the surviving original ends after use had worn away the rest; the exceptions are *9644* and *9651* which have two broken ends and are presumably part of the shaft of the original object. *9647* is the largest and thickest of the range and is more squared in cross-section with horizontal cuts on three surfaces and a worn fourth surface. *9652* is a rod with a faceted circular cross-section and a worn flat surface near the base. The bases of *9641, 9643, 9649* and *9652* are all slightly angled, possibly as a result of being held down against a work surface and a blade being stroked up and down against the shaft. The end of *9639* forms a slight foot which might have been caused by a similar process.

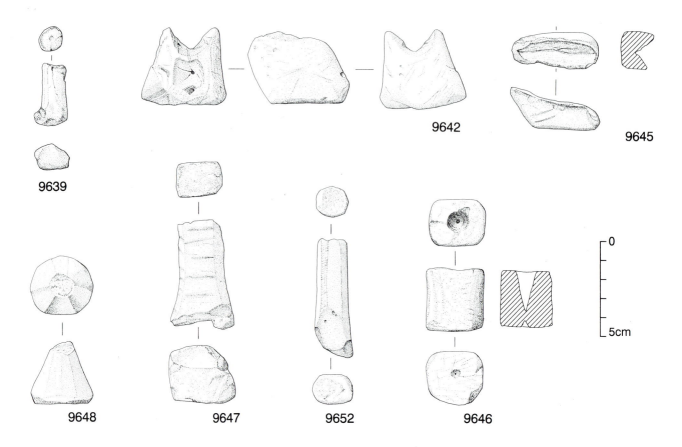

Fig.1227 *Chalk cores and burnishers from 16–22 Coppergate. Scale 1:2*

The second group comprises objects which have worn holes or perforations (*9646, 9650, 9654, 9656, 9658, 9659*). Two of them (*9646* and *9656*) are approximately square (c.20–25mm²) and have cone-shaped regular depressions worn more than half-way though the object. The larger of the two objects (*9646*) also has a small cone-shaped hole worn into the other end. *9654* is square-shaped but flatter and has a hole worn right through one surface and has worn or bevelled edges. A smaller cube (10mm²) from Period 6, *9658*, has holes through all six faces, all apparently worn by a point as the holes are cone-shaped. This may be an unusual bead or playing piece but needs at least to be considered with this group. Similarly *9659* (also from Period 6) may have been a simple disc-bead with a wide central perforation but it too may be related to this group. The final piece in this group (*9650*), although broken, is more irregular in form and is perforated right through.

The third group comprises five chalk lumps of various shapes all of which show similar signs of wear. Two of them, *9642* and *9660*, have hollowed,

concave channels on one surface as the result of wear and, in addition, *9642* has two flattened, smooth surfaces and a conical depression of the sort seen on two from the first group. *9660* also has another smoothed surface. *9653* is a flat, approximately tri-angular, piece with one surface worn smooth and *9655* is a broken fragment of a flat disc with worn, slightly faceted edges; it might have been broken off a larger cone of the type described above. *9645* is a small boat-shaped piece with a smooth base which has been worn flat, two smooth sides and a worn, almost V-shaped, central depression. A deep scratch at the base of this worn centre suggests a point has been used to produce this result.

The distribution of these objects across the site is interesting. Of the 22, there are nine from Periods 4A and 4B which are from the front and centre of Tenement B, one of them (*9642*) from the floor level in the wattle building. A further four from these early periods are from the front and centre of Tenement C, two from floor levels in the wattle building. Three are from the front and centre of Tenement D, one from the floor

Table 240   Location of chalk objects at 16–22 Coppergate

	Tenement			
	A	**B**	**C**	**D**
Front		9639 (4A)	9830 (5A)	9653 (5A)
		9640 (4A)	9826 (4B)	9656 (5B)
		9641 (4A)		
		9652 (5A)		
Floor level	9651 (4B)	9642 (4B)	9979 (4B)	9830 (4B)
			9645 (4B)	
Centre	10445 (3)	10351 (3)	9650 (4B)	9647 (4B)
		9644 (4B)		9646 (4B)
		11075 (4B)		
		9648 (4B)		
Rear		9818 (4B)	9657 (4B)	

level of one of the buildings. There is a single Period 4B example from the rear of Tenement B and a residual example (*9660*) from the back of Tenement C. The objects are clearly associated with an activity which took place in and around the structures. One possible explanation is that the objects were the source of chalk powder which, mixed with oil, was used as a mild abrasive to polish the surface of amber and possibly jet. The distribution pattern, with its emphasis on Tenement B, offers some support for this suggestion in relation to the amber.

Excavation at 6–8 Pavement in York produced a much larger but similarly shaped chalk cone with faceted cuts around it. The discussion of that object includes references to other examples from late 11th and 12th century contexts in Oxford (*379*, p.77, Fig.39, *AY* 17/3) and similar objects were also recovered from Flaxengate, Lincoln (Mann 1982, 39, *411–24*, fig.45). Many of the Lincoln examples are described as tapering blocks of rectangular, circular, ovoid or polygonal section, and the illustrated examples have parallels amongst the Coppergate group. Mann also concludes that the uneven facing is the result of wear rather than cutting and suggests a use as 'rubbers' in some finishing process. Most were recovered from later 11th and 12th century contexts, indicating a slightly later date than the York examples. It may be significant that the jet working evidence from Flaxengate is also 11th century in date, and there may be a connection between the use of powdered chalk or chalk blocks for jet working on Flaxengate and their proposed use in an earlier context for amber or jet working at Coppergate.

Glass Manufacturing Evidence

By J. Bayley and R. Doonan

Introduction

Around the 10th century a new type of glass came into use in Britain, for beads, rings and other trinkets (e.g. Bayley 1985); from the 9th–13th century it was commonly used for similar objects in eastern Europe (Ullrich 1989). Unlike most earlier glass, of which the main components were soda, lime and silica, it was a lead glass, containing up to 70% by weight lead oxide, the rest comprising silica, with only low levels of other elements. Although some lead is found in opaque-coloured glass and enamels in earlier periods, these only contain a maximum of 30% lead oxide. The new high-lead glass was a translucent yellow colour, though copper was often added to produce a translucent green or, when present in larger quantities, a much darker opaque green that can look almost black. Glass of this type was not used to make vessels in north-west Europe until the 13th–early 14th century (Baumgartner and Kreuger 1988; Tyson 1996).

York is one of the few English towns that has produced evidence for the working of high-lead glass; the others include Gloucester (Bayley 1979) and Lincoln (Gilmour 1988, 70). The evidence is mainly

Table 241 High-lead glass and glass working finds from York

| Site | Crucible sherds | | Waste | Objects | Date of activity and/or objects |
	Stamford	Other			
16–22 Coppergate	259	–	yes	beads, rings	mid-10th century onwards
16–22 Coppergate	–	47	–	slick-stones	late 10th century onwards
22 Piccadilly	1362	1	yes	beads	10th/11th century onwards
34 Shambles	–	11	yes	beads	?12th–early13th century
6–8 Pavement	–	–	–	beads, rings	Anglo-Scandinavian
7–13 Pavement	–	–	–	beads, rings	Anglo-Scandinavian
Clifford Street	–	–	yes	beads	Anglo-Scandinavian

in the form of the crucibles in which the glass was melted, but there are also part-made and failed objects and glass waste.

This report discusses the analyses of some of this glass working debris and some of the possible products of the industry from two sites in York: 16–22 Coppergate and 22 Piccadilly. Although some tables are reproduced here, others are reproduced in the Ancient Monument Laboratories report (Bayley and Doonan 1999).

High-lead glass working in York

A number of York sites, all within 200 metres of each other, have produced evidence for the working of high-lead glass. Other sites in the same area have artefacts made of this type of glass, though no manufacturing waste has been identified from them (p.226, *AY 17/4*). Table 241 summarises these finds.

A number of different types of pottery were used as crucibles. Eleven sherds came from 34 Shambles, one in a fine red fabric, three of a buff gritty fabric and seven of a red gritty fabric. The forms were probably fairly shallow bowls with a simple rim with a diameter of 105–50mm.

Nearly 85% of the Coppergate crucibles, and all but one of the Piccadilly crucibles, are Stamford ware. Most are bowls, twice as wide as they are deep, with a slightly flanged rim and a diameter of 120–150mm, sloping sides and a flattish base (*AY 16/5*, p.472,

fig.205, *2345*). The remainder of the Coppergate crucibles are in oxidised gritty fabrics, with similar forms but simple rims (*AY 16/5, 2357–66*), like those from 34 Shambles (*AY 16/3*, p.229, fig.91, *845–50*). A single sherd from Piccadilly was of this type, and a further sherd from the site was a Stamford ware metal-melting crucible that had been used to melt high-lead glass.

The Coppergate and Piccadilly high-lead glass

The Coppergate crucibles mainly contain dark green or almost black glass. This is true of a large proportion of the 24 crucible sherds from context 17890, and also 85% of the sherds from Piccadilly. About 10% of the Piccadilly sherds had blue alkali glass on them; they are discussed below (pp.2525–8). A sample of the main group of Piccadilly crucible sherds was analysed qualitatively by X-ray fluorescence (XRF). This showed the major element present in the glass was lead, together with some copper. Samples cut from nine sherds were examined and analysed quantitatively using an energy-dispersive analyser on a scanning electron microscope (SEM).

The SEM images showed the glass all contained subrounded silica particles. These were larger than the silica temper in the crucible fabric, and so could not have eroded out from the crucible surface. They

Fig.1228 *High-lead glass beads from 16–22 Coppergate: (from top left)* 10071, 10170, 10138, 10081, 10260, 10240. *Actual diameter of* 10071 *is 7·2mm*

Table 242 High-lead glass waste from 16–22 Coppergate. The elements are listed in order of decreasing abundance; question marks denote uncertainty. Where no catalogue number is recorded, the find was not given a small find number

Catalogue Number	Context	Description	Elements	Period
9968	27819	Black glass fragment (?high-lead glass)	–	P3
9969	27819	Green high-lead melted glass	–	P3
9971	30189	'Black' high-lead glass on fired clay	–	P3
9975	27017	Fired clay with golden-brown high-lead glass	Pb Fe Cu ?Zn	P4B
–	6284	Fired clay interleaved with green high-lead glass	–	P5B
–	6785	Fired clay interleaved with green/yellow high-lead glass	Pb Fe Cu Zn	P5B
9977	16882	Green high-lead glass lump (24 x 18 x 8mm)	–	P5B
9983	6774	Green glass on iron wire	Pb Fe Cu Zn	P5Cr
–	6774	Fired clay interleaved with green high-lead glass	–	P5Cr
9979	15311	High-lead green glass waste on fired clay	Pb Fe Cu	P5Cr
–	5348	Hearth lining with Pb/Cu-rich vitrified surface layer	Pb Cu Fe Zn ?Sn	P6 (C6e1/D6a16)
–	5781	Fired clay interleaved with green high-lead glass	Pb Fe Cu Zn	P6 (C6e6)
–	9224	Lump of golden-brown high-lead glass (35 x 33 x 20mm)	–	P6 (C6e9)
–	16525	Fired and vitrified clay with green high-lead glass	–	P6 (D6a13–14)
–	9305	Fired clay interleaved with green high-lead glass	Pb Cu Fe Zn	P6 (D6a24)
–	9801	High-lead brown glass lump (15 x 12 x 10mm)	Pb Fe Zn Cu	P6 (D6y1)

must therefore have been a deliberate component of the glass melt. This suggests that the glass had been made, rather than just melted, in the crucibles. Heraclius, probably writing in the 12th century (Merrifield 1967, 216), gives a recipe which involved heating together equal volumes of lead oxide, sand (silica) and colouring the resulting glass by adding copper. Heraclius' recipe gives a composition similar to that found by analysis.

The analyses, which were made of areas without unreacted quartz grains, show that the glass in most of the crucibles has a consistent composition, typically 60–70% lead oxide (PbO), 25–30% silica (SiO_2) and 5–10% copper oxide (CuO), though there is some variation between different areas on the same sherd (Bayley and Doonan 1999). The levels of alkalis (Na_2O, K_2O) and alkali earths (MgO, CaO) are very low compared with most glasses, suggesting they are accidental contaminants, rather than deliberate additions. No other elements are present at high enough levels to be deliberate.

On about 3% of the Piccadilly sherds some or all of the glass is opaque red, orange or ginger-brown rather than green/black, but its chemical composition is no different. This colour change was caused by melting conditions becoming more reducing, so some of the copper was present as finely divided metal or as Cu_2O rather than as CuO. In several crucibles droplets of metallic lead were also found in the glass, another indicator of insufficiently oxidising conditions. No tin or zinc was detected in any of the quantitatively analysed glass, although traces of both metals were found on some sherds that were analysed by XRF. This suggests that both pure copper and a range of copper alloys were used as colourants; all these metals were present on the Coppergate site (p.809, Fig.357, AY 17/7), as were c.30kg of scrap and waste lead (p.810, ibid.).

The glass on two of the analysed sherds was a lead silicate, like the rest, but had a copper content. of under 1%. This suggests that high copper contents were not necessary to produce the desired green colour.

Table 242 lists a group of finds from 16–22 Coppergate which provide additional evidence of high-lead glass working. There are pieces of fired clay, interleaved with high-lead glass, and lumps of glass of this type. They probably represent glass that was spilt from the crucibles and soaked into the hearth

Table 243 Measured density of a sample of beads from 16–22 Coppergate

Catalogue Number	Density	Colour	Comments
10072	5·92	yellow	
10083	5·74	yellow	
10097	5·75	yellow	
10099	5·51	yellow	
10134	5·74	yellow	
10148	5·59	yellow	
10150	4·45	yellow	tapering hole does not fully perforate bead
10177	5·72	yellow	
10181	5·62	yellow	
10182	6·80?	yellow	density measurement unreliable
10231	6·75?	yellow	very small, glass looks opaque. Density measurement unreliable

Table 244 XRF analysis of selected glass beads from 16–22 Coppergate. The results of the SEM analysis are presented in Bayley and Doonan 1999

Catalogue Number	Context	Colour	SEM	Elements detected by XRF
10071	18489	yellow	–	Pb Fe ?Cu
10081	3543	yellow	–	Pb Fe ?Cu
10094	15592	yellow	–	Pb Fe ?Cu
10132	15432	yellow	yes	Pb Fe ?Cu
10138	6927	black	yes	Pb Fe ?Cu
10151	15311	black?	–	Pb Fe
10170	12412	green	yes	Pb Cu Fe ?Mn
10171	9801	green	–	Pb Cu Fe
10173	16734	yellow	yes	Pb, Fe
10240	6866	black	–	Pb Fe ?Cu
10257	7782	green	–	Pb Cu Fe
10264	31389	opaque orange	–	Cu Sn Fe
10265	25350	opaque red	–	Cu Zn Sn Fe
10335	16733	green	–	Pb Cu Fe

lining. Most of the glass is green/black and contains appreciable amounts of copper, like the glass on most of the crucibles, but a few pieces have far lower copper levels or are effectively copper-free. These are mainly yellow to golden-brown in colour. *9983* is green high-lead glass on an iron wire, and is probably a bead in the making.

With all this evidence for glass making and working, it is necessary to consider what objects were being made from it. Glass finds from the Coppergate and Piccadilly sites include beads of a range of forms and colours, rings and slick-stones; a selection of them have been analysed, so their compositions can be compared with those of the glass working debris.

Some of the beads from Coppergate had their density determined. The values (Table 243) indicate that most of these beads have lead oxide contents of around 70–75%; they are made of high-lead glass.

A second group of beads were analysed by XRF; the results (see Table 244) show that the yellow, green and black beads all had the same high-lead composition (Fig.1228). The yellow colour appears to be due to traces of iron, while the black beads have higher iron contents; the green beads are coloured by small amounts of copper. The opaque red and orange beads were both coloured by copper, but contained no detectable lead.

Samples were removed from four beads and analysed in the SEM. These results confirm the interpretation of the XRF data. The yellow beads contain less iron than the black bead (*10138*), but one of them (*10173*) had copper levels similar to that in the green bead (*10170*). These results are comparable to those obtained by Henderson (pp.224–5, *AY* 17/4). None of the beads contain nearly as much copper as the glass on most of the crucibles, and two of them have far more iron. It is therefore most unlikely that any

Fig.1229 *Glass working debris from 22 Piccadilly: (top left) waster or trail with pincer marks, 10639; (bottom left) two rod ends with pincer marks, 10638; (right) manufacturing debris with ceramic/stone inclusions, 10642. Actual length of 10639 is 18mm*

Table 245 Other glass working finds from 16–22 Coppergate

Cat. No.	Context	Comments	Period
9972	15688	melted colourless glass	P4B
	22633	metalworking crucible with black glass	P4B
9973	24556	blue glass droplet	P4B
9974	22797	blue glass waste fragment	P4B
	15177	potash-glass lump/flow	P5B
9978	6284	blue glass on fired clay lump	P5B
9981	18366	melted colourless glass	P6 (B6a5)
9980	11886	blue glass tessera (XRF Pb Fe Sb Cu Co)	P6 (B6f4)
10253	1346	part-melted half opaque orange bead (XRF Pb Cu Fe)	P6 (C6z1)

of the analysed beads were made of glass from the crucibles found on the Piccadilly site, though the green glass stuck on an iron wire (*9983*) is probably of similar composition to that of the translucent green beads and so is probably a part-made bead. Some of the glassy waste listed in Table 242 (p.2520) has only traces of copper and may therefore be of a similar composition to the yellow beads.

Five of the slick-stones from 16–22 Coppergate have been shown to be high-lead glass, three from Anglo-Scandinavian levels (*6593, 9994–5*) and two from medieval contexts (sfs1487, 3356, see Ottaway and Rogers, *AY* 17/– in prep.); lower lead levels were detected in several more (Mortimer 1995). They are all dark green/black in colour and are reported as containing no copper; the colour was due to significant amounts of iron. These pieces probably have a similar composition to that of the black bead (*10138*) but no quantitative analyses have been carried out.

There are problems in interpreting most of the glass artefacts from Coppergate and Piccadilly as

Fig.1230 *Potsherd discs from 22 Piccadilly used for melting blue glass. Actual diameter of sherd at top right 35mm*

Fig.1231 *Malformed blue glass beads from 22 Piccadilly: (clockwise from top left)* 10669, 10674, 10654, 10655. *Actual width of 10669 is 10·5mm*

Table 246   Glass melting crucibles (after Table 51, *AY* 16/5, with additions). SW = Stamford Ware; O = Other

Coppergate Period	Piccadilly Period	High-lead Glass		Non-lead Glass	
		SW	O	SW	O
3	–	–	–	–	1
4A	–	–	–	–	–
4B	–	7	–	–	–
5A	–	2	2	–	1
–	3	3	–	–	–
5B	–	24	22	–	1
4/5	–	2	1	–	–
–	4/1	918	1	120	–
5C	–	33	11	–	1
–	4/2	–	–	–	–
6	–	191	11	–	17
–	4/3	1	–	–	–
–	6	438	–	21	–

products of the local glass industry because of the mismatches in composition and appearance. The lead content of the glass on the crucibles is, on average, a little lower than that of the glass beads from both Coppergate and Shambles. In general, glass that looks similar has different copper and iron contents, while some pieces where the analyses are in good agreement appear different colours. A larger programme of analyses might help resolve these difficulties, but, as high-lead glass is only used in England and eastern Europe for a limited period (Ullrich 1989; Bayley forthcoming), it is most unlikely that all the artefacts are imports to the site.

Alkali glass melting

About 10% of the crucible sherds from Piccadilly had glass of a different type, with only traces of lead

Table 247 Sherds with translucent blue glass from 16–22 Coppergate

Cat. No.	Context	Comments	Period
9970	26732	Glass appears colourless	P3
9976	8023	Colourless glass on sherd	P5A
	6284		P5B
	19270		P5Cr
	3493		P6 (A6c1)
	3407		P6 (A6e1/B6c3)
	3366	Glass appears colourless	P6 (A6g1/B6g1)
	17890		P6 (B6a1/A6n1)
	18331	Pale blue	P6 (B6a5/A6n2)
	18668		P6 (C6d4)
	12363		P6 (C6e5/B6c3)
	9276		P6 (C6e7)
	4620/A	Glass includes other vitrified material	P6 (C6e9/D6e1)
9982	16612	Glass appears colourless	P6 (D6a1/C6a1)
	9453		P6 (D6a15)
	16130		P6 (D6a16/C6e1)
	6245		P6 (D6a6)
	12674	Clear scrape mark	P6 (D6b1)
	1604	Clear scrape marks	P6 (D6e3/C6e11)

present. Most of these pieces of glass were a transparent or translucent blue, though some were so pale they appeared colourless. The blue is normally produced by low concentrations of cobalt, and XRF analyses detected cobalt in most of this glass, along with small amounts of manganese, iron, copper, lead and antimony. On two pieces the glass was turquoise rather than blue, a colour produced by copper in a low-lead or lead-free glass. In these cases, traces of tin and zinc were also present. On a few pieces the glass appeared an opaque buff or white, but in the majority of cases closer examination showed these to be devitrified glass; their appearance was similar to that of decayed potash glass.

The fabric of the sherds with the low-lead glass was similar to Stamford ware in texture, but had a pale buff rather than pale grey colour. This may be due to the glass being melted under more strongly oxidising conditions. These sherds were not parts of complete vessels that had contained molten glass, like the crucibles described above. Instead they were sherds from larger pots that had been cut into rough

Fig.1232 *Blue glass beads from 22 Piccadilly: (top left and centre)* 10655; *(top right)* 10651; *(bottom)* 10670. *Actual diameter of* 10651 *11·3mm*

circles, 30–40mm across, and then had a small amount of glass placed on their concave side which was melted and scraped off, apparently to make a bead. Not all the sherds are complete discs, but they were all fragments of pieces of this size and shape (Fig.1230). The glass on them does not usually reach the curved edge; if it does, it flows over the broken edge. A total of 21 similar sherds, used in the same way, are known from the Coppergate site, although on five of them the glass appears colourless rather than blue (see Table 247).

From 22 Piccadilly there were malformed blue beads (e.g. *10669*; Fig.1231) and also a number of irregularly shaped pieces of blue glassworking waste (Fig.1229), some of which had pincer marks (e.g. *10638*); Table 248 provides a full list. Some of these pieces were also analysed by XRF and three samples in the SEM. The results show the blue glasses are soda glass, coloured by traces of copper and cobalt and containing some antimony; the composition is very consistent. Varying redox conditions mean that some of the glass was decolourised by the antimony, while in other cases it is opaque, or contains opaque white swirls. Under the SEM these can be seen to be due to calcium antimonate particles in the transparent glass. The composition of the blue glass is comparable to that of Roman blue glass; however, although over 2,200 Roman vessel glass fragments were recovered during excavations at Coppergate, less than a dozen pieces of deep blue glass were found, and it is therefore very unlikely that such glass was collected locally (H.E.M. Cool, pers. comm.) Alternatively, glass that was still being made to this recipe in the

Table 248   XRF analyses of blue glass beads and waste from 22 Piccadilly. The results of the SEM analyses are presented in Bayley and Doonan 1999

Catalogue Number	Context	Object	XRF	Comments
10638	2162	Chip and two ?rod ends with pincer marks	yes	SEM analysis
10639	2162	Waste/trail with pincer marks	yes	
10640	2162	Two bead fragments		
10641	2187	Two glass fragments and ceramic inclusions		
10642	2042	Six glass chunks with ceramic/stone inclusions		SEM analysis
10649	2162	Malformed bead		
10651	3035	Bead	yes	
10652	2042	Malformed bead	yes	Bubbles in glass make it looks opaque
10653	2186	Bead fragment	yes	
10654	2162	Two beads and two fragments		
10655	2162	Six bead fragments and one malformed	yes	SEM analysis
10656	2186	Bead fragment	yes	
10657	2187	Malformed bead		Bubbles and ?sand in the glass
10658	2089	Bead fragment		
10667	2089	Bead fragment		
10669	2162	Malformed bead	yes	Bubbles and ?sand in the glass
10670	2162	Six beads	yes	
10672	2243	Bead fragment	yes	
10673	2254	Bead fragment		
10674	2112	Bead fragment		Glass not hot enough so imperfectly shaped; joins visible
10676	2042	Bead and 'core'		

eastern Mediterranean may have been imported. The glass was remelted on the makeshift ceramic discs, scraped up when soft, and manipulated to make beads of gadrooned or conical shapes.

XRF detected the following elements at low levels in almost all the analysed beads and waste (Table 248): Manganese (Mn), Iron (Fe), Cobalt (Co), Copper (Cu), Lead (Pb) and Antimony (Sb). Cobalt was not detected in *10652* and Nickel (Ni) was also probably present in one rod end (*10638*).

There are a few further finds from Coppergate which appear to be related to this blue glass working (Table 245). There is some blue glass on a lump of fired clay (*9978*), as well as a droplet and piece of waste (*9973, 9974*). A blue tessera (*9980*) is possible raw material for this small-scale remelting industry. Theophilus mentions tesserae as a good source of coloured glass (Hawthorne and Smith 1979, 59), though vessel fragments or cullet would have been equally suitable.

Dating the glass working

At Coppergate, the earliest Stamford ware crucibles with high-lead glass date from the mid 10th century, but nearly three-quarters are from Period 6 (later 11th century onwards) (Table 246). Three sherds from Piccadilly are from Period 3 (10th/11th century) but almost 68% are from Period 4/1 (early/mid 11th century), with almost all the rest from 14th/15th century contexts (Table 246), where they are presumably residual, as Stamford ware had stopped being made by the mid 13th century. It appears that the main period of high-lead glass manufacture was in the 11th century, and probably earlier rather than later. It has been suggested that the effectively unstratified material from 34 Shambles was probably of 12th or early 13th century date. If this is correct, it may mean that high-lead glass continued to be used to make beads in York after its original floruit in the 11th century.

The chronological distribution for the crucibles with blue, Roman-type glass is very similar to that of the high-lead glass (Table 246); the two glass working traditions appear to be contemporary.

Most of the post-11th century contexts containing glass working finds are build-up or levelling dumps, so it is likely that the finds are residual in them, reinforcing the suggestion that the main floruit for the industry on 16–22 Coppergate and 22 Piccadilly was in the 11th century.

Conclusions

High-lead glass was being made in Stamford ware crucibles, and used to make objects, on or near the 16–22 Coppergate and 22 Piccadilly sites. No quantitatively analysed objects had compositions that fully matched the glass on the crucibles so we cannot demonstrate what types of objects were being made.

Blue soda glass of Roman-type composition was being remelted on small discs cut from sherds of Stamford ware and turned into beads. Both these industries appear to have started in the 10th century but their main production was in the 11th century.

Evidence for Textile Production

An overview of the evidence for textile production at 16–22 Coppergate and an interpretation of its significance has already been published (*AY* 17/11). That summary, however, contains only a select catalogue and account of the artefacts; a more inclusive report of all the textile working items relevant to this fascicule is now presented. Catalogue entries for objects previously published are reprinted at the start of the relevant section of the catalogue in this fascicule.

Spinning equipment

Spindle whorls (Fig.1233)

A total of 243 spindle whorls were recovered from Anglo-Scandinavian Coppergate, of which 84 are of stone, thirteen of lead and one (*6852*) of fired clay. The rest are of other materials (*AY* 17/11).

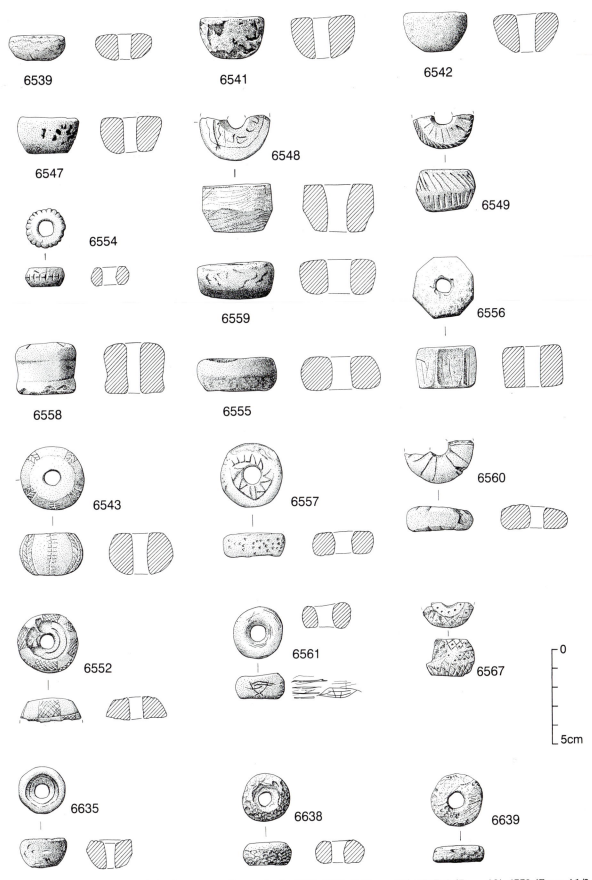

Fig.1233 *Spindle whorls from 16–22 Coppergate. Stone whorls, 6539, 6541–2 (Form A1), 6547–9 (Form A2), 6552 (Form A1/2 or B), 6554–61 (Form B), 6567 (Form B/C); lead whorls, 6635 (Form A1), 6638–9 (Form B). Scale 1:2*

Table 249 Lead alloy spindle whorls from 16–22 Coppergate by type and period

Period	4A	4B	5A	5B	5C	u/s	Total
A1	–	5	–	–	–	1	6
A2	2	1	–	–	–	–	3
B	–	3	–	–	–	1	4
Untyped	–	1	–	–	–	–	1
Total	2	10	–	–	–	2	14

Lead spindle whorls

Eleven of the thirteen finished lead whorls (*6635, 6638–9, 10545–52*) are of Anglo-Scandinavian form (p.1743, *AY* 17/11). All appear to have been cast in moulds, with a former for the spindle hole (ibid.); an incompletely cast example with an incomplete perforation (*10545*) may indicate their manufacture on the site (see pp.2478–9 and also *AY* 17/7 for more evidence of lead alloy working at Coppergate). *6636* and *6640*, from Period 4B deposits, are thought to be residual Roman whorls (p.1743, *AY* 17/11).

It is unclear whether there is any significance in the non-appearance of lead alloy whorls after Period 4B. Whorls of both stone and bone are more common than those of lead alloy in all periods associated with Anglo-Scandinavian occupation at Coppergate

(Table 146, *AY* 17/11), and other sites, such as Winchester, indicate a similar preference for these materials (Woodland 1990, 216–25).

Stone spindle whorls (Fig.1233)

By P. Walton Rogers

There are 78 stone spindle whorls from Anglo-Scandinavian deposits at 16–22 Coppergate, and at least fourteen whorls of Anglo-Scandinavian form re-deposited in 11th–14th century levels (Period 6). These whorls, used to weight the spindle while hand-spinning, form part of a large collection of textile-manufacturing tools, which also includes spindles, a spinner's distaff and whorls of bone, antler, lead, clay and potsherd (pp.1731–49, *AY* 17/11).

Dr G.D. Gaunt's study of the geological sources of the stone spindle whorls shows that, with rare exceptions, the raw materials can be found within 30km of York (Table 250). His identifications of individual whorls can be found in the catalogue. The most commonly used stone was chalk. The majority of the chalk whorls are made from a white, very fine-grained, variety which is common throughout the Cretaceous Chalk Group succession, and which can be found in most parts of the Yorkshire Wolds. The other chalk whorls are generally more greyish-white and are fine-grained (i.e. slightly coarser than the majority). They are attributed to the Ferriby Chalk Formation, which comprises the lowest c.26m of the Chalk Group succession, and which occurs in the steep slopes of the Wolds facing north and west across the Vales of Pickering and York respectively. Two

Table 250 The geological origin of Anglo-Scandinavian whorls from 16–22 Coppergate (identified by G.D. Gaunt)
[* *6556* and *9266* are either Ferriby Chalk or Jurassic Limestone]

Geology / Period	Chalk Group	Ferriby Chalk Formation	Jurassic Limestone	Magnesian Limestone	Argillaceous stone	Sandstone	Uncertain
3	3	1	–	–	2	1	–
4A	1	2	1	–	2	–	–
4B	18	5	7	3	2	1	2*
5A	5	1	–	2	–	–	–
5B	7	6	1	–	2	–	2
5C	1	–	–	–	–	–	–
6 (Form A)	9	2	1	–	1	–	1
Total	44	17	10	5	9	2	5

Table 251 Sources of raw materials for spindle whorls from sites of the 6th to 14th century in Great Britain

Site	Raw materials of spindle whorls	Reference
Jarlshof, Shetland	21 steatite 2 claystone 1 sandstone	Hamilton 1956
Aberdeen, Grampian (Broad Street and St Paul's Street)	2 part-metamorphosed micaceous mudstone 1 metamorphic	Trewin 1982
Perth, Tayside (Canal Street)	1 Lower Old Red Sandstone 1 phyllite–Dalradian	Holdsworth 1987
Hartlepool, Cleveland (Church Close)	5 limestone	Daniels 1990, 366
Beverley, E. Yorks. (Eastgate and Lurk Lane)	22 chalk 9 Jurassic limestone 1 Magnesian limestone	Foreman 1991, 110–12 Foreman 1992, 123–4
Lincoln (Flaxengate, Hungate, Danes Terrace, Broadgate East)	38 Lincolnshire limestone 1 (or 3) Carboniferous limestone 2 chalk 2 mudstone 1 sandstone	Mann 1982, 22–5 J.E. Mann, pers. comm.
Goltho, Lincs.	9 'sandstone and chalk'	Beresford 1987, 194–5
Northampton, Northants. (St Peter's Street)	11 limestone 1 sandstone 1 siltstone	Oakley and Hall 1979
King's Lynn, Norfolk	20 similar, of which 2 are definitely limestone (calcite mudstone) probably from Bristol-Mendip region	Ellis in Clarke and Carter 1977
Norwich, Norfolk	5 Jurassic limestone	Margeson 1993, 184–5
Thetford, Norfolk	5 chalk 4 limestone 1 shale	Rogerson and Dallas 1984, 111–12
Mucking, Essex	[25 fired clay] 5 shale (re-used Roman)	Hamerow 1993, 64–6
London	8 calcite mudstone	Pritchard 1984; 1991
Oxford (St Aldate's)	6 Oxfordshire limestone	Durham 1978, 152
Winchester, Hants.	63 chalk 3 limestone 1 micaceous ironstone	Woodland 1990

types of limestone have also been used. One is fine- to medium-grained and almost certainly of Jurassic origin, from eastern Yorkshire. The other is Dolomitic, from the Permian Lower Magnesian Limestone which occurs along the western edge of the Vale of York — although on textural evidence some at least of these whorls may have been made from building stone which the Romans brought to York. A few whorls are made of sandstone and argillaceous rocks (i.e. siltstone and mudstone), most of which are probably from Pennine Upper Carboniferous sources, although Jurassic origins cannot be precluded. Only one whorl, 9301, from Period 5B, is likely to have come from further afield: it is of possibly thermally metamorphosed siltstone, probably from the Lake District, Cheviot Hills or southern Scotland.

The 92 whorls have been made by several different methods. Only about a quarter have the smooth profile and fine encircling lines which show they have been made on a lathe (e.g. 6536–7), which contrasts with middle and late Anglo-Saxon Flixborough, Lincs. (Fig.1299, 8, p.2606), and with later (Period 6) levels at Coppergate, where most whorls were lathe-turned. Instead, many of the Anglo-Scandinavian whorls have sharp, irregular facets, which indicate they have been cut with a knife (e.g. 6540, 6545). Some of these have been given a surface smoothing, although the facets are still visible. Other whorls have broad, round-edged facets, as if they have been rubbed against an abrasive surface (e.g. 6555, 6559), while some have been marked by a tool like a rasp (6548, 9261).

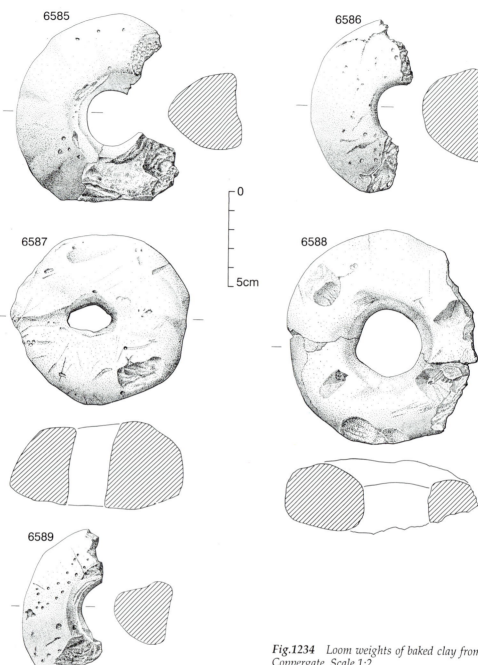

6585

6586

6587

6588

6589

0

5cm

Fig.1234 *Loom weights of baked clay from 16–22 Coppergate. Scale 1:2*

All the stone whorls — even the most roughly made — have been neatly drilled to make a spindle hole of standard diameter, 9–11mm. The same is true of the bone whorls, where cattle femur heads have been roughly chopped and trimmed and then neatly drilled (pp.1964–5, *AY* 17/12). As there is evidence that the bone and lead spindle whorls were made at Coppergate (pp.1741–3, *AY* 17/11), it seems likely that the stone whorls were too, although the only possible piece of debris from their manufacture is a

chalk whorl, *6567*, which has been drilled through, then re-drilled crossways, before fracturing.

The whorls have been made in a wide range of shapes and sizes. Although there is a chronological shift from whorls with one main flat face (Forms A1 and A2) to whorls with two equal flat faces (Form B) over the period in question (Fig.805, *AY* 17/11), within these general categories there is considerable variety (Figs.806–7, *AY* 17/11). Again, this contrasts with the more standardised shapes and weights of the later globular whorls (Form C from Period 6).

The knife-cut whorls are also the ones that are most commonly decorated with incised straight-line patterns (ladder, herring-bone, zig-zag, etc.), ring-and-dot generally being reserved for the lathe-turned whorls. Several of the whorls (e.g. *6544*) show designs similar to those seen on bone and clay whorls from Frisia (Roes 1963; 1965). *6544* has been decorated with arcs and semicircles, in a distinctive cross design which can be matched exactly in one Frisian bone whorl (Roes 1963, pl.34, 10). The stone from which these whorls are made is the same white chalk as many of the other Coppergate whorls, and they may result from the known Frisian presence in York (MacGregor 1978, 37; *AY* 1, 131–2) rather than trade with the Continent.

The great variation in shape, size and method of manufacture seen in the Anglo-Scandinavian whorls tends to support the impression given by the other textile tools from the site, of a domestic, peasant-style textile industry, where tools were made up only as the spinner or weaver required them, from easily obtained raw materials.

The use of stone of local origin is entirely typical of the period. Table 251 shows how most collections of stone spindle whorls of the 6th to 14th century reflect the geology of the region in which they have been found. The exceptions are those sites placed in areas of clay or alluvium, such as the Anglo-Saxon village at Mucking, Essex, which is the only site where fired clay whorls outnumber stone ones; and 10th–12th century London and King's Lynn, which have both yielded white calcite mudstone whorls, probably brought in by sea from the Mendips-Bristol region. Elsewhere, there may have been some regional exchange of whorls. At Beverley, for example, whorls were mainly made from local chalk, but limestone from the North York Moors, 50km away, accounted for a certain number. These, as Foreman suggests, may have been brought to Beverley with wool for the textile industry (Foreman 1992, 123). In the Anglo-Scandinavian collection from Coppergate, however, there is little difference in shape, ornament or method of manufacture between whorls from the Pennines and adjacent areas and those from the Wolds. The most likely conclusion here is that the stones were picked up on a casual basis

Table 252 Loom weights from 16–22 Coppergate according to period

			Period			
3	4A	4B	5A	5B	5Cr	6
5	1	12	2	11	1	2

during journeys into the hinterland — perhaps collected at the foot of sea-cliffs or inland escarpments — and brought back to York for shaping.

Weaving equipment

Loom weights (Fig.1234)

Fragments of 34 loom weights were recovered from Coppergate and one unstratified fragment from 22 Piccadilly. The Coppergate examples were distributed through the whole of the sequence (see Table 252). Two fragments recovered from Period 6 deposits are likely to be residual from earlier deposits. The loom weights have been discussed by Penelope Walton Rogers (p.1753, *AY* 17/11), together with the other textile making equipment. She remarks that this is a small collection given the size of the area excavated, and believes that these loom weights represent the last stages of the use of the warp-weighted loom in towns and that many of those in later levels may be residual from earlier Anglo-Scandinavian deposits.

Stitching equipment

Needles (Fig.1235)

Out of 243 needles found in Anglo-Scandinavian levels, only seven are of copper alloy (*6623–5, 10361–4*), the vast majority (89%) being of iron (Table 150, *AY* 17/11). There were also three of bone (*6680–2*, p.1968, *AY* 17/12). The copper alloy needles appear to share common methods of manufacture with their iron counterparts. The eye is formed in one of two ways, either by flattening the upper end and punching a circular eye through, or by splitting the upper end into two and rejoining it at the top leaving an oval gap for the eye (p.544, *AY* 17/6). Three of the copper alloy needles have a punched circular eye (*6623, 10363–4*), and the remainder have elongated oval eyes.

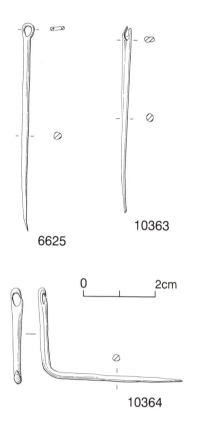

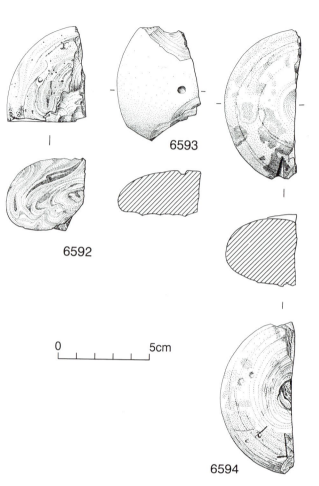

Fig. 1235 *Copper alloy needles from 16–22 Coppergate. Scale 1:1*

Fig. 1236 *Glass slick-stones from 16–22 Coppergate. Scale 1:2*

6623 stands out from the other copper alloy needles in terms of its length (90·6mm) and shape, over two-thirds of its shank being flat with a spatulate tip. Known as a bayonet-point, it was used in leatherwork (p.1785, *AY* 17/11). The remaining complete needles range in length from 49·2mm (*10363*) to 59·2mm (*10364*). The diameters range from 1·7mm (*6624*) to 2·2mm (*10363*). These needles would have been used to sew a variety of materials including silks, linens and wool.

Finishing equipment

Slick-stones (Fig.1236)

There were 25 glass slick-stones or linen-smoothers and three stone ones from Anglo-Scandinavian contexts on the site (a further fifteen glass ones were recovered from medieval contexts). Their appearance and use is described in *AY* 17/11

(pp.1775–9, Figs.826–8). The cataalogue entries for the slick-stones are reproduced in the relevant material sections in the catalogue of this fascicule.

Evidence Relating to Fishing (Fig.1237)

The excavations at 16–22 Coppergate produced scant artefactual evidence of fishing, despite the site's proximity to the River Foss, and evidence of the consumption of riverine, estuarine and marine fish, as provided by fish bones (*AY* 15/3, 195–8). Two net sinkers, both of pure lead, were recovered (*10553–4*), both deriving from build-up deposits, the former from Period 4B, the latter from Period 5B. A possible third (*9816*), produced by drilling a hole in a pebble, was found in a Period 5Cr context. These supplement the only other evidence for fishing from the site, seven iron fish hooks (*2991–7*, pp.600–1, *AY* 17/6). The cylindrical sinkers have been made by wrapping a piece of lead around a rope forming the lower edge of a fishing net; they are open at both ends, enabling them to be slid on or off as required. Similar net sinkers, thought to have been used on hand nets, were recovered in Anglian and 11th century levels at 46–54 Fishergate (*5477–83*, p.1320, *AY* 17/9).

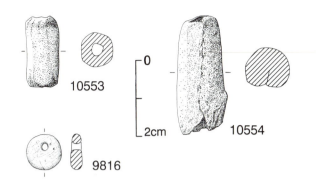

Fig.1237   *Fish-net sinkers from 16–22 Coppergate:* 9816 *made of stone,* 10553–4 *made of lead. Scale 1:1*

Discussion

The picture that emerges of the character of this part of Anglo-Scandinavian York is one of small workshops, set up in and around structures which probably serve a domestic purpose. Some of the activities described or referred to above seem to focus on particular tenements at different times. The scale and professionalism of the various enterprises also varies from what is clearly routine household production to mass production for commercial purposes.

Textile production in the Anglo-Scandinavian period seems to be the clearest example of the former mode of production. Walton Rogers has pointed out that 'the even spread of textile equipment laterally across the tenements ... is that to be expected from a common domestic occupation' (p.1825, *AY* 17/11). The fact that there is a greater quantity of such evidence at Coppergate than at other contemporary sites in the city might suggest that more cloth was made there. Against this, however, is the fact that some of the textile tools, especially the iron needles, wool-comb spikes and possibly other iron textile tools, were being made on the site, thereby inflating the numbers.

Smaller-scale or shorter-lived crafts for which there is evidence includes amber and jet working. The quantity of evidence for these crafts is very small given that the period in question spans two centuries, or eight to ten generations. The jet working evidence shows little patterning across the Coppergate site, but there is some indication that the amber working at

Coppergate was focused around Tenement B, especially in Period 4B. If the contemporary chalk pieces (Fig.1227, p.2518), also from Tenement B, are correctly interpreted as being related to polishing and burnishing, this strengthens the argument for a small workshop operating from here during the 10th century. The Clifford Street amber workshop may well have been a larger operation, and possibly a little later in date, though both these statements are impossible to confirm. On the evidence recovered from these sites it seems unlikely that either jet or amber working could have been the sole means of support for a family. It is more reasonable to suggest that this was a sporadic activity, carried out by skilled individuals, when the raw materials were available. The same interpretation may apply to the scant evidence for the manufacture of hones from imported raw material. Some investment in specialist tools was required, particularly a small lathe and a drill, as well as a range of knives, and possibly saws and files. These may not have been in the tool-kit of every family, but could have been relatively easily acquired.

Similar sporadic activity by skilled individuals has been suggested for the working of bone and, more particularly, antler at 16–22 Coppergate and elsewhere in the city (*AY* 17/12). The production of antler combs seems to have been focused in Tenements B and C in Period 4B, with a shift in emphasis in Period 5B to the building set back from the street-frontage in Tenement C (Fig.881, *AY* 17/12). Again, despite the impressive quantity of material recovered from the site, the scale of activity over 200 years cannot have been great, and is insufficient to propose a long-term settled workshop. One of the possibilities is that itinerant comb-makers operated periodically from these tenements before moving on to the next manor, village or urban centre. This proposed mode of production would be less likely for the amber or jet worker, whose raw materials were less ubiquitously obtained and whose skills were less specialised. As with jet and amber working, no particular structural modifications, other than a work-bench or area and lighting, would be required for bone or antler working, and all these occupations could have been carried out in a structure that was otherwise domestic in function.

The other industries that operated from 16–22 Coppergate and from 22 Piccadilly were on a different scale. Glass working, non-ferrous and ferrous metalworking all need hearths or furnaces. They also require an advanced level of skill, specialist tools or utensils and they produce obnoxious fumes and waste products. At Coppergate the metal-working evidence is focused on Tenements C and D in Periods 4B and 5B, while substantial amounts of glass working evidence derives from 22 Piccadilly.

Everyday Life

Household Equipment

Glass vessels (Figs.1238–9)

By M. Stiff

Fifty-six of the glass small finds recovered during the Coppergate excavations were from Anglo-Scandinavian contexts or displayed characteristics usually associated with early medieval vessel forms. A further six fragments characteristic of this period were found during excavations at the nearby 22 Piccadilly site. The sherds from these sites were compared to others found at similar settlements in England and Continental Europe (Stiff 1996).

At the time of inspection the 56 glass small finds from Coppergate consisted of over 140 individual sherds. This can be accounted for by the instability of the devitrified material, which has further degraded and divided since excavation. The 34 glass finds showing the clarity normally associated with soda-lime-silica glass consist of only 35 fragments. Soda glass dominated glass production in Europe until the appearance of high-potash glasses towards the end of the first millennium. This change reflects a move away from glass made using a soda-rich alkali to one with a high potash content, probably resulting from a move from a mineral to a vegetable source (Sanderson and Hutchings 1987). The devitrified Coppergate finds are all from Period 4 or 5 contexts and include *10018* (Period 4A), *10007, 10029, 10031* (Period 4B), *10021, 10042* (Period 5A), *10012–13, 10022* (Period 5B), *10015–16, 10060* (Period 5Cr). The poor condition of many of the fragments makes it difficult to determine whether some finds derive from the same vessel. The 34 soda-lime-silica finds, however, are probably all from separate vessels. Of the 56 finds, twelve have sherds from vessel rims, five from bases and the remainder consist only of body fragments.

Vessel types

Only eight of the Coppergate fragments are sufficiently diagnostic for the vessel type to be determined with certainty. The earliest of these (*10020*) is a light green-blue base fragment from a vessel decorated with optic-blown ribbing (Fig.1239). An arm

from a base cross is visible on this light sherd, and there is evidence of bosses placed both on and between the cross arms. This form of decoration was used principally on palm cups and tall palm cups from the late 6th to the early 8th century, although it is also to be found on some pouch bottles and squat jars (Harden 1956; Winfield-Smith 1957). Optic-blown palm cups tend to mirror the evolution of the plain variety into the funnel beaker form, the body becoming progressively narrower and more elongated (Ypey 1964). The narrower profile of the

Fig.1238 *Fragments of squat jars with opaque yellow marvered trails from 16–22 Coppergate: (top) 10010 , (bottom) 10019. Actual length of 10010, 20mm*

Coppergate fragment suggests that it derives from a tall palm cup, probably dating from the late 7th to early 8th century. This fragment was found in a dump deposit belonging to Period 5A. A fragment from a similar vessel was recovered from a late 11th–early 12th century context at the 22 Piccadilly site (*10643*).

Three fragments belong to funnel beakers dating from the 8th to 9th century. *10009* is a very light blue-green sherd with an outsplayed fire-rounded and thickened rim. Two more fragments may also come from funnel beakers. *10006* is a light green-blue sherd from the fire-rounded and thickened rim of a funnel beaker or tall beaker. This fragment was recovered from deposits dated to Period 3, and is similar to 9th century fragments found in sites such as Dorestad, Ribe and Hedeby. *10014* is another light green-blue sherd from the outsplayed rim of a funnel beaker, although this was recovered from Period 5B deposits.

The remaining four identifiable sherds are probably from squat jars. Three are rim fragments and one is from a kicked base. *10011* is a light green-blue rim sherd, possibly folded internally prior to fire rounding. It is decorated with a horizontal, opaque yellow marvered trail laid around the outer edge of the rim and neck. This form of decoration is similar to squat jar fragments recovered from 8th century contexts in Ipswich, London and Hamwic. *10011*, however, was recovered from dump deposits dated to Period 5A. Sherds of this type are often decorated with vertical *reticella* trails. *10010* is another jar fragment, this time discovered in Period 4B occupation layers (Fig.1238). It is from the internally folded rim of a vessel that was decorated with opaque yellow, horizontal marvered trails around the rim and neck. This fragment appears black in reflected light but is probably made of very dark red glass. A very similar fragment dating from the 8th century was recovered during the excavations at Fishergate (*4641*, p.1338, *AY* 17/9). Two further fragments were also found in Period 4B. Another rim sherd, *10008*, may also belong to a squat jar (Fig.1239). This piece is of dark blue glass with a plain, outsplayed fire-rounded and thickened rim. The base fragment, *10019*, is of very dark grey-green glass and is decorated with horizontal, opaque yellow marvered trails (Fig.1238). Fragments from the shoulder of a jar with similar colour and decoration were found in the earliest workshop layers (VH1) at Nicolajgade 8 in Ribe. This

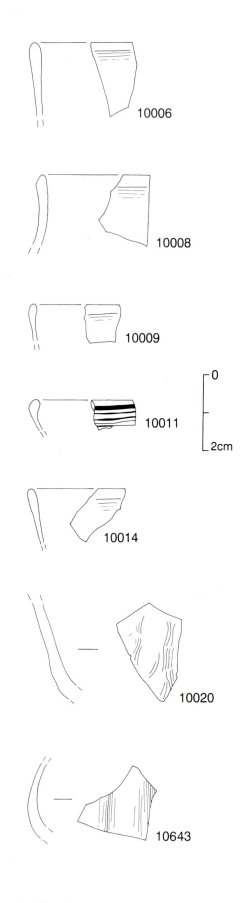

Fig.1239 *Vessel glass from 16–22 Coppergate and 22 Piccadilly (10643). Scale 1:1*

phase is thought to date around 815–20 (Frandsen and Jensen 1987, 182; Stiff 1996, 171–3). Similar fragments have also been found in 8th century contexts at Ipswich, London and Hamwic.

Of the remaining 48 finds, six contain vessel rims and three bases. Five of the rims are of severely devitrified glass, two of which (*10012*, *10016*) may come from jars or small beakers. *10016* consists of five fragments of glass, one with a fire-rounded and thickened edge, and is significant due to the relative flatness of these sherds. It is possible that they may be heat-distorted, although they may have belonged to a piece of window glass. The sixth rim sherd, *10017*, is of very light blue-green soda glass and comes from just below the edge of an outsplayed rim with an inward fold. This fragment is decorated with fine opaque yellow marvered trails. Ten fragments from funnel beakers with this form of decoration have been found at Hamwic, and other examples are known from Dorestad, Ribe and London. The inward fold is more commonly detected on squat jars, however, and similar examples have been found at Ipswich, London, Hamwic, Dorestad and Hedeby (Stiff 1996, Appendix C, D, F and G) (Fig.1299, **12**, **13**, **15**, p.2606; Fig.1300, **3**, **4**, p.2608)

The three base fragments are all of devitrified glass. *10018* is a very dark opaque brown-grey sherd from a vessel with a broad kicked base. It was recovered from a dump deposit belonging to Period 4A. *10021* is an opaque brown fragment from a Period 5A dump deposit and is kicked, with the remains of a pontil wad. These sherds probably belonged to jars or bottles. The third of these fragments (*10022*) is of a dark opaque brown-grey colour and belongs to a vessel with a flattened base. This sherd was found in the backfill of a linear feature dating to Period 5B.

Decoration

The remaining fragments can only be discussed in terms of their decoration and colour. Four of these show evidence of optic-blown decoration. *10043* is from a spherical or hemispherical vessel, decorated with vertical or diagonal optic-blown corrugations. This sherd is also overlaid with a curving, transparent yellow trail heavily marvered into the vessel wall. Such a combination of decorative features is extremely rare on vessel glass of this period. *10026*,

10027 and *10038* are all of strongly coloured glass, more usually associated with jars or bottles, although all are too small for the vessel profile to be determined. *10026*, a brown-yellow sherd, and *10027*, a dark grey-green fragment, were both recovered from build-up deposits belonging to Period 3. Optic-blown decoration is most commonly found on vessels of the palm cup/funnel beaker series, squat jars and pouch bottles.

Nine finds contain fragments with trailed decoration. *10044* is a light green-blue sherd with an opaque yellow marvered trail. A second fragment, *10040*, may also have been decorated with opaque yellow or white marvered trails, although these have decomposed, leaving only indentations in the surface of the metal. *10041* is a very light yellow-green sherd decorated with opaque orange-red trails. This colour is unusual, although self-coloured trails streaked with opaque red are often found. An example of this can be seen on a light green-yellow sherd found at Coppergate (*10061*). The remaining sherds are all decorated with self-coloured trails. *10037* and *10045* are from Period 5 contexts, although both are of a colour and style more in keeping with vessels of the 8th century or earlier. *10045* is of light brown-yellow glass and has a thick vertical trail; *10037* is dark brown-green in colour with a horizontal trail, and may derive from the neck of a small jar. *10007*, *10031* and *10046* are all of opaque grey or opaque brown devitrified glass. Of these, *10031* is the most significant since it consists of sherds which are similar in fabric and decoration to the devitrified jars found in graves 739 and 750 at Birka (Fig.1300, **1**, p.2608). Arbman has dated these vessels to the first half of the 10th century (Arbman 1940, 193, 2–3 and 194, 2–3; Arbman 1943, 263–72; Stiff 1996, 65–6).

22 Piccadilly

Six fragments of vessel glass were recovered from 22 Piccadilly. Only one was from a recognisable vessel form: a base sherd from a tall palm cup decorated with vertical, optic-blown ribbing, *10643*. This fragment is decorated with a moulded cross with raised bosses placed between the cross-arms in the form of a quincunx. Of the remaining six sherds, only one is decorated, *10646*. This fragment is light green-yellow and has a fine, self-coloured trail. The remaining sherds are undiagnostic fragments of light yellow-green, green-blue and blue-green glass.

Discussion

Because of the condition of many of the devitrified sherds in late 9th to 11th century contexts at Coppergate, little can be added to our knowledge of the range of vessel types and decorative techniques employed during this period. What is of particular note, however, is the large number of sherds that appear to pre-date the period of occupation for this site (Table 253). Although some could be accounted for by the disturbance of Period 3 layers, others, such as the tall palm cup fragment (*10020*) and several of the jar sherds, could not be dated later than the middle of the 8th century. These fragments, along with those found at 22 Piccadilly, have more in common with the finds from Fishergate, and their presence at Coppergate is perplexing given the relative lack of other Anglian finds in Period 2 layers.

One possibility is that these fragments represent cullet brought into the settlement for reworking. This seems unlikely, however, since the sherds are quite widely dispersed and there is little related evidence to support such a hypothesis. For glass fragments such as these to be identified as cullet there must be either evidence that the pieces have been systematically recovered and kept together for recycling, or evidence for contemporaneous glass working activity on the site. Although glass working did take place at Coppergate, the earliest fragments of Stamford ware crucibles with glass remains date from Period 4B and over three-quarters come from Period 6 contexts (see Table 246, p.2525). Whilst some of the glass sherds do come from Period 4B and 5 contexts (which would allow for contemporaneous glass working), others are from Period 3 and Period 4B contexts, indicating the presence of this type of material prior to any evidence of a glass industry on this site.

It is also worth asking where such glass would have been found for the purposes of recycling. It is probable that the glass workers would have brought supplies of scrap glass and other raw materials with them, or would have located readily available sources nearby. Anglian glass would need to be obtained either by robbing burials or sifting through the remains of earlier settlement sites. The tall palm cup fragments date from the late 7th or early 8th century and are therefore unlikely to have been buried as grave goods. In any case, glassware is only rarely found with burials, even when the deposition of

grave goods was still taking place. Instead, such sherds are more likely to represent domestic refuse. In order to recover such material, the Coppergate glass workers, or the people from whom they obtained their raw materials, would have needed to dig through refuse in areas of earlier Anglian occupation such as the Fishergate settlement. However, the fact that the Anglians themselves would in all probability have recycled their glass would have made this a fruitless exercise. Study of glass from trading settlements of the 7th to 9th century indicates that the careful gathering and re-use of vessel glass was widespread. Estimating the percentage of fragments surviving from each vessel can be problematic given the poor rates of recovery without the use of wet sieving (Stiff forthcoming). Nevertheless, some indication can be given from the excavations at Ribe where 100% sieving of the soil removed during the 1990–1 excavations at the Post Office site produced 1,373 sherds of vessel glass. Lund has estimated that these represent the remains of up to 1,119 vessels (Lund 1993, 19). This suggests that care was taken to recover fragments from broken vessels, and that these were not disposed of along with the other domestic refuse.

During the excavations at the Royal Opera House site in London (ROP 95) 5,578 litres of samples were processed resulting in 37 vessel glass finds. It can be estimated that the sieving of at least two tonnes of soil would be required to produce enough glass to make one small vessel. Assuming a similar density of finds in Anglo-Scandinavian York, this quantity should probably be multiplied tenfold given that the inhabitants of Coppergate would not have had access to the tools available to modern archaeologists (this is the approximate recovery rate in London without the use of wet sieving; Stiff forthcoming). The improbability of such expenditure of effort is increased still further when we consider that the remains of Roman York would have provided far richer sources of scrap glass.

A different explanation is therefore required for the presence of pre-Viking glass on this site. As can be seen, no fragments were found in contexts dating from before the mid 9th century, despite the fact that several of the sherds found can be dated on stylistic grounds to no later than the mid 8th century. Of these sherds, several come from Period 4 and 5 contexts.

Table 253 Glass finds from 16–22 Coppergate by period

Period	3	4A	4B	5A	5B	5C	6	u/s
Number of fragments	7	1	14	8	21	3	1	1

These can be best explained through residuality, although the presence of this material in Period 3 layers and the lack of any such material in Period 2 contexts is still puzzling. Given the presence of nearly 200 fragments of Anglian pottery sherds at Coppergate, the glass tends to support Mainman's assertion that there was Anglian activity in the general area prior to the mid 9th century, despite the absence of Anglian structures at this site (*AY* 16/5, 487). The discovery of the 8th century Anglian helmet at Coppergate also supports this, and Hall has suggested the possibility of an early ecclesiastical foundation at St Mary, Castlegate (p.1691, *AY* 17/11). (Fig.1187, **13**, p.2452). Difficult as it is to explain, it seems most likely that the early vessel sherds from this site represent residual material imported from nearby. Further excavation should help to reveal the extent of the mid–late Anglian settlement and provide the answers to some of these problems.

Stone vessels (Figs.1240–2)

Vessels, all probably bowls, made from sandstone, talc schist and steatite were recovered from Anglo-Scandinavian levels on the site, though none are earlier than Period 4B. There is no clustering of fragments in any one tenement, but those from the Period 4B and 5A levels are from the front of the site where the structures had stood and where the vessels were presumably used (Fig.1241). The steatite examples from Period 6 are believed to be residual and so are included here.

Dr G.D. Gaunt suggests that the steatite probably originated in the Dalradian Supergroup in Shetland and also suggests a similar provenance for the fragments of talc schist vessels recovered from Periods 4B, 5B and 6. Three fragments were recovered from Tenement C and may be part of the same bowl. A sandstone bowl fragment was also recovered from a Period 4B deposit.

The steatite and talc schist bowls are large, thick-walled open forms. The most complete example (*9671*, Figs.1240, 1242), and one of the earliest, is of an open bowl with a flat, squared-off rim. The outside surface is heavily sooted and there are clear blade marks showing how the surface was carved and finished. Approximately 15mm below the rim edge are two holes 30mm apart with another pair 25mm immediately below these. These holes penetrate right through the wall of the vessel and were used to position a flattened iron loop, the top of which protrudes 15mm above the rim. The lower pair of holes secured the ends of the iron loop, the pointed ends of which are flattened upwards against the inner surface to secure it. The top pair of holes held another smaller iron strip, one end of which was folded horizontally against the iron hoop on the outside, and the pointed end was also flattened to grip the inner surface. Only part of one of these strips survives but the position of the other holes implies that there were originally two whose function was to give additional strength to the suspension loop. This, however, created a weak spot and it is at this point that the vessel broke, across one of the holes.

A second rim fragment from another vessel (*9680*, Fig.1240) has a single hole drilled into the surviving piece 60mm below the rim edge. This may also have been to allow the vessel to be suspended, but not enough of the vessel survives to show how. A rim fragment (*9692*) from a Period 6 deposit is likely to be residual from Anglo-Scandinavian levels.

Table 254 The incidence of stone bowls from 16–22 Coppergate

Period	4B	5A	5B	6
Sandstone	1	0	0	1
Talc schist	2	0	10	1
Steatite	2	2	1	2
Total	5	2	11	4

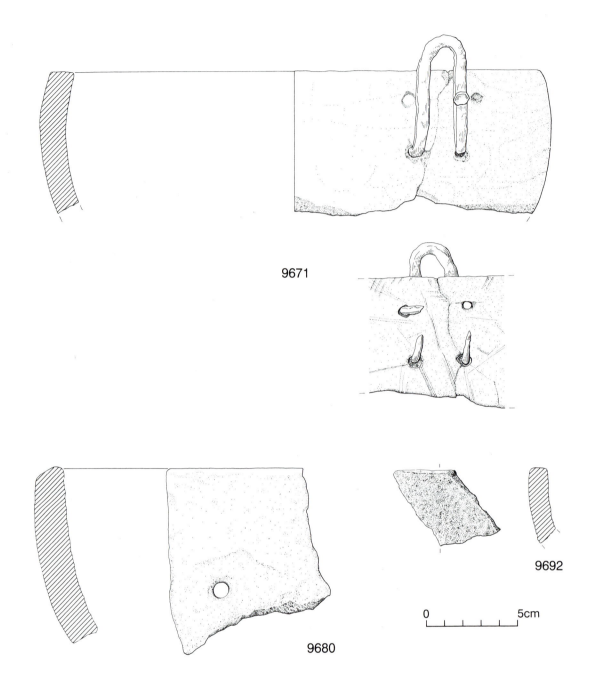

Fig.1240 *Carved stone bowls from 16–22 Coppergate. Scale 1:2*

There are other fragments which are all probably sherds from similar vessels. The thickness of the walls range from 12 to 25mm with most clustering around 19–20mm. The sherds are often blackened on the outside (e.g. *9671–2, 9677*), but just as commonly on the inside (e.g. *9676–7, 9680*), where a blackened residue adheres to the surface. In some cases the exterior has been well finished to give a smooth surface (e.g. *9672, 9676–7, 9680*), while in other cases it is still quite rough (e.g. *9689*). This might imply they were unfinished, though the softness of the stone may mean that this is the result of wear and tear. In support of the former suggestion it is worth remarking that there are a number of smaller fragments,

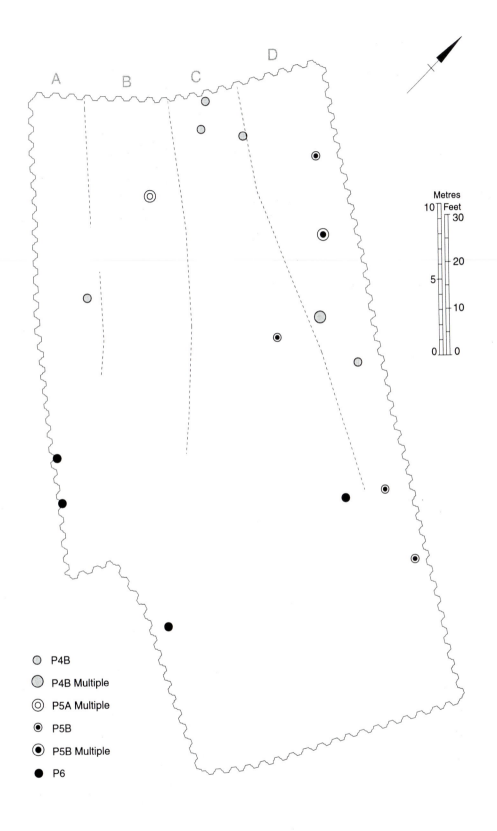

A   B   C   D

Metres
10 ┌ ┐ Feet
│ │ ┌ ┐ 30
│ │
│ │ 20
5 │ │
│ │ 10
│ │
0 └ ┘ └ ┘ 0

○ P4B

◉ P4B Multiple

◎ P5A Multiple

⊙ P5B

◉ P5B Multiple

● P6

Fig.1241   *Distribution of stone vessels from 16–22 Coppergate in all periods
(tenement divisions A–D relate only to Periods 4B, 5A and 5B)*

Fig.1242 *Steatite bowl from 16-22 Coppergate, 9671. Actual height 74·0mm*

mostly from a single context (29263) in Period 5B (*9683–8*). Some might be small abraded parts of bowls, others might be waste from the finishing of bowls which were brought part-made to the site.

Elsewhere in this report (p.2478), Dr Gaunt has suggested that if the ingot moulds made from these materials originated in Britain, their most likely source is from outcrops in the Shetland Isles which were known to be exploited in the Viking period. While vessels made from these materials occur widely on Norse sites in Scotland, they are unusual in England. Their appearance in York, however, is consistent with Viking trading patterns which can be reconstructed through the occurrence of different materials and object types in the city. The trade routes which brought goods from the Scandinavian homelands would no doubt encompass the Viking settlements in Orkney and Shetland and these stone bowls support this. The terminal of a Pictish penannular brooch (*10425*) found at Coppergate (see pp.2570–1) must also have originated in the Northern Isles and may have arrived, somewhat earlier, by the same seaways.

Stone lamps (Figs.1243–4)

Fragments of nine stone lamps were recovered from Anglo-Scandinavian contexts and one unstratified find may be of similar date. Those from the earlier contexts (Period 3 and 4A) (*9661–3*) are all of dolomitic limestone from the Permian Lower Magnesian Limestone, as is one of the later (Period 5Cr) examples (*9669*). *9665* and *9668* are also limestone but of Middle or Upper Jurassic origin. The remaining lamps are sandstone (*9664, 9667*) and chalk (*9666*).

Dr G.D. Gaunt remarks that *the relict oolitic or micro-cellular textures of the Lower Magnesian Limestone lamps (9661–3) from the earlier contexts suggest that they may well have been made from old Roman building stone in York, which has these textures.*

One of the earliest examples, *9662*, is a flattened bun-shaped lamp with smooth surfaces and a wide deep recess for the oil. The outside is blackened and there are some simple tool marks visible. The other Period 3 lamp (*9661*) is a larger, irregular, now fragmentary, block which has been shaped into an ovoid

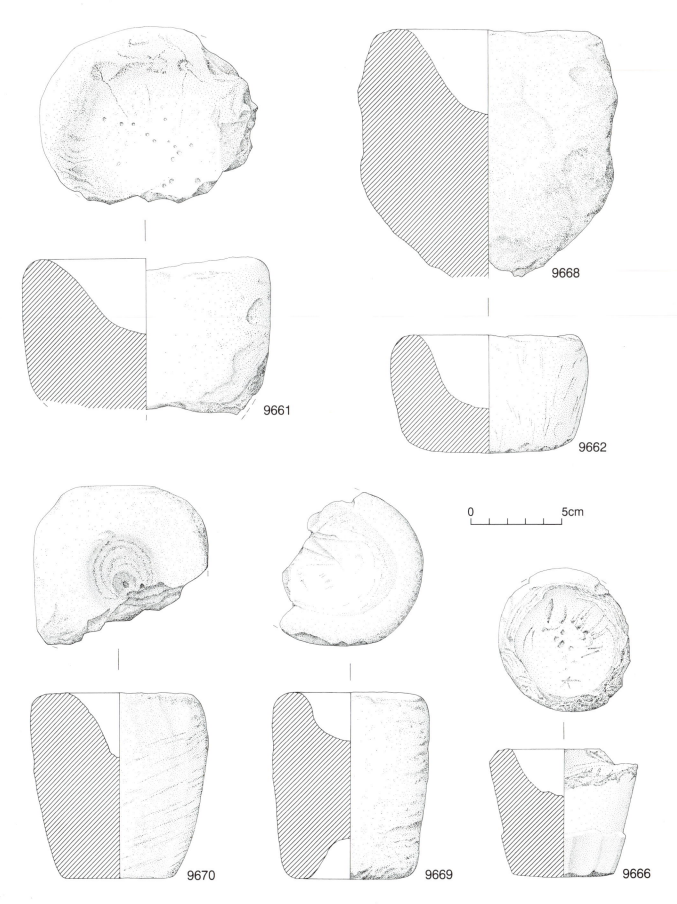

Fig.1243 *Stone lamps from 16–22 Coppergate. Scale 1:2*

9668

9661

9662

0   5cm

9670

9669

9666

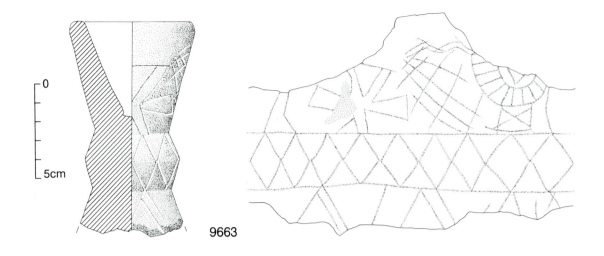

Fig.1244 *Decorated stone lamp from 16–22 Coppergate. Scale 1:2*

with a central recess. Once again the outside is blackened, this time on the top surfaces.

The most elaborate lamp, in terms of form and decoration, *9663*, comes from Period 4A (Fig.1244). It is made from limestone and has a carinated plinth and a deep recess cut into the top surface. The outer surfaces of the plinth and the bowl of the lamp are covered with shallow, simple incised decoration which forms criss-crosses, star designs and roundels with infilled borders. The lamp is incomplete so the full decorative scheme cannot be recreated.

The sandstone lamp, *9667*, has roughly squared edges and base and a single quite deep recess cut into the top. Only about a quarter of *9668* survives, indicating a cup-shaped lamp with a wide deep recess pecked into the top. The outer surface of both are crudely shaped and blackened.

9669 is roughly cylindrical with, somewhat unusually, recesses at both ends. The second recess was presumably made when the original recess was damaged but as only just over half the lamp survives it is impossible to tell which is the primary and which the secondary recess. Both show peck marks and are soot blackened. Another lamp, *9665*, also has recesses at both ends but in this case only one seems to have been used for oil. The recess on the other end forms

a deep, narrow cone which might have been placed over a stake set in an earth floor to make the lamp more stable. The second recess in *9669* may have functioned in a similar way although it is much more shallow and broad.

The chalk lamp, *9666*, is incomplete but enough survives to show the original height of the rim, and indicates a shallow recess produced by pecking. The base of the lamp has been roughly chipped to produce a simple plinth or footring, possibly to give extra weight for stability, or maybe simply as decoration. The outside is blackened over much of the surface.

9670 is unstratified but is similar to many of the other lamps in being roughly cylindrical with a small recess pecked deeply into the top. The lamp tapers towards the base, the sides are roughly faceted and the base simply cut away.

9664 may have served as a lamp at some time but this is unlikely to have been its primary purpose. It stands 243mm tall and has only a small recess in the top. The only indication that this was a lamp is some blackening of the top surface. It is a massive piece and the recess may have served as a door-pivot.

When discussing the lighting of the buildings, these stones lamps need to be considered together with the pottery lamps, which were more plentiful (*AY* 16/5, figs.154, 156, 158, 169, 186, 188–9) and the iron candle-holders and lamps (Fig.293, *AY* 17/6) also recovered from the site. None of these would individually have produced much light in the dark interiors, but would have supplemented the light from the hearth.

Spoons (Fig.1245)

Two copper alloy spoons were recovered (*10365–6*); although very different in size, both may have had similar uses. The smaller of the two spoons is *10365*, found in a Period 4B build-up deposit. With a narrow tapering stem and shallow oval bowl, it measures just 50·2mm in length. Its size indicates a possible function as a toilet instrument (see pp.2600–1), although it lacks any evidence of suspension which is typical of most of these objects from the Anglo-Saxon or Anglo-Scandinavian periods (see for example Birka; Arbman 1940, taf.171–3). Individual toilet spoons are, however, known from the Roman period, where they have been identified as having a range of possible functions, including cleaning out ears and extracting cosmetics from flasks or small pots (Crummy 1983, 59). It seems possible, therefore, that *10365* is a Roman spoon.

An unstratified double-ended spoon *10366* is three times the length of *10365* and it is paralleled by six tin-plated iron spoons, also from Coppergate (*2998–3003*, pp.601–4, *AY* 17/6). As with the iron spoons, *10366* has spatulate-like bowls, but it is larger than any of the iron examples and has a spirally twisted stem. All the iron spoons came from Period 4B contexts in Tenements C or D (p.603, *AY* 17/6), and it seems likely that *10366* is Anglo-Scandinavian in date. A thorough review of parallels for the iron spoons revealed that these implements, both single- and double-ended, are uncommon in the pre-Norman period (ibid.). Indeed, only one other double-ended spoon is known from this period; this is the silver example found at Sevington, Wiltshire, and dated to the 9th century (Wilson 1964, 61, no.68). The precise function of these implements remain obscure, although they are generally thought to have had a domestic use (ibid., 62); it has been suggested that the spatulate nature of the bowls on the Coppergate spoons may indicate use in holding and measuring viscous or solid materials such as drugs or spices (p.603, *AY* 17/6).

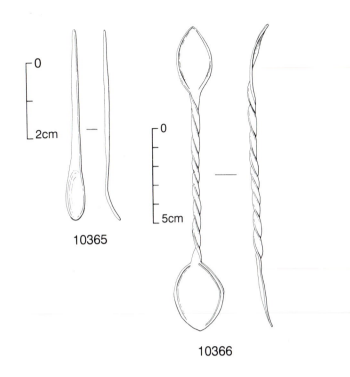

Fig.1245 *Copper alloy spoons from 16–22 Coppergate: 10365, scale 1:1; 10366, scale 1:2*

Querns (Figs.1246–9)

Rotary querns, used to grind cereals, were found throughout the Anglo-Scandinavian sequence. Forty-one fragments were recovered of which 24 were lava, sixteen were sandstone and one, unusually, was made of limestone (Table 255).

The distribution pattern of the quern fragments reflects the areas where successive structures had stood at various times. In Periods 3 and 4A, for example, most fragments are found on the street-frontage with only five fragments in the backyard areas. In Period 4B fragments were found in each of Tenements B, C and D, mostly towards the rear of where the buildings would have stood or in the central area of the site. Only two fragments were found at the rear of the site, nearest to the River Foss. In Period 5A fragments were limited to two each in Tenements C and D, while in Period 5B, they are distributed across all tenements in the structures and in the central part of the site.

2547

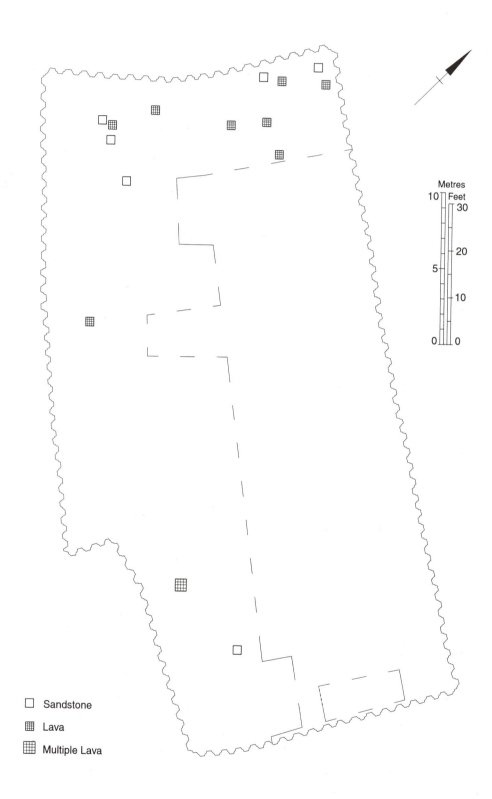

Fig.1246 *Distribution of querns in Period 3 at 16–22 Coppergate*

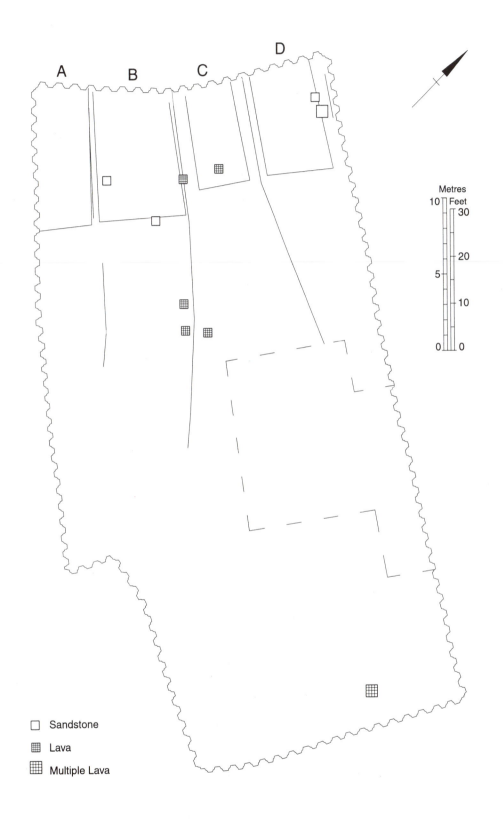

A   B   C   D

Metres
10 Feet
        30

        20

5
        10

0   0

☐ Sandstone

▦ Lava

▦ Multiple Lava

Fig.1247 *Distribution of querns in Period 4B at 16–22 Coppergate*

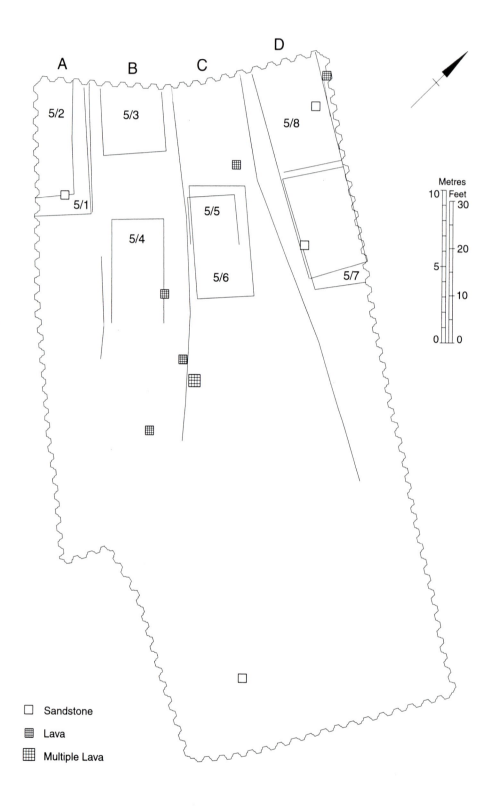

Fig.1248 *Distribution of querns in Period 5B at 16–22 Coppergate*

Most of the querns, especially the lava querns, are very fragmentary and in only a few cases can upper and lower stones be identified. *9693, 9698, 9700* and *9714* have part of the socket for the turning handle surviving. Part of the central perforation survives on several examples and, in the case of *9707*, there is a raised rim around the perforation, perhaps indicative of how it was set on the spindle. Some examples, such as *9706*, have clear dressing marks on the upper surface. *9697* may have had a secondary function as a grinding surface as one of the flat faces is quite worn. A single quern fragment with a part of the grinding edge surviving was recovered from 22 Piccadilly (*10635*).

Lava querns were shipped from the quarries in Mayen, in the Eifel region of Germany, to sites throughout north-western Europe including many

Table 255 Querns from 16–22 Coppergate according to period and material

Period	3	4A	4B	5A	5B	5C	Total
Lava	10	–	7	1	6	–	24
Sandstone	6	–	4	2	4	–	16
Limestone	–	1	–	–	–	–	1
Total	16	1	12	3	10	–	41

in Britain (Parkhouse 1976, 186). These include other sites in York, for example, 6–8 Pavement (p.74, *AY* 17/3) and 46–54 Fishergate (*4463–512, 4514, 4516–27, AY* 17/9). The stone used for the sandstone querns is almost invariably Millstone Grit and, less com-

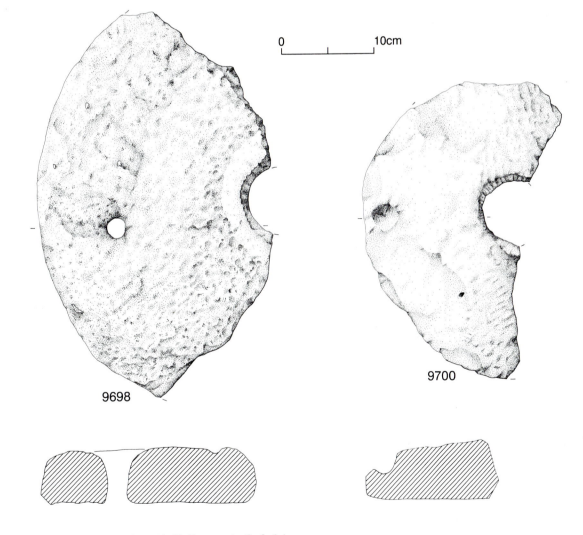

0   10cm

9698

9700

Fig.1249 Sandstone querns from 16–22 Coppergate. Scale 1:4

monly, from the Coal Measures. Limestone querns are rare and a source in the Howardian Hills near York has been suggested by Dr G.D. Gaunt for *9733*. Querns from more local sources have also been recovered from elsewhere in York; for example, 6–8 Pavement (*374–7, AY 17/3*) and from Parliament Street (*682, AY 17/4*).

The relatively small number of fragments from Coppergate is in contrast to the greater number recovered from 46–54 Fishergate, where 76 fragments, all lava, were found in Anglian levels and a further 26 from Anglo-Scandinavian contexts. The eighteen smaller fragments from later contexts are believed to be residual Anglo-Scandinavian (p.1322, *AY* 17/9). Only five examples of sandstone querns were recovered from Fishergate, including complete upper and lower stones from an Anglo-Scandinavian pit. This pattern of preference for lava as a material in the Anglian period, seen at Fishergate, is consistent with the findings from Coppergate where the greater number of lava fragments are from the earliest deposits (Table 255). The relative paucity of evidence from Coppergate raises the question of how much basic processing of cereals was carried out on this site.

Structural Fittings and Furnishings

Fittings

A number of non-ferrous fittings were found, many of which are more commonly made of iron; these include hasps, hinges, strip fittings and bindings, nails and bolts. The majority of these are most likely to have been used on small pieces of wooden furniture, such as boxes or caskets, for which they may have been chosen as a more decorative alternative to iron fittings; the smaller fittings may have been applied to textile or leather.

Stapled hasp (Fig.1250)

10367 is a copper alloy stapled hasp which was found in Period 5B backfill in Structure 5/7 on Tenement D. Similar in form and size to iron hasps found at Coppergate (*3495–8*, pp.645–6, *AY* 17/6), it has been decorated on the upper face.

Hinge fittings (Fig.1250)

Found in a Period 3 dump deposit, *10368* is a looped hinge fitting of copper alloy with a decoratively shaped terminal and a loop at the other end, with which another plate, now missing, would have engaged. Perhaps from a box, *10368* is similar in form to an iron hinge also found at Coppergate (*3480*, p.641, *AY* 17/6). Another hinge fitting fragment, from a Period 3 build-up deposit, *10369*, has a rounded terminal with an iron rivet through, below which it expands towards the other broken end; similar hinges, decorated with ring-and-dot motifs were found at Birka (Arbman 1940, taf.261, no.1a).

Strip fittings (Fig.1250)

10370–3, 10377 and *10382* form a group of decoratively bossed strip fittings, the largest of which (*10370–1*) retain traces of the wood to which they were originally attached (*8929, AY* 17/13). The wood traces on both are mineralised and unidentifiable to species. Unlike a similar iron fitting from Coppergate, which is unpierced (*3389*, p.632, *AY* 17/6), all the copper alloy bossed fittings retain rivets or have rivet holes. Possibly a hinge fragment, *10370* is a folded strip with the remains of an iron ring through the loop; only one half of the strip is decorated, this presumably being the side that would have been visible. *10371–2* are from the same build-up deposit, and may both derive from the same object. Similarly shaped to *10370*, and also possibly a hinge fitting, *10376* is decorated on its upper face with incised Z-shaped motifs. Other strip fittings include *10375*, which bears incised diagonal lines, and *10373*, of which only a small fragment remains, decorated with a stamped ring which has a perforation through it. Two undecorated strip fittings (*10381, 10383*) and *10379*, with lateral incised lines, all have an axial row of rivet holes. Although now lacking any rivet holes, a

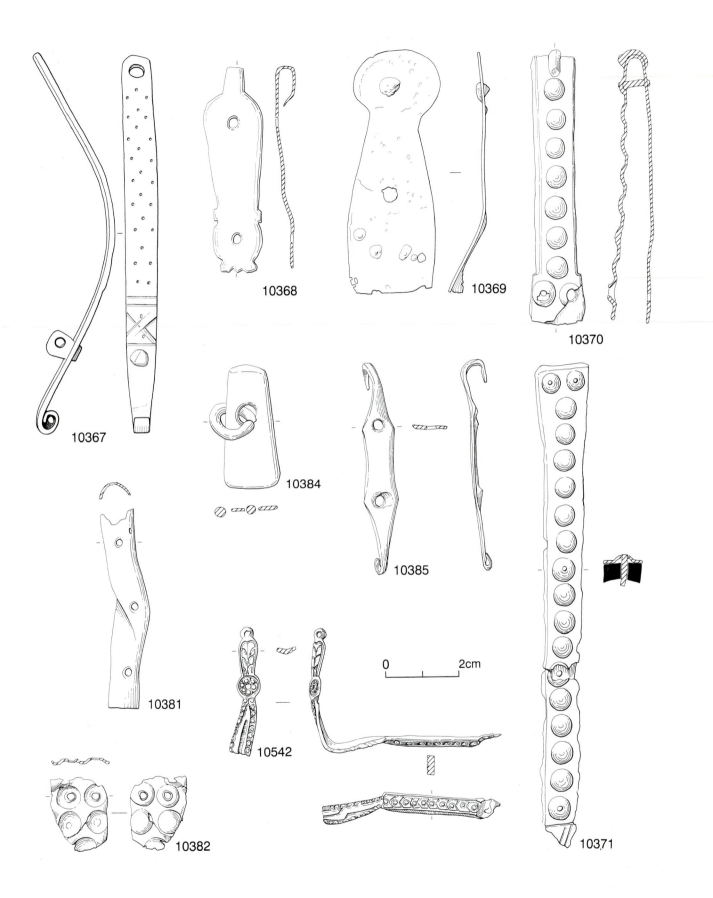

10368

10369

10370

10367

10384

10385

10381

10542

10382

0 2cm

10371

Fig.1250 *Fittings from 16–22 Coppergate. Scale 1:1*

fragmentary decorated strip *10374* may also have been a fitting. Nine of the strip fittings come from Period 4B contexts, with three (*10370, 10373, 10378*) being found in the floor level of the wattle building on Tenement B.

Possible fittings (Fig.1250)

A fitting of uncertain function is *10384* which comprises a trapezoidal plate, with an incomplete ring looped through an off-centre perforation. *10385* comes from a Period 5Cr deposit; it is subrectangular with two axial perforations, and both ends hooked over. It is similar in shape to an iron object found at Coppergate which was described as a clip, perhaps for a belt or strap (*3797*, p.693, *AY* 17/6).

Possible decorative fitting (Fig.1250)

Made of silver, *10542* was found in a Period 5Cr dump. Its function is also uncertain, but close to the terminal there is a large perforation, which may have been for attachment to an object; it is broken at the other end. Whatever its function, its extensive decoration, which is primarily made up of punched dots, indicates that it was meant to be very visible.

Studs (Figs.1251–3)

Decorative studs or bosses were found at both Coppergate (*10536, 10541, 10555–6*) and 22 Piccadilly (*10682*).

M.E. Hutchinson comments upon the silver stud *10541*:

The metal has the typical appearance of slightly corroded silver-gilt, and previous analysis in the Ancient Monuments Laboratory confirmed the mercury gilded debased silver. Although the surface of the glass paste is much worn, the metalwork is in quite good condition. The round glass paste is in a band setting surrounded by two rows of decorated wire, the inner twisted from two wires and the outer beaded. As there are eight 'beads' to 4mm, this is fine work. Theophilus describes a method for making such beaded wire (Theophilus, Book III; IX).

Examination of the inner space and glass paste by low-powered microscope revealed spherical bubbles, identifying the stone as a blue glass. As light will pass through the stone, the glass is technically translucent, but this is not apparent to the eye; it may have been intended to look like lapis lazuli. Inspection with a Chelsea filter showed it to

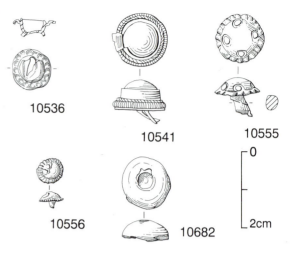

Fig.1251 *Studs from 16–22 Coppergate: 10536 gold; 10541 silver; 10555–6 lead alloy. Copper alloy stud 10682 from 22 Piccadilly. Scale 1:1*

be coloured by cobalt, which is what the colour suggests. It is c.10·0mm in diameter.

As the mount is damaged, it was possible to see behind the glass. There is a layer of something underneath the stone, but it does not look like a reflective foil, as it is dark and appears to be fibrous. However, setters will use anything to hand to raise a stone up to the correct height for the setting (a ring from St Augustine's Abbey, Canterbury, has a piece of cloth behind it), and this material may be something which was used to raise the stone. In any case, a stone, whether natural or imitation, which looks opaque has no need of a foil.

Fig.1252 *Detailed view of beading on 10541*

Fig.1253 *Gold stud from 16–22 Coppergate (10536). Actual diameter 10.0mm*

This stud represents another of the Anglian objects from the site, although it was found residually in a Period 5B dump/build-up deposit. There are two prongs on the reverse to attach the stud, possibly to a precious metal bowl similar to that found in the cemetery at Ormside, Cumbria. The Ormside bowl has a plain gilt-bronze inner bowl and a decorated silver-gilt outer bowl with separate decorated inner and outer base-plates, the whole held together by rivets (Webster and Backhouse 1991, 173, pl.134). The inner base-plate is decorated with a cross with expanded arms, and false filigree collared bosses containing blue glass cabochons, the settings which *10541* strongly resembles. The bowl itself is dated by its ornament to the second half of the 8th century although decorative rim-clamps indicated a repair in the 9th century, and the bowl is thought to have come from a Viking grave (ibid.).

Another stud with a filigree collar, but made of lead alloy (*10556*), may represent a cheaper version of a decorative boss for a vessel. *10556* was found in a floor level of the Period 4B wattle building on Tenement D.

The gold stud *10536* comes from a Period 4A build-up deposit (Fig.1253). With its flattened rim decorated with punched dots, it may be compared to a number of decorative mounts and pendants recovered from the cemetery at Birka (Arbman 1940, taf.97, nos.23–4).

A second lead alloy stud (*10555*) has a decorative head, with stamped rings on it; it was found in a Period 3 pit backfill. A copper alloy stud, recovered at 22 Piccadilly (*10682*) has a plain domed head, centrally perforated; traces of pewter on the underside indicate that it may originally have been attached to a pewter vessel.

Mounts (Fig.1254)

Some small fittings which appear to be decorative rather than functional are made of copper alloy. From a Period 5B build-up deposit, *10389* is a subcrescent-shaped piece of sheet with two rivet holes, decorated with rocked-tracer ornament along the edges and ring-and-dot motifs in the central field. A pendant from Birka is similarly shaped (Arbman 1940, taf.98, no.13). Also decorated with ring-and-dot, through which a rivet hole has been made, *10386* is a tiny mount fragment from a floor level in the Period 4B wattle building on Tenement B. Tongue-shaped, *10387* is decorated with a cross-shaped arrangement of ring-and-dot motifs. Perhaps a mount for a belt, *10388* is centrally domed, and has lugs on the back for attachment; it was found in a possible floor level in the Period 5B Structure 5/8 on Tenement D. *10390* is subrectangular, and decorated with an incised herring-bone pattern.

From an unstratified context at the Vicars Choral College at the Bedern comes a fragment of a large gilded copper alloy openwork mount (*10708*), into which crossing tendrils and part of a spiral, elements typical of Ringerike-style decoration, have been deeply carved. Although incomplete, the fragment retains two rivet holes for attachment, and has a stepped profile to one side on the reverse — it may have been re-used or repaired, as one of the rivet holes appears to be a secondary addition. It represents one of only two non-ferrous metal objects of clearly Anglo-Scandinavian origin from the College (the other being the ring-headed pin, *10709*), and one of the very few examples of Ringerike-style motifs in the north of England.

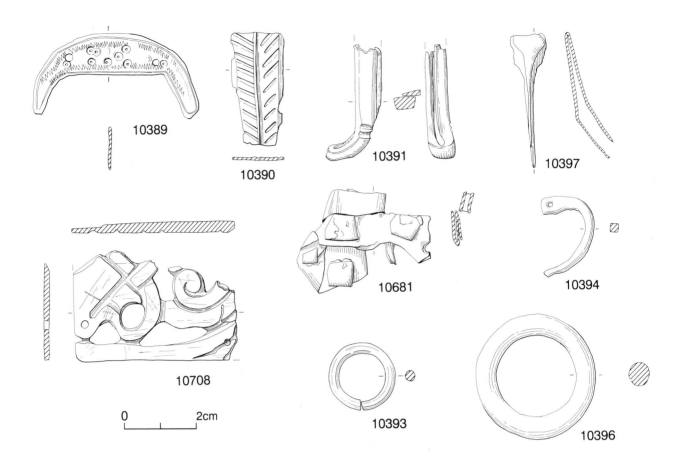

Fig.1254 *Copper alloy fittings: mounts,* 10389 *from 16–22 Coppergate,* 10708 *from Bedern; rings,* 10393 *and* 10396, *and ring-shaped object* 10394 *from 16–22 Coppergate; binding from 16–22 Coppergate,* 10391; *double-spiked loop from 16–22 Coppergate,* 10397; *patch of folded sheet from 22 Piccadilly,* 10681. *Scale 1:1*

Binding (Fig.1254)

Found in a Period 5Cr dump, *10391* appears to be a fragment of a curved edge-binding, made from a semi-circular strip folded into two, and broken across perforations. Its shape suggests that it was more likely to have been applied to leather or textile than wood, but its precise function is uncertain.

Rings (Fig.1254)

Miscellaneous rings of copper alloy (*10392–3, 10396*), lead alloy (*10557–9*) and of tin (*10619*) were recovered from contexts dating from the mid 9th/ early 10th to mid 11th centuries. They vary in diameter from 12mm (*10619*) to 32·9mm (*10396*), the latter being mercury gilded. Two incomplete ring-shaped objects (*10394–5*) have one end which has been flattened and perforated. Precise uses cannot

be ascribed to this varied group of rings, but possible functions include finger-rings, suspension rings or looped handles for boxes.

Double-spiked loop (Fig.1254)

The identity of *10397* is uncertain, but it may be a fitting for attaching a ring handle to a box. The projecting spikes would have been set into the box, and the ring passed through a loop at the top; the upper end of *10397* is not looped, but may have been flattened. Copper alloy fittings of this type are known from the Roman period (Crummy 1983, 119–20, fig.125).

Nails (Fig.1255)

Lead alloy nails recovered from early 10th–mid 11th century deposits at Coppergate (*10560–5*) rep-

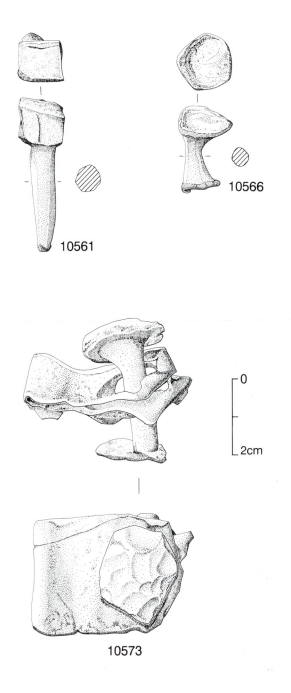

Fig.1255 *Lead alloy nail (10561) and clench bolts from 16–22 Coppergate. Scale 1:1*

Clench bolts (Fig.1255)

In addition to over 80 iron clench bolts and roves from Anglo-Scandinavian levels at Coppergate (*3066–151*, pp.615–18, *AY* 17/6), ten lead alloy examples were also found (*10566–75*). A further three found in late 11th–mid 13th century dumps may be residual (*10576–8*). These non-ferrous clench bolts differ from their ferrous counterparts in having shanks of circular or subcircular rather than square section. They are also shorter on average, the complete examples ranging in length from 14mm (*10568*) to 38·5mm (*10573*), the majority being 20–30mm long; this compares to a range amongst the iron clench bolts of 24–107mm, the majority being 27–45mm long (p.616, *AY* 17/6). Where the roves survive, these are either subcircular or lozenge-shaped. Those bolts which have been analysed have proved to be pure or nearly pure lead.

Two of the lead alloy clench bolts had been driven through perforations in lead alloy strips (*10570, 10573*) suggesting that they had different uses to iron bolts, which were used to join timbers in the construction of both clinker-built ships and buildings (ibid., p.615). The use of non-ferrous rather than ferrous material for these bolts may indicate use externally on structures, since lead alloy bolts would not rust as iron bolts would.

Perforated strips

Two incomplete perforated lead strips (*10579–80*), similar to those found with clench bolts in situ were recovered. The strips derive from late 10th–late 11th century contexts, a period when the use of lead for roofing is known (Foreman 1991a, 158); two strip fragments are, however, insufficient to indicate the use of lead roofing on the site. Copper alloy perforated strips of uncertain function were also found at Coppergate (*10398*) and 22 Piccadilly (*10683*).

Window cames

Two fragments of window came of H-shaped section were found in Period 5B deposits, *10581* in build-up and *10582* in a scoop. Although more commonly found on medieval sites, window cames have been recovered in small numbers from Saxon sites, for example at Jarrow (Cramp 1969, 48).

resent another type of object more commonly found in iron. Four of the six nails are complete, and exhibit a narrow range of lengths from 35·1mm (*10565*) to 40·1mm (*10561*). The precise functions of these objects are uncertain; as with the smaller iron nails from Coppergate, they may have been used on boxes or caskets (p.613, *AY* 17/6), and, as with tin-plated iron nails, may have served a decorative role (ibid., p.614).

Miscellaneous non-ferrous objects

Two copper alloy tube fragments from 16–22 Coppergate made from rolled up sheet (*10399–400*) are of unknown function. A fragment of folded copper alloy sheet with folded sheet rivets was found at 22 Piccadilly (*10681*; Fig.1254). It may have acted as a patch, perhaps on a non-ferrous vessel, but its precise function is unknown. Also of unknown function is *10401*, an incomplete object of copper alloy sheet, which appears to have broken along one edge, across two perforations.

Horse Harness (Fig.1256)

In addition to ferrous horse equipment including parts of snaffle bits (*3840–50*), horseshoes (*3851–6*) and horseshoe nails (*3857–904*, pp.704–9, AY 17/6) found at 16–22 Coppergate, three non-ferrous objects have been tentatively identified as horse harness fittings (*10402–4*). *10402* was found in a Period 4A (late 9th–early 10th century) build-up deposit. Broken at one end, it curves to a pointed terminal, and has prominent looped projections, single on one side and double on the other, between which it is decorated with an enamelled design, originally red. There appears to be no known parallel to this object, but it has been suggested that it may form part of a strap-distributor, the missing part of the object probably being a second pointed terminal symmetrically balancing the first. It may derive from a suite of enamelled harness mounts (C. Bourke, R. Ó Floinn, pers. comm.). The animal-like features on the terminal invite comparison with 9th century strap-ends, such as *5317* and *5321* from 46–54 Fishergate (pp.1350–1, AY 17/9), both of which were also decorated with enamel. Graham-Campbell has noted a series of enamelled harness mounts from the Isle of Lewis, Isle of Man, Ireland and Norway, which he considers to be 8th–9th century (Graham-Campbell 1986, 281–4). Moreover, Raghnall Ó Floinn notes that the loops are reminiscent of those on harness mounts found in a Viking burial at Kiloran Bay, Colonsay (Fig.1299, **1**, p.2606) (Grieg 1930, fig.30); he suggests that *10402* may have functioned in a similar fashion to a strap-distributor also found in the burial, which had three loops through which strap-ends were fastened. He also cites a further looped mount with geometric enamelled cells found complete with a strap mount of the Kiloran Bay type in excavations at Christchurch Place, Dublin (unpublished).

A much plainer object from a Period 5A dump, *10403*, may also be an incomplete strap distributor with loops for three straps, and one fixed arm, now broken. Distributors such as these are more commonly made of iron (Goodall 1990, 1043, nos.3885A, 3886; Goodall 1991, 135, no.566) but copper alloy examples have also been found in Scandinavia, in Uppland, Sweden (Arbman 1935–7, 270–2, fig.7).

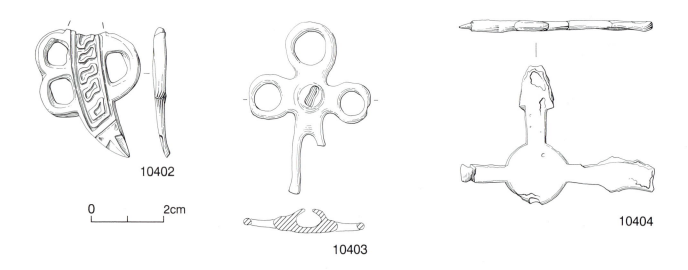

10402

0   2cm

10403

10404

Fig.1256   Copper alloy horse harness equipment from 16–22 Coppergate. Scale 1:1

A possible harness mount, *10404* from a Period 5B dump appears originally to have been cross-shaped. It has a central roundel, and arms with shaped terminals; it is made of copper alloy and has been gilded. It may represent a simple version of very elaborate harness mounts found in 9th century Scandinavian burials, at Navan, Co. Meath, Ireland (Youngs 1989, 118, no.113), and Soma, in Norway (Wamers 1985, 100, no.91). In both instances, the burials contained assemblages including richly decorated cross-shaped mounts or plaques, with central circular fields and arms with variously shaped terminals. These were found in association with bits from a horse's harness, leading to their identification as harness mounts (Youngs 1989, 118).

Trade and Exchange

Balances (Figs.1257–8)

Beam balances

Anglo-Scandinavian contexts at Coppergate produced fragments of hand-held balances of both types known from this period, that is with either a rigid arm (*10409*) or folding arms (*10405–6, 10410, 10412*) from which scale pans were hung (Kruse 1992, 68). Fragments from balances whose type could not be determined were also found (*10407, 10411, 10413–14*). In addition to the well-stratified Anglo-Scandinavian balances, other balance fragments recovered from medieval contexts may also be from this period (*10415–16*).

Both folding and non-folding balance types appear to have been used contemporaneously at Coppergate, as noted at other sites in Anglo-Scandinavian England (Kruse 1992, 72). The most complete example of a folding beam balance from Coppergate is *10405* on which both of the arms are

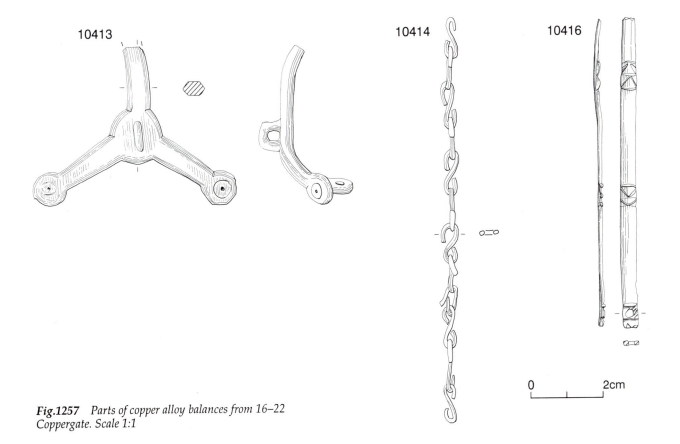

Fig.1257 *Parts of copper alloy balances from 16–22 Coppergate. Scale 1:1*

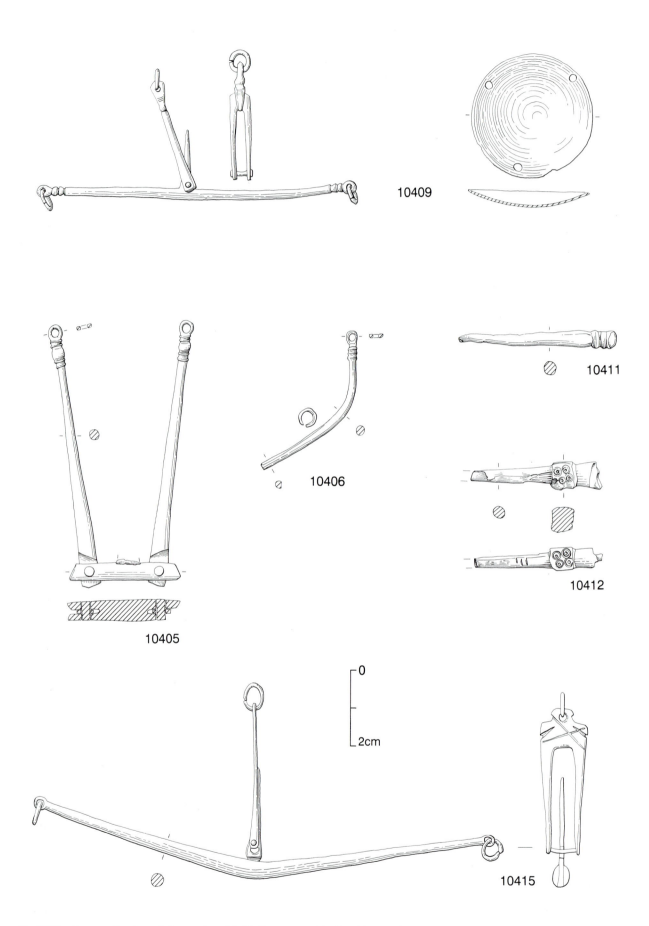

10409

10411

10406

10412

10405

0

2cm

10415

Fig.1258 *Copper alloy beam balances from 16–22 Coppergate, 10409 with one of its two scale pans. Scale 1:1*

still attached to the beam, hinging on rivets, and the pointer appears to have been soldered on. Fragments of folding beam balance arms (*10406, 10410, 10412*) are identified as such by the remains of the pivotal part of the arm; *10412* from a Period 5B deposit is decorated close to the pivotal end where the arm assumes a square section with ring-and-dot motifs, a characteristic which Kruse notes could be of Scandinavian or Baltic inspiration (ibid., 73), but which is also found on a balance from a 13th century context at Winchester (Biddle 1990c, 923–5, fig.284, no.3211). The non-folding balance *10409* retains its stirrup for suspension and its pointer, and was found complete with two scale pans, each with three suspension holes.

Other parts of balances include *10413*, a suspension bracket from which a pan would have hung by three chains, and which would itself have been attached to the balance arm by chain. This can be seen on a balance found at the 9th century Kilmainham-Islandbridge cemetery complex, Dublin (Roesdahl et al. 1992, 320, no.356). Of less certain identification, *10411*, which was found in a Period 5A context, may be a balance arm fragment; it has a moulding at one end which is similar to those on the arms of *10405* and *10409*. *10407* appears to be part of a balance stirrup, while a fragment of chain of S-shaped links (*10414*) may also once have hung from a pair of scales. A single S-shaped copper alloy chain link found at 22 Piccadilly (*10690*) may possibly derive from a balance.

A balance and other fragments recovered from Period 6 deposits at Coppergate may also be Anglo-Scandinavian. With a rigid arm, and retaining its stirrup, *10415*, which was found in a 12th–13th century cut, is very similar to a folding balance from 9 Blake Street, York, recovered from a Period 6 (10th/11th century onwards) context, but thought possibly to be Roman (*6343*, p.1551, *AY* 17/10). The Blake Street example is similarly decorated with an asymmetrical saltire on the stirrup, although it has been applied using a rocked tracer as opposed to the simple incised ornament on *10415*. These balances are probably contemporary, but their dating is uncertain; the stirrup shape is seen on other 10th/11th century balances from Ipswich (Kruse 1992, fig.4), suggesting that this may be the most likely period of origin for the two York balances, but Kruse considers the shape simple and undiagnostic (ibid., 76). Although from a late 14th–early 15th century build-up/dump, *10416* is another possible Anglo-Scandinavian stirrup fragment; very similar fragments from early–mid 11th century contexts on the PK Bank site in Lund, Sweden (Fig.1300, **5**, p.2608), were identified as such (Molander 1976, 187, fig.131).

Weights (Figs.1259–60)

Weights of copper alloy (*10408*), of lead alloy (*10584–7, 10589*) and of lead (*10592*) or iron coated with non-ferrous metals (*10356–60*) were found at Coppergate. Other possible lead alloy weights include the ship-shaped *10583*, and several discs (*10588, 10590–1, 10593–8*).

Copper alloy weight

A survey of scales and weights from burials of the 6th and 7th centuries in England noted that all but two of the weights were of copper alloy (Scull 1990, 187); this contrasts with later Anglo-Saxon weights which tend to be of iron or lead (Kruse 1992, 78). The only copper alloy weight from Coppergate (*10408*) was found in a Period 4B dump, and may

Table 256   Weights from Anglo-Scandinavian contexts at 16–22 Coppergate

Catalogue Number	Period	Material	Weight
10356	3	Iron + Cu, Zn coating	21.90g
10357	3	Iron + Cu, Zn coating	26.97g
10358	4B	Iron + Cu, Zn, Pb coating	97.20g
10359	4B	Iron + Pb coating	25.00g
10360	5Cf	Iron + Cu, Zn coating	18.50g
10408	4B	Heavily leaded copper	1.50g
10583	4B	Lead	26.37g
10584	4B	Fairly pure lead	53.09g
10585	4B	Lead alloy	27.24g
10586	4B	Fairly pure lead	58.60g
10587	4B	Fairly pure lead	28.08g
10588	4B	Lead	4.84g
10589	4B	Fairly pure lead	12.03g
10590	5A	Lead	14.91g
10591	5A	Lead	4.60g
10592	5B	Lead + Cu coating	35.65g
10593	5B	Lead	2.79g

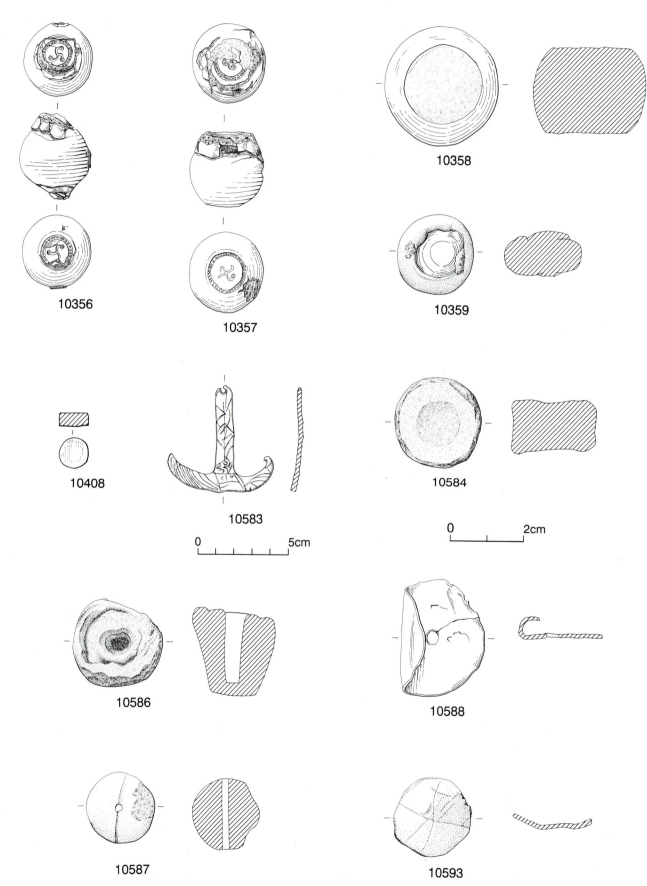

Fig.1259 *Weights from 16–22 Coppergate: iron 10356–9; copper alloy 10408; lead alloy 10583–4, 10586–8, 10593. Scale 1:1, 10583 1:2*

Fig.1260 Pair of iron weights coated in brass from 16–22 Coppergate: (left) 10356, diameter 19·0mm; (right) 10357, diameter 21·0mm

possibly derive from pre-Anglo-Scandinavian activity on the site.

Lead alloy weights

These are variously cylindrical (*10584*), truncated conical (*10585*), inverted truncated conical (*10586*) and spherical (*10587*). The discs are plain (*10591*) or with incised markings (*10593*), perforated centrally (*10588*) or at the edge (*10590*). Kruse notes that plain lead weights are the most common type recovered (ibid., 79), but that there are difficulties in identifying such objects as weights with certainty, particularly the discs, some of which could be counters or pendants. Furthermore, there are few contemporary examples of lead weights from England, apart from individual finds from East Anglia at Thetford, St Neots and Ipswich (ibid.).

Sheathed in copper alloy, *10592* resembles the more commonly found iron weights with copper alloy coatings (see below); it was recovered from the Period 5B backfill of Structure 5/6 on Tenement C. Coated lead weights have been found previously, however, both in Anglo-Saxon England and in Viking Ireland (Kisch 1965, 83). The similarity in shape between *10592* and the iron weights from Coppergate, which are certainly from the Viking period (see below), indicates that *10592* is probably contemporary with them. A discoidal lead weight with a decoratively cast and turned copper alloy shell was also found in a late 12th century context at Fishergate (Ottaway and Rogers, *AY* 17/– in prep.).

10583 has been variously described as anchor-shaped (Kruse 1992, 83) and ship-shaped (Hall 1984, 106). It is of uncertain function, but may be a weight, although it has previously been published as a pendant (ibid.). It was found in a Period 4B dump deposit, and has been broken at the upper end through a perforation which was presumably for suspension. Similarly shaped lead objects found in Dublin have been interpreted as weights (Wallace 1987, 212), and it appears significant that at 26·37g, *10583* is extremely close to the basic unit of weight of 26·6g identified amongst 200 examples from Dublin (ibid.).

From elsewhere in York, a lead alloy weight with an enamelled mount was recovered during excavations at the site of the Clementhorpe nunnery (*AY* 7/2, *81*); the mount, which appears to be of 8th or

9th century date (Tweddle 1983, 24), has been cut down and set into the weight. The origin of the mount is uncertain, but the re-use of mounts in this way appears to be a Scandinavian tradition, parallels coming from Viking graves at Kiloran Bay, Colonsay, in the Hebrides, and from the Kilmainham-Islandbridge cemetery outside Dublin (Kruse 1992, 81).

Iron weights

The five iron weights, which range from 18·5g (*10360*) to 97·2g (*10358*), are all approximately globular, flattened top and bottom, and encased in non-ferrous coatings; four of the coatings are of brass, the fifth (*10359*) is of lead. The coatings completely cover the weights, apart from *10358* on which the coating is absent from the top and bottom faces. Iron weights with non-ferrous coatings appear to be the most common type found in Viking Age Scandinavia and the Baltic, normally having copper alloy coatings (Kruse 1992, 80); the use of lead alloy coating on *10359* is unusual (ibid., 83).

10356–7 form a pair (Fig.1260); there is approximately 5g in weight between them, and they were found within a metre of each other in Period 3 levels. That they are a pair is indicated by the decoration each has on the flattened top and bottom faces. It is more clearly defined on *10356*, where a stamped 'triskele' motif of linked curves with three dots appears within a circle of stamped dots; the motif on *10357* is less clear, but appears to incorporate four linked dots within the same defining circle. A set of five weights found in a 10th century male cremation at Hemlingby, Valbo, Gästrikland in Sweden, contains weights identical to *10356–7*; four of the five weights have the stamped circles containing motifs of linked curves and dots, incorporating one, three, four or five dots, while the fifth weight is illegible (Roesdahl and Wilson 1992, 266, no.151). It is thought that such weights probably had oriental prototypes (Kisch 1959, 167), but were also associated with the medieval Scandinavian system of *marks*, *öre* and *örtugar*. The Hemlingby weights appear to represent half an *öre* and one, three, four and five *örtugar* (ibid.). That this type of weight was long-lived is evident from the recovery of an example from a 12th century deposit at Lund, Sweden (Molander 1976, 194, fig.134), while an undecorated globular weight of this type came from a similarly dated deposit at the Vintry site in London (J. Stevenson, pers. comm.). Three sites in Norfolk have also produced weights of this type (Margeson 1996, 56). While most of the Coppergate weights could have been made on the site, these two decorated examples of more complex manufacture appear more likely to be imports, probably from Scandinavia, an assumption also made by Wallace in relation to the contemporary Dublin weights (Wallace 1987, 212).

Another possible set of weights from Coppergate comprises *10584–5* which are of lead, *10358*, which is iron coated in brass, and *10359* which is iron coated in lead. Three were recovered in the floor level of the Period 4B wattle building on Tenement D, the fourth, *10359*, from a scoop backfill from the same building. Although varying considerably in form, the possibility that they once derived from the same set is reinforced by the recovery of other sets incorporating a variety of forms, such as a group found in a bag together with a pair of scales at Jåtten, Hetland, Rogaland, Norway (Roesdahl and Wilson 1992, 266, no.150).

Many attempts have been made to correlate archaeologically recovered weights with postulated Anglo-Saxon, Scandinavian or medieval units of measurement (see for example Kruse 1992, 86–9; Drinkall and Stevenson 1996, 5–9). These researchers were looking at assemblages considerably larger than that from Coppergate, and, as both failed to provide clear patterns of association of shapes or weights with any particular system of measurement, no attempt has been made similarly to analyse and link the Coppergate weights to any known metrological system.

Gaming Pieces

Stone counters (Fig.1262)

There are thirteen stone objects which have been classed as counters and a further five which might be pot lids. These are typically roughly chipped flat stone discs which can be grouped on the basis of diameter. The group of smallest counters comprises five examples (*9737, 9739–40, 9743, 9749*) with diameters of around 20–25mm and thicknesses of 3–5mm; *9739* has been cut down from a pebble so has a naturally domed top. Dr G.D. Gaunt has identified them all as sandstone with the exception of *9749*, which is probably an indurated siltstone or silty mudstone. Apart from this object, which is from Period 5B, all these small examples are from Period 4B and were found near the street-frontage in Tenements C and D.

The rest of the sandstone chipped discs are larger and thicker. Of these, four (*9734, 9747–8, 9751*) have diameters between 35 and 40mm and thicknesses between 5 and 12mm. *9751* and the fragmentary *9747* are better finished than the cruder, more angular *9748*. The remaining four (*9735, 9741, 9744–5*) have diameters between approximately 45 and 55mm and thicknesses between 10 and 16mm. Three have been chipped into rough discs (*9745* is fragmentary), but *9741* is much more angular and crudely shaped. This group is well distributed through the sequence from

Period 3 onwards but once again most of the counters are from the street-frontage in Tenements C and D; *9748* was found near the street-frontage in Tenement A.

Some of the stone discs are perhaps too large to be considered as simple counters or playing pieces and may have served as lids for wooden or ceramic vessels, though the vessels they covered could only have been small. Into this category have been placed *9736* (Period 4A), *9738* (Period 4B), *9742* (Period 4B), and *9750* (Period 5B). Most are roughly chipped discs of between 13 and 20mm thickness and all are made from sandstone. *9738* has much smoother edges and is more circular than the others. Slight wear around one edge might indicate that it was pushed firmly into the neck of some vessel.

Dr Gaunt suggests that the predominance of stone counters and possible pot lids with Elland Flags-type lithology implies a more readily available source of

Fig.1261   Hnefatafl *board and gaming pieces of bone, chalk and jet from 16–22 Coppergate. Width of wooden board 109mm*

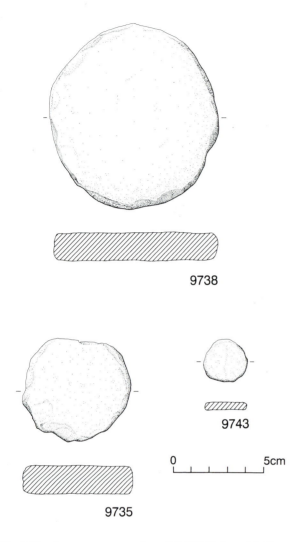

Fig.1262 *Stone counters and pot lid (9738) from 16–22 Coppergate. Scale 1:2*

his stone than its nearest outcrops, 32km away, namely the abundant old Roman roofing stones with this lithology found in situ in York (pers. comm.).

Pottery and tile counters

There are also twelve counters made from cut-down and shaped pottery sherds or tile fragments. The majority, seven, are made from Roman pottery and might be of Roman date and residual in Anglo-Scandinavian contexts. Four counters are made from samian ware body-sherds, *9956–7*, *9959* (Period 3) and *9961* (Period 4B), two are made from Roman grey wares, *9958* (Period 3) and *9960* (Period 4B), and one from a Roman colour-coated ware (*9962*) (Period

5B). Equally, however, they may have been fashioned in the Anglo-Scandinavian period from sherds which had been brought to the surface.

Of the others, *9965* (Period 5Cr) is made from Torksey-type ware, *9964* (Period 5A) from an Anglo-Scandinavian grey ware and *9963* (Period 4B) from a coarse fabric with a splash of glaze or glassy residue. Two counters are cut down from tile, presumably of Roman date, *9966* (Period 4B) and *9967* (Period 5B). These counters are all roughly discoidal and have been smoothed to a greater or lesser extent.

The samian and colour-coated ware have diameters ranging between 22 and 30mm with thicknesses varying between 4 and 12mm depending on the thickness of the original sherd. One of the Roman grey ware counters (*9958*) has a diameter of 35mm, while the other (*9960*) is larger at 60mm. The Torksey ware (*9965*) and the Anglo-Scandinavian grey ware (*9964*) counters are 21 and 22mm respectively, while the sherd with the splash of glaze (*9963*) has been used to produce a larger counter (50mm). The two tile counters, *9966* and *9967*, are both thicker (17mm and 19mm respectively) and larger (70mm and 60mm respectively).

The purpose of the chipped stone and fired clay discs is uncertain. All could have functioned as counters or playing pieces, or, in the case of the larger ones, as pot lids or covers.

Stone playing pieces (Figs.1261, 1263)

The function of another group of stone objects is, however, much clearer. Eight domed chalk pieces *9752–9* of comparable shape and size are believed to be *hnefatafl* pieces. All of them, with the exception of *9758–9*, were found in the floor levels of the Period 4B wattle building on Tenement C, and it is tempting to see them as part of a set. *9758* was found further down the same tenement in a later context but may well have been part of the same group. The diameter of all the bases is a millimetre or two either side of 20mm and their height is also approximately 20mm. Two of the pieces are slightly pointed (*9755*, *9757*), the rest are dome-shaped (e.g. *9752*). *9756* is covered with red ochre and there are traces of the same colouration on *9758*. It is not clear whether the colouration on *9756* formed a pattern, but some patches are thicker than others.

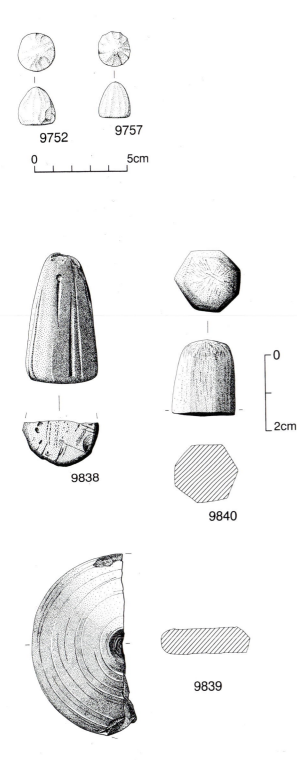

Fig.1263 *Playing pieces from 16–22 Coppergate: 9752, 9757, chalk, scale 1:2; 9838–40, jet or shale, scale 1:1*

Playing pieces in a number of different materials have been recovered from the site. There are other *hnefatafl* pieces in jet, antler, ivory and bone. The form and size of the antler ones (*7731–2*, p.1982, Fig.940, *AY* 17/12), which were also found in Period 4B just west of the wattle building, are the most similar to these chalk ones. A fragment of an oak gaming board (*9032*, *AY* 17/13), probably used for *hnefatafl*, was recovered from a Period 5B dump or backfill within Structure 5/1 on Tenement A, and may well have been associated with these pieces (Fig.1261).

9749 is a small highly polished flat stone which has been listed with the counters (p.2564). It might have received its glossy surface as a result of frequent handling and may have been a playing piece or used as a burnisher.

Jet and shale playing pieces and counters (Fig.1263)

A broken shale playing piece (*9838*) of conical form was recovered from a Period 3 deposit, near the front of what was to become Tenement A. It is decorated very simply with irregular vertical incised lines and is probably also a *hnefatafl* piece. Another, much more finely made and highly polished jet *hnefatafl* piece (*9840*) was recovered from a medieval deposit in the backyard area of the site. It is of heptagonal section with a rounded top, and is probably a residual Anglo-Scandinavian piece.

The only other possible jet gaming piece or counter from Anglo-Scandinavian levels is a large fragmentary lathe-turned discoid object which was found in Period 5B levels at the back of Tenement B (*9839*). An alternative interpretation is that it might be a lid, possibly of Roman date (L. Allason-Jones, pers. comm.)

Other medieval jet gaming pieces have been recovered from York, from Nessgate (Fig.1187, **15**, p.2452) (Waterman 1959, 94, fig.21.1) and Union Terrace (YAT 1972.18), and from Coppergate; sf1380 (Period 6) may be another unfinished piece. There are also jet dice from medieval deposits (Ottaway and Rogers, *AY* 17/– in prep.). In addition to the above pieces, eighteen glass counters were recovered from Roman to medieval contexts at Coppergate; these are thought to be Roman in date and will be published in *AY* 6/2 (forthcoming).

Personal Ornament and Dress Accessories

Buckles (Fig.1264)

Only two non-ferrous buckles, both of copper alloy, were found in Anglo-Scandinavian levels at Coppergate (*10417–18*); both are from build-up deposits or dumps, the former from Period 4A, the latter from Period 5A. This is in contrast to almost 100 iron buckles or buckle fragments from Anglo-Scandinavian contexts (p.681, *AY* 17/6). The most common form of iron buckle found at Coppergate is D-shaped (p.683, ibid.). *10417* shares this form, which is commonly found on mid 9th to 11th century sites both in England and Scandinavia. The shape of the larger buckle, *10418*, is also paralleled amongst the iron examples (*3686, 3696, 3726, 3734, AY* 17/6). Some effort has been made to enhance the appearance of this buckle, however, as it appears to have been coated with silver. Buckles such as *10417* and *10418* are often found in association with horse fittings, but may also have been used on costume (Hinton 1996, 8). A third possible buckle, *10419*, is incomplete, and its identification uncertain.

Strap-guide (Fig.1264)

Another belt fitting is *10420* which is probably a strap-guide or loop through which a strap would pass after going through a buckle. Iron strap-guides were recovered at Coppergate (Fig.297, pp.688–90, *AY* 17/ 6), but *10420* has clearly been designed to be more decorative than its iron counterparts, having been ornamented with ring-and-dot motifs. It was found in a floor level of the Period 4B wattle building on Tenement B.

Strap-ends (Fig.1265)

There are five non-ferrous strap-ends from Coppergate, four of copper alloy (*10421–4*) and one of pure lead (*10599*). These are in addition to one antler and two bone strap-ends (*6800–1, 7697, AY* 17/12), and five iron strap-ends (*3789–93, AY* 17/6) found on the site.

10424 has a plain split end with a single central rivet for attachment. The lower end incorporates stylised zoomorphic features with a rounded tip for a snout, drilled eyes and incised 'lunate' ears. It belongs to a distinctive group of strap-ends found widely across the area of the Danelaw (G. Thomas,

pers. comm.), including two other examples from York, one from Fishergate (*5320*, p.1351, *AY* 17/9), the other from excavations at St Mary's Abbey (*AY* 7/2, *58*, fig.71). Both contain several pairs of eyes and ears. From the nearby Yorkshire Wolds, two similar strap-ends from Cottam (Fig.1299, **6**, p.2606) have been published (Haldenby 1990, 56, fig.4, no.7; Haldenby 1992, 28–30, fig.3, no.1), with a note that a further eight examples are known, the majority from the East Riding of Yorkshire. Further afield, this strap-end form has been found in Norwich (Margeson 1993, 34, fig.20, no.1) (Fig.1299, **11**), Northumberland (Wilson 1964, 29, no.12) and in a souterrain near Dundee, Scotland (Taylor 1982, 229, 248, fig.6, no.30). These strap-ends may be compared to clasps associated with strap-distributors found in Viking contexts, particularly one from Västergötland, Sweden, and a second from a Viking burial at Cronk Moar, Isle of Man (both in Bersu and Wilson 1966, 74–5). The Viking burial was tentatively dated from the mid 9th–mid 10th centuries (ibid., 87), which may suggest a possible date for *10424*, recovered from a mid 12th century build-up/dump.

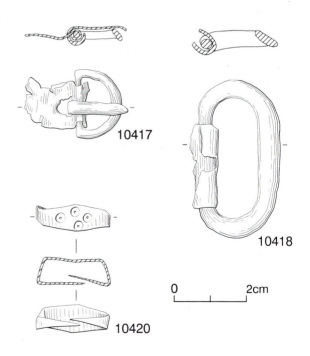

Fig.1264   Buckles 10417–18 and strap-guide 10420 from 16–22 Coppergate. Scale 1:1

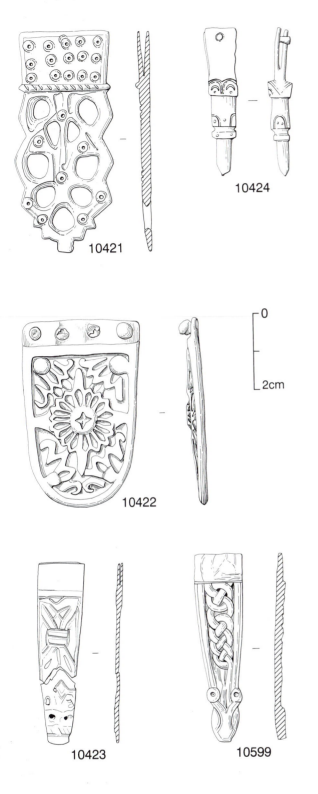

behind the animal head contains ribbon interlace in low relief within plain borders. The use of interlace within borders is also seen on incomplete strap-ends from Fishergate (*5319*, p.1352, *AY 17/9*) and from Meols, Cheshire (Bu'lock 1960, 12, fig.4e) (Fig.1299, **7**, p.2606), the latter a site with evidence of Norse-Irish connections (ibid., 14–19). Other examples come from Ipswich (Thomas forthcoming), and also from Aggersborg, Denmark (Roesdahl 1981, 115, fig.13). *10599* was recovered from a Period 5A dump deposit, but is probably contemporary with *10424*.

Also from a Period 5A dump deposit, *10423* has an animal head terminal, though here it has a squarer snout, and mere dots for eyes. Although its form is similar to many other Anglo-Saxon strap-ends, Scandinavian influence can be seen in its Borre-style ring-chain interlace decoration, also seen on a strap-end found at St Mary Bishophill Senior in York (Roesdahl et al. 1981, 108, YD39) (Fig1187, **22**, p.2452). Richardson (1993) notes that the use of a triquetra with the upper looping system of the interlace is a feature of a group of double-sided strap-ends from the Irish Sea area. The 'muzzled' or square snout also suggests an Anglo-Scandinavian attribution. The use of the Borre style dates the two York strap-ends to the late 9th–early 10th centuries, when it was current in England (*AY 8/2*, 163). Several other artefacts found in York have used Borre-style motifs, including a decorated antler tine from 22 Piccadilly (*7953*, *AY 17/12*), a wooden spoon from Clifford Street (Roesdahl et al. 1981, YDL11) (Fig.1187, **14**) and a stone cross-head fragment from St Mary Castlegate (*AY 8/2*, 160–3) (Fig.1187, **13**). The recovery of two such similar strap-ends from the city suggests that they may have been made in York, perhaps at Coppergate itself, where a unique iron mould for making strap-ends was discovered (*2250*, p.523, *AY 17/6*).

A very different form is represented by *10421*, an openwork strap-end, with a split upper end, and the whole decorated with stamped ring-and-dot motifs; it was found in a Period 4B dump. The openwork appears to incorporate vine scroll, a design that, as a result of Carolingian influence, was adapted by, and ultimately replaced by, acanthus leaf as the preferred ornamental style during the 10th century (Webster 1984, 88; Roesdahl et al. 1981, 108, YD36). The use of vine scroll indicates that *10421* pre-dates several examples recovered at Winchester which are decor-

Fig.1265 *Strap-ends from 16–22 Coppergate: 10421–4, copper alloy; 10599, lead alloy. Scale 1:1*

The lead strap-end, *10599*, has a large moulded animal head terminal, with prominent eyes and well-rounded ears set in relief. The field of decoration

ated with either inhabited (Hinton 1990a, 494–7, nos.1056–7) or uninhabited (ibid., no.1060) acanthus leaf, and which have flat, butt ends. A second, albeit very corroded, openwork strap-end from York was found on the Lloyds Bank, Pavement, site and is decorated with uninhabited acanthus leaf (*451*, p.89, *AY* 17/3) (Fig.1187, **9**, p.2452). The split upper end on *10421* is paralleled on an openwork strap-end from Middle Harling, Norfolk (Margeson 1995, 60, fig.41, no.75).

The last in the sequence of strap-ends from Coppergate is *10422*, which has a broad, tongue shape, is decorated with acanthus leaf ornament surrounding a central rosette, and was fixed to the strap by four iron rivets. Its acanthus leaf design indicates a 10th century date, as does its broad shape and flat, butt end (Wilson 1964, 62), which accords with its recovery from a possible floor level in the Period 4B wattle building on Tenement A. Its ornament suggests that it was either imported from the Carolingian empire, or that it is a native copy of a Carolingian design. Similarly shaped strap-ends incorporating acanthus leaf motifs found in Muysen, Belgium (Fraenkel-Schoorl 1978, 349–50), and Rijs, Friesland, Netherlands (ibid., 369–71), were both thought to have been made in northern France (ibid., 391). *10422* is one of a growing body of Carolingian (or Carolingian inspired) strap-ends being discovered in the Danelaw area, several having been recovered in Lincolnshire in the recent past (G. Thomas, pers. comm.).

Brooches

Brooches of several different types — penannular, bow, disc and cross-shaped — were recovered from Coppergate.

Penannular brooch (Fig.1266)

10425 is a squarish, expanded terminal with cusped sides, a central setting which may have originally contained a glass stud (no trace now survives), and bosses in each corner; part of the hoop also survives. A comparable terminal was found at 46–54 Fishergate (*5333*, p.1359, *AY* 17/9). The shape of both terminals from York resembles the square terminal found on brooch no.19, one of a series of Pictish penannular brooches found in a hoard on St Ninian's Isle, all of which are thought to have been in fashion in the late 8th century (Wilson 1973, 90–101). The layout of the design on *10425* is also

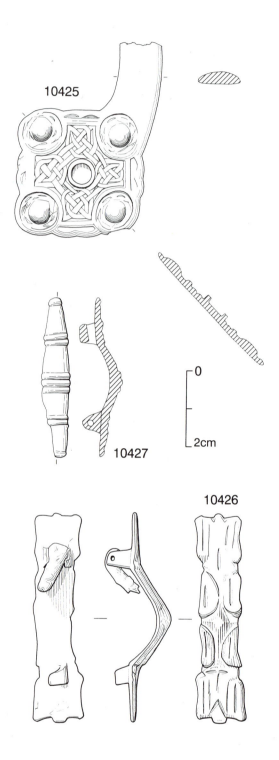

Fig.1266 *Brooches from 16–22 Coppergate: terminal of a penannular brooch,* 10425; *ansate brooches,* 10426–7. *Scale 1:1*

paralleled by that on the terminal of a brooch found at Hålen, Norway, in a grave of the early Viking period (Petersen 1951, 54, fig.58), and on a silver brooch from Ballynagloch, Co. Antrim, Ireland, which may have come from the same workshop as the Hålen brooch (Youngs 1989, 102, no.85). Recovered from a mid 9th–early 10th century build-up deposit at Coppergate, *10425* must have been of some age when it was discarded, as evidenced by its worn appearance. It forms part of a small group of objects recovered from the site, including ringed pins for example (pp.2580–2), which reflect the links between the Viking kingdom of York and other areas of Viking activity including Scotland and Ireland.

Ansate brooches (Fig.1266)

Two copper alloy examples of this type, also known as equal-armed bow brooches, were found at 16–22 Coppergate in Period 4B contexts (*10426–7*); an unfinished lead bow brooch (*4147*) was also found (p.2475). These brooches are characterised by a narrow arched bow and terminals at head and foot of identical form, and the finished Coppergate brooches are both of a variant known as the 'caterpillar' which have terminals which barely expand, if at all, beyond the width of the bow (Hattatt 1987, 325). *10426* comes from a possible floor level in the Tenement C wattle building, and is subrectangular with mouldings very reminiscent of a brooch from Suffolk (ibid., 383, no.1425). A similar example was found in Ravendale, Lincolnshire (K. Leahy, pers. comm.). Found in a pit backfill on Tenement B, *10427* is of a rather simpler design with rounded terminals and transverse mouldings, and is similar to a brooch found in excavations on Fishergate, Norwich (Williams 1994, 14). Both brooches are paralleled by examples found in London (Pritchard 1991, 143–4, nos.94–5), and Domburg, at the mouth of the Rhine (Capelle 1976, taf.2, no.17; taf.3, no.26) (Fig.1300, **6**, p.2608).

Hattatt noted that these equal-armed brooches were essentially from the late 7th–9th century or later in north-west Europe, with the 'caterpillar' variety being more geographically limited to areas bordering the North Sea from Denmark to France (Hattatt 1987, 325). However, Hinton has suggested that the quantity now known in England may indicate manufacture here of some types, borne out by the recovery of an unfinished example in Norwich (Hinton 1996, 3), and apparently supported by the recovery of the unfinished brooch *4147*. He also speculates that these brooches may have maintained their popularity into the 10th century (ibid.), a suggestion supported by the Coppergate brooches and the recovery of the Ravendale brooch in association with 10th century coins (K. Leahy, pers. comm.).

Disc brooches (Figs.1267–9)

Coppergate produced a total of nine disc brooches, of which one was made of copper alloy (*10428*), two of copper alloy and iron (*10429–30*), four of pewter (*10600–3*), and one of lead alloy with possible silvering on the front (*10604*). The ninth brooch was found during the watching brief at Coppergate (*10629*) and is made of lead alloy.

All three copper alloy brooches (*10428–30*) derive from Period 4B dumps or build-up deposits, and all incorporate a backward-looking animal motif, although two different designs can be recognised. *10428* has been cast, and it retains parts of the attachment and catch plates; it appears to have been in use for some time as it is heavily worn, and a perforation at one side suggests that it was either repaired or possibly re-used as a pendant. The animal motif is set within a billeted border, and it lacks an eye. The other two brooches (*10429–30*) have been manufactured in a different manner. Both have iron backings with iron pin attachments, onto which a disc of copper alloy foil of slightly larger diameter has been placed, with the edge turned over all round the circumference. An unusual manufacturing technique, this is also used on a bronze nummular brooch from Sulgrave, Northamptonshire (Dolley 1971, 333–5), and on circular medallions which ornament the 7th or 8th century belt-shrine from Moylough, Co. Sligo, Ireland (O'Kelly 1965, 169). The attached discs on both brooches have *repoussé* decoration with a pair of beaded borders containing the animals. The backward-looking animal motif, within either billeted or beaded borders, was once thought to be exclusively found in East Anglia (Wilson 1964, 37; Smedley and Owles 1965, 174). However, in addition to the Coppergate brooches, they have also been recorded from North Lincolnshire (Leahy 1982, 107–8), while an enamelled mount with the same motif was found at 46–54 Fishergate (*5325*, pp.1354–6, *AY* 17/9). The three brooches from Coppergate represent the most northerly distribution of this type so far recovered, and the 10th century contexts from which they derive fit well with the 9th–10th century date for brooches with this motif (ibid., 1356).

A different style of backward-looking animal decorates one of the pewter disc brooches, *10604*, which was found in a Period 5B build-up deposit. Within a billeted frame, a contoured and hatched quadruped extends its tongue between its hind legs.

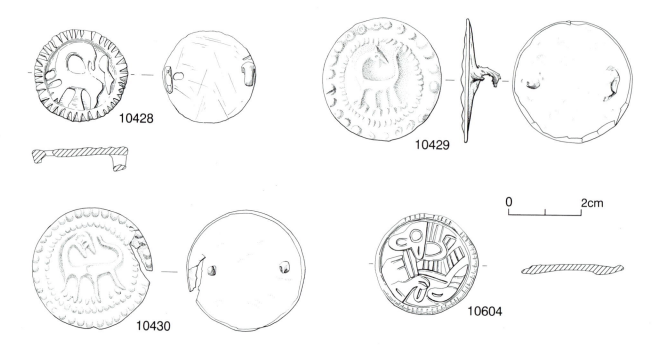

Fig.1267 *Disc brooches from 16–22 Coppergate: 10428–30, copper alloy; 10604, lead alloy. Scale 1:1*

Although in this instance found on a brooch, the design can also be seen on 10th century disc pendants, such as one from Nomeland, Valle, Aust-Agder in Norway (Petersen 1928, fig.155), and three from graves at Birka (Callmer 1989, 26, Abbs.3.6–3.8), and while not a classical representation of the Jellinge style, it clearly has Jellinge-style attributes (ibid., 23; C. Richardson, pers. comm.). Another almost identical pewter (previously identified as silver) brooch has been found in York, unfortunately from an unrecorded site (Waterman 1959, 79, fig.10, no.9; Graham-Campbell 1980a, 38–9, no.134), while at least eight copper alloy examples, some with gilding, have been recovered across Norfolk (Margeson 1997, 24; H. Geake, pers. comm.), and another is known from South Ferriby, Lincolnshire (K. Leahy, pers. comm.). The quality of the casting of *10604* is poor, with casting bubbles visible, and it may be another example of a reject made on the site.

The use of a cast scrollwork design links two brooches from Coppergate. *10603* has been cast in imitation filigree, and is decorated with scrolls and loops in a cross-shaped arrangement with a central quatrefoil. This design appears again on *10601*; here it surrounds a boss within the central field, which is itself encircled by eleven concentric bands of alternating fine and coarse beading, the whole possibly silver plated originally. A find from Louth in Lincolnshire provides a very similar example (K. Leahy, pers. comm.), while a simplified version of *10601* incorporating six bands of beading, with three scrolled loops around a central boss, was also found at Wellington Row in York (YAT 1987.24, sf8579) (Fig.1187, **17**, p.2452). A fragmentary brooch with the same central motif as the Wellington Row brooch has also been recovered at Appleton-le-Street (P. Rahtz, pers. comm.). Elsewhere, the scroll design appears on a gold filigree brooch recovered from Hedeby, Germany, where it may have been made, but was more likely imported (Graham-Campbell 1980a, 40–1, nos.140–1). Of similar form to *10601*, but lacking the scrollwork, is *10602*. It has six plain bands of moulding, and at its heart, a central boss within a circular field divided into quadrants, each with its own smaller pinched up boss. A parallel from Lincolnshire was found at Binbrook (K. Leahy, pers. comm.), while a pewter brooch from Barwick, Norfolk, has five bands of beading around a central boss (H. Geake, pers. comm.).

All these brooches are contemporary with, and in some way related to, the large silver coin brooches of the 10th century, which had a central imitation coin

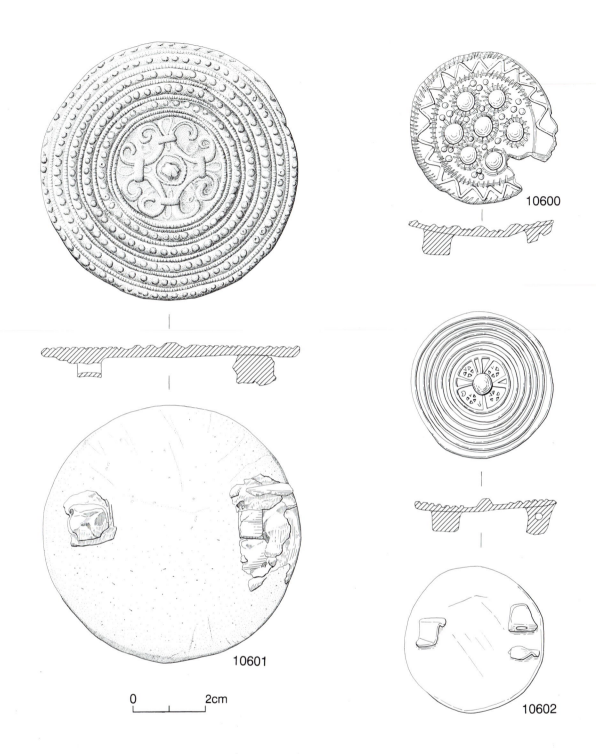

10600

10601

10602

0   2cm

Fig.1268 *Lead alloy disc brooches from 16–22 Coppergate. Scale 1:1*

surrounded by circles of imitation filigree. An example from York has a copy of a coin of Valentinian at its centre (*AY 7/2, 103*; Roesdahl et al. 1981, 105, YD7). The Coppergate brooches derive from Period 4B pit backfill (*10601*), Period 5A pit backfill (*10602*) and a floor level in the Period 5B Structure 5/6 (*10603*).

The fifth pewter disc brooch from Coppergate is *10600* from a floor level in the Period 4B wattle building on Tenement C. It differs from the three brooches above in having a frame filled with geometric ornament which surrounds a circular field containing one central and six satellite bosses, each

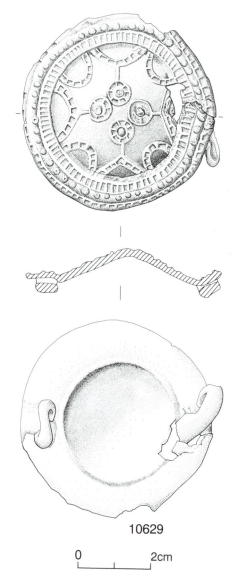

Fig.1269 Lead alloy disc brooch from the Coppergate watching brief site. Scale 1:1

with a beaded collar. A similar copper alloy brooch was found on Pavement in York (Waterman 1959, 104, fig.25, no.5). Bosses also feature at the centre of the lead alloy disc brooch found during the watching brief at Coppergate (*10629*). This has a billeted circumferential frame encircling an eight-pointed star also defined by billeted frames, and containing four bosses at its heart. This design appears to be related to that on a large disc brooch from Parliament Street, York (*AY 7/2, 136*; Waterman 1959, 77–9, fig.10, no.8), which in turn closely resembles a brooch found in the late 9th century Beeston Tor hoard (Wilson 1964, 29–30, no.3).

It seems probable that many, if not all, of the disc brooches found at Coppergate were manufactured locally. It has been suggested that pewter brooches are typical urban finds indicative of mass-production of cheap goods (Graham-Campbell 1980a, 39), and other evidence of non-ferrous jewellery being made at Coppergate is considerable (pp.2475–8).

Cross brooch (Fig.1270)

Made of copper alloy, *10431* was recovered from Period 4B build-up, but may be one of the earliest pieces of metalwork recovered at Coppergate. With its pairs of bosses on each arm, it fits into a group of cross brooches studied by Wamers (1994, 138–9), who noted examples from southern Ireland, Norway, France, Germany and the Netherlands, the latter producing two at the 8th–9th century trading centre of Domburg (ibid., 138–40, liste 32). Wamers dates these brooches to the second half of the 8th–the first half of the 9th century, and suggests a Frisian influence on the design of the York and other north European examples. Other examples from England come from West Rudham, Norfolk (H. Geake, pers. comm.), and South Ferriby, Lincs. (K. Leahy, pers. comm.), the latter complete with iron pin.

Kite brooch (Figs.1270–1)

10535 is a filigree foil fragment, one of only three gold objects found at Anglo-Scandinavian Coppergate. It was recovered from a Period 3 pit backfill. Almost certainly incomplete, the fragment comprises a two-strand simple pattern interlace, delineated by a three-strand filigree band consisting of a central beaded wire flanked on either edge by a finer spiral-beaded wire. The damaged filigree foil has been pierced and placed on a flat foil back-plate; the damage to the filigree indicates the incompleteness of the foil, suggesting that it may originally have been part of a larger panel.

The construction technique employed on this foil has a long history, and it has been used on some high-quality objects, including the late 6th–7th century Kentish Kingston brooch and Faversham bird-buckles (Whitfield 1997a, 224), the late 7th–early 8th century Hunterston annular brooch (Stevenson 1974, 25, pls.XVI, XVII), the 8th century Derrynaflan paten (Ryan 1989, 131–2, pl.125a) and the 9th–10th century Clonmacnoise kite brooch (Whitfield 1997b, 500). It also survived for a long period in Scandinavia,

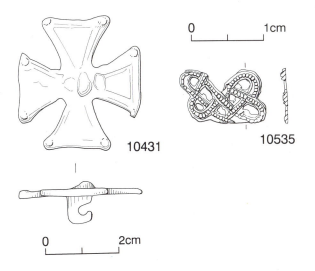

Fig.1270 *Copper alloy cross brooch 10431 from 16–22 Coppergate, scale 1:1. Gold kite brooch fragment 10535, also from 16–22 Coppergate, scale 2:1*

occurring on 6th century Scandinavian sword and scabbard fittings, and on Viking Age Terslev brooches (Whitfield 1997a, 224). The three-strand band of beaded wire similarly appears to belong to a long-lived tradition, appearing on the probably 7th–8th century gold filigree panel from Ireland in the collections at Alnwick Castle, Northumberland (Whitfield forthcoming), and on the Clonmacnoise kite brooch.

The fragmentary nature of *10535*, and the wide range of possible dates of its manufacture indicated by the parallels noted above, combine to make identification of its function and original provenance difficult. It could be an archaic piece of Anglo-Saxon work which found its way to late 9th–10th century Coppergate; perhaps more plausibly, it has been suggested that it could possibly be a panel fragment from a kite brooch (N. Whitfield, pers. comm.), in which case it could be contemporary with its context, and is likely to have originated in Ireland.

Brooch pins (Fig.1272)

10432–4 are pins which are looped at one end, and have become separated from brooches. Of particular interest is *10432* which is a copper alloy brooch pin

Fig.1271 *Kite brooch fragment 10535 from 16–22 Coppergate. Actual length 11·4mm*

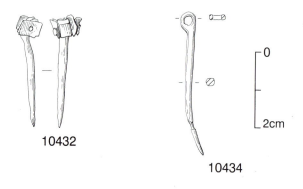

Fig.1272 *Copper alloy brooch pins from 16–22 Coppergate.*
Scale 1:1

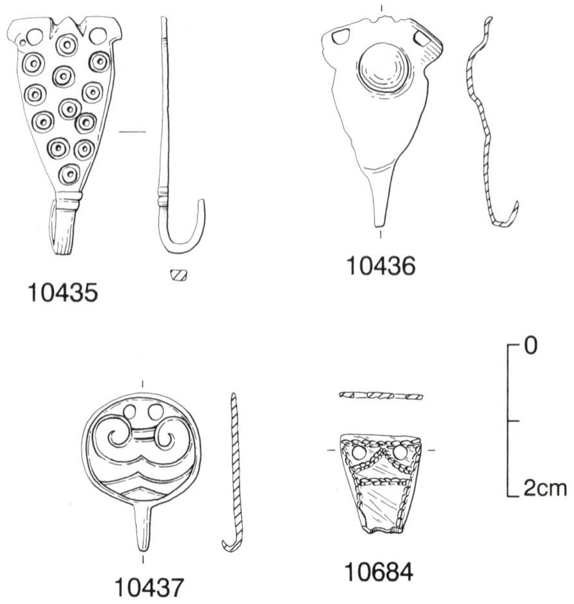

Fig.1273 *Copper alloy hooked tags from 16–22 Coppergate*
(10435–7) and 22 Piccadilly (10684). Scale 1:1

attached to the remains of a silver hinge with a brass
hinge-pin; it was found in a Period 5A dump deposit.

Hooked tags (Fig.1273)

Three of these objects were found at Coppergate
(*10435–7*), and a fourth was recovered at 22 Piccadilly
(*10684*). *10437* is circular, while the others have
triangular plates; all have hooked tips.

Also termed garment hooks by some (e.g. Roesdahl et al. 1981, 107), the precise function of these
fittings is uncertain. They have frequently been found
in burials, but in association with several different
parts of the skeleton, including skull, waist and knees
(p.88, *AY 17/3*). More recently, a pair found in Rome
have been interpreted as possible purse fasteners
(Graham-Campbell and Okasha 1991, 223). Whatever
the function, the insubstantial nature of all indicates
that they must have acted only as some sort of light
fastener, probably on clothing or dress accessories.
They appear to have had a long period of currency;
amongst the earliest are several dated to the 7th
century found at Shakenoak Farm, Oxon. (Dickinson
1973, 116), while at Winchester their use appeared to
continue into the 11th century (Hinton 1990b, 549).

The Coppergate and 22 Piccadilly tags come from
contexts ranging from a Period 3 build-up deposit
(*10435*) to a Period 6 levelling dump (*10437*).
Although three of the four tags from Coppergate and
22 Piccadilly are triangular, non-ferrous metal tags
found previously in York have all been circular (see
for example Waterman 1959, 76–7, fig.10, no.11; *450*,
pp.87–8, *AY 17/3*; pp.1359–60, *5334–5, AY 17/9*). Tri-

angular tags have also been found previously in the
region, at Cottam on the Yorkshire Wolds (Haldenby
1994, 54, fig.3), and at Whitby (Peers and Radford
1943, 60, fig.12, no.10). Three triangular iron tags were
also found at Coppergate (p.697, Fig.302, *AY 17/6*).

Apart from *10436*, all the tags bear some form of
incised or punched decoration. The decoration on
10437 incorporates a scroll motif, characteristic of the
Ringerike style, which developed in Scandinavia
during the early years of the 11th century, but became
current in England during the reign of King Cnut, in
the second quarter of the century (Graham-Campbell
1980b, 149). The Ringerike style has previously been
associated particularly with the south of England,
but an increasing number of artefacts are known from
the north of England. In addition to *10437*, Coppergate has also produced the lead alloy cross *10556*
(p.2476), while an incomplete boxwood knife handle
was recovered at 22 Piccadilly (*9195, AY 17/13*). An
almost identical tag to *10437* made of silver was
recovered from Scopwick, Lincs. (K. Leahy, pers.
comm.). An openwork mount from the Bedern
(*10708*) is also of Ringerike style (p.2555–6).

Dress pins (Figs.1274–6)

These were the most frequently recovered type
of non-ferrous object found at 16–22 Coppergate, the

assemblage comprising 60 copper alloy pins and pin fragments; 22 Piccadilly and Bedern each produced two.

The pins have been classified into types according to head shape, with subdivision amongst one type, the ringed pins. Initially, Hinton's classification of the Hamwic pins was copied with the York pins; he divided the dress pins from Hamwic by head type, and subdivided according to head decoration, the presence or absence of a collar and the nature of the shank (Hinton 1996, 14). It became clear, however, that, as with the Hamwic pins, no pattern of correlation between head and shank type was present at Coppergate. Most types had examples which did or did not have decorative collars, and did or did not have the swelling or hip on the shank which acted to prevent slippage of the pin during use, and so the classification was abandoned in favour of a simpler typology.

Seventeen of the pins are no longer extant (10446–7, 10458–61, 10463, 10469–70, 10486–7, 10492–7), having been destroyed during analysis, the results of which are held in an archive report. The author is grateful to Dr Christopher Caple for his notes on these pins which were never seen by the author.

Type 1: Globular head

Ten examples of this head type were recovered at Coppergate (10438–47) making it the most numerous. Only 10442 has any decoration on the head, but an incised spiral motif was noted on the shank of 10447; a similar design appeared on the shank fragment 10493. This type of dress pin appears to predominate across the country during the Anglo-Saxon period (Hinton 1996, 20). It has previously been found in some numbers in York at Fishergate (pp.1361–2, Fig.662, AY 17/9), 6–8 Pavement (Fig.48, AY 17/3) and elsewhere in the city (Waterman 1959, 78–9, fig.11), as well as at other sites in the north of England including Whitby (Peers and Radford 1943, fig.14) and Cottam on the Yorkshire Wolds (Haldenby 1990, 54–5; 1994, 51–2). Bu'lock suggested that this type was not often found on Viking sites (Bu'lock 1960, 9, fig.3b), and it is worth noting that seven of the ten recovered at Coppergate derive from Period 3 and Period 4A levels (see Table 257, p.2582) in the earliest stages of the Anglo-Scandinavian settlement of the site. Two iron pins with this head type were also found at the site in Period 3 contexts (3800–1, p.93, Fig.300, AY 17/6).

Type 2: Polyhedral head

Five pins (10448–52) have squat faceted polyhedral heads. All but one of these have heads decorated with either punched dots (e.g. 10449) or punched ring-and-dot motifs (e.g. 10450). This pin type has been found on the same range of sites as Type 1. As with Type 1, iron pins of this design were found at Coppergate (3805, 3811, p.693, Fig.300, AY 17/6). Apart from a single example from Period 1/3, all the Type 2 pins were found in contexts of Period 4B or later (see Table 257), perhaps indicating a longer lifespan than Type 1.

Type 3: Baluster head

This type is differentiated from Type 2 by its narrowness and its lozenge-shaped facet on top of the head. There are three pins from Coppergate of this type (10453–5) and two are decorated with punched dots (Fig.1274). Unlike Types 1 and 2, this pin type does not seem to be found elsewhere in Anglo-Saxon or Anglo-Scandinavian England, the only other examples known also coming from York, in Anglian levels at Fishergate (5350, Fig.662, AY 17/9) and from Rougier Street (YAT 1981.12, sf4) (Fig.1187, 18, p.2452). This head shape is also recognised on ringed pins (pp.2580–3), on which it appears in combination with spiral rings and plain rings. The earlier spiral-ringed examples have been recovered in pre-Viking deposits in Ireland at sites including Garryduff I, Co. Cork, Lagore Crannog, Co. Meath, and Carraig Aille, Lough Gur, Co. Limerick (Fanning 1994, 13). The Fishergate pin comes from the first half of the 9th century, and two of the three Coppergate pins come from Period 3 build-up deposits (see Table 257), suggesting that this unperforated design may have arrived in York in pre-Viking times, where it remained a local variant.

Type 4: Biconical head

All four pins of this type are undecorated and are equally split into those with faceted biconical heads (10457, 10459) and those with plain biconical heads (10456, 10458). They have appeared on many of the same sites as Type 1, with which they are clearly contemporary.

Type 5: Spiral head

Coppergate produced five examples of this type (*10460–4*). In addition to the decoratively spiralled head, *10461* also had incised circumferential rings at the top of the shank. This type has been found previously on middle Saxon sites such as Flixborough, Lincs. (Webster and Backhouse 1991, 97, no.69j, k), the monastery at Hartlepool (Jackson 1989, 182, fig.33, 8) and at Hamwic where eleven were recovered (Hinton 1996, 29, fig.11) (Fig.1299, **2, 8, 15**, p.2606). It has been suggested that these pins had their floruit in the 7th–8th century (Webster and Backhouse 1991, 97), but examples from York indicate a longer term of use. Of two such pins from Fishergate, one came from an 11th–12th century grave (*5369*, Fig.664, p.1363, *AY 17/9*), and, as Table 257 shows, all the Coppergate pins derive from contexts of the mid 9th–mid 11th centuries.

Type 6: Inverted plano-convex head

There are three pins in this category from Coppergate (*10465–7*), and one from 22 Piccadilly (*10685*); *10467* has been decorated with incised spiral grooves around the head (*wrythen* decoration) and an incised saltire on the top, while the others are undecorated. This head shape is not clearly paralleled elsewhere, although the *wrythen* decoration on *10467* is seen on Type 1 pins from Hamwic (Hinton 1996, 16, fig.7, Type Ab) and Brandon, Suffolk (Webster and Backhouse 1991, 85, no.66k — labelled i on the illustration). The York pins derive from mid 9th–11th/13th century build-up or dump deposits.

Type 7: Linked pin

Almost certainly the earliest pin type of all those recovered at Coppergate, and one of the few Anglian objects to have been found there, *10468* retains two links of the chain by which it would originally have been joined to its partner. In the past, this pin form has mainly been found in 7th–8th century graves; examples in precious metals were retrieved from the cemetery at Roundway Down, Wiltshire (Leeds 1936, 109, fig.23b; Youngs 1989, 53–4, pl.40), and from a grave at Hamwic (Hinton 1996, 33–4, fig.13), while a bronze pin was one of several found at Winnall, Hampshire (Meaney 1970, 37, fig.9). Settlements have also produced these, however, with two copper alloy linked pins being found at Fishergate in an 8th century deposit (*5366–7*, p.1363, *AY 17/9*). *10468* must be residual in its Period 4B build-up deposit.

Type 8: Flat oval head

Two pins (*10469–70*) have incomplete flat heads which appear to have originally been oval, and both have ring-and-dot decoration. It is tempting but probably misplaced to compare these with the well-known flat, disc-headed type of middle Saxon pin found previously in York as noted by Waterman (1959, 78, fig.11, no.3); although both heads are incomplete, it seems clear that neither are of a size comparable to these. Similar examples to the two Coppergate pins have, however, been found both in York, at the Friends Burial Ground site (*AY 7/2, 75*), and elsewhere in England. Whitby produced one plain oval flat-headed pin and one which was perforated (Peers and Radford 1943, 63, fig.14), and at Hamwic one example which may be comparable was found (Hinton 1996, 33, fig.13, Type H). The Rhineland trading centre of Domburg has also produced a similar pin (Capelle 1976, taf.14, no.258). All these parallels to the two Coppergate pins suggest a possible 9th century date for this pin type; this indicates that *10469* may be contemporary with its context (Period 4A pit backfill), but that *10470* may be residual in its context (Period 5B build-up deposit).

Type 9: Flat trapezoidal head

Recovered from a Period 5B (late 10th–early/mid 11th century) pit backfill, *10471* is identical to a pin found previously near The Mount in York (Waterman 1959, fig.11, no.4; *AY 7/2, 113*), and a similar example was found at Jewbury (YAT 1983.5) (*AY 7/2, 89b*); another was found at the site of the Anglo-Saxon monastery at Hartlepool, where it was recovered from cultivation levels post-dating the monastery and pre-dating late 11th/early 12th century occupation (Jackson 1988, 182, fig.33, no.7, illustrated upside down). Possibly allied to these pins is one with an undecorated head from Whitby (Peers and Radford 1949, fig.14). The Hartlepool pin appears to derive from a context of similar date to *10471* and thus a 10th–mid 11th century origin for this pin type may be indicated.

Type 10: Flat, sub-figure-of-eight shaped head

Standing out on its own amongst the Coppergate pins is *10472* with its double lobes containing rings and its perforated ring-and-dot motifs. Another possible example, however, is *10686* from 22 Pic-

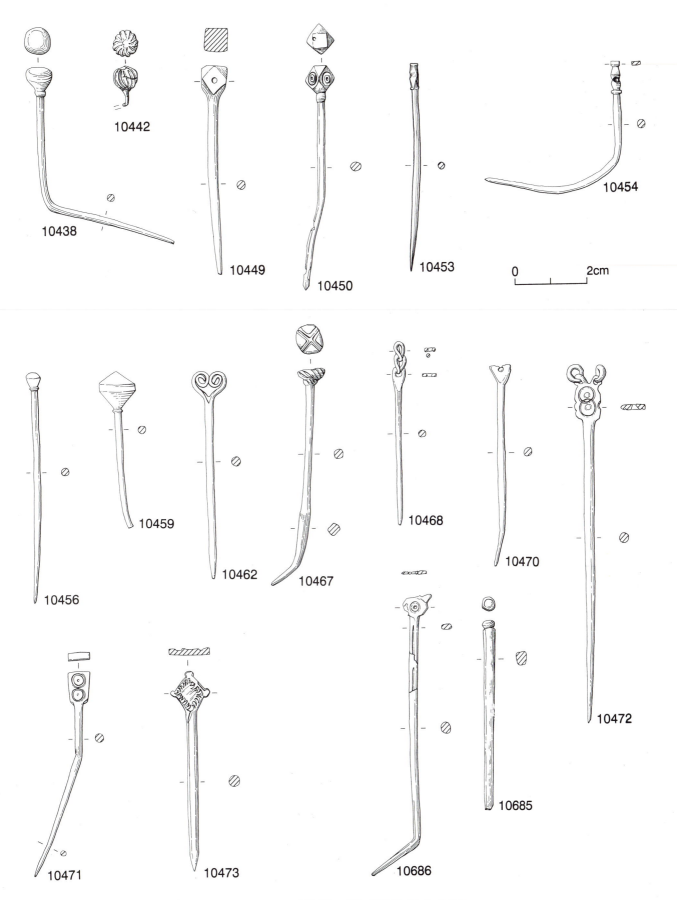

10442

10438

10449

10450

10453

10454

10456

10459

10462

10467

10468

10470

10471

10473

10686

10685

10472

Fig.1274 *Copper alloy pins from 16–22 Coppergate and 22 Piccadilly (10685–6). Scale 1:1*

cadilly with a head which, although incomplete, bears some similarity in shape and decoration to *10472*. Both the Coppergate and Piccadilly pins of this type derive from 11th century contexts.

Type 11: Flat polygonal head

10473, from a Period 5Cr pit backfill, has a lozenge-shaped head with knops and rocked-tracer decoration. Several pins similar to *10473* have been found previously in York, including two at Fishergate (*5371–2*, p.1363, Fig.664, *AY 17/9*) and another which is unprovenanced from within the city (Waterman 1959, 79, fig.11, no.15). An example from the College of the Vicars Choral at Bedern (*10710*) was retrieved residually from a mid 14th century deposit. Another example which comes from the grave at Ely of the early 11th century Archbishop Wulfstan of York may originally have been gilded or silvered (Way 1847, 21–2; also pp.1363–4, *AY 17/9*).

This pin type is thought to have originated in Ireland (Armstrong 1922); individual examples have also come from Birsay (Curle 1982, 62, Ill.39) and London (Pritchard 1991, 150). Hinton suggests that pins with lozenge-shaped heads decorated with ring-and-dot motifs from Southampton (Hinton 1996, 32, Group F) may represent a middle Saxon precursor of the more elaborate knop-headed pins such as *10473*.

Type 12: Ringed pins (Fig.1275)

A total of seven ringed pins were recovered at Coppergate (*10474–80*); of these five retained their rings. Fanning's typology of the ringed pins from Dublin divides them by ring form and head shape (Fanning 1994, 7–8); this typology is followed in the analysis of the Coppergate pins.

Ring form

Fanning notes seven ring forms at Dublin; the most common of these is the plain ring, and all the complete Coppergate pins have rings of this form. Two rings which have separated from pins (*10481*, *10483*) are also of this type; both retain part of the hinge which swivelled within the perforation of the pin head. A third ring (*10482*) may also be from a pin, although its ends lack a clearly defined hinge or pivot.

Head shape

Five different head shapes are described by Fanning; three of these are represented at Coppergate.

Type 12a: Loop-headed

This pin head shape was present on two pins (*10474–5*), both of which had lost their rings, which seem likely to have been plain. Fanning notes that loop-headed pins with plain rings are the simplest of all ringed pin forms (Fanning 1994, 15). Pins of this form of both copper alloy and of iron are known from pre-Viking and Viking contexts in Ireland, and it is the dominant type in most Viking areas outside Ireland, including Scandinavia (ibid., 16). In Scotland, seven have been recovered from late 9th to early 10th century Viking graves (Fanning1983b, 325–6), while elsewhere in Britain, they have been found on the Isle of Man and at Meols, Cheshire (Fanning 1994, 19). At Coppergate, *10474* was found in a floor level in the Period 4B wattle building on Tenement C, while *10475* was found in a late 11th century levelling dump, in the same context as a Ringerike hooked tag (*10437*). An iron pin of this type was found in a Period 3 context at Coppergate (*3802*, pp.693–5, *AY 17/6*), and another at All Saints, Pavement, York (*1233*, p.229, *AY 17/4*).

Type 12b: Baluster-headed

Three pins of this type were found at Coppergate (*10476–8*). *10476* and *10477* were both recovered from Period 5A build-up deposits, while *10478* is unstratified. This type is characterised by a square-sectioned head with a central lozenge-shaped portion with collars above and below. The narrow facets on such heads leave little space for decoration, though simple decoration has been placed on both *10477* and *10478*, the former comprising stamped dots, the latter an incised saltire. *10478* is also the only Coppergate ringed pin to have decoration on its shank. Though only eleven pins of this type were recorded by Fanning from Dublin, the majority derived from contexts approximately contemporary with the stratified pins from Coppergate, leading Fanning to date the main floruit of this type to the 10th century (Fanning 1994, 24). This assessment appears to stand despite changes to the dating of the contexts of the Coppergate pins since Fanning's report. Waterman records another example of this pin type from York, found at Pavement (1959, 102–3, fig.25, no.1).

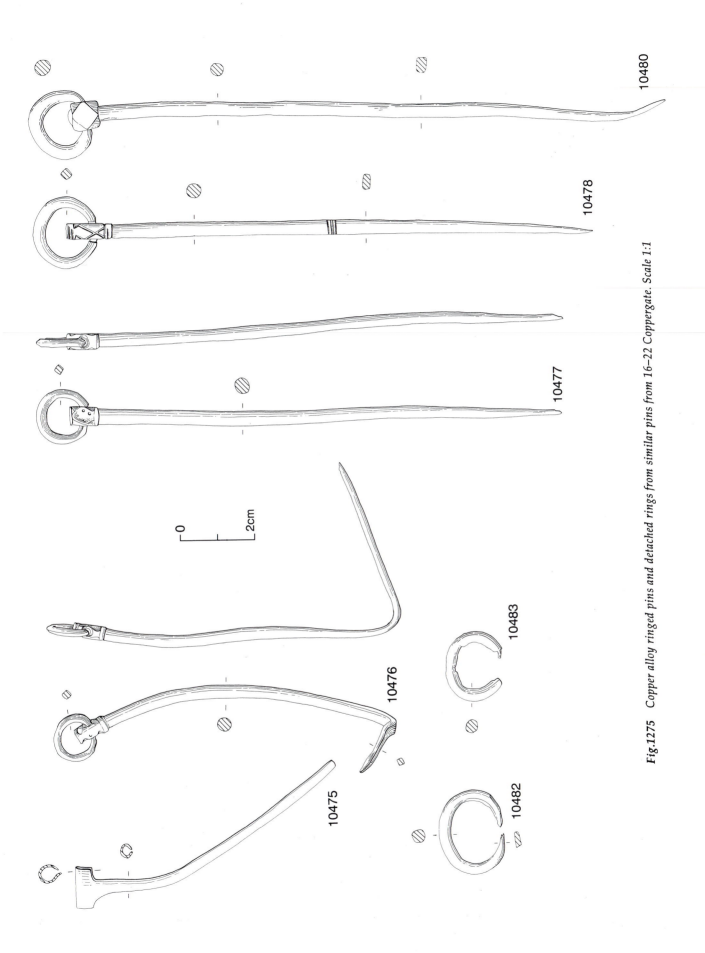

10480

10478

10477

10483

10476

10482

10475

0 2cm

Fig.1275 Copper alloy ringed pins and detached rings from similar pins from 16–22 Coppergate. Scale 1:1

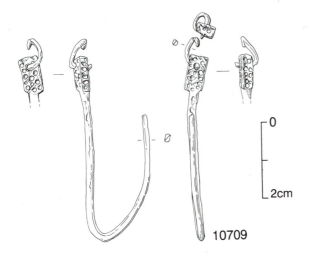

Fig.1276 Copper alloy pin from the College of Vicars Choral at Bedern. Scale 1:1

Unusually, *10478* is composed of a bronze pin and a brass ring, indicating that the ring had been made separately from the pin, and was possibly a replacement.

Type 12c: Polyhedral-headed

Two pins from Coppergate fall into this group (*10479–80*) which Fanning considers to be closely associated with the baluster-headed, plain-ringed pins noted above (Fanning 1994, 23). The head of *10479* (from a Period 5B pit backfill) is simply decorated with punched dots, a design also found on one of two pins of this type from York noted by Waterman (1959, fig.11, nos.13–14), and also on two from Meols (Bu'lock 1960, fig.5b, 5c). The simple faceting on the head of *10480* is also seen at Meols (ibid., fig.5e, 5f). This pin type forms the largest group amongst the ringed pins recovered in Dublin (Fanning 1994, 25). It also appears to be the most frequently found type on British sites of the Viking period, being the most common of all types found in Scotland (Fanning 1983b, 327), and also recovered from the Isle of Man (Fanning 1983a, 27–30), Lincoln and Derby (Fanning 1994, 32).

The significance of these ringed pins amongst the Coppergate assemblage lies primarily in the connections they indicate between Dublin and York during the 10th century, when all of these pin types were current. It is uncertain whether the York pins are products from Dublin itself or copies inspired by contacts with Viking Ireland (Fanning 1994, 33), but they certainly provide archaeological confirmation of links, both political and trading, between the two cities (Hall 1994, 19).

Table 257   The typology of complete dress pins at 16–22 Coppergate according to period

Type	Period 1/3	3	4A	4B	4/5	5A	5B	5Cr	6	u/s	Total
1	–	5	2	–	–	–	–	2	–	1	10
2	1	–	–	2	–	–	1	–	1	–	5
3	–	2	–	1	–	–	–	–	–	–	3
4	–	2	1	–	–	–	1	–	–	–	4
5	–	2	–	2	–	–	1	–	–	–	5
6	–	2	–	–	–	–	–	–	1	–	3
7	–	–	–	1	–	–	–	–	–	–	1
8	–	–	1	–	–	–	1	–	–	–	2
9	–	–	–	–	–	–	1	–	–	–	1
10	–	–	–	–	–	–	–	–	1	–	1
11	–	–	–	–	–	–	–	1	–	–	1
12a	–	–	–	1	–	–	–	–	1	–	2
12b	–	–	–	–	–	2	–	–	–	1	3
12c	–	–	–	–	–	–	1	–	–	1	2
Total	1	13	4	7	–	2	6	3	4	3	43

Miscellaneous pins (Fig.1276)

A pin from the College of Vicars Choral at Bedern (*10709*) has a head of rectangular shape and section, which is covered in punched dot decoration, and has a transverse perforation containing an incomplete ring. It was recovered from a Period 1 (mid–late 13th century) pit in the long trench, but seems likely to be contemporary with the other dress pin from the site (*10710*). It has previously been published as coming from 36 St Andrewgate (MacGregor 1978, 46, fig.28. no.5).

10484–5 from Coppergate may be headless pins, a type that has been found elsewhere in York, for example at Fishergate (pp.1364–6, *AY 17/9*). Alternatively, they may represent pins in the process of being cut down or repaired. In addition, there were twelve pin shank fragments which cannot be attributed to any type (*10486–97*).

Comparison of the York pins with pins from elsewhere show both similarities and differences. Types 1–5 as described above were also found in York's Anglian settlement at Fishergate (pp.1361–7, *AY 17/9*), and as Table 257 shows, around 75% occurred in the earlier levels (Periods 3–4B) at Coppergate. The only pin types which are likely to have been unknown in pre-Viking York are Types 11 and 12, probably originating in Ireland, and subsequently being adopted by Norse settlers. In common with the pins found on other sites in York, none of the Coppergate pins is made of an alloy more precious than copper; this differs from sites elsewhere in England, such as Hamwic, where certain types were manufactured in silver as well as copper alloy (Hinton 1996, 20–1).

Lead alloy pin

A lead alloy pin (*10605*), of which only the shank survives, may be a cheap imitation of a copper alloy pin.

Wire rings with twisted ends (Fig.1277)

These simple rings are of single-strand wire, or of wire wound around a core, with ends twisted around each other to complete the hoop. Manufactured in gold, copper alloy, lead alloy or tin, they were found on both Coppergate (*10498–506, 10537, 10606–7, 10617*) and 22 Piccadilly (*10687*). The knotting of ends is a common feature of Viking rings of various sizes and functions, and rings such as these have been used in jewellery, on brooches (Graham-Campbell 1980a, 38–9, nos.132, 137), necklaces (ibid., 45, no.154), some types of ringed pin (ibid., 58, no.205) and pendants (Roesdahl and Wilson 1992, 276, nos.180, 198). There is also evidence for their use as suspension loops for implements such as tweezers *10531* (p.2600) and hone *9609*. Indeed, the ring from 22 Piccadilly (*10687*) was found alongside a pair of tweezers (*10690*) for which it may originally have been the suspension ring (p.2600). The gold ring *10537* was recovered from an early 12th century dump, but seems likely to be residual.

Large twisted wire rings (Fig.1277)

Two copper alloy rings, both made from two wires twisted together (*10507–8*) are of uncertain function. Twisted wire arm-rings are well known from the Viking period, several examples of silver coming from a hoard found at Birka for example (Graham-Campbell 1980a, 87, no.302), but with diameters of 46mm (*10507*) and 37mm (*10508*), these rings from Coppergate appear to be too small to be arm-rings unless, like *10608* (see below), they were intended for children. They derive from a Period 3 dump (*10507*) and a 4B scoop backfill (*10508*).

Arm-rings (Fig.1278)

Two rings made of lead alloy rods (*10608–9*) and a third made of a twisted rod of tin (*10618*), all with ends twisted together to form the hoop, were found at Coppergate. The smaller lead alloy ring (*10608*) is made of pewter, while the larger is of pure lead. Both *10608* and *10618* appear to have been made for children, perhaps of about 12–15 years of age (see Crummy 1983, 36). Arm-rings of precious metals are common finds in Viking Age Scandinavia, occurring particularly in hoards, where they represented an alternative form of storing gold or silver (Graham-Campbell 1980a, 30). Many were also present in the Cuerdale silver hoard, deposited in the early 10th century near the River Ribble in Lancashire (ibid., 87, no.301). In York, a silver arm-ring was found in a burial at St Mary Bishophill Junior (Roesdahl et al. 1981, 109, YD51). The arm-rings all come from Period 4B contexts at Coppergate, *10609* and *10618* from build-up deposits, and *10608* from a floor level in the Tenement C wattle building, and all are typical 9th–early 10th century forms (Graham-Campbell

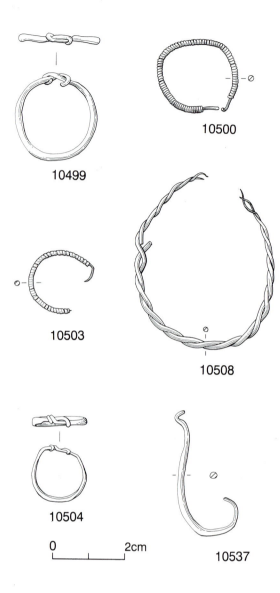

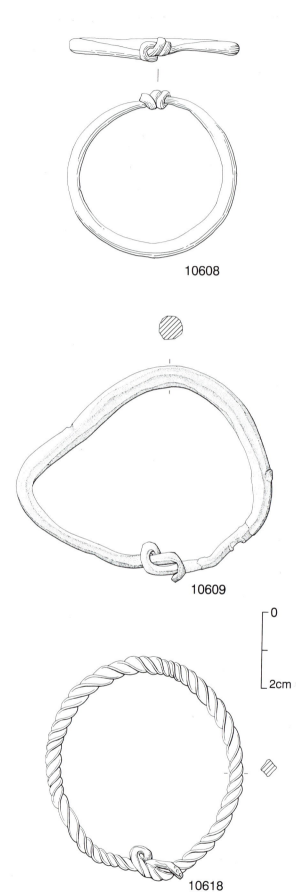

Fig.1277 *Copper alloy and gold (10537) wire rings with twisted ends from 16–22 Coppergate. Scale 1:1*

1980a, 61, no. 218). Together with three possible arm-rings of iron (*3827–9*, pp.696–7, *AY 17/6*) they are presumably cheap imitations of forms well known in more precious metals.

Fig.1278 *(right) Arm-rings from 16–22 Coppergate: 10608–9 made of lead alloy; 10618 made of tin. Scale 1:1*

Finger-rings

Non-ferrous metal finger-rings (Fig.1279)

As with the other non-ferrous jewellery from 16–22 Coppergate and 22 Piccadilly, the 23 finger-rings which were recovered are predominantly made of non-precious metals, only three being of silver (*10539–40, 10543*). The remainder are made of copper alloy (*10509–23, 10688*), or lead alloy (*10611–14*). Two copper alloy penannular rings (*10524, 10689*) may also be finger-rings.

The silver ring (*10543*), which was found in an unstratified context, represents part of a small group of finger-rings found in the north of Britain, which are decorated with Trewhiddle-style backward-biting beasts. Another was found near Selkirk, Scotland, a third at Hale, Cheshire (Webster and Backhouse 1991, 237–8, nos.203–4), and a gold example at Riby in Lincolnshire (K. Leahy, pers. comm.). Webster asserts that the decoration on these finger-rings is a simplified regional version of the Trewhiddle style, probably dating to the end of the 9th century (ibid.). The faceted hexagonal brass ring, *10513*, was found in a floor level in the Period 4B wattle building on Tenement C, and may be a simplified copy of the silver ring which originally formed part of the Trewhiddle hoard (Wilson and Blunt 1961, 85, pl.XXVIId). The site at Fishergate also produced a silver ring of this style (Fig.668, *5436*, p.1371, *AY* 17/9).

Graham-Campbell has noted that finger-rings in the Viking era were often miniaturised versions of neck- and arm-rings (1980b, 118), and this can be seen at Coppergate in *10511, 10518, 10520, 10540, 10613* and *10614*, all of which were recovered from Period 4B–5B deposits. *10614*, which was found in a floor level in the Period 5B Structure 5/3, is made of plaited lead alloy rods and has a flat bezel. The other rings have been made by twisting together two rods or strands of silver, copper or lead alloy. These were clearly inspired by larger rings such as the gold arm-ring from Oxna, Shetland (Graham-Campbell 1980a, 62, no.225), and silver arm-rings from Fyrkat, Jutland, Denmark (ibid., 61, no.218). A gold ring, similar to *10614*, was found on Hungate in York (Waterman 1959, 80, fig.10, no.14) (Fig.1187, **10**, p.2452). A fragment of twisted double-strand silver wire, *10538*, may be debris from the manufacture of twisted wire finger-rings.

Found with the arm-rings at Fyrkat was a silver finger-ring (Graham-Campbell 1980a, 61, no.219), similar in form to three finger-rings from Coppergate. All are made of flat bands tapering to ends which have been knotted together or overlapped. *10515* and *10517* have been decorated with ring-and-dot motifs, and *10522* with incised lines. This finger-ring design has been commonly found in Viking graves and hoards of the later 9th and early 10th centuries (ibid.). The Coppergate rings came from Period 4B and 5B dump or build-up deposits.

Three rings, *10510, 10512* and *10514*, are all of similar design, with triangular sections, decorated on each side of an axial rib. *10512* has the most intricate decoration with interlacing strands running along each facet; the other two are decorated with punched dots. A lead alloy ring, *10612*, is similar, but with decoration on the rib as well as on each side of it. Three bands (*10509, 10521, 10611*) also have some simple decoration; others are plain hoops (*10516, 10519, 10523, 10539*). The sole ring from 22 Piccadilly (*10688*) is also plain, the section thinning out towards the separated ends, which were originally connected by a scarf joint.

The two penannular rings (*10524, 10689*) may be either finger-rings or ear-rings. Similar rings were recovered from 10th–11th century deposits at Thetford (Goodall 1984, 69, fig.110, nos.17–20), and four more examples were found at Fishergate (*5411–14*, pp.1370–1, *AY* 17/9).

Glass finger-rings (Fig.1280)

Coppergate produced three glass finger-rings (*10062–4*) from Period 5B deposits. Two further glass rings (*10065–6*) may be residual in their medieval contexts. *10065* derives from 11th–13th century build-up, and *10066* from early 13th century features. Apart from *10064* which is yellow, all the finger-rings are dark green or black, colours which are also well represented amongst the glass beads (pp.2592–4), and may be indicative of the use of high-lead glass in their manufacture (pp.2521–4).

Sites in York contemporary with Coppergate have also produced glass rings; these include two sites on Pavement, where glass rings, beads and evidence of their manufacture were recovered (*411–13*, p.91, *AY* 17/3; Waterman 1959, 104). Elsewhere in England, excavations at Flaxengate, Lincoln, and Gloucester

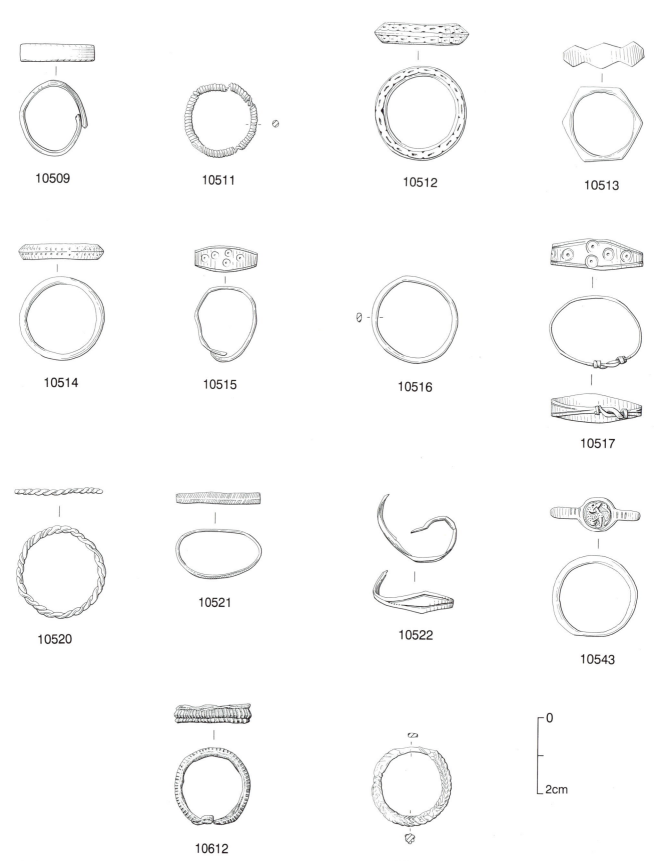

Fig.1279 *Finger-rings from 16–22 Coppergate: 10509, 10511–17, 10520–2, made of copper alloy; 10543, made of silver; 10612, 10614, made of lead alloy. Scale 1:1*

10509

10511

10512

10513

10514

10515

10516

10517

10520

10521

10522

10543

10612

10614

0

2cm

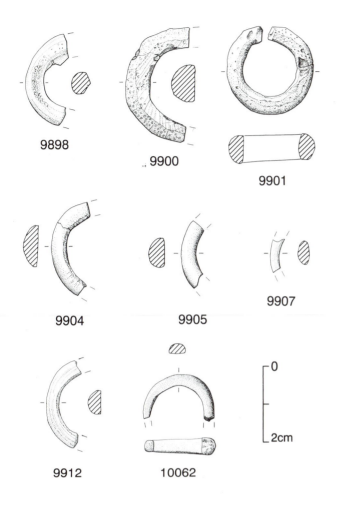

Fig.1280 *Finger-rings from 16–22 Coppergate: 9898, 9900–1 (roughouts), 9904–5, 9907, 9912 (finished), made of amber; 10062, made of glass. Scale 1:1*

have produced similar evidence (Roesdahl et al. 1981, 138, YAJG14). Two green glass finger-rings were also found at Winchester in 10th and 11th century deposits (Charleston 1990, 652–3).

Amber finger-rings (Fig.1280)

Fragments of fifteen amber finger-rings in various stages of production were recovered from Period 3 onwards at 16–22 Coppergate and fourteen from Clifford Street. The Coppergate examples include some with broad plain bands (e.g. *9904*) and others with thinner, more rounded (*9901*) or ovoid (*9907*) bands. Some are highly polished (*9905*), indicating much wear prior to loss. The unfinished Clifford Street finger-rings all appear to be intended to be broad plain bands with rounded D-shaped profiles (Fig.1220, p.2506). The broken fragment of a com-

pleted one (*10795*) is clearly of this form, as is the fragment from 16–22 Coppergate (*9912*).

Jet finger-rings (Fig.1281)

Fragments of simple plain rings in jet and jet-like material were recovered from Anglo-Scandinavian contexts. Many of these could be paralleled by Roman finds in York and elsewhere (L. Allason-Jones, pers. comm.), and could themselves be Roman. These simple forms have no diagnostic features and have been included here on stratigraphic grounds, though some question of their date must remain. However, there are various objects of jet and related material which are certainly of Roman manufacture, on typological grounds; eight from Period 3 levels (sfs9500, 9587, 10421, 12326, 14386–7, 14402, 15929), seven from Period 4B (sfs8583, 8684, 8985, 8992, 9701, 12482, 13822), one from Period 5A (sf11407) and two from Period 5B (sfs5679, 8270). These are all likely to be residual, although they could have been found and used in the Anglo-Scandinavian period. Unfortunately, a further five finds, including three ring frag-

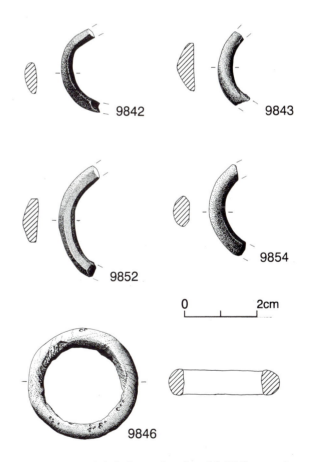

Fig. 1281 *Jet and shale finger-rings from 16–22 Coppergate. Scale 1:1*

ments from Period 4B (sfs7596, 7632, 7681), a fragment (sf7724) and a bead from Period 5A (sf6607), all recorded as jet, were stolen shortly after excavation was completed so no more detailed record exists. Finger-rings of jet and similar materials have been recovered from Viking Age sites in the British Isles and Scandinavia (e.g. Graham-Campbell 1980, 66; Shetelig 1940b, 207).

The earliest of the plain jet rings is a fragment of a broad band (9841) from Period 3, found in the centre of the site. Apart from the possible finger-ring rough-out (9834, Fig.1217, p.2500), Period 4B produced a number of ring fragments made from jet (9842–5) and jet-like material (9846). Period 5B produced further jet (9847–51) and shale (9852) finger-rings, and a ring fragment (9853). These were well distributed across the site, showing no tendency towards spatial clustering. Finally, a jet finger-ring (9854) was found in Period 5Cr in the backyard of Tenement A.

Pendants

Non-ferrous metal pendants (Fig.1282)

The manufacture of pendants, amongst other lead alloy and pewter jewellery, appears to have taken place on or near 16–22 Coppergate (pp.2478–9). A range of finished pendants of copper alloy (10525–6) and tin (10620) from Period 4B contexts, and of lead

alloy (10615–16) from Period 5A deposits were also recovered.

The pendants are all circular, apart from 10525, which is tongue-shaped. Two are plain, 10526 which has a punched perforation for suspension, and 10616, also plain, but with a perforated lug for suspension. Both 10615 and 10620 are decorated with a boss at the centre. On 10615, this boss is surrounded by crescent-shaped motifs, a design repeated in the border, where bosses and crescents alternate around the edge. On 10620, the boss is at the centre of a circle divided into quadrants, with further bosses in each quadrant, and the border divided by relief lines into eight. All four circular pendants are small, ranging in diameter from 14·3mm (10616) to 21mm (10615), and were probably originally part of necklaces. Intact necklaces of glass beads found in Viking Age graves, such as those at Birka, sometimes incorporated a number of metal pendants (Arbman 1940, 210–13, taf.119).

From a Period 4B dump, 10525 is an elongated tongue-shaped pendant, on which the original surfaces have, unfortunately, been considerably altered by corrosion, and have consequently suffered a substantial loss of detail. Scratched markings on both faces of the object were thought to be possible runic letters, and have been studied by Professor Ray

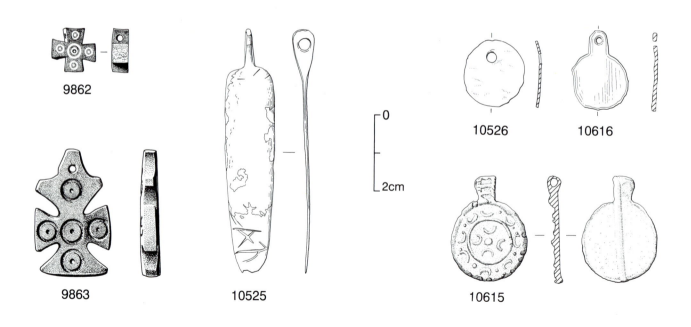

Fig.1282 Pendants from 16–22 Coppergate: 9862–3 made of jet; 10525–6 made of copper alloy; 10615–16 made of lead alloy. Scale 1:1

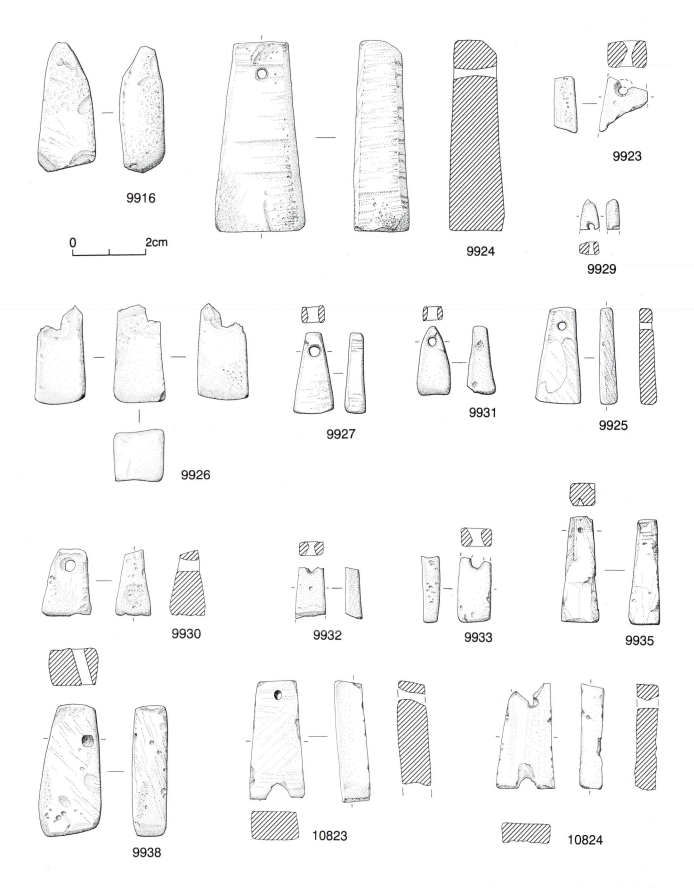

Fig.1283 *Amber pendants from 16–22 Coppergate, 9916, 9923–7, 9929–33, 9935, 9938, and from an unknown location in York, 10823–4. Scale 1:1*

Page of Corpus Christi College, Cambridge, and Professor Michael Barnes of the Department of Scandinavian Studies, University College, London. Both concluded that, while certain of the markings had the appearance of runes, they were not certainly runic; both noted that the condition of the piece made a definite interpretation difficult.

Amber pendants (Fig.1283)

Twenty-seven pendants, including both complete and unfinished examples, were recovered from Coppergate, the earliest occurring in Period 4B deposits. Most of these are incomplete (*9913–20*), having been broken or discarded at various stages of production. *9924*, however, is a fine, unusually large example, in more or less pristine condition, though showing some polish through wear. The pendant is wedge-shaped, as are most of the pendants, with slightly bevelled edges and a perforation at the narrow end of the wedge, showing wear from a narrow thong used for suspension. Perforations are usually centrally positioned, but are occasionally strikingly off-centre (*9938*). *9925*, from Period 5A, is of similar form though smaller and flatter, again with bevelled edges. Thinner, finer, examples exist (*9927, 9929*), as do thicker (*9926*) and more simple examples (*9930–1*). Most of the Clifford Street examples are quite short though their thickness varies (Fig.1221, p.2507). *10816*, for example, is bell-shaped with a thick base, while *10802* is flat and thin. *10821* is unusually long for the Clifford Street assemblage.

Fig.1284 Jet pendants from 16–22 Coppergate: (left) 9862, (right) 9863. Actual length of 9863 is 33·7mm

The two unprovenanced examples recovered from the city (*10823–4*) are unusual as they both have simple notches cut into their wider ends. In addition to these, the notes of the antiquarian collector, William Hewett, refer to 'an amber pendant one and a half inches long pierced' being recovered from 25–7 High Ousegate. This item does not survive amongst his collection in Hull museum, but another amber pendant does. It is described as being found 'Twelve feet down Old Coach and Horses Corner off Nessgate Oct 1906 purchased on the spot by W. Hewett from Navvies'. It is a wedge-shaped pendant similar to the Coppergate material.

Jet pendants (Figs.1282, 1284)

Two jet crosses were recovered from 12th century dumps at Coppergate, but have been included here because of the uncertainty concerning their date. They could be correctly stratified in the contexts where they were found, but there is a great deal of residual material in these dumps. The uncertainty over their date, especially *9862*, was raised soon after excavation (Roesdahl et al. 1981,137). *9862* is an equal-armed cross, decorated with ring and dot design, inlaid with an unidentified substance, possibly orpiment. The other (*9863*) is larger, has a pierced projecting loop, broad flaring arms and the same arrangement of ring-and-dot. In this case the inlay has been identified as orpiment.[1]

In considering the date of these crosses, a number of parallels need to be taken into account. *9862* is similar to a jet cross found on a skeleton from Scarborough (Rowntree 1931), where ring-and-dot decoration is part of a more elaborate design (Muller 1987, fig 3.8). In this case the skeleton was dated to the 10th century. A much simpler example was recovered from Guisborough Priory, in a grave which may pre-date the 12th century Norman aisle where it was found (Heslop 1995, 93–4, fig.17,2). Another cross from St John's Priory, Pontefract, was found in the grave of a child (G 79) within the sacristy which might date to the later 12th century (Bellamy 1965, 93). This cross has the same arrangement of ring-and-dot with one in the centre and the others on each of the flaring arms, and is very similar to *9863*.

These crosses raise the possibility that both *9862* and *9863* are indeed 12th century in date, as their contexts suggest, but this remains uncertain. Cross pendants and crucifixes in other materials have been found in a number of clearly Viking Age contexts in Scandinavia (e.g. Graham-Campbell 1980a, 341, 527–33, Petersen 1928, 171–3, fig.166).

A very fine jet pendant in the form of a coiled serpent was found during 19th century work at York Railway Station (Waterman 1959, fig.21, 3), and is closely paralleled by an example from Longva, Haram, in Norway (Muller 1987, fig.3.7). These finds are of a more pagan character than the crosses and attest to the attraction jet held in Scandinavia. As jet does not occur anywhere in Scandinavia, the most likely source is the Whitby area.

Beads

Glass beads (Figs.1285–90)

Over 300 glass beads and fragments of varying shapes and colours were recovered from the excavations and watching brief at 16–22 Coppergate and 22 Piccadilly. It is not possible to be certain of the exact numbers, as many have deteriorated since excavation, and in other cases fragments with separate find numbers may have originally been part of the same bead. They have been grouped by shape, resulting in seven main categories. In addition, there are Roman forms and others of uncertain form. The beads are predominantly translucent, but opaque glass beads were also recovered (Tables 262, 264, p.2593).

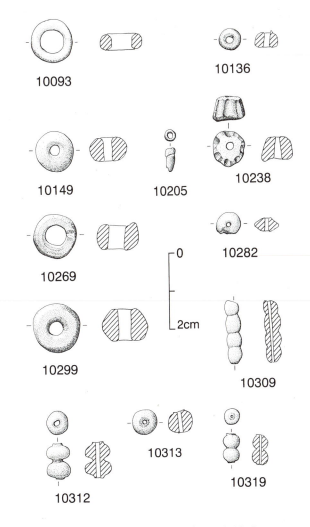

Fig.1285 *Monochrome glass beads from 16–22 Coppergate. Type 1, 10093; Type 2, 10136, 10149; Type 3, 10205; Type 4, 10238; Type 5, 10269; Type 6, 10282, 10299; Type 7, 10309, 10312–13, 10319. Scale 1:1*

Table 258 Glass beads from 16–22 Coppergate according to type and period

Period	1–3	4A	4B	5A	5B	4/5	5Cf	5Cr	6	u/s	Total
Type 1	1	–	2	–	12	–	1	6	15	1	38
Type 2	2	–	14	7	26	1	1	8	32	2	93
Type 3	2	–	8	3	11	–	–	3	19	–	46
Type 4	–	–	–	–	7	–	1	4	17	1	30
Type 5	1	–	4	1	4	–	–	3	6	–	19
Type 6	3	–	2	1	1	–	–	1	13	1	22
Type 7	1	1	12	5	1	1	–	1	–	–	22
Unknown	–	–	5	2	5	–	1	1	3	–	17
Roman	1	–	–	–	1	–	–	–	–	–	2
Total	11	1	47	19	68	2	4	27	105	5	289

Table 259 Glass beads from 22 Piccadilly according to type and period

Period	1–3	4/1	4/2	4/3	6	Total
Type 1	–	2	–	1	1	4
Type 2	–	1	–	–	–	1
Type 3	–	–	–	–	–	0
Type 4	–	13	1	–	2	16
Type 5	–	3	1	–	2	6
Type 6	–	12	1	–	3	16
Unknown	–	–	–	–	1	1
Roman	–	–	–	–	–	0
Total	0	31	3	1	9	44

Forms

Type 1: Annular; this form is defined as having a height to diameter ratio of less than 1:2 (see p.1380, *AY* 17/9).

Type 2: Globular; the beads of this form have a height to diameter ratio of more than 1:2.

Type 3: Cylindrical.

Type 4: Gadrooned/dimpled.

Type 5: Barrel-shaped.

Type 6: Biconical.

Type 7: Segmented; this type includes beads of mainly single or double spherical segments, although triple-segmented and quadruple-segmented beads were also found.

In addition to the identifiably Anglo-Scandinavian beads, two Roman beads were found at Coppergate, which may have been re-used; a bead of hexagonal section from Period 3 (*10339*) and a bead of subsquare section from Period 5B (*10355*). There was also a group of unidentifiable form consisting

Table 261 Translucent glass colours associated with post-Roman beads from 16–22 Coppergate

Type Colour	1	2	3	4	5	6	7	?	Total
Blue	3	8	2	14	–	15	5	1	48
Green	6	23	26	11	–	–	1	3	70
Blue/green	1	4	–	–	–	–	1	1	7
Yellow	20	25	2	–	–	–	4	2	53
Black	2	18	9	5	–	–	–	2	36
Red	–	1	1	–	–	–	–	–	2
Colourless	–	1	–	–	–	1	5	–	7
Orange/foil	–	–	1	–	–	1	–	–	2
Colourless/foil	–	–	–	–	–	–	2	–	2
Polychrome	5	–	–	–	1	3	–	1	10
Orange	–	1	–	–	–	–	–	–	1
Brown	–	–	–	–	–	–	–	1	1
Total	37	81	41	30	1	20	18	11	239

mainly of bead fragments. The only bead from the watching brief belongs to this group (*10628*).

Fabric and colour

The beads are primarily monochrome — only around 10% are polychrome — and include a range of colours such as blue, blue-green, green, yellow, red, orange and white. Others are so darkly coloured they appear black, whilst some are colourless. A gold-coloured overlay was used on two beads (*10215*,

Table 260 Bead types from 16–22 Coppergate and 22 Piccadilly as a percentage of all post-Roman beads

Type	1	2	3	4	5	6	7	% Total
Coppergate	14.0	34.5	17.0	11.3	7.3	7.8	8.1	100
22 Piccadilly	9.4	2.3	–	37.2	13.9	37.2	–	100

Table 262 Opaque glass colours associated with post-Roman beads from 16–22 Coppergate

Type / Colour	1	2	3	4	5	6	7	?	Total
Green	–	–	1	–	–	–	–	–	1
Yellow	1	5	4	–	1	–	4	6	21
Orange	–	–	–	–	15	2	–	–	17
Brown	–	6	–	–	–	–	–	–	6
Red	–	–	–	–	2	–	–	–	2
Blue	–	1	–	–	–	–	–	–	1
Total	1	12	5	–	18	2	4	6	48

Table 263 Translucent glass colours associated with beads from 22 Piccadilly

Type / Colour	1	2	3	4	5	6	Total
Blue	3	1	–	14	–	13	31
Green	1	–	–	–	–	–	1
Black	–	–	–	1	–	–	1
Total	4	1	–	15	–	13	33

Table 264 Opaque glass colours associated with beads from 22 Piccadilly

Type / Colour	1	2	3	4	5	6	?	Total
Orange	–	–	–	–	2	3	–	5
Brown	–	–	–	–	1	–	–	1
Orange/ brown	–	–	–	–	2	–	1	3
Red	–	–	–	–	1	–	–	1
Pink	–	–	–	1	–	–	–	1
Total	–	–	–	1	6	3	1	11

10291; Fig.1286), while two segmented beads contained a gold-coloured layer (*10315, 10322*). The fabric of a number of the beads was analysed. Analysis of yellow, green and black translucent beads from Coppergate revealed that all have a high-lead composition. The colourants were iron, which featured as traces in the yellow beads and in higher amounts in the black beads, while the green beads were coloured by copper. The opaque orange and red beads were also coloured by copper, but unlike the other beads, contain no detectable lead (see Table 244, p.2522). Unfortunately, the foiled beads were not analysed, but it is likely that a silver foil with a yellow/amber glass layer covering the silver was used on the two segmented beads (*10315, 10322*), the

Fig.1286 Beads covered in gold foil from 16–22 Coppergate: 10215 (top), 10291 (bottom). Actual diameter of 10215 is 9·0mm

2593

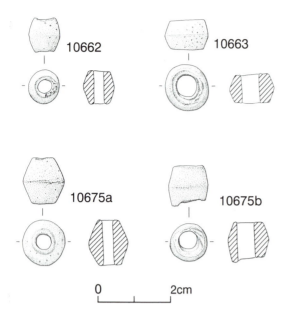

10662   10663

10675a   10675b

0   2cm

Fig.1287 Barrel-shaped and biconical (10657a) beads from 22 Piccadilly. Scale 1:1

method utilised at Kaupang and Birka (Astrup and Andersen 1987, 226–7). Opaque glass was used primarily in the Type 5 (barrel-shaped) beads (see Tables 262, 264). At 22 Piccadilly, a high proportion of the beads (32 out of 44) are translucent blue. Analysis indicated these are made of soda glass,

Fig.1288 Polychrome glass bead from 16–22 Coppergate, 10350. Actual diameter 14·5mm

coloured by traces of copper and cobalt and containing some antimony (see pp.2519–28). Of the remaining beads, eight are opaque orange or red, of the same fabric as the Coppergate examples.

Table 260 (p.2592) demonstrates that certain types predominated at each site: Types 1–4 were the most common at Coppergate, while at 22 Piccadilly Types 4 and 6 were the most frequently found. The report on glass working at the two sites (pp.2525–8) indicated that blue beads were being manufactured at 22 Piccadilly. Analysis of the colours of the bead types (Tables 261–4) shows that 27 out of 32 of all the Type 4 and Type 6 beads and fragments from the site are blue. These are likely to be products of the site.

Discussion of the post-Roman glass beads

Beads of the four main groups recovered from Coppergate (Types 1–4) have been found in considerable numbers elsewhere in York, including Fishergate, where they derived from well-stratified levels (pp.1380–6, *AY* 17/9), two sites on Pavement at Lloyds Bank (p.89, *AY* 17/3) and at 7–13 Pavement (Waterman 1959, 104, fig.25), and also at 34 Shambles, where there was evidence that they were being manufactured during the 12th or early 13th century (pp.210–26, *AY* 17/4). The globular form (Type 2), which was the most commonly found at Coppergate, was also the primary type recovered at Fishergate (p.1380, *AY* 17/9) and at the Shambles (pp.210–13, *AY* 17/4). Annular beads (Type 1) also derive from these sites. Both the globular and annular shape are known Roman forms, and appear long-lived. The small wire-wound cylindrical bead (Type 3) was similarly represented at both Coppergate and Fishergate, and was found predominantly in green (pp.1380–1, *AY* 17/9). Despite being a known Anglian type (p.1381, ibid.), the gadrooned or lobed form (Type 4) does not make its first appearance at Coppergate until Period 5B, and at 22 Piccadilly in the contemporary Period 4/1; this is not easily explained. The longevity of this form is hard to determine, but it may have continued to be used into the medieval period. The appearance of this type in 12th century contexts at Lurk Lane in Beverley lends support to this view (Henderson 1991, 125).

By contrast, the other main bead types found at Coppergate (Types 5, 6 and 7) have rarely been retrieved previously in York. They were not found at Anglian Fishergate, and only one example each of the biconical-shaped beads (Type 6) and segmented beads (Type 7) has been found elsewhere in the city, both noted by Waterman (1959, 95–6, 103–4). Indeed these beads appear to be unknown in England outside York, although segmented beads have been found on Norse sites in Scotland, such as the Brough of Birsay (Curle 1982, 83) and Jarlshof (Hamilton 1956, 152). A necklace of 44 such beads was recovered from a 10th century Viking grave at Kneep, Isle of Lewis (Welander et al. 1987, 163–5). Segmented beads are also a known Roman type (Guido 1978, 94). All three types are common finds in Scandinavia

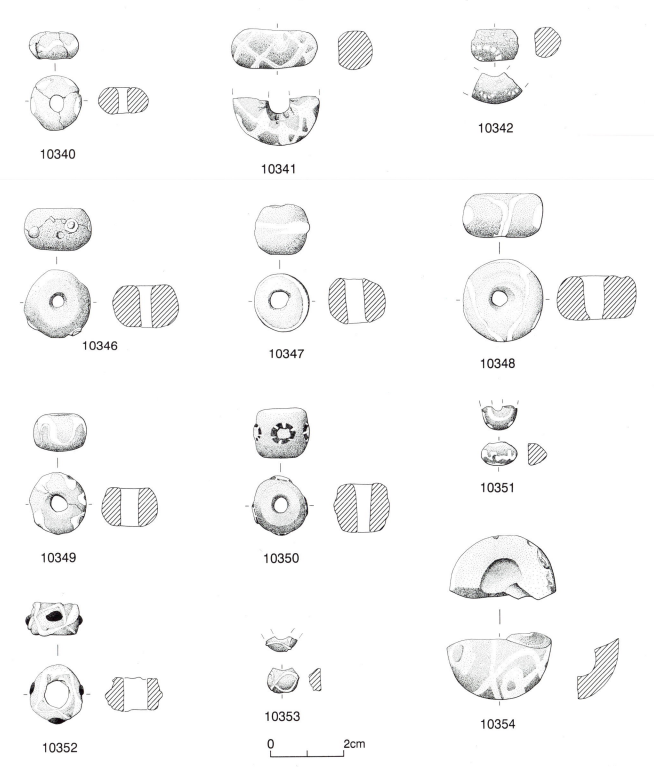

10340

10341

10342

10346

10347

10348

10349

10350

10351

10352

10353

10354

0   2cm

Fig.1289 *Polychrome glass beads from 16–22 Coppergate. Scale 1:1*

(Callmer 1977, Types A, B, E). The biconical beads (Type 6) appear in quantity in 5th and 6th century levels at Helgö, Sweden, where the 500 or so Types 5 and 6 together represented 50% of the beads recovered (Lundström 1981, 9). At the 8th–10th century settlement of Paviken in Gotland, Sweden, Type 6 was absent, but both Types 5 and 7 were represented (ibid.). At both sites, there was evidence of bead manufacture (Lundström 1976, 3). Hedeby, in north Germany, has also produced Type 5 and 7 beads and debris from their manufacture (Dekówna 1990, 34–6). The use of gold foil as a decorative element on beads is also paralleled on Scandinavian sites such as Paviken and Ribe, where not only beads but also the raw material consisting of glass tesserae with foil overlays were recovered (Lundström 1976, 4–5).

Polychrome beads (Figs.1288–90)

Sixteen polychrome beads were recovered from Coppergate. All consist of a monochrome bead, with an applied decorative design, usually created from a single motif, but occasionally incorporating two. The most commonly used motif is a wave, sometimes single, as on *10340*, but more frequently two waves crossing, as on *10352*. Another popular motif is a blob, incorporated on *10352* and also seen to great effect on *10350*, where green blobs are surrounded by red circles with yellow lines through. Cable, as on *10342*, and spirals, as on *10344*, are also used. All the Coppergate beads are paralleled by examples from Helgö (Lundström 1981, 9–15), and elsewhere in Scandinavia (Callmer 1977, pls.4–20).

Beads from the Bedern

The medieval site of the College of Vicars Choral at the Bedern also produced nine glass beads of the types described above. All were recovered, residually, in contexts ranging from the mid 13th century to the post-medieval period. Of the monochrome beads, two are of Type 1 (*10699–700*), two are Type 2 (*10701–*

Fig.1290 *Polychrome glass beads from 16–22 Coppergate: (from top) 10352, 10351, 10347. Actual diameter of 10352 14·1mm*

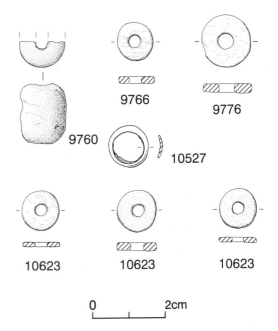

Fig.1291 *Beads from 16–22 Coppergate: 9760, 9766, 9776, made of stone; 10527, made of copper alloy; 10623, made of an uncertain material. Scale 1:1*

2), two are Type 3 (*10703–4*) and one each of Type 5 (*10705*) and Type 6 (*10706*). The single polychrome bead from the Bedern (*10707*) is globular, and is dark appearing black with yellow marvered blobs.

Copper alloy bead (Fig.1291)

Globular in shape and centrally perforated, *10527* was recovered from a Period 3 scoop backfill. Non-ferrous beads are known from sites of the Anglo-Scandinavian period. Petersen notes their use by the Norse (Petersen 1928, 163), and a number were recovered at Birka, including one of the same form as *10527* (Arbman 1940, taf.114, no.15). They often appear to have been used on necklaces, together with beads of other materials, such as glass, amber and precious stones (Arbman 1943, 88–9, Grab.306).

Amber beads (Fig.1292)

A total of 34 complete and unfinished amber beads were recovered from Coppergate. Bead rough-outs were recovered from Period 3 onwards (e.g. *9864, 9867*) and finished beads from Period 4A (e.g. *9881*). These are generally quite wide (9mm to 16mm), thick and roughly discoidal, with central or off-centre perforations. The perforations are usually drilled from both sides resulting in an hour-glass cross-section. Profiles can be D-shaped (e.g. *9896*), ovoid or biconical in section (e.g. *9881*). In some cases the outer surfaces are highly polished (*9891, 9896*), and in other cases the inside of the perforations are worn smooth (*9891, 9894*), both resulting from wear. *9896* has an unusually small perforation, and is also more rounded than many of the others. *9883* is flatter than many other Coppergate examples and shows little sign of wear around the perforation, although the surfaces are all well polished. *9895* is clearly unfinished and appears to have been carved rather than lathe-turned as the surfaces and edges all show irregular knife-trimming marks.

The Clifford Street beads are mainly unfinished, so their final form is sometimes uncertain (Fig.1219, p.2505). The majority are, like the Coppergate examples, thick with rounded edges (e.g. *10779*); some are very chunky (e.g. *10780*), others are clearly intended to be thin, flat discs (e.g. *10781*).

Other examples of amber beads, believed to be Anglo-Scandinavian in date, derive from King's Square (YAT 1988.8), where two fragments of com-

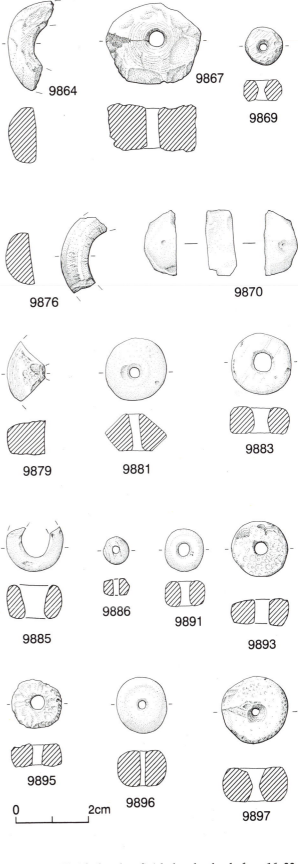

Fig.1292 *Finished and unfinished amber beads from 16–22 Coppergate. Scale 1:1*

pleted beads were recovered, in addition to others broken in production (Fig.1187, **5**, p.2452). One is closely paralleled in the Coppergate collection (e.g. *9886*). The other is rather different, being a fragment of a flat plain discoid bead, now quite decayed; it is paralleled by a similar example from 7–9 Aldwark which is of uncertain date (YAT 1985.5). Beads which are typologically and technologically similar to the Coppergate beads have also been recovered from Coffee Yard (YAT 1987.1) and 12–18 Swinegate (YAT 1989.28) (Fig.1187, **2**, **3**). A related, more square-cut, though incomplete, example was found on the City Mills site at Skeldergate (YAT 1983.2) (Fig.1187, **23**).

Stone beads (Fig.1291)

There are nineteen stone beads from Anglo-Scandinavian deposits at Coppergate. In addition, one from a Period 6 deposit and two unstratified examples are probably part of the same group.

The earliest examples are from Period 4B (*9760–1*). *9760* is a fragment of a plain, quite simply finished cylindrical bead with a horizontal perforation. It is made from steatite and represents the only use of this material apart from vessels and moulds. *9761* is a tiny flat plain disc bead (4mm in diameter) made from a crinoid ossicle of calcite.

Most of the beads are from Period 5B deposits and constitute a group of simple flat disc beads. These vary in diameter from 9mm (*9771*) to twice that size (*9768*). The majority, however, are between 10mm and 13mm diameter, with thicknesses usually between 1mm and 2·5mm. The beads are most frequently made of mudstone, and occasionally marble or possibly quartz. The mudstone appears dark grey and matt, while the marble and possible quartz examples are paler and more shiny.

There are other virtually identical beads from the site made of bone, antler and shell (probably oyster). Some of these occur in earlier deposits (Period 4B and Period 5A) but in some cases examples were found in the same contexts as the stone beads, and beads of different materials may well have originally been strung together. For example, eight stone beads and two bone beads were found together in a pit fill in Tenement C. Four of the marble beads (*9767, 9772–4*) and one of the mudstone ones (*9771*) are all very closely matched in size at 10mm. Three beads of uncertain material (*10623*) and six shell beads (*10621–*

2) were also recovered together in a dump or backfill deposit in Structure 5/4 on Tenement B.

Dr G.D. Gaunt remarks:

The most probable sources of the mudstone and silty mudstone beads are, on the grounds of proximity to York, the Lower Palaeozoic of southern Scotland and Cumbria, the Carboniferous of the Pennines and Lower Jurassic of north-eastern Yorkshire. Pennine Carboniferous rocks, notably in the Great Scar Limestone and Wensleydale groups (formerly the Carboniferous Limestone and Yoredale sequences respectively), are the sources also for the cylindrical calcitic crinoid ossicles utilised as beads. The marble beads appear to be made from 'true' marble (of metamorphic origin), not 'false' marble (sedimentary limestone of ornamental quality such as the Cotham, Forest, Frosterley and Purbeck 'marbles', as long referred to by the quarrying industry). In the British Isles 'true' marbles are virtually confined to small areas in north-western Scotland and western Ireland. There is, however, little or no evidence of the exploitation of these marbles except in their surrounding regions, and on the basis of known trade in other marble items such as statuary it is more likely that the marble beads had a non-British origin, probably from circum-Mediterranean regions. They may, of course, have been made from fragments of earlier imported marble items. Similarly, although the steatite bead (9760) was almost certainly derived from the Dalradian Supergroup in the Shetlands, it may well be secondarily derived from a fragment of an earlier imported steatite bowl or mould.

Use of the beads

There seems little doubt that the majority of the Coppergate and Piccadilly beads were originally strung onto necklaces, although beads were also used to adorn other objects, such as tweezers (*10531*) during the Viking period. Viking Age graves at Birka have produced several necklaces, some composed almost entirely of glass beads (Graham-Campbell 1980, 44, no.153), others incorporating silver pendants and rings (ibid., 45, no.154). These complete necklaces show how beads of many different forms could be strung together on one necklace, although others, incorporating single bead types, are also known, such as the segmented bead necklace from Kneep, Isle of Lewis (Welander et al. 1987, 163–5). A necklace of 71 beads of glass, amber and jet was found close to the head of a 10th century Viking female burial at Peel, Isle of Man, with a further two amber beads and a perforated fossil found at the waist, perhaps as components of a belt or pendant (Holgate 1987, 15).

Jet and shale bracelets (Fig.1293)

Bracelet fragments in jet and related material were recovered from Coppergate. As with the finger-rings it is difficult to be certain that these are not Roman in date. Only those which are plain rounded or D-profile bands are included here and their inclusion is only justified by their recovery in Anglo-Scandinavian deposits. Bracelets, or arm-rings, of jet and other similar materials, have been found elsewhere in the British Isles in Viking Age contexts (e.g. Graham-Campbell 1980a, 66; Hamilton 1956, fig.56.5–8; Greig 1940, 85, fig.48).

The earliest from Coppergate is a shale fragment from Period 3 in what was to become Tenement A (*9855*). Similar fragments were recovered from Period 4A (*9856–7*) and Period 4/5 (*9861*), all in shale or jet-like material rather than true jet. Period 4B produced two bracelet fragments, *9858* made from jet, and *9859* made from jet-like material. Two shale bracelets were recovered from Period 5A levels (*9860* and sf344). The latter may well be Roman in date. There is no real pattern to the distribution of this material but most of it is from the front half of the site. A small fragment recovered from a medieval context at Bedern (*10698*) may possibly be of Roman date.

Other personal items

Bell (Fig.1294)

10528 is a bell which was found in a Period 5A build-up deposit. It is largely complete, although it lacks a clapper and has an incomplete suspension loop. Its hexagonal body and scalloped or fluted lower edge is paralleled by a number of other bells found on contemporary sites, most with Scandinavian connections. An example decorated with ring-and-dot motifs was recovered from Freswick Links, Caithness (Batey 1988, 213–16), while a plain bell was found at Meols (Bu'lock 1972, fig.9m). Closer to York, another decorated bell was found at Cottam, in the Yorkshire Wolds, which has also produced metalwork with Jellinge-style decoration (Haldenby 1990, 58–9, figs.5, 6.1). Batey (1988, 215) suggests a possible Norse origin for these bells, and dates them to the 10th century, a date range into which *10528* fits comfortably.

Although iron bells were also found in Anglo-Scandinavian levels at Coppergate (*2751–5*, pp.557–8, *AY* 17/6), these are larger than *10528* and are thought to have been for cattle or sheep. The more delicate nature of *10528* and other contemporary copper alloy bells suggests a more likely function as charms or parts of necklaces (Batey 1988, 215).

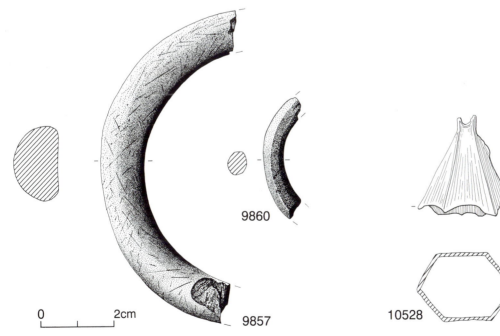

9860

9857

Fig.1293   Shale bracelets from 16–22 Coppergate. Scale 1:1

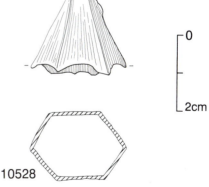

10528

Fig.1294   Copper alloy bell from 16–22 Coppergate. Scale 1:1

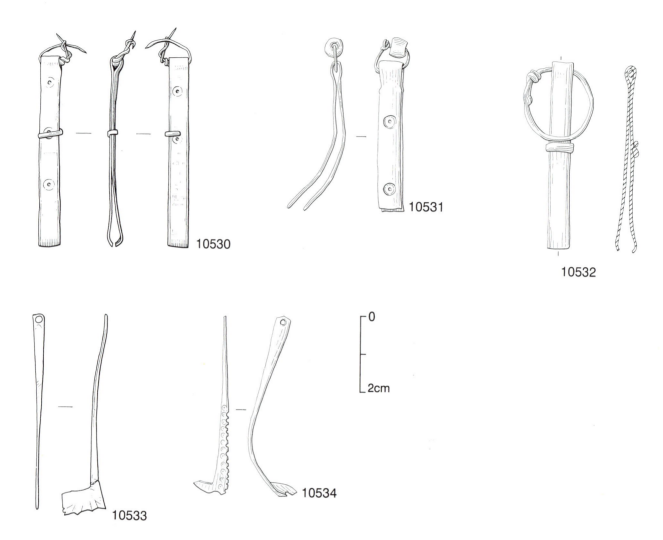

Fig.1295 *Copper alloy toilet implements from 16–22 Coppergate: 10530–2, tweezers; 10533–4, possible toilet implements of unknown function. Scale 1:1*

Toilet implements (Fig.1295)

Tweezers

The three pairs of tweezers (*10530–2*) recovered from Period 4/5–5B contexts at Coppergate are all made from folded strips, and all retain a twisted wire suspension ring which on *10531* carries a white glass bead. Ring-and-dot motifs decorate both *10530* and *10531*, while *10530* and *10532* retain the remains of slides. A pair found at 22 Piccadilly (*10690*) has no ring but has a slide. Presumably used primarily for cosmetic purposes, these simple toilet implements are common finds of the Saxon and Viking periods. The narrow strip form of the Coppergate and Piccadilly tweezers lacks the expanded ends of those found at Fishergate (*5420*, pp.1387–8, Fig.678, *AY*

17/9), and Hamwic (Hinton 1996, 44–6, fig.18), but bears more similarity to examples from Winchester, which date from the 10th century onwards (Biddle 1990b, 690–2), and others from Hedeby (Müller-Wille 1973, 34, abb.8, 5–6). *10529*, a ring of rectangular section, may be a slide from a pair of tweezers.

Possible toilet implements

Two unusual objects which may derive from the same toilet set are *10533* and *10534*, both found in the floor level of the Period 4B wattle building on Tenement C at Coppergate, and both made of brass. The objects are of similar lengths, 50mm and 48mm respectively, and both have stems of rectangular section with a perforation for suspension at one end. At the other end, *10533* has what appears to be a blade with one serrated edge, while *10534* has a serrated edge and projecting lobe, the stem decorated with ring-and-dot motifs. So far, no parallels for these objects have been found.

A fragment of glass, sf7941, which was recovered from a Period 4B deposit, has tentatively been identified as Roman mirror glass, and will be published in *AY 6/2* (in prep.).

Miscellaneous Stone Objects

Sculpture

Several pieces of stone sculpture were recovered from the 16–22 Coppergate site. Some of these have been fully described and discussed in the *Corpus of Anglo-Saxon Sculpture* by J.T. Lang and his work is summarised here.

Grave-marker (Fig.1298)

Part of a small limestone grave-marker (*10827*; Lang 1991, 103, Ills.333–6) was recovered from a Period 5B context. It is broken at the top and on one face but is otherwise in crisp condition. The stone tapers and Lang describes it as follows.

Broad face A: A double flat edge moulding flanks a plain long stemmed cross in low relief. The arm-type is uncertain, probably type B11. The tapering stem is flanked by a row of bold pellets at each side.

Narrow faces B and D: A flat edge moulding flanks a vertical run of broad chevrons, partly broken away on face D.

Broad face C: The edge moulding is flat. Within is a plain rectangular moulding, also flat, framing a vertical run of broad chevrons.

Probable cross fragments

The 25 fragments of which *10825* is comprised are believed to derive from a cross and may all be part of the same monument. They have been discussed by Lang (1991, 104–5, Ills.337–8) and also by Tweddle in *AY 7/2* (23–4). Their conclusions are summarised here. The fragments are of fine-grained oolitic limestone. Two fragments are of a shaft of rectangular section (sfs2163 and 7112) which are described by Tweddle:

Face A has a prominent roll moulding on the edge with inside it a smaller roll moulding. Only the margin of the face survives, decorated with a curved incised line. Faces

B and C are destroyed. Face D is destroyed apart from the common corner roll moulding with Face A and a smaller inner roll moulding. The smaller fragment consists of part of the corner roll moulding and fragmentary inner moulding.

The other fragments may be part of the same monument, which Tweddle suggests may have been decorated with one or more equal-armed crosses with curved mouldings in the re-entrant angles. Both Lang and Tweddle agree that the carving is very crisp and believe that the small size of the fragments suggests that they represent the debris from dressing the stone for re-use. Lang suggests a date between the late 8th and early 9th century, while Tweddle gives a broader date range of 8th or 9th century. Most of the pieces were recovered from a single context within Period 5A, but one or two are from Periods 4A and 4B.

Grave-cover (Figs.1296–7)

Fragments of a Magnesian Limestone grave-cover, *10826*, were recovered from a Period 5B context. This stone is also a fine-grained limestone and, although much broken, is still very crisp. It is probably an unfinished reject (Lang 1991, 103, Ills.327, 329–30). Lang describes it as follows.

Face B: A flat perimeter moulding surrounds the end of the panel. Within the moulding is a drilled fix-point hole. The panel contains half a pattern of two interlocked profile beasts, one upside-down. The upright beast has an incised double outline. The long neck tapers from a substantial chest which has a scroll in relief immediately above the junction of the fore-leg. The leg is double-outlined and has a four-toed paw. The head has an incised elliptical eye and an unfinished triple nose-fold. The lower jaw hangs open. The ear is extended into a median-incised fetter band which binds both animals.

Fig.1296 *Face B of limestone grave-cover* 10826 *from 16–22 Coppergate. Actual length 230mm*

Fig.1297 *Face E of limestone grave-cover* 10826 *from 16–22 Coppergate. Actual width 110mm*

The unfinished foot of the reversed beast lies in the mouth of the upright one. Its body has an incised double outline and median-incised tail. A fix-point hole lies on the incised contour.

Face E: The perimeter moulding is broad and flat. It also has fix-point markings. Within the panel is the head of a profile beast with double outline. The head is domed with a small, pricked ear and snub jowl. The incised eye is elliptical. The mouth is a closed slit and from it droops a frondy element. A forepaw has three toes.

He draws similarities between this piece and part of a cross-shaft from Newgate and part of a grave-cover from Clifford Street, and suggests that they may be the products of the same craftsman. He notes similarities between the beast-head of Face B and English manuscript styles of the late 9th century.

Although Lang's *Corpus* gives a deposition date for the Coppergate fragments of not later than c.960, more recent analysis of the site suggests a date sometime after c.975.

Grave-cover (Fig.1298)

This fragment, *10828*, is of Millstone Grit from a Period 5B context and could be a re-used Roman ashlar (Lang 1991, 104, Ills.339–41). It is very broken and worn and is decorated only on the upper surface. Lang describes this as follows.

A (top): A flat edge moulding turns the angle of the panel. Within are the remains of indecipherable interlace using flat strands, and terminating in a twist.

He draws parallels with a piece from Stonegrave, North Yorkshire, as the interlace cannot be matched in York.

Fossils

Forty fossils were recovered from 16–22 Coppergate and these are described individually in the catalogue.

Dr G.D. Gaunt reports: *Some were probably erratics and a few may have been brought to York with building*

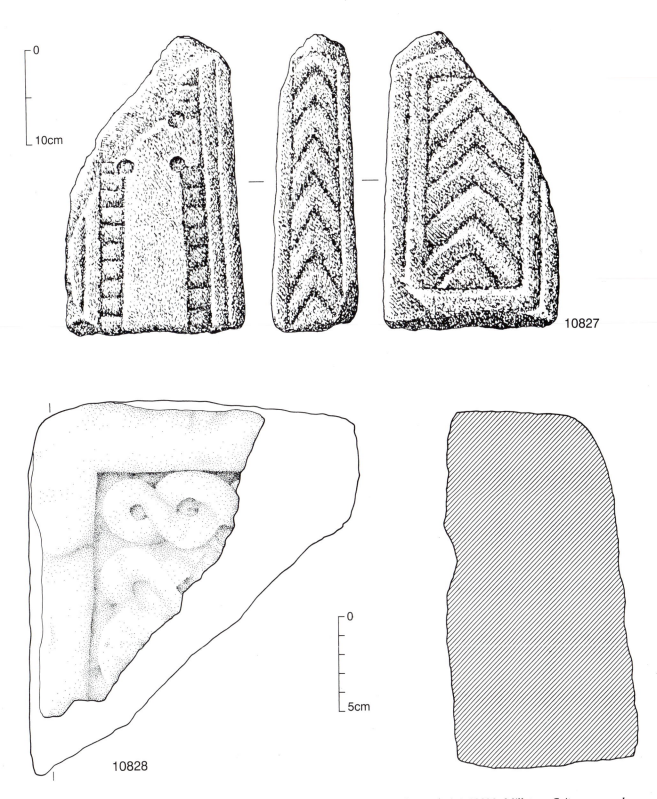

Fig.1298 *Stone sculpture from 16–22 Coppergate: 10827, limestone grave-marker, scale 1:4; 10828, Millstone Grit grave-marker, scale 1:2*

and artefactual stone. However, many of the fossils have little or no adhering stone and, since they do not occur naturally near York, were presumably brought there because of their decorative, curiosity, esoteric or talismanic value. They include crinoid ossicles (known as St Cuthbert's beads), Gryphaea, especially G. arcuata (devil's toe-nails), ammonites (snakestones or St Hilda's serpents) and bivalves (stone hearts). Some brachiopods *were used in children's games instead of pebbles, and echinoids of an appropriate weight were known as 'poundstones'. Corals were presumably prized for their internal structural patterns.*

The fossils are generally well distributed across the site and show no concentration in any one period or position.

Highly polished fragments

Five fragmentary items (*9817–21*) have been included here which are almost certainly Roman in origin, but which may have had a function in the Anglo-Scandinavian period. They come from contexts ranging from Period 3 to Period 6. They are made from very fine-grained rock and are polished; in the case of *9818*, very highly polished. They may have originally been part of Roman composite objects but may have been re-used in the post-Roman period, possibly in portable altars and reliquaries (Lynn 1984). Sites in both Scotland and Ireland have produced nineteen similar fragments in contexts ranging in date from the 9th to the 18th century. Some of these were recovered from Viking Age levels at Wood Quay in Dublin and there are other examples from early Christian deposits in Dublin and elsewhere (ibid., 28).

Stone fragments

Inevitably collections of this size produced a number of pieces which cannot be firmly identified and, in some cases, they may be unmodified from their natural state.

These include, for example, worked sandstone fragments (*9825*), which join to form a right angle, but whose purpose is unclear. Similarly, *9827*, is a rectangular limestone fragment, with one worked surface. A large lump of limestone with two parallel grooves in it (*9824*) may have formed part of a structure, but its purpose is unclear. A sandstone fragment with glaze on it from metalworking or glass working, *9829*, was also recovered.

Smaller items include a fragment of schist (*9828*) and Norwegian Ragstone pebbles (*9826, 9830*). *9826* has one worn surface and may have been used as a burnisher or polisher, while *9830* comprises two pebbles with naturally occurring holes in them, which might have been collected as amulets. Finally, *9823* is an ironstone fragment with faceted sides, whose purpose remains uncertain.

Discussion

All the sites under consideration here, with the exception of Bedern, are situated in an area which has long been believed to be part of the core of Anglo-Scandinavian York. York Archaeological Trust excavations since 1972, and other small investigations and observations in the area over the last century, have produced a considerable body of artefactual evidence to illustrate the period between the late 9th and late 11th century.

This evidence, in particular that from 16–22 Coppergate, includes material which pre-dates the Anglo-Scandinavian period and traditionally sits more comfortably in an 8th and early 9th century context. This material is almost always found in early Anglo-Scandinavian contexts but occurs sporadically throughout the period. The presence of early material has been recognised before in relation to the pottery; Continental imports, Ipswich wares and hand-made wares of Anglian date were recovered throughout the sequence (AY 16/5, 392–400). There are also a few pre-Viking Age coins, for example a single porcupine sceat (720–40), three coins of Eanred (810–41) and five coins of Æthelred (841–4) (AY 18/1, 3, 15, 19–21, 25, 28, 30–1). The evidence in this report provides further indications of activity in the area in the 8th and early 9th century. The glass, for example, incorporates a small but significant group of 8th or even 7th century forms, all from later contexts. Amongst the non-ferrous metalwork there are also types which are more likely to be Anglian rather than Anglo-Scandinavian. The cross brooch (10431), the linked pin (10468) and the silver stud (10541), for example, are all types which have their closest parallels in the 8th and early 9th centuries. Some of the sculptural fragments are clearly part of 8th century monuments which were apparently broken up in the Anglo-Scandinavian period.

All these finds were recovered from late 9th–early 11th century contexts, and can be classed either as residual, or individual earlier items with long life-spans, or styles and classes of artefact which continue into the middle decades of the 9th century. If they are residual, this begs the question of their original source, whether on the site or adjacent to it. There are a few features at 16–22 Coppergate, between the Roman and Anglo-Scandinavian levels, which may represent Anglian occupation but these are difficult

to interpret (p.2547). Similarly, at 22 Piccadilly, closer to the course of the River Foss, there is a small collection of early types of pottery and early forms of bone combs (AY 7/2, 263, 94; 7926, 7951, AY 17/12). It is becoming increasingly clear that there was some form of occupation in this part of the city in the 8th century and/or early to mid 9th century, but its character remains elusive.

This scatter of Anglian objects and features is in marked contrast with the picture that emerges in the subsequent periods. The topographical organisation which is seen on the site, the laying out of boundaries and the erecting of structures, is paralleled by an explosion of activities both of a domestic and industrial character, much of which is reflected in the material culture. New types of raw materials are available through trade and external contacts, new forms and styles of decoration and design are adopted and new technologies developed.

The range of raw materials used by the Anglo-Scandinavian population is greater than in the previous period, and must reflect the wider geographical orbit in which these people operated. Amber, although in evidence throughout the Anglo-Saxon period, was imported into the city in far greater quantities to supply workshops such as those indicated at Coppergate and Clifford Street, and to satisfy a new demand for a range of personal ornament. Steatite was imported either as finished or roughed-out bowls from the Scandinavian settlements in Shetland. The penannular brooch 10425 may also have come from Shetland. Access to sources of schist and phyllite in Norway and/or Shetland resulted in a change in preference of stone type for the production of honestones. The importation of Niedermendig lava for quernstones continued a connection which had originally been forged by the Romans.

A wide range of contacts is also reflected by completed objects. It is often unclear whether these are imported items or local products made under the influence of the various foreign styles and types which were circulating. The ringed pins, for example, are probably of Irish origin though there is nothing to preclude them being made locally. The ansate brooches, similarly, show typological and stylistic influences from the Continent but may have an

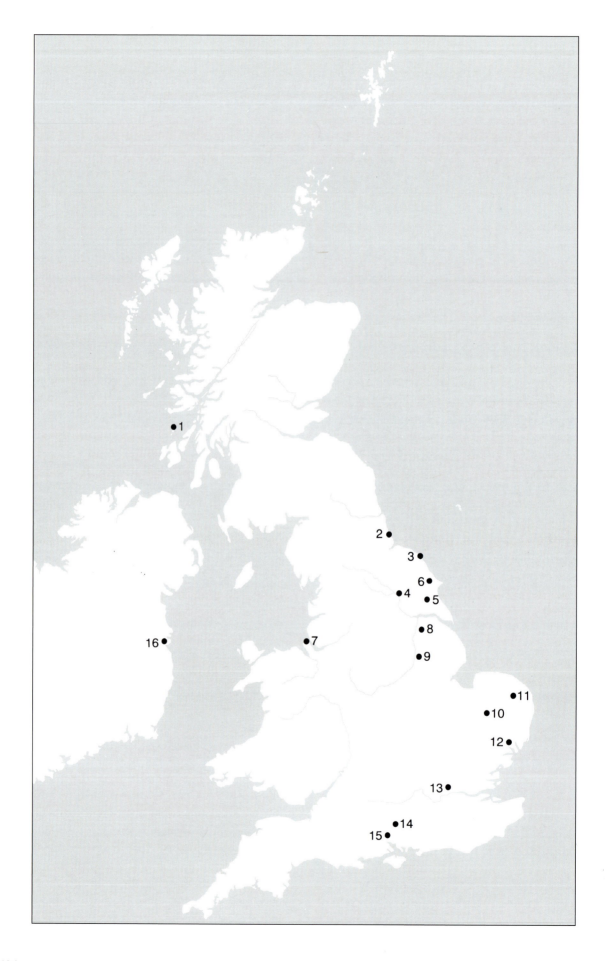

English source. Many of the originally Scandinavian art styles became popular and were widely adopted and developed in England. The Jellinge style seen on disc brooch *10604* and grave cover *10826*, the Borre style on strap-ends such as *10423* and open-work badges *4277–8*, and the Ringerike style on mount *10708* from Bedern, lead alloy cross matrix *10544* and hooked tag *10437* all confirm the position of York in a cultural milieu where these styles and influences were well known and popular. Taken together with other evidence, such as imported pottery (*AY 16/5*), silks (pp.313–14, 361–76, 381–2, *AY 17/5*), walrus and ivory (*AY 17/12*), this new evidence increases our understanding of the position of York within an international network of contacts.

Local and regional sources for raw materials, however, were also widely exploited. In the case of the stone there is clear evidence for deliberate selection according to the intended function. The properties of Millstone Grit (from the Pennines), used for the rotary grindstones, make it most suitable for sharpening metal-edged tools and blades, and it was selected for the same reason for some of the larger hones. Limestone was the preferred material for lamps. A ready source of small blocks suitable for the relatively simple modifications necessary was provided by the Roman ashlar blocks which must have littered the streets of York. This, coupled with the relative softness of the stone, must have influenced the choice of raw material. Chalk from the Yorkshire Wolds, which is also easily worked, was used both for fashioning small playing pieces and spindle whorls, and was probably used in powdered form for polishing.

Seams bearing jet are known on the North Yorkshire Moors as well as along the North Yorkshire coast. The evidence for jet working is only slight by comparison with that for amber working and this must indicate a clear cultural preference for amber jewellery by the population served by the artisans of York.

The sources of ores used in metalworking processes have not been pinpointed but many would have been in the Pennine areas, although tin may have come from further afield. Gold and silver would both have been circulating as jewellery and, in the case of silver, as coins to be melted down and re-used. The raw materials for glass making would also have been available regionally although cullet could be collected from the city itself. Once again this new evidence for regional networks needs to be considered together with previously published material. The area around the city would have provided a source for the antler, bone, leather and wood from which many of the other artefacts were produced.

York's role as a consumer of raw materials, imported objects and cultural influences cannot be considered without paying equal attention to its importance as a producer. The evidence at 16–22 Coppergate for the manufacture of ferrous and non-ferrous objects, of items of antler and bone, of textiles, of a range wooden artefacts and leather goods is supplemented by the new evidence described above. Some of these crafts, for example the jet working, were carried out on a very limited scale; in other cases, such as amber working, there is some evidence for short-lived workshops which may represent no more than the output of a season or two. Glass production seems to have been focused in one area of the site (the northern strip of 16–22 Coppergate and 22 Piccadilly), indicating a workshop in that area. Settled workshops of uncertain duration can also be hypothecated in the case of the non-ferrous and ferrous metal industries.

The absence of excavated sites of this period in the hinterland of York makes it difficult to establish where the market for these products lay. The urban population must have been a significant consumer of the output of the workshops and craftsmen identified on these sites, but some must also have reached those areas which were the sources of so much of the raw material. It is perhaps significant

Fig.1299 (*facing*) *Map of Britain and Ireland showing the main sites referred to in the text*

1	Kiloran Bay, Colonsay	7	Meols	12	Ipswich
2	Hartlepool	8	Flixborough	13	London
3	Whitby	9	Lincoln	14	Hamwic
4	York	10	Thetford	15	Winchester
5	Beverley	11	Norwich	16	Dublin
6	Cottam				

Fig.1300 *Map of Northern Europe showing the main sites referred to in the text*

1	*Birka*	4	*Dorestad*
2	*Ribe*	5	*Lund*
3	*Hedeby*	6	*Domburg*

how little there is in the way of finished items of jewellery at 16–22 Coppergate, in contrast with the waste and rejects associated with production. This is true of the amber and non-ferrous metalwork — the numbers of obviously worn and lost items is quite small in relation to the area excavated. The non-ferrous assemblage in particular appears considerably smaller than might be expected for a site of this size, and may attest to the efficiency of recycling materials for this industry. The recent increase in evidence gathered by metal detectorists in the area around York indicates that metal objects of this period found their way onto many rural sites; some may well be the products of urban workshops such as those excavated at Coppergate. It is reasonable to assume that objects made from other materials were similarly distributed.

The excavated structures were dwellings as well as workshops, and there is inevitably the detritus of everyday life amongst the assemblages; this is seen more markedly in terms of the pottery, leather, wooden artefacts, iron, bone and antler. Textile production should be classed as a domestic activity rather than a commercial one (*AY* 17/11); food preparation, in the form of cooking, is indicated by the quantities of pottery recovered (*AY* 16/5), but the relatively small number of quernstone fragments, in contrast with the Anglian site at 46–54 Fishergate, raises questions about other stages of food processing. Objects associated with leisure such as the playing pieces described above and elsewhere, and a range of simple musical instruments, help to elucidate the character of the sites (*AY* 17/12; *AY* 17/13). The overwhelming impression which is gleaned from the material covered in this report, and from assemblages already published, is that the Coppergate area was occupied by a community of artisans involved in a wide range of commercial enterprises and craft activities. These included procuring the raw materials, by means of intermediaries or by direct contact, fashioning the various products using a range of technologies and skills, and trading them for cash or using them in barter. We have a few of their personal possessions, lost in the course of everyday life, and the picture these give is not of a wealthy population, but of individuals with moderate means and a range of strategies for securing their livelihood.

Catalogue

The catalogue numbers follow consecutively those on p.2432, *AY* 17/13, except for items previously catalogued in fascicules in *AY* 17 which appear at the start of relevant sections. Each entry ends with the small find number, prefixed sf, preceded by context number; a list of provenances appears on pp.2661–3. If a catalogue entry incorporates more than one item or fragment, the dimensions given relate to the largest item. Entries for items attributed to Period 6 are followed by a code denoting Tenement (A–D), Period (6), phase and sequence. It should be noted that since 1994 the Yorkshire Musuem accession codes have been prefixed YORYM.

Abbreviations: L. = length; W. = width; T. = thickness; D. = diameter; H. = height; Wt. = weight

Finds from 16–22 Coppergate (1976–81.7)

Stone

Ingot moulds

Note: Full catalogue entries for *3990, 3992, 3994–5, 3997–4001* appear in *AY* 17/7.

All moulds are made of talc schist unless specified otherwise.

3990   Steatite. Roughly rectangular section, with a total of six bar-shaped grooves of varying lengths cut in three of the faces. The fourth face has both a Thor's hammer shape and a narrow hole drilled deep into it. L.82.0, W.50.0, T.34.0mm 3729 sf9645 (P3) (*Fig.1199*)

3992   Re-used as a spindle whorl. Traces of a minimum of five bar-shaped grooves to take molten metal survive. L.58.0, W.51.0, T.25.0mm 27504 sf10065 (P4B) (*Fig.1200*)

3994   Incomplete, with parts of a total of six bar-shaped grooves and one conical hole surviving on the four faces and a further hole in the end. L.60.0, W.38.0, T.37.0mm 34207 sf12890 (P4B) (*Fig.1200*)

3995   Bar-shaped groove cut in both surviving faces. L.112.0, W.20.0, T.26.0mm 25341 sf8664 (P4B) (*Fig.1200*)

3997   One bar-shaped groove cut into surviving face. L.67.0, W.28.0, T.25.0mm 22090 sf7376 (P5A) (*Fig.1200*)

3998   Steatite. Bar-shaped groove cut into each long face L.76.0, W.49.0, T.39.0mm 14625 sf5479 (P5B) (*Fig.1199*)

3999   Fragment. Bar-shaped groove cut into each surviving face. L.107.0, W.19.0 T.27.0mm 19632 sf9198 (P5B)

4000   Steatite. Four bar-shaped grooves, two on one of the long faces and one on each of two others. L.180.0, W.70.0, T.60.0mm 21961 sf9987 (P5B) (*Fig.1199*)

4001   Rim sherd from steatite vessel re-used as an ingot mould. Two shapes are cut in it, on one side a groove for a bar ingot and on the other a cross or part of a Thor's hammer. L.44.0, W.24.0, T.12.0mm 9802 sf3109 (D6y1; late 12th/early 13th century) (P6) (*Fig.1199*)

9247   Possible mould, pebble fragment with a single long shallow groove and traces of a second cut parallel into the surface, the rest is broken away. L.50, W.33, T.30mm 22421 sf7697(4B)

9248   Fragment. Broken along the groove. L.80.0, W.21.0, T.17.0mm 5759 sf2013 (D6a6; late 11th/early 12th century) (P6)

Spindle whorls

Note: Full catalogue entries for *6536–42, 6545–9, 6552–63* and *6567* appear in *AY* 17/11. These are illustrated on Figs.806–8.

Where whorls are incomplete, measurement of the incomplete dimension is given in brackets [ ]. In these cases an estimated original weight has been added after the present weight.

6536   Almost complete. Truncated hemispherical shape, with four encircling incised lines; form A1. Mudstone, medium to dark grey, micromicaceous, slightly fissile, silty; probably Coal Measures, but could be Millstone Grit. D.33.7, T.14.7, perforation D.10.6mm, Wt.20.4g 27422 sf9732 (P4A)

6537   Hemispherical shape with deep rilling around circumference and around hole; form A1. Chalk, greyish white, fine-grained. Chalk Group, possibly Ferriby Chalk Formation. D.33.0, T.19.6, perforation D.9.8mm, Wt.24.8g 20427 sf6995 (P4B)

6538   Hemispherical shape; undecorated; form A1. Chalk, white, very fine-grained; Chalk Group. D.30.0, T.14.7, perforation D.10.0mm, Wt.14.8g 22679 sf7945 (P4B)

6539   Flattened hemispherical shape; undecorated; form A1. Chalk, white to pinkish-fawn (?burnt) very fine-grained; Chalk Group. D.30.2, T.12.6, perforation D.9.7mm, Wt.14.5g 22911 sf8104 (P4B) (*Fig.1233*)

6540   Fragment only. Truncated spherical; undecorated; form A1. Chalk, white, very fine-grained; Chalk Group. L.26.8, T.19.8mm, Wt.[6.1 est.18]g 22800 sf8340 (P4B)

6541   Hemispherical shape; undecorated; form A1. Chalk, pale greyish-fawn, fine-grained; Chalk Group, possibly Ferriby Chalk Formation. D.36.8, T.22.0, perforation D.9.9mm, Wt.33.3g 22815 sf8360 (P4B) (*Fig.1233*)

6542   Hemispherical; form A1. Limestone, pale grey, fine-grained, silty, with few thin calcite veins, few small casts and moulds of shell debris and a few calcite minute shell fragments, including paired shells, possibly ostracods; 'granular' limestone, provenance uncertain. D.34.7, T.18.9, perforation D.10.7mm, Wt.28.0g 19390 sf8884 (P4B) (*Fig.1233*)

6545   Rounded truncated cone shape; undecorated; form A2. Chalk, white, very fine-grained; Chalk Group. D.33.1, T.16.6, perforation D.9.0mm, Wt.27.4g 22845 sf8037 (P4B)

6546   Rounded truncated cone shape; undecorated; form A2. Limestone, pale brownish-grey, fine- to medium-grained, with moderately sorted subangular to rounded grains; 'granular' limestone, provenance uncertain. D.35.4, T.21.5, perforation D.9.4mm, Wt.33.9g 22713 sf7884 (P4B)

6547   Rounded truncated cone shape; undecorated; form A2. Limestone, pale brownish-grey, fine- to medium-grained, with moderately sorted, subangular to rounded grains; 'granular' limestone, provenance uncertain. D.35.4, T.21.5, perforation D.9.4mm, Wt.33.9g 22713 sf7884 (P4B) (*Fig.1233*)

6548   Fragment only. Asymmetrical, truncated biconical; tooling marks on sides; decorated on bottom with two roughly incised encircling lines, filled with diagonals; form A2. Chalk, white, fine-grained; Chalk Group, possibly Ferriby Chalk Formation. D.37.7, T.24.7mm, Wt.[23.3, est.47]g 22309 sf7526 (P5A) (*Fig.1233*)

6549   Fragment only. Asymmetrical, truncated biconical; all faces decorated with incised oblique and vertical lines; form A2. Chalk, white, fine-grained, with few scattered small ?quartz grains, spicules and foraminifera; Chalk Group, probably Ferriby Chalk Formation. D.32.0, T.20.5, Wt.[11.6, est.29]g 7232 sf1291 (P5B) (*Fig.1233*)

6552   Fragment only. One flat face, with curving sides (original shape not clear); sides decorated with fields of incised cross-hatching; two encircling grooves around perforation; form A1/2 or B. Limestone, pale grey with pale brown mottling, fine-grained, almost entirely dolomite, with pseudo-septarian ?dessication cracks on split surface; probably Lower Magnesian Limestone but could be Upper Magnesian Limestone. D.31.6, T.11.3mm, Wt.14.1g 19390 sf9049 (P4B) (*Fig.1233*)

6553   Fragment only. One flat face with curving sides, possibly hemispherical originally; decorated with incised ring-and-dot, in a row around sides; form A1/2 or B. Siltstone, medium grey, micaceous, slightly fissile; probably Coal Measures but could be Millstone Grit. D.35.7, T.[7.6]mm, Wt.[12.2]g 19390 sf9108 (P4B)

6554   Shallow, rounded cylindrical shape with vertical rilling; form B. Chalk, white, very fine-grained; Chalk Group. D.21.9, T.9.0, perforation D.9.3mm, Wt.42.7g 25350 sf8558 (P4B) (*Fig.1233*)

6555   Irregular, rounded cylindrical shape; undecorated; form B. Chalk, white, very fine-grained; Chalk Group. D.42.7, T.16.5, perforation D.12.0mm, Wt 30.4g 23700 sf7793 (P4B) (*Fig.1233*)

6556   Octagonal cylinder; undecorated; form B. Limestone or chalk, greyish-white, fine- to medium-grained, comprising closely packed subangular to subrounded grains with slight intergranular porosity; probably 'granular' limestone of uncertain provenance, but could be abnormally coarse-grained chalk from Ferriby Chalk Formation of Chalk Group. D.30.5, T.20.5, perforation D.9.1mm, Wt.29.3g 22415 sf7678 (P4B) (*Fig.1233*)

6557   Rounded cylindrical shape; appears to be light brown with white coating; incised zig-zag decoration on both flat faces; form B. Chalk, very fine-grained; Chalk Group. D.33.9, T.12.1, perforation D.10.8mm, Wt.15.9g 15173 sf4199 (P5A) (*Fig.1233*)

6558   Uneven cylindrical shape; incised lines radiating from upper and lower faces; form B. Chalk, white, very fine-grained, with foraminifera; Chalk Group. D.35.2, T.25.0, perforation D.9.6mm, Wt.30.0g 18536 sf7043 (P5A) (*Fig.1233*)

6559   Almost complete. Irregular cylindrical shape; undecorated; form B. Limestone, pale brownish-grey with slightly pinkish tinge in places (?burnt), fine-grained, microcellular dolomitic; upper part of Lower Magnesian Limestone. D.40.7, T.17.7, perforation D.12.8, Wt.32.8g 18536 sf7044 (P5A) (*Fig.1233*)

6560   Fragment only. Shallow rounded cylindrical shape; incised lines radiating from central hole, top and bottom; form B. Chalk, white, very fine-grained; Chalk Group. L.36.5, T.12.7mm, Wt.[9.6, est.21]g 20181 sf7060 (P5A) (*Fig.1233*)

6561   Shallow cylindrical shape, with rounded sides; three groups of incised lines around circumference. Form B. Off-white with light brown coating. Chalk, white, very fine-grained; Chalk Group. D.28.3, T.12.6, perforation D.10.4mm, Wt.9.6g 14922 sf6960 (P5A) (*Fig.1233*)

6562   Almost complete. Cylindrical shape; undecorated; chipped; form B. Chalk, very fine-grained; Chalk Group. D.37.1, T.17.8, perforation D.11.0mm, Wt.28.5g 1092 sf318 (P5B)

6563   Irregular shallow cylindrical shape; undecorated; form B. Chalk, white, very fine-grained; Chalk Group. D.35.8, T.10.4, perforation D.11.2mm, Wt.15.9g 15663 sf4569 (P5B)

6567   Fragment only. Faceted, subspherical shape, with incised decoration of zones of dots, diamonds, zig-zags and cross-hatching; appears to have been re-used, as second hole has been drilled crossways to first. Form B/C. Chalk, white, very fine-grained; Chalk Group. L.26.2, T.18.8mm, Wt.[5.4, est.16]g sf3339 3543 (P5Cr) (*Fig.1233*)

9249   Irregularly shaped, flattened hemispherical/disc-shaped; undecorated; form A1. Siltstone or silty mudstone, medium grey micaceous; probably Coal Measures, but could be Millstone Grit. D.31.1, T.7.8, perforation D.9.6mm, Wt.9.8g 26181 sf8645 (P1/3)

9250   Incomplete. Truncated biconical shape, with band of incised lines around one face; form A1 or A2. Siltstone, medium to dark grey, slightly micaceous; probably Coal Measures but could be Millstone Grit. D.37.5, T.[15.8]mm, Wt.[31.4, est.36]g 26200 sf9078 (P3)

9251   Fragment only. Original shape/form not known; two deep grooves around central hole on only surviving face. Sandstone, pale brownish-grey, fine-grained, slightly micromicaceous, slightly calcareous, silty; Coal Measures or (Middle Jurassic) Ravenscar Group. D.29.9, T.[7.7]mm, Wt.[4.8]g 30713 sf12008 (P3)

9252   Hemispherical shape, with deep encircling grooves on upper face and sides; form A1. Crizzled appearance. Chalk, pale greyish-brown, fine-grained; Chalk Group, possibly Ferriby Chalk Formation. D.38.0, T.17.1, perforation D.10.0mm, Wt.26.4g 33072 sf12706 (P3)

9253   Deep hemispherical shape; undecorated; form A1. Chalk, white, very fine-grained; Chalk Group. D.38.7, T.21.4, perforation D.11.5mm, Wt.39.2g 32549 sf13202 (P3)

9254   Almost complete. Hemispherical shape, undecorated; form A1. Chalk, white, very fine-grained; Chalk Group. D.40.0, T.22.2, perforation D.11.1mm, Wt.34.1g 34244 sf13640 (P3)

9255   Incomplete. Rounded biconical shape, undecorated; cracked; form C. Chalk, white, very fine-grained; Chalk Group. D.33.0, T.24.7mm, Wt.[11.6, est.25]g 32969 sf13905 (P3)

9256   Incomplete. Flattened and rounded hemispherical shape; undecorated; form A1. Chalk, greyish-fawn, fine-grained; Chalk Group, possibly Ferriby Chalk Formation. D.38.8, T.17.2mm, Wt.[17.3, est.29]g 26427 sf8833 (P4A)

9257   Flattened hemispherical shape; undecorated; form A1. Chalk, brownish-white, fine-grained; Chalk Group, possibly Ferriby Chalk Formation. D.27.9, T.11.8, perforation D.8.7mm, Wt.11.2g 26616 sf8877 (P4A)

9258   Almost complete. Truncated hemispherical shape, with four encircling incised lines; form A1. Mudstone, medium to dark grey, micromicaceous, slightly fissile, silty; probably Coal Measures, but could be Millstone Grit. D.33.7, T.14.7, perforation D.10.6mm, Wt.20.4g 27422 sf9732 (P4A)

9259 Hemispherical shape, undecorated; form A1. Chalk, white, very fine-grained; Chalk Group. D.24.8, T.13.4, perforation D.8.6mm, Wt.9.1g 30132 sf10600 (P4A)

9260 Incomplete. Hemispherical shape; pale grey with black coating, which covers all worked surfaces, except where chipped; undecorated; form A1. Limestone, pale grey lower part with sharp, apparently bedded, junction with pale brownish-grey upper part, fine-grained, silty, with moderately sorted angular to subrounded grains and scattered white, brown and 'hollow' short parallel streaks; 'streaky granular' limestone, provenance uncertain. D.31.0, T.20.6mm, Wt.[18.1, est.36]g 30274 sf11034 (P4A)

9261 Thin fragment with one flat face; undecorated; form A or B. Mudstone, medium slightly brownish-grey, ?ferruginous, slightly calcareous, silty, non-fissile, with subconchoidal fracture. Upper Carboniferous or Jurassic. D.36.7, T.[6.2]mm, Wt.[4.8]g 30352 sf11475 (P4A)

9262 Hemispherical shape with deep rilling around circumference and around hole; form A1. Chalk, greyish-white, fine-grained; Chalk Group, possibly Ferriby Chalk Formation. D.33.0, T.19.6, perforation D.9.8mm, Wt.24.8g 20427 sf6995 (P4B)

9263 Fragment only. Truncated conical shape, undecorated; form A2. Chalk, white, very fine-grained; Chalk Group. L.30.7, T.19.6mm, Wt.[6.58, est.18]g 20667 sf7553 (P4B)

9264 Rounded truncated cone, undecorated; form A2. Chalk, pale yellowish-fawn, fine-grained; Chalk Group, possibly Ferriby Chalk Formation. D.35.9, T.20.7, perforation D.12.8mm, Wt.31.6g. 23531 sf7619 (P4B)

9265 Complete but with flaking surface. Rounded truncated cone shape; single groove around circumference; form A2. Sandstone, pale greyish-brown, with ?ferruginous pale orange-brown patches, soft, friable, porous, very fine-grained, silty and ferruginous; Coal Measures or one of non-marine parts of (Middle Jurassic) Ravenscar Group. D.33.7, T.19.4, perforation D.9.7mm, Wt.32.0g 22590 sf7738 (P4B)

9266 Rounded cylindrical; undecorated; form B. Limestone or chalk, greyish-white, fine- to medium-grained, comprising closely packed subangular to subrounded grains with slight intergranular porosity; probably 'granular' limestone of uncertain provenance but could be abnormally coarsely-grained chalk from Ferriby Chalk Formation of Chalk Group. D.34.7, T.15.2, perforation D.9.2mm, Wt.25.8g 22560 sf7785 (P4B)

9267 Incomplete, fragmented. Hemispherical shape; shallow incised lines around lower hole; form A1. Limestone, pale yellow to brownish-grey, fine-grained, almost entirely dolomitic; probably Lower Magnesian Limestone but could be Upper Magnesian Limestone. D.34.8, T.[18.1]mm, Wt.[22.3, est.30]g 22679 sf7942 (P4B)

9268 Hemispherical shape; undecorated; form A1. Chalk, white, very fine-grained; Chalk Group. D.30.0, T.14.7, perforation D.10.0mm, Wt.14.8g 22679 sf7945 (P4B)

9269 Truncated biconical shape; decorated on sides with incised diagonals and cross-hatching; form B. Chalk, white, very fine-grained; Chalk Group. D.33.5, T.26.0, perforation D.13.4mm, Wt.37.9g 22679 sf7950 (P4B)

9270 Fragment only. Truncated biconical shape, with sharply cut facets; incised zig-zag decoration top and bottom; form B. Chalk, white, very fine-grained; Chalk Group. D.[26.6], T.21.6mm, Wt.[5.6, est.22]g 23794 sf7988 (P4B)

9271 Rounded cylindrical shape; undecorated; form B. Chalk, white, very fine-grained; Chalk Group. D.31.2, T.21.3, perforation D.11.3mm, Wt.20.6g 22845 sf8023 (P4B)

9272 Hemispherical; fine incised lines around circumference; form A1. Chalk, white, very fine-grained; Chalk Group. D.31.9, T.18.0, perforation D.9.8mm, Wt.21.0g 22590 sf8085 (P4B)

9273 Fragment only. Hemispherical shape; undecorated; form A1. Chalk, greyish-white, fine-grained; Chalk Group, possibly Ferriby Chalk Formation. L.31.7, T.14.6mm, Wt.[10.0, est.20]g 25257 sf8329 (P4B)

9274 Incomplete, fragmented, ?hemispherical shape with groove around circumference; form ?A1. Mudstone, dark grey fissile, micaceous silty; probably Coal Measures but could be Millstone Grit. D.28.4, T.9.1mm, Wt.[7.5, est.?]g 24241 sf8449 (P4B)

9275 Shallow cylinder with deep rilling on top, bottom and sides; form B or C. Chalk, white, very fine-grained, with scattered foraminifera; Chalk Group. D.42.0, T.15.6, perforation D.8.9mm, Wt.29.4g 24787 sf8484 (P4B)

9276 Fragment only. Rounded truncated cone shape; undecorated; form A2. Limestone, pale grey, fine- to medium-grained, with moderately sorted subangular to subrounded grains, numerous thin, short, parallel hollows, giving a 'streaky' appearance, and a small ?shell mould; 'streaky granular' limestone, provenance uncertain. L.28.7, T.21.4mm, Wt.[9.8, est.34]g 25350 sf8586 (P4B)

9277 Rounded truncated cone shape; undecorated; form A2. Limestone, pale grey, fine- to medium-grained, with moderately sorted subangular to rounded grains; 'granular limestone', provenance uncertain. D.33.1, T.17.6, perforation D.8.9mm, Wt.23.1g 25450 sf8638 (P4B)

9278 Almost complete but fragmented. Rounded truncated cone shape, with fine encircling incised lines arranged in two zones; form A1. Limestone, pale grey with ?ferruginous pale orange-brown mottling, fine-grained, substantially dolomitic; probably Lower Magnesian Limestone but could be Upper Magnesian Limestone. D.30.8, T.18.5mm, Wt.[17.0]g 19390 sf9059 (P4B)

9279 Incomplete. Flattened hemispherical shape; chipped; black patches, ?charred; undecorated; form A1. Chalk, greyish-white, fine-grained; Chalk Group, possibly Ferriby Chalk Formation. D.33.1, T.14.3mm, Wt.[17.0, est.23]g 26254 sf9153 (P4B)

9280 Incomplete. Shallow, rounded cylindrical; shallow grooves radiating from central perforation at top and bottom; form B. Chalk, white, very fine-grained; Chalk Group. D.33.8, T.10.8mm, Wt.[12.4, est.14]g 25725 sf9510 (P4B)

9281 Hemispherical shape; undecorated; form A1. Chalk, white, very fine-grained; Chalk Group. D.40.7, T.24.8, perforation D.9.5mm, Wt.54.8g 25725 sf9514 (P4B)

9282 Fragment only. Irregular, chamfered biconical shape; undecorated; form C. Chalk, white, very fine-grained; Chalk Group. L.37.9, T14.5mm, Wt.[10.7, est.27]g 25780 sf9654 (P4B)

9283 Fragment only. Shallow, truncated cone shape; undecorated; form A2. Chalk, pale grey, fine-grained, with scattered subangular to subrounded ?microbioclastic grains in creamy white matrix; Chalk Group, possibly Ferriby Chalk Formation. L.42.5, T.14.6mm, Wt.[15.6, est.39]g 25860 sf9784 (P4B)

9284 Fragment only; part of same whorl as 9285. Truncated biconical shape with two deep grooves around central hole; form B, or perhaps C. Chalk, white, very fine-grained; Chalk Group. L.34.2, T.16.7mm, Wt.[8.8, est.30]g 27509 sf10037 (P4B)

9285 Fragment only; part of same whorl as 9284. L.27.0, T.16.7mm, Wt.[6.6, est.30]g 27504 sf10054 (P4B)

9286 Fragment only. Rounded cylindrical shape, slightly tapering; vertical scratches on sides; form A2. Limestone, pale grey fine- to (slightly) medium-grained, with moderately sorted angular to subrounded grains; 'granular' limestone, provenance uncertain. D.32.8, T.19.6mm, Wt.[14.4, est.29]g 28356 sf10401 (P4B)

9287 Irregularly worked cylindrical shape; undecorated; form B. Chalk, white, very fine-grained; Chalk Group. D.33.1,

T.14.2, perforation D.11.3mm, Wt.15.4g 27341 sf12368 (P4B)

9288 Fragment only. Flattened hemispherical shape; undecorated; surfaces stained, probably with iron oxide; form A2. Limestone, greyish-white with orange ?ferruginous patches, fine- to medium-grained, silty, with moderately sorted angular to subrounded grains and scattered white and hollow, short, parallel streaks; 'streaky granular' limestone, provenance uncertain. L.34.4, T.14.6mm, Wt.[10.3, est.23]g 35451 sf13950 (P4B)

9289 Fragment only. Hemispherical shape, with flat base; undecorated; surfaces stained, probably with iron oxide; form A2. Limestone, greyish-white with pale yellowish-brown ?ferruginous patches; fine- to medium-grained silty, with moderately sorted angular to subrounded grains and scattered white and hollow, short, parallel streaks; 'streaky granular' limestone, provenance uncertain. L.36.4, T.18.7mm, Wt.[12.9, est.39]g 35483 sf13977 (P4B)

9290 Fragment only. Rounded cylindrical shape; undecorated; form B. Limestone, pale brownish-grey, fine-grained, microcellular dolomitic; upper part of Lower Magnesian Limestone. L.31.9, T.12.6mm, Wt.[6.6, est.13]g 22309 sf7538 (P5A)

9291 Fragment only. Shaved biconical shape; grooves around central perforation at top; form B, or perhaps A2. Chalk, white, very fine-grained, with spicules and foraminifera; Chalk Group. D.43.5, T.14.5mm, Wt.[14.8, est.30]g 26868 sf9379 (P5A)

9292 Fragment only. Rounded broad cone shape; undecorated; form A1. Limestone, pale grey, fine-grained, silty; 'granular' limestone, provenance uncertain. L.29.8, T.16.1mm, Wt.[7.6, est.26]g 8011 sf669 (P5B)

9293 Fragment only. Hemispherical with tapering lower half; undecorated; form A1. Uncertain lithology: dark grey, hard, non-carbonate, cryptocrystalline material with few minute subrounded voids and a thin (c.1mm wide) white streak parallel to, but c.2–4mm inside, outer surface of whorl; provenance uncertain. L.32.0mm, T.20.4mm, Wt.[9.9, est.26]g 7204 sf1000 (P5B)

9294 Rounded cylindrical shape; undecorated; lathe marks; form B. Chalk, greyish-white, fine-grained; Chalk Group, possibly Ferriby Chalk Formation. D.34.8, T.24.4, perforation D.11.6mm, Wt.40.8g 1595 sf1554 (P5B)

9295 Fragment only. Shaved globular; undecorated; form B. Chalk, brownish-white, fine-grained; Chalk Group, possibly Ferriby Chalk Formation. D.36.4, T.17.2, perforation D.12.0mm, Wt.[14.8, est.30]g 7473 sf1732 (P5B)

9296 Irregular shallow cylindrical shape; undecorated; possibly abraded and therefore diminished in size; form B. Chalk, white, very fine-grained; Chalk Group. D.26.6, T.10.4, perforation D.10.3mm, Wt.[6.53]g 9726 sf3010 (P5B)

9297 Shaved globular shape; encircling grooves at upper edge, middle and bottom; form A1. Chalk, very fine-grained; Chalk Group. D.25.9, T.14.8, perforation D.7.3mm, Wt.8.42g 14005 sf4180 (P5B)

9298 Fragment only. Rounded cylindrical shape; undecorated; form B. Chalk, greyish-white, fine-grained; Chalk Group, possibly Ferriby Chalk Formation. L.35.9, T.17.2mm, Wt.[12.8, est.32]g 6429 sf5307 (P5B)

9299 Fragment only. Rounded cylindrical shape; scratches top, bottom and sides; form B. Chalk, greyish-white with pink tinge in places (?burnt), fine-grained with rounded ?microbioclastic grains; Chalk Group, possibly Ferriby Chalk Formation. L.24.5, T.18.8mm, Wt.[7.86, est.30]g 6433 sf6202 (P5B)

9300 Thin fragment, representing upper face only. Original shape not clear. Chalk, white, hard, very fine-grained; Chalk Group. L.34.0, T.[6.6], perforation D.7.6mm, Wt.[6.6,est.?]g 20052 sf6327 (P5B)

9301 Flattened hemispherical shape; undecorated; form A2. Siltstone, medium grey micro-mottled, with numerous minute dark grey polygonal to rounded masses in a paler matrix and with small void, possibly a shell-mould; probably Lower Palaeozoic or Upper Carboniferous. D.39.8, T.16.2, perforation D.9.5mm, Wt.36.6g 19285 sf6669 (P5B)

9302 Incomplete. Hemispherical shape; undecorated; surface crizzled; form A1. Chalk, white, very fine-grained; Chalk Group. D.45.6, T.24.5mm, Wt.[45.8, est.50]g 19320 sf6838 (P5B)

9303 Fragment only. Irregularly rounded cylindrical shape; undecorated; form B. Chalk, greyish-white, fine-grained; Chalk Group, possibly Ferriby Chalk Formation. D.34.3, T.15.8mm, Wt.[10.2, est.20]g 19460 sf7029 (P5B)

9304 Rounded truncated cone shape; undecorated; chipped; form A1. Chalk, white, very fine-grained; Chalk Group. D.35.0, T.21.4, perforation D.12.0mm, Wt.32.2g 21382 sf8609 (P5B)

9305 Incomplete? Hemispherical, upper face broken; encircling grooves on lower part; form A1. Siltstone, medium to dark grey, slightly micaceous, slightly fissile, calcareous; probably Lias Group (Lower Jurassic) but could be from Upper Jurassic. D.35.4, T.[13.8]mm, Wt.[22.2]g 26245 sf9168 (P5B)

9306 Fragment only. Shallow rounded biconical shape, with depression around hole at top and bottom; undecorated; form C. Chalk, white, very fine-grained; Chalk Group. D.34.9, T.13.8mm, Wt.[8.3, est.17]g 21597 sf9235 (P5B)

Hones

Sandstone

4409 Fragment with streaks of haematite on two of its sides. Of squarish section, both ends and part of two surfaces broken away. Evidence of burning and heat fractures throughout. Signs of wear on all surviving surfaces. Pale greyish-red, fine-grained with angular to subangular grains, moderately to fairly well sorted and fairly well compacted, with scattered muscovite. Upper Carboniferous, probably Coal Measures. Reddish colour probably due to heat. L.62.0, W.36.0, T.25.0mm 27819 sf10624 (P3)

9307 Fragment of subrectangular section with rounded end. The other end and part of the surface is roughly broken away and there are large cracks throughout the hone. Pale to medium grey, fine- to medium-grained with angular to subrounded grains, poorly sorted and well compacted, with appreciable scattered muscovite (including some large rounded flakes) and sparse dark minerals and/or rock fragments. Lower Palaeozoic or (more probably) Carboniferous. L.60.0, W.34.0, T.15.0mm 26181 sf9165 (P1/3)

9308 Fragment, of rectangular section, one end broken and the other worn to a rounded point. All four surfaces show signs of wear. Pale grey, fine-grained with angular to subangular grains, well sorted and well compacted, with sparse muscovite. Upper Carboniferous, probably Coal Measures. L.60.0, W.42.0, T.15.0mm 32755 sf14203 (P1/3)

9309 Rectangular section at one end tapering towards the other. All surfaces show signs of wear. Medium grey, fine-grained with angular to subangular grains, moderately sorted and well compacted, with appreciable scattered muscovite and sparse dark minerals and/or rock fragments, and ?silica matrix. Lower Palaeozoic or (more probably) Carboniferous. L.57.0, W.30.0, T.22.0mm 30585 sf1820 (P3)

9310 Fragment, broken away at one end. Of rectangular section, all four surfaces show signs of wear. Long shallow depression worn into upper surface. Pale grey, fine-grained with angular to subangular grains, well sorted and fairly well compacted, with appreciable muscovite mainly concentrated on fissile laminae. Coal Measures of Elland Flags type. L.102.0, W.39.9, T.9.0mm 24946 sf8819 (P3) (*Fig.1205*)

9311 Fragment, one end broken away. Of square section, all four surfaces worn, part of one surface not dressed. Pale grey, very fine- to fine-grained with subangular to subrounded grains, well sorted and moderately compacted, with strongly calcareous matrix (almost sandy limestone). Middle or Upper Jurassic. L.60.0, W.25.0, T.23.0mm 26202 sf9243 (P3)

9312 Roughly square section but now rounded due to wear on all surfaces. Medium to dark grey, fine-grained with indiscernible grain shapes, well sorted and well compacted, with scattered muscovite and some dark minerals and/or rock fragments. Lower Palaeozoic or (more probably) Carboniferous. L.128.0, W.30.0, T.20.0mm 26631 sf9436 (P3) (*Fig.1205*)

9313 Fragment, one end broken away. Of roughly rectangular section but worn smooth and rounded on all surfaces and edges. Pale to medium grey, fine-grained with subangular to subrounded grain, well sorted and fairly well compacted, with sparse muscovite, sparse dark minerals and/or rock fragments, and slightly calcareous matrix. Carboniferous or Jurassic. Worn, non-elongate, shape suggests erratic. L.63.0, W.47.0, T.17.5mm 28066 sf10071 (P3)

9314 Fragment, broken axially and at both ends. Two surviving surfaces show signs of wear. Sandstone, pale grey to partly greyish-pink, fine-grained with angular to subangular grains, well sorted and well compacted. Upper Carboniferous, probably Coal Measures. Partly worn shape suggests fragment of erratic. Pink colour suggests heat. L.22.0, W.25.0, T.18mm 27819 sf10740 (P3)

9315 Fragment. Both ends and most of three surfaces broken away; where surfaces survive these are worn smooth. Pale to medium brownish-grey, fine-grained with angular to subangular grains, well sorted and fairly well compacted, with abundant muscovite and sparse bronze-coloured mica (including large flakes) concentrated on fissile laminae. Coal Measure of Elland Flags type. L.50.0, W.25.0, T.25.0mm 25990 sf10744 (P3)

9316 Fragment, of ovoid section. One end broken away and all other surfaces smoothed and rounded. Medium grey, fine-grained with angular to subangular grains, well sorted and highly compacted, with sparse muscovite and dark minerals and/or fragments. Lower Palaeozoic or (less probably) Carboniferous. L.55.0, W.33.0, T.18.0mm 31061 sf10935 (P3)

9317 Rectangular section at one end tapering towards the other. All surfaces show signs of wear. Sandstone, medium grey, fine-grained with angular to subangular grains, moderately sorted and well compacted, with appreciable scattered muscovite and sparse dark minerals and/or rock fragments, and ?silica matrix. Lower Palaeozoic or (more probably) Carboniferous. L.57.0, W.30.0, T.22.0mm 30585 sf11820 (P3) (*Fig.1205*)

9318 Roughly ovoid section. All surfaces worn and rounded, especially in the centre of the hone. Pale brownish-grey, fine-grained with angular to subangular grains, moderately sorted and fairly well compacted, with sparse muscovite. Upper Carboniferous, probably Coal Measures. L.88.0, W.20.0, T.14.0mm 33017 sf12625 (P3) (*Fig.1205*)

9319 Fragment, broken away at one end. Of roughly rectangular section but worn rounded at end and on edges. Medium grey, fine-grained with angular to subangular grains, moderately sorted and fairly well compacted, with sparse muscovite. Upper Carboniferous, probably Coal Measures. L.64.0, W.52.0, T.15.0mm 20893 sf12718 (P3)

9320 Fragment, broken away at both ends. One plane either not dressed or flaked off; the three other surfaces show signs of wear. Upper plane has a shallow rectangular depression worn into the surface. Pale grey, fine-grained with subangular to subrounded grains, fairly well sorted and fairly well compacted, with sparse muscovite, a few minute ovoid masses (possibly ooliths) and a slightly calcareous matrix; slightly fissile along vague laminae. Middle or Upper Jurassic. Traces of brick-red mortar adhering. L.47.0, W.30.0, T.14.0mm 25593 sf9062 (P4A)

9321 Fragment, lower plane flaked off. Little evidence of wear on most surfaces. Medium grey, fine-grained with angular to subangular grains, moderately sorted and fairly well compacted, with scattered muscovite (including large flakes up to 25mm wide). Upper Carboniferous, probably Coal Measures. L.103.0, W.29.0, T.19.0mm 27440 sf9873 (P4A)

9322 Square section. Two surfaces and one edge roughly dressed, the other edges and surface worn smooth. Medium to dark grey, fine-grained with angular to subangular grains, moderately sorted and well compacted, with abundant scattered muscovite and some dark minerals and/or rock fragments. Lower Palaeozoic or (more probably) Carboniferous. L.34.0, W.29.0, T.35.0mm 27485 sf9894 (P4A) (*Fig.1205*)

9323 Fragment, both ends broken away, of rectangular section. Two dressed surfaces of which one worn smooth. Pale grey, fine-grained with angular to subrounded grains, moderately to well sorted and fairly well compacted, with abundant muscovite concentrated on fissile laminae. Coal Measures of Elland Flags type. L.35.0, W.14.0, T.8.0mm 25987 sf10132 (P4A)

9324 Fragment, of rectangular section. Broken away at one end and one edge. Surviving surfaces and edge show signs of wear. Pale to medium grey, fine-grained and silty with subangular to subrounded grains, well sorted and fairly well compacted, with appreciable muscovite and some bronze-coloured mica partly concentrated on fissile laminae. Coal Measures of Elland Flags type. L.61.0, W.48.0, T.8.0mm 9487 sf2075 (P4B)

9325 Flat ovoid shape and ovoid section, worn on edges and one surface. Pale grey, fine-grained with mainly subangular grains, well sorted and fairly well compacted, with scattered muscovite. Upper Carboniferous, probably Coal Measures. L.94.0, W.48.0, T.18.0mm 4793 sf7072 (P4B)

9326 Fragment, of triangular section. One end roughly dressed, the other broken away, all surfaces worn smooth. Medium grey, fine-grained with mainly angular grains, well sorted and highly compacted, with siliceous matrix. Lower Palaeozoic or (less probably) Carboniferous. L.23.0, W.16.0, T.10.0mm 22306 sf7571 (P4B) (*Fig.1205*)

9327 Fragment, one end broken away. Of rectangular section and all surfaces and edges worn smooth. Medium brownish-grey, fine-grained with mainly subangular grains, well sorted and well compacted, with sparse muscovite. Upper Carboniferous, probably Coal Measures. L.77.0, W.60.0, T.36.0mm 25330 sf8405 (P4B) (*Fig.1205*)

9328 Fragment, one end broken away. Of subrectangular section; all surfaces and ends worn smooth and rounded. Pale grey with thin medium grey layers, fine-grained with angular to subangular grains, moderately well sorted and well compacted, with appreciable scattered muscovite. Lower Palaeozoic or (more probably) Carboniferous. L.91.0, W.31.0, T.23.0mm 26171 sf8820 (P4B)

9329 Fragment. Split axially so one entire surface missing. Roughly rectangular in shape with axial perforation drilled into top. Pale to medium grey, fine-grained and silty with mainly subangular grains, well sorted and well compacted, with appreciable muscovite partly concentrated on slightly fissile laminae. Coal Measures of Elland Flags type. L.52.0, W.19.0, T.8.0mm 26491 sf9032 (P4B) (*Fig.1205*)

9330 Fragment. Of ovoid section which flattens towards top. Broken away across axial perforation at the top. Perforation drilled from two sides. All surfaces and edges worn smooth and rounded, apart from one plane where surface sheared off. Medium to dark grey, fine-grained with angular to subangular grains, moderately sorted and well compacted, with abundant scattered muscovite, sparse biotite, and some dark minerals and/or rock fragments. Lower Palaeozoic or (more probably) Carboniferous. L.82.0, W.30.0, T.18.0mm 25622 sf9327 (P4B) (Fig.1205)

9331 Square section. All surfaces and edges worn smooth. Dark grey, fine-grained with indiscernible grain shapes, moderately sorted and well compacted, with scattered muscovite, sparse biotite, appreciable dark minerals and/or rock fragments, and ?siliceous matrix. Lower Palaeozoic or (more probably) Carboniferous. L.49.0, W.18.0, T.16.0mm 19634 sf9651 (P4B) (Fig.1205)

9332 Fragment, of rectangular section. Broken at one end and roughly dressed at other. Surfaces and edges worn smooth. Very shallow short linear grooves worn into one surface. Medium grey, fine-grained with angular to subangular grains, well sorted and well compacted. Upper Carboniferous, probably Coal Measures. L.62.0, W.32.0, T.18.0mm 26960 sf9662 (P4B)

9333 Fragment, of roughly rectangular section, worn on one surface. Pale grey, fine-grained with angular to subrounded grains, moderately sorted and fairly well compacted, with appreciable muscovite on bedding-plane surfaces, and sparse dark minerals and/or rock fragments. Coal Measures of Elland Flags type. L.19.0, W.21.0, T.14.0mm 25934 sf9999 (P4B)

9334 Fragment, rectangular section, little sign of wear. One end sawn, the other broken. Pale grey, fine- to medium-grained with angular to subrounded grains, poorly sorted and moderately compacted, with scattered muscovite. Upper Carboniferous. L.24.0, W.9.0, T.8.0mm 25934 sf10002 (P4B)

9335 Fragment, medium grey, fine-grained with angular to subangular grains, moderately sorted and well compacted, with appreciable scattered muscovite, sparse dark minerals and/or rock fragments, and ?siliceous matrix. Lower Palaeozoic or (more probably) Carboniferous. L.21.0, W.20.0, T.5.0mm 25934 sf10005 (P4B)

9336 Fragments (4). One or two worn surfaces on each fragment. Pale to medium brownish-grey, fine-grained with angular to subangular grains, fairly well sorted and fairly well compacted with appreciable muscovite and some bronze-coloured mica concentrated on fissile laminae. Coal Measures of Elland Flags type. L.41.0, W.13.0, T.10.0mm 25934 sf10101 (P4B)

9337 Fragment of trapezoidal section, broken at both ends. All surfaces worn smooth. Pale grey, fine- to medium-grained with angular to subrounded grains, moderately sorted and moderately compacted, with sparse scattered muscovite. Upper Carboniferous. L.25.0, W.15.0, T.9.0mm 25934 sf10112 (P4B)

9338 Fragment. Square section, worn on two surfaces. Pale grey, fine- to medium-grained with angular to subrounded grains, moderately sorted and fairly well compacted, with sparse muscovite. Upper Carboniferous. L.14.0, W.14.0, T.14.0mm 25934 sf10139 (P4B)

9339 Rectangular section. Upper and lower surfaces and one edge worn smooth, other edge surface broken away. Both ends roughly dressed. Pale grey, fine-grained with angular to subangular grains, well sorted and fairly well compacted, with sparse muscovite; thin bedded and apparently grain-size layered. Upper Carboniferous, probably Coal Measures. L.72.0, W.31.0, T.12.0mm 28904 sf12571 (P4B)

9340 Ovoid section. Both ends sawn and roughly dressed, all other surfaces worn smooth and rounded. Pale brownish-grey, fine- to (slightly) medium-grained with angular to subrounded grains, moderately sorted and fairly well compacted, with sparse muscovite. Upper Carboniferous, probably Coal Measures. L.70.0, W.31.0, T.25.0mm 20747 sf12617 (P4B) (Fig.1205)

9341 Flattened ovoid section. All surfaces worn smooth and rounded. Medium to dark grey, fine-grained with indiscernible grain shapes, apparently fairly well sorted, highly compacted. Lower Palaeozoic or (less probably) Carboniferous. L.84.0, W.35.0, T.20.0mm 19643 sf12724 (P4B)

9342 Flattened ovoid section. All surfaces worn smooth and rounded except one edge which is worn flat. Medium grey with pale grey laminae, fine-grained with indiscernible grain shapes, apparently fairly well sorted and well compacted, with laminae disrupted by bioturbation or slumping. Upper Carboniferous. L.104.0, W.30.0, T.24.0mm 31478 sf12892 (P4B) (Fig.1205)

9343 Fragment, of rectangular section. One end and part of one surface broken away, the other end is roughly dressed. Three surfaces worn smooth. Medium grey, fine-grained with angular to subangular grains, moderately sorted and fairly well compacted, with sparse muscovite. Upper Carboniferous, probably Coal Measures. L.83.0, W.45.0, T.28.0mm 19719 sf12904 (P4B)

9344 Fragment, flat profile. Medium grey, fine-grained with angular to subrounded grains, moderately sorted and well compacted, with appreciable scattered muscovite and some dark minerals and/or rock fragments. Lower Palaeozoic or (more probably) Carboniferous. L.29.0, W.12.0, T.3.0mm 25934 sf19608 (P4B)

9345 Rectangular section. Two surfaces and both ends worn smooth; one surface slightly worn and the other roughly dressed. Dark grey with thin irregular medium grey layers and lenses, very fine-grained (fine-grained in paler layers) with indiscernible grain shapes, well sorted and highly compacted, with ?siliceous matrix. Lower Palaeozoic or (less probably) Carboniferous. L.80.0, W.19.0, T.15.0mm 14974 sf6581 (P5A)

9346 Roughly ovoid section. One end and two surfaces broken away; remaining end sawn and surfaces worn smooth and rough. A groove has been roughly chipped along the centre and a shallow groove worn into one edge. Medium grey, fine-grained with angular to subangular grains, moderately sorted and well compacted, with appreciable scattered muscovite, sparse dark minerals and/or rock fragments, and single minute fish fragment, possibly scale. Lower Palaeozoic or (more probably) Carboniferous. L.50.0, W.35.0, T.17.0mm 20185 sf7034 (P5A) (Fig.1206)

9347 Ovoid section, worn on three surfaces. Pale brownish-grey, fine-grained with angular to subrounded grains, moderately sorted and moderately compacted, with sparse muscovite, strongly calcareous matrix, and abundant thin elongate black ?carbonaceous plant fragments all with same alignment. Probably Middle Jurassic of north-eastern Yorkshire, but could conceivably be Lower Cretaceous of south-eastern England. L.119.0, W.50.0, T.30.0mm 20719 sf7102 (P5A)

9348 Fragment, of rectangular section. Both ends broken away; four surfaces worn smooth, one flaking away. Medium grey, fine- to medium-grained with angular to subangular grains, moderately sorted and well compacted, with appreciable scattered muscovite and sparse dark minerals and/or rock fragments. Lower Palaeozoic. L.43.0, W.48.0, T.30.0mm 22050 sf7236 (P5A)

9349 Rectangular section; all surfaces smoothed and rounded. Medium grey, fine-grained with subangular to subrounded grains, well sorted and fairly well compacted, with sparse muscovite; moderately fissile. Upper Carboniferous, probably Coal Measures. L.76.0, W.25.0, T.10.0mm 22192 sf7379 (P5A) (Fig.1206)

9350 Fragment; one worn surface, all other surfaces, end and section are roughly broken away. Medium grey, fine-grained with subangular to subrounded grains, well sorted and fairly well compacted, with sparse muscovite; apparently laminated but not obviously fissile. Upper Carboniferous, probably Coal Measures. L.85.0, W.20.0, T.25.0mm 22166 sf7383 (P5A)

9351 Flattened ovoid section. All surfaces and both ends worn smooth and rounded; two chips missing, one from each end. Medium to dark grey, fine-grained with angular to subrounded grains, moderately sorted and fairly well compacted, with sparse muscovite and sparse dark minerals and/or rock fragments, and moderately calcareous matrix. Carboniferous or Jurassic. L.127.0, W.40.0, T.15.0mm 22128 sf7455 (P5A) (Fig.1206)

9352 Rectangular section. Both ends sawn, three surfaces worn, the other roughly dressed. Pale to medium grey, fine-grained with angular to subangular grains, well sorted and well compacted, with scattered muscovite and some dark minerals and/or rock fragments. Upper Carboniferous, probably Coal Measures. L.100.0, W.50.0, T.25.0mm 26792 sf9720 (P5A) (Fig.1206)

9353 Rectangular section. One end sawn, the other sawn then broken across; four worn surfaces. Medium grey, fine-grained with angular to subangular grains, moderately to well sorted and well compacted, with some scattered muscovite and sparse dark minerals and/or rock fragments; possibly fissile. Upper Carboniferous probably Coal Measures. L.80.0, W.35.0, T.15.0mm 2875 sf593 (P5B)

9354 Rectangular section. One end sawn, the other broken away; two surfaces worn, the other two broken away. Pale brownish-grey, fine- to (slightly) medium-grained with angular to subangular grains, moderately sorted and fairly well compacted, with some scattered muscovite, sparse ?biotite and other dark minerals and/or rock fragments, and sparse pinkish-white rounded minerals, possibly degraded feldspar; possibly fissile. Upper Carboniferous, probably Coal Measures. L.82.0, W.40.0, T.15.0mm 9722 sf2294 (P5B)

9355 Rectangular section. One end chipped across top, end rounded; very shallow beginnings of perforation drilled on one side; four smoothed surfaces. Dark grey, fine-grained with angular to subangular grains, moderately sorted and well compacted, with abundant scattered muscovite and sparse biotite, other dark minerals and/or rock fragments, and ?siliceous matrix. Lower Palaeozoic or (more probably) Carboniferous. L.90.0, W.24.0, T.14.0mm 9722 sf2996 (P5B) (Fig.1206)

9356 Ovoid section; worn rounded on all surfaces. Medium to dark grey, fine-grained with indiscernible grain shapes, well sorted and highly compacted, with sparse muscovite, biotite and dark minerals and/or rock fragments. Lower Palaeozoic or (less probably) Carboniferous. L.140.0, W.40.0, T.40.0mm 15371 sf4242 (P5B) (Fig.1206)

9357 Approximately square section. One end sawn, the other roughly dressed; four surfaces worn, one has pronounced groove worn into lower part pale grey, fine-grained with angular to subrounded grains, well sorted and fairly well compacted, with some scattered muscovite. Upper Carboniferous, probably Coal Measures. L.63.0, W.30.0, T.22.0mm 15870 sf5125 (P5B) (Fig.1206)

9358 Rectangular section. Three worn surfaces, fourth is broken away. Medium grey with thin dark grey layers, fine-grained with angular to subangular grains, well sorted and highly compacted, with ?siliceous matrix; slightly fissile along darker, ?silty layers. Lower Palaeozoic or (less probably) Carboniferous. L.50.0, W.25.0, T.15.0mm 6425 sf5574 (P5B)

9359 Fragment, of rectangular section. Two ends broken away; four smooth surfaces. Medium to dark grey, fine-grained and mainly angular-grained, well sorted and highly compacted, with siliceous matrix. Lower Palaeozoic. L.21.0, W.21.0, T.12.0mm 15999 sf5713 (P5B)

9360 Rectangular section. Two ends sawn and then worn smooth; all other surfaces worn smooth. Pale brownish-grey, fine-grained with subangular to subrounded grains, fairly well sorted and fairly well compacted. Upper Carboniferous, probably Coal Measures. L.62.0, W.47.0, T.33.0mm 14633 sf6570 (P5B) (Fig.1206)

9361 Fragment, of square section. One end sawn, other end and one surface broken away; three surfaces worn. Medium grey, very fine- to fine-grained with angular to subangular grains, well sorted and highly compacted, with scattered muscovite, sparse biotite, and ?siliceous matrix. Lower Palaeozoic or (less probably) Carboniferous. L.36.0, W.23.0, T.21.0mm 14973 sf6727 (P5B)

9362 Approximately rectangular section; all surfaces worn smooth. Medium grey, fine-grained with angular to subangular grains, moderately sorted and highly compacted, with sparse dark minerals and/or rock fragments. Lower Palaeozoic. L.50.0, W.23.0, T.15.0mm 21919 sf9983 (P5B)

9363 Fragment of irregular section and shape; one worn surface. Medium grey, fine- to medium-grained with angular to subrounded grains, moderately sorted and fairly well compacted, with some scattered muscovite and ?siliceous matrix. Upper Carboniferous. L.78.0, W.65.0, T.23.0mm 20205 sf6441 (P5Cr)

Schist

All schist hones are of Norwegian Ragstone type unless otherwise specified.

9364 Fragment, of rectangular section, both ends broken. Upper surface very worn, especially in one area. Pale grey, fine-grained, quartzitic, micaceous (mainly muscovite). L.60.0, W.34.0, T.15.0mm 26181 sf12245 (P1/3)

9365 Fragment. Both ends broken and all but one worn surface sheared away. As 9364, with biotite. L.70.0, W.28.0, T.9.0mm 26059 sf8787 (P3)

9366 Fragment. Both ends broken away. Upper flat surface and two sides show signs of wear, lower surface not dressed. Two long shallow grooves worn into upper surface. As 9364. L.160.0, W.38.0, T.17.0mm 24766 sf9947 (P3) (Fig.1207)

9367 Fragment, of triangular section and one end broken away. Long deep groove worn into each of the three surfaces, two surfaces show signs of wear elsewhere. As 9364, but slightly darker, with sparse biotite. L.110.0, W.35.0, T.17.0mm 27413 sf10129 (P3) (Fig.1207)

9368 Fragment, broken away at both ends. Of triangular section, upper surface shows signs of wear. As 9364. L.64.0, W.25.0, T.8.0mm 32702 sf14237 (P3)

9369 Fragment, both ends broken away. One plane worn smooth, the other plane and edges not dressed. As 9364, but slightly darker. L.47.0, W.23.0, T.5.0mm 25987 sf10830 (P4A)

9370 Fragment. One surviving edge worn smooth, the other surfaces and ends broken away. Pale to medium grey, very fine- to fine-grained (almost phyllite), quartzitic, micaceous (mainly or all muscovite). ?Norwegian Ragstone type. L.39.0, W.24.0, T.9.0mm 30273 sf11157(P4A)

9371 Fragment, of rectangular section. Broken away at one end, roughly finished at other. Signs of wear on all four faces. Pale grey, fine- to medium-grained, mainly quartzitic (almost metaquartzite, with markedly elongate quartz), moderately micaceous (mainly muscovite). L.58.0, W.11.0, T.22.0mm 9450 sf1945 (P4B) (Fig.1207)

9372 Fragment, of irregular section; two smoothed surfaces partly broken away. As *9370*. ?Norwegian Ragstone type. L.70.0, W.22.0, T.14.0mm 15685 sf4574 (P4B)

9373 Fragment, of rectangular section; one surface shows signs of wear. As *9364*. L.46.0, W.21.0, T.9.0mm 20749 sf7156 (P4B)

9374 Fragment, broken across one end and sawn at the other, worn in the middle. As *9364* with sparse biotite. L.78.0, W.28.0, T.8.5mm 23125 sf7351 (P4B)

9375 Fragment, of roughly triangular section. Wear on one surface. As *9364*. L.40.0, W.16.0, T.9.0mm 22416 sf7604 (P4B)

9376 Fragment, of roughly triangular section. One end partially sawn, other end broken away; two worn surfaces survive. As *9364*. L.60.0, W.28.0, T.10.0mm 22415 sf7682 (P4B)

9377 Fragment, of square section. Saw marks round one end which has been roughly broken away; other end possibly sawn and then worn; signs of wear on all four faces. As *9364*. L.23.0, W.9.0, T.7.5mm 22523 sf7742 (P4B) (*Fig.1207*)

9378 Rectangular section. Perforation at one end, other end roughly broken away. As *9364*. L.40.0, W.10.0, T.6.0mm 23669 sf7748 (P4B) (*Fig.1207*)

9379 Rectangular section, worn on one edge, sawn at both ends. As *9364*, but slightly darker, with sparse biotite. L.11.3, W.28.0, T.9.0mm 22631 sf7780 (P4B)

9380 Rectangular section. Perforation at one end, both ends sawn; signs of wear on three surfaces. As *9364*. L.70.0, W.15.0, T.6.0mm 22631 sf7781 (P4B) (*Fig.1207*)

9381 Roughly triangular section. One end broken away, the other end smoothed; one surface smooth. As *9364*. L.105.0, W.19.0, T.16.0mm 22713 sf7891 (P4B)

9382 Fragment, of rectangular section. Both ends broken away, all surfaces worn. As *9364*. L.48.0, W.25.0, T.9.0mm 23788 sf7920 (P4B)

9383 Fragment, of irregular section. One surface shows signs of wear. As *9364*. L.45.0, W.8.0, T.5.0mm 22679 sf7930 (P4B)

9384 Irregular section. One surface shows signs of wear. As *9364*. L.29.0, W.5.0, T.3.0mm 22679 sf7931 (P4B)

9385 Fragment, of triangular section. Both ends broken away, no obvious sign of wear on any surface. As *9364*. L.42.0, W.6.0, T.6.0mm 22747 sf7969 (P4B)

9386 Irregular; no signs of wear. As *9370*. ?Norwegian Ragstone type. L.133.0, W.34.0, T.15.0mm 22745 sf7976 (P4B)

9387 Fragment, of irregular section. Both ends broken away; slight wear on one surface. As *9364*. L.54.0, W.9.0, T.5.0mm 22748 sf7981 (P4B)

9388 Fragment, of irregular section. No obvious sign of wear on any surface. As *9364*. L.50.0, W.9.0, T.6.0mm 22748 sf7985 (P4B)

9389 Fragment, of irregular section. Both ends broken away; no obvious signs of wear. As *9364* with sparse pale green ?chlorite. L.35.0, W.9.0, T.5.0mm 22748 sf7986 (P4B)

9390 Fragment, of irregular section. No obvious signs of wear. As *9364*. L.22.0, W.5.0, T.4.0mm 22748 sf7987 (P4B)

9391 Irregular ovoid section. Roughly dressed at both ends, two surfaces show signs of wear, one worn smooth and rounded. As *9364*, but slightly darker, with biotite. L.45.0, W.16.0, T.22.0mm 22815 sf8031 (P4B)

9392 Roughly rectangular section. Both ends and three surfaces broken away, other surface worn smooth. As *9364*. L.43.0, W.9.0, T.5.0mm 22845 sf8039 (P4B)

9393 Fragment, of irregular section. Both ends broken away, one edge shows signs of wear; other surfaces roughly dressed. As *9364*. L.53.0, W.20.0, T.5.0mm 22816 sf8126 (P4B)

9394 Fragment, of rectangular section. One end sawn and the other broken away; all four surfaces show signs of wear; tapers in middle and edges rounded. As *9364*, with sparse biotite. L.50.0, W.15.0, T.9.0mm 24003 sf8235 (P4B)

9395 Fragment, of irregular section; all surfaces broken. As *9364*. L.38.0, W.6.0, T.5.0mm 25285 sf8346 (P4B)

9396 Fragment, of irregular section, all surfaces broken away. As *9364*. L.50.0, W.15.0, T.9.0mm 25285 sf8349 (P4B)

9397 Fragment. Three surfaces show signs of wear, fourth surface broken away or unfinished; sawn/rounded both ends. As *9364*. L.55.0, W.11.0, T.10.0mm 25085 sf8398 (P4B)

9398 Fragment, of trapezoidal section; both ends broken away; three surfaces worn smooth, one has a central long narrow groove worn into it; fourth surface roughly dressed. As *9364*, with sparse biotite. L.50.0, W.24.0, T.16.0mm 25380 sf8480 (P4B)

9399 Rectangular section. No signs of wear on any surface. As *9364*. L.70.0, W.25.0, T.14.0mm 25380 sf8483 (P4B)

9400 Fragment. One end broken off, worn on all surfaces. As *9364*. L92.0, W.18.5, T.9.0mm 24556 sf8659 (P4B)

9401 Square section. One end is roughly dressed, the other is broken away; diagonal striations worn across one surface and longitudinal striations worn across another. As *9364*. L.32.0, W.16.0, T.16.0mm 25698 sf9467 (P4B)

9402 Fragment, of irregular section. No signs of wear on any surface. As *9364*, but slightly coarser-grained. L.33.0, W.18.0, T.6.0mm 25934 sf9984 (P4B)

9403 Fragment, of square section. Four surfaces worn smooth; broken away at both ends. As *9364*, but slightly darker. L.32.0, W.16.0, T.12.0mm 25934 sf10001 (P4B)

9404 Fragment, of irregular section. No obvious signs of wear; one end is sawn, possibly by-product of production. As *9364*. L.73.0, W.15.0, T.8.0mm 24808 sf10030 (P4B)

9405 Rectangular section and triangular profile. Sawn away at one end and worn away at other; all four surfaces worn. As *9364*. L.58.0, W.12.0, T.14.0mm 26748 sf10050 (P4B) (*Fig.1207*)

9406 Trapezoidal section and triangular profile; broken away at one end and worn away at the other. As *9364*. L.29.0, W.12.0, T.13.0mm 25934 sf10053 (P4B) (*Fig.1207*)

9407 Approximately triangular section. Broken away at one end and sawn at the other, two surfaces worn rounded, other surfaces broken away. As *9364*. L.40.0, W.15.0, T.9.0mm 25934 sf10056 (P4B)

9408 Rectangular section. One end sawn off and the other roughly dressed; three surfaces worn smooth and the other uneven. As *9364*. L.40.0, W.15.0, T.13.0mm 25934 sf10070 (P4B)

9409 Rectangular section. Both ends roughly dressed; three surfaces worn smooth and two roughly dressed. As *9364*. L.40.0, W.15.0, T.17.0mm 25934 sf10079 (P4B)

9410 Triangular section. One surface worn smooth, other two surfaces irregular. As *9364*. L.39.0, W.9.0, T.7.0mm 25934 sf10087 (P4B)

9411 Fragment. As *9364*, but slightly darker. L.18.0, W.16.0, T.3.0mm 25934 sf10091 (P4B)

9412 Roughly rectangular section. Both ends broken away, all four surfaces worn. As *9370*. ?Norwegian Ragstone type. L.28.0, W.10.0, T.10.0mm 25934 sf10096 (P4B)

9413 Fragment. As *9364*. L.17.0, W.9.0, T.3.0mm 25934 sf10098 (P4B)

9414 Fragment all surfaces broken away. As *9364*, but slightly darker, with sparse biotite. L.45.0mm 25934 sf10105 (P4B)

9415 Square profile. As *9364*, with sparse biotite. L.12.0, W.15.0, T.12.0mm sf10107 (P4B)

9416 Fragment of irregular section; one end and one surface smoothed, other end and surfaces broken away. As *9364*, but slightly darker, with sparse biotite. L.27.0, W.14.0mm 25934 sf10137 (P4B)

9417 Fragment of irregular section. One end rounded, the other broken away. As *9364*. L.29.0, W.9.0, T.9.0mm 25934 sf10138 (P4B)

9418 Square section. Sawn at both ends, three surfaces show signs of wear. As *9364*, with some thin quartz-rich bands. L.34.0, W.22.0, T.22.0mm 25934 sf10142 (P4B) (*Fig.1207*)

9419 Fragment of irregular section. One end sawn, signs of wear on three surfaces, the other surface and end broken away. As *9364*. L.45.0, W.10.0, T.6.0mm 25934 sf10153 (P4B)

9420 Square section, worn on three surfaces, one end sawn the other broken away. As *9364*, but slightly darker, with sparse biotite. L.45.0, W.15.0, T.14.0mm 25934 sf10158 (P4B)

9421 Triangular section. Sawn at both ends, four surfaces worn. As *9364*, with sparse biotite. L.133.0, W.45.0, T.35.0mm 28808 sf11359 (P4B) (*Fig.1207*)

9422 Fragment, of irregular section. Two worn surfaces survive; other surfaces and ends broken away. As *9364*. L.70.0, W.30.0, T.20.0mm 27509 sf11591 (P4B)

9423 Fragment, of roughly square section. One end broken away, three worn surfaces, one roughly finished, other end smoothed. As *9370*. ?Norwegian Ragstone type. L.50.0, W.11.0, T.16.0mm 24808 sf11721 (P4B)

9424 Fragment. Both ends and two surfaces broken away, two worn surfaces. As *9370*. ?Norwegian Ragstone type. L.50.0, W.10.0, T.7.0mm 26247 sf11913 (P4B)

9425 Rectangular section, all surface worn. Perforation begun from both sides but not drilled through. Possible re-use of a broken end from a longer original. As *9364*, with some slightly darker bands ?Norwegian Ragstone type. L.45.0, W.10.0, T.9.0mm 28967 sf12441 (P4B) (*Fig.1207*)

9426 Fragment or unfinished. Both ends and all surfaces roughly broken away, no signs of wear. As *9364*, but slightly darker and with slightly reddish bands. Reddish colour possibly due to heat. L.48.0, W.13.0, T.8.0mm 28904 sf12572 (P4B)

9427 Two fragments. One is tiny, the other of roughly triangular section; two surfaces show signs of wear. As *9364*. L.28.0, W.11.0, T.5.0mm, Smallest L.23.0mm 25380 sf12774 (P4B)

9428 Thin rectangular section. Sawn at one end, roughly broken away at other; two surfaces worn. As *9364*. L.43.0, W.18.0, T.4.0mm 31476 sf12855 (P4B)

9429 Fragment of irregular section. Both ends roughly sawn; drilling of perforation begun at one end on one surface only; that surface and one side show signs of wear. As *9364*, but slightly darker. L.46.0, W.18.0, T.9.0mm 31476 sf12978 (P4B)

9430 Fragment of thin rectangular section. Both ends broken away, two flat surfaces show signs of wear. As *9370*. ?Norwegian Ragstone type. L.55.0, W.20.0, T.5.0mm 32217 sf13050 (P4B)

9431 Fragment of rectangular section. One end broken away, other end sawn, three surfaces worn, one broken away. As *9364*. L.100.0, W.17.0, T.10.0mm 34670 sf13133 (P4B)

9432 Fragment; part of two worn surfaces survive, other surfaces and end broken away. As *9364*. L.46.0, W.30.0, T.15.0mm 34412 sf13329 (P4B)

9433 Fragment; all surfaces broken away. As *9364*. L.60.0, W.24.0, T.18.0mm 32465 sf13354 (P4B)

9434 Rectangular section; sawn both ends, four surfaces worn. As *9364*, with sparse biotite. L.66.0, W.20.0, T.10.0mm 35147 sf13867 (P4B)

9435 Square section. Broken away at both ends and one surface; other three surfaces show signs of wear; one impregnated with red ?haematite. As *9364*, with more quartzitic bands folded isoclinally. L.85.0, W.32.0, T.28.0mm 32993 sf14044 (P4B)

9436 Rectangular section. Sawn at one end, broken away at other, four surfaces worn. As *9364*. L.155.0, W.36.0, T.21.0mm 36434 sf14057 (P4B) (*Fig.1207*)

9437 Roughly rectangular section. One surface shows signs of wear, both ends broken away. As *9364*, but slightly darker. L.30.0, W.24.0, T.12.0mm 34492 sf14245 (P4B)

9438 Fragment, of roughly triangular section. Three surfaces show signs of wear; broken away at both ends. As *9364*. L.50.0, W.20.0, T.12.0mm 8251 sf1117 (P5A)

9439 Large fragment, all surfaces broken away, one end sawn and broken across, other end roughly broken. As *9364*. L.110.0, W.44.0, T.18.0mm 8491 sf1740 (P5A)

9440 Fragment, of flat ovoid section broken away at one end; all other surfaces and edges worn smooth and thin. As *9364*. L.80.0, W.27.0, T.7.0mm 8367 sf4653 (P5A)

9441 Fragment, of rectangular section, broken away at one end; four surfaces show signs of wear. As *9364*. L.64.0, W.10.0, T.6.0mm 18286 sf4924 (P5A) (*Fig.1207*)

9442 Fragment, of irregular section; two smooth surfaces survive. As *9364*, but slightly coarser-grained. L.55.0, W.18.0, T.16.0mm 2078 sf4938 (P5A)

9443 Complete. One end flattened, the other end pointed, both ends sawn. Rectangular section. All surfaces worn and an elongated groove worn into one surface may result from the sharpening of small points. As *9364*. L18.0, W.22.5, T.17.5mm 20105 sf5942 (P5A)

9444 Fragment, of rectangular section, sawn at both ends to approximately trapezoidal shape; two smoothed surfaces survive. As *9364*, but slightly coarser-grained. L.85.0, W.45.0, T.21.0mm 14874 sf6019 (P5A) (*Fig.1207*)

9445 Rectangular section. One end sawn at an angle, the other end broken. Worn on one surface halfway down the length of the hone, the rest remains rough possibly to facilitate grip. As *9364*. L.14.7, W.24.0, T.17.0mm 20105 sf6048 (P5A)

9446 Rectangular section, both ends sawn. Four worn surfaces, sawn incised line across top 5mm from top, possibly for a suspension thread. As *9370*. ?Norwegian Ragstone type. L.80.0, W.12.0, T.8.0mm 20604 sf7078 (P5A) (*Fig.1207*)

9447 Two fragments; one surface on each show signs of wear; irregular surfaces and sections. As *9364*, but slightly darker. L.50.0, W.12.0, T.4.0mm 20143 sf7141 (P5A)

9448 Fragment; irregular surfaces and section, no obviously worn surfaces. As *9364*, but slightly darker. L.59.0, W.14.0, T.19.0mm 20718 sf7149 (P5A)

9449 Square section, no perforation; four smooth surfaces, both ends sawn. As *9364*. L.72.0, W.9.0, T.10.0mm 22084 sf7190 (P5A)

9450 Fragment. Two worn surfaces, other surfaces and ends broken away. As *9364*, but slightly darker. L.21.0, W.9.0, T.5.0mm 18571 sf7201 (P5A)

9451 Fragment; one end sawn, other end and all surfaces broken away. As *9364*, but slightly darker. L.57.0, W.25.0, T.13.0mm 23000 sf7344 (P5A)

9452 Fragment, little signs of wear, broken on all surfaces. As *9364*, but slightly coarser-grained, and with sparse biotite. L.76.0, W.34.0, T.5.5mm 22090 sf7368 (P5A)

9453 Fragment, of irregular section. Both ends broken away, two worn surfaces. As *9364*. L.55.0, W.22.0, T.24.0mm 22166 sf7471 (P5A)

9454 Rectangular section. One end roughly dressed, the other broken away; three surfaces worn, one roughly finished.

As *9364*, with slightly darker bands. ?Norwegian Ragstone type. L.55.0, W.20.0, T.10.0mm 22122 sf7534 (P5A)

9455 Fragment, of approximately rectangular section. Both ends broken away, one surface worn, other surfaces smoothed. As *9364*, but slightly darker. L.62.0, W.22.0, T.7.0mm 22309 sf7549 (P5A)

9456 Fragment, of irregular section, worn on one surface. As *9364*. L.40.0, W.220.0, T.9.0mm 26496 sf9065 (P5A)

9457 Fragment. Both ends and all surfaces roughly dressed. As *9364*. L.42.0, W.17.0, T.10.0mm 26953 sf9810 (P5A)

9458 Fragment, of roughly rectangular section. One end broken away; other end smoothed and well rounded. As *9364*, but slightly darker. L.46.0, W.24.0, T.10.0mm 27118 sf10077 (P5A)

9459 Fragment, of roughly square section. Broken away at both ends; one worn surface. As *9364*. L.71.0, W.20.0, T.16.0mm 22124 sf11016 (P5A)

9460 Roughly rectangular section. One end sawn, the other worn and rounded smooth; three surfaces worn smooth, the other roughly dressed. As *9364*, with sparse biotite. L.74.0, W.25.0, T.10.0mm 27804 sf11049 (P5A)

9461 Rectangular section. One end sawn, the other worn thin; three worn surfaces, other roughly dressed. As *9364*, but slightly darker. L.78.0, W.14.0, T.8.0mm 26871 sf12355 (P5A)

9462 Roughly rectangular section. One end sawn and smoothed, the other broken away; three surfaces worn, one broken away. As *9371*. L.140.0, W.34.0, T.30.0mm 1473 sf431 (P5B)

9463 Rectangular section. Sawn at both ends; two worn surfaces, two roughly dressed. As *9371*. L.40.0, W.10.0, T.9.0mm 2801 sf491 (P5B)

9464 Square section, sawn at one end, other end broken away, little sign of use except on one surface, possibly unfinished. As *9371*. L.115.0, W.27.0, T.25.0mm 2875 sf599 (P5B) (*Fig.1211*)

9465 Irregular section. One smooth rounded surface, other surfaces and both ends broken away. As *9364*, but variably pale grey to reddish-brown, with sparse pale green ?chlorite. Reddish colour suggests heat. L.61.0, W.30.0, T.12.0mm 2875 sf619 (P5B)

9466 Fragment of square section; one end sawn, the other broken away; four worn surfaces. As *9364*. L.58.0, W.25.0, T.19.0mm 7123 sf745 (P5B)

9467 Irregular section. Two worn surfaces, other surfaces and both ends broken away. As *9370*. L.58.0, W.21.0, T.14.0mm 7204 sf1005 (P5B)

9468 Fragment of square section. One smooth surface, the other surfaces and both ends broken away. As *9364*, with some darker bands containing biotite. L.55.0, W.25.0, T.21.0mm 7204 sf1013 (P5B)

9469 Square section. Two ends broken away; four worn surfaces. As *9364*. L.60.0, W.21.0, T.19.0mm 8051 sf1118 (P5B)

9470 Square section. Both ends sawn; two worn surfaces, two roughly dressed. As *9364*. L.39.0, W.14.0, T.10.0mm 7377 sf1438 (P5B)

9471 Square section. Two surfaces worn; two chipped and cut, both ends sawn and smoothed. As *9364*. L.36.0, W.16.0, T.14.0mm 7500 sf1538 (P5B)

9472 Fragment of irregular section. Both ends and two surfaces broken away; two worn surfaces. As *9364*. L.88.0, W.27.0, T.14.0mm 9360 sf1885 (P5B)

9473 Fragment of rectangular section. Both ends broken away; three worn surfaces and one roughly dressed. As *9364*, but slightly coarser-grained. L.37.0, W.14.0, T.10.0mm 5321 sf2284 (P5B)

9474 Fragment of irregular section. One worn surface; both ends and other surface broken away. As *9364*. L.64.0, W.22.0, T.8.0mm 13716 sf3568 (P5B)

9475 Fragment of irregular section. One worn surface survives; all other surfaces and ends broken away. As *9364*. L.38.0, W.12.0, T.8.0mm 13716 sf3578 (P5B)

9476 Fragment of rectangular section. Both ends broken away; two worn surfaces. As *9364*. L.23.0, W.10.0, T.5.0mm 14403 sf4037 (P5B)

9477 Irregular section. Part of one worn surface survives; both ends and other surfaces broken away. Partly schist, as *9364*, but pale brownish-grey, and partly phyllite, lithology as *9524*, in sharp contrast along schistosity. L.120.0, W.25.0, T.18.0mm 15192 sf4316 (P5B)

9478 Rectangular section. Both ends sawn; four worn surfaces; erratic saw marks on one surface. As *9364*, but slightly darker. L.44.0, W.14.0, T.11.0mm 15587 sf4444 (P5B)

9479 Rectangular section. One end sawn, the other where it is worn thin, broken away; four worn surfaces. As *9364*. L.150.0, W.35.0, T.19.0mm 16882 sf4477 (P5B) (*Fig.1208*)

9480 Rectangular section. One end sawn, the other broken away. Four worn surfaces; worn thin towards broken end. No evidence that it broke across perforation. As *9364*, with sparse biotite. L.76.0, W.18.0, T.12.0mm 15608 sf4486 (P5B)

9481 Rectangular section. One end sawn across diagonally, other end has 'V' chipped into it, no sign of drilling; four worn surfaces. As *9364*, but slightly darker, with sparse biotite. L.70.0, W.30.0, T.21.0mm 15645 sf4563 (P5B) (*Fig.1208*)

9482 Fragment of rectangular section. Both ends broken away; two worn surfaces, two surfaces laminated off. As *9364*. L.29.0, W.12.0, T.9.0mm 14851 sf5915 (P5B)

9483 Triangular section. Broken away at both ends; two worn surfaces, others laminated off. As *9364*, but slightly darker. L.90.0, W.23.0, T.14.0mm 14887 sf6080 (P5B)

9484 Fragment of square section. Both ends broken away; four worn surfaces, one with shallow grooves cut into it, and which disappear over broken edges. As *9364*. L.40.0, W.23.0, T.20.0mm 6787 sf6161 (P5B)

9485 Roughly rectangular section, more worn on one side than another, broken across half the perforation. As *9364*. L.56 W.22.5 T.12mm 6925 sf6496 (P5B)

9486 Triangular section. One end sawn, one roughly dressed; three slightly worn surfaces. As *9364*. L.62.0, W.40.0, T.29.0mm 6933 sf6603 (P5B)

9487 Rectangular section. Sawn at one end, broken away at other; one surface worn, three others roughly dressed. As *9364*, but slightly coarser-grained. L.65.0, W.29.0, T.26.0mm 6870 sf6829 (P5B)

9488 Rectangular section, unusually long, worn on all surfaces, sawn at both ends. as *9364*, with sparse biotite. L.330.0, W.37.5, T.29mm sf6930 (P5B)

9489 Fragment of rectangular section. Both ends sawn and roughly dressed; four worn surfaces. As *9364*. L.40.0, W.15.0, T.11.0mm 19285 sf7113 (P5B)

9490 Fragment of triangular section. Both ends possibly sawn, one surface worn, others roughly dressed. As *9364*, with sparse biotite. L.45.0, W.25.0, T.12.0mm 21245 sf8320 (P5B)

9491 Fragment of rectangular section. Both ends and one surface broken away; three worn surfaces. As *9370*. L.38.0, W.35.0, T.13.0mm 21245 sf8440 (P5B)

9492 Fragment of irregular section. Both ends and two surfaces broken away; scratch marks on surface. As *9364*, with sparse biotite. L.22.0, W.15.0, T.6.0mm 21245 sf8462 (P5B)

9493 Fragment of triangular section. One end sawn, the other and one surface broken away; two worn surfaces. As *9364*. L.107.0, W.33.0, T.34.0mm 26015 sf8703 (P5B)

9494 Fragment of irregular section. All surfaces and both ends broken away. As 9370. L.70.0, W.17.0, T.8.0mm 21478 sf9003 (P5B)

9495 Fragment, of rectangular section. Three worn surfaces; two broken ends and one surface broken away. As 9364. L.49.0, W.15.0, T.13.0mm 21512 sf9064 (P5B)

9496 Fragment of rectangular section. Broken across at both ends; two worn surfaces, other two surfaces roughly dressed or flaked off. As 9364, with some thin quartz-rich bands. L.48.0, W.35.0, T.23.0mm 21512 sf9131 (P5B)

9497 Fragment of square section. Both ends and two surfaces broken away; two worn surfaces. As 9370. L.30.0, W.14.0, T.11.0mm 21543 sf9163 (P5B)

9498 Fragment of rectangular section. One end broken away, other end rounded and a perforation begun from both sides but incomplete; four worn surfaces. As 9364. L.31.0, W.15.0, T.10.0mm 14515 sf9751 (P5B) (Fig.1208)

9499 Flat rectangular section. One edge notched, beginning of perforation at other end on one surface; sides worn but not surfaces. As 9364. L.60.0, W.11.0, T.5.0mm 14515 sf9830 (P5B) (Fig.1208)

9500 Fragment of irregular section. All surfaces and both ends broken away. Partly schist, as 9364, and partly phyllite, as 9524, in sharp contact along schistosity. L.53.0, W.19.0, T.10.0mm 21660 sf9936 (P5B)

9501 Suboval profile, broken at one end and sawn at the other, all surafces worn. As 9364. L.75.0, W.19.0, T.28.0 29045 sf10172 (P5B)

9502 Fragment of rectangular section. One end sawn and snapped, the other broken away; four worn surfaces. As 9370. L.51.0, W.12.0, T.10.0mm 21919 sf10594 (P5B)

9503 Fragment of rectangular section. Both ends sawn and snapped; three worn surfaces, fourth is broken away. As 9364, but with slightly darker bands. L.55.0, W.30.0, T.15.0mm 29263 sf10675 (P5B)

9504 Fragment of square section. One end sawn and snapped, the other broken away; surfaces not worn but roughly dressed. As 9364, but slightly darker. L.97.0, W.20.0, T.20.0mm 29263 sf10713 (P5B) (Fig.1211)

9505 Square section. Both ends broken away, three worn surfaces, one partially survives. As 9364. L.44.0, W.23.0, T.25.0mm 29263 sf10756 (P5B)

9506 Rectangular section. Broken away at both ends; two worn surfaces; two surfaces broken away. As 9364. L.46.0, W.18.0, T.14.0mm 29263 sf10846 (P5B)

9507 Rectangular section. One end sawn and snapped, one sawn and smoothed; worn perforation at top end; all surfaces worn. As 9364, but slightly darker. L.38.0, W.9.0, T.5.0mm 21769 sf10870 (P5B) (Fig.1208)

9508 Fragment. Both ends sawn, one on the diagonal, all surfaces roughly dressed but not worn; possible roughout. As 9364, but slightly darker and with thin reddish bands and sparse pale green ?chlorite. Reddish colour possibly due to heat. L.110.0, W.25.0, T.14.0mm 29263 sf10955 (P5B) (Fig.1211)

9509 Fragment, of rectangular section. Sawn across one end, other end broken away; two worn surfaces, others broken away. As 9364, with sparse pale green ?chlorite. L.98.0, W.20.0, T.10.0mm 21554 sf11386 (P5B)

9510 Incomplete. Four surfaces and two ends roughly dressed; no signs of wear. As 9364. L.100.0, W.30.0, T.25.0mm 29263 sf11589 (P5B) (Fig.1211)

9511 Fragment of rectangular section. Both ends broken away as are two surfaces; two worn surfaces. As 9370. L.55.0, W.30.0, T.23.0mm 21678 sf11684 (P5B)

9512 Fragment of rectangular section. Both ends and two surfaces broken away; two worn surfaces. As 9364, with sparse biotite. L.39.0, W.14.0, T.13.0mm 24899 sf12562 (P5B)

9513 Both ends sawn on diagonal; surfaces show little sign of wear. As 9364. L.85.0, W.40.0, T.30.0mm 9797 sf3550 (P5Cf)

9514 Roughly square section. Four worn surfaces; especially worn at one end where hone has worn away; other end sawn and snapped. As 9364, but pale brownish-grey and slightly darker grey banded. ?Norwegian Ragstone type. L.90.0, W.24.0, T.19.0mm 14179 sf3627 (P5Cf)

9515 Fragment, of rectangular section. Four worn surfaces, one partially broken away, two ends broken away. As 9370, but with pale reddish-brown bands and thin lenticular quartz bands or veins. ?Norwegian Ragstone type. Reddish colour suggests heat. L.110.0, T.20.0, W.18.0mm 3445 sf2594 (P5Cr)

9516 Rectangular section. Three worn surfaces, striations across worn surface. Pale grey, fine-grained, quartzitic, micaceous (mainly muscovite, some biotite), with sparse dark non-micaceous minerals. L.87.0, W.11.0, T.8.0mm 3577 sf3621 (P5Cr)

9517 Irregular section; several grooves worn deeply into each section causing a very irregular appearance. Unusual configuration of deeply worn surfaces suggests use for trimming and sharpening woodworking gouges. As 9364. L.14.0, W.22.0, T.3.0mm 16763 sf4621 (P5Cr)

9518 Rectangular section. Axial perforation at top; other end sawn across, four worn surfaces. As 9364, with trace of isoclinally folded thin coarser-grained layer across one surface. L.59.0, W.15.0, T.5.0mm 18744 sf5826 (P5Cr)

9519 Fragment, of rough rectangular section. One end worn down, other end and three surfaces broken away; other surface worn smooth. As 9364, but slightly coarser-grained. L.92.0, W.32.0, T.10.0mm 6781 sf5962 (P5Cr)

9520 Fragment, of irregular, triangular section. One end broken away and the other roughly finished. Three worn surfaces, snapped in middle where worn thin. As 9364. L.50.0, W.22.0, T.10.0mm 18931 sf5992 (P5Cr)

9521 Fragment, of irregular section. Two worn surfaces, other surfaces and both ends broken away. As 9364. L.50.0, W.18.0, T.8.0mm 21044 sf6954 (P5Cr)

9522 Fragment of rectangular section. One surface worn, all other surfaces unfinished and rough. As 9364, with sparse biotite. L.35.0, W.22.0, T.16.0mm 21107 sf7053 (P5Cr)

9523 Rectangular section. Three worn surfaces; middle very worn to end where snapped off. Groove chipped into one surface but no sign of subsequent wear. As 9364. L.100.0, W.28.0, T.21.0mm 19190 sf7130 (P5Cr) (Fig.1208)

Phyllite

All phyllite hones are of purple-phyllite type unless otherwise specified.

9524 Rectangular section. Lower end sawn, top broken across axial perforation; four worn surfaces. Medium grey, very fine-grained, quartzitic, micaceous (mainly or all muscovite). L.50.0, W.23.0, T.5.0mm 9797 sf3525 (P3)

9525 Fragment, both ends broken away. Two surfaces sheared off, the remaining upper and side surface worn. As 9524. L.70.0, W.19.0, T.10.0mm 24770 sf9370 (P3)

9526 Fragment, of rectangular section. One end broken away, all four surfaces show signs of wear. As 9524. L.60.0, W.18.0, T.10.0mm 28239 sf10234 (P3)

9527 Fragment, broken away at one end. Of rectangular section, worn smooth on all surfaces and edges. As 9524. L.35.0, W.16.0, T.6.0mm 25759 sf9753 (P4A)

9528 Fragment. One surviving surface and edge worn smooth, other surfaces and ends broken away. As 9524. L.45.0, W.17.0, T.5.0mm 25994 sf10212 (P4A)

9529 Roughly square section, worn towards the centre, slightly pointed end has three notches cut into each corner and notched end tapers. As *9524*. L.56.0, W.11.0, T.11.0mm 22323 sf7578 (P4B)

9530 Fragment. Part of one surface remains and is worn, the other surface and ends broken away. As *9524*. L.41.0, W.19.0, T.10.0mm 22238 sf7579 (P4B)

9531 Complete, rectangular section, worn on all four surfaces, sawn at both ends. As *9524*, but with thin paler layers, apparently coarser-grained (almost schist). ?Purple-phyllite type. L.91.0, W.13.0, T.7.5mm 22415 sf7674 (P4B)

9532 Fragments. Part of one surface remains and is worn, the other surfaces and ends broken away. As *9524*. L.59.0, W.20.0, T.6.0mm 22574 sf7764 (P4B)

9533 Fragment. Part of one surface remains and is worn, the other surface and ends broken away. As *9524*. L.80.0, W.17.0, T.10.0mm 22560 sf7807 (P4B)

9534 Fragment, broken away at one end. Of rectangular section, part of one plane broken away irregularly but newly exposed surface also partially worn. As *9524*. L.66.0, W.20.0, T.9.0mm 22560 sf7809 (P4B) (*Fig.1209*)

9535 Fragment, broken away at both ends. Part of one plane broken away but where surfaces survive these are worn smooth. As *9524*. L.45.0, W.11.0, T.5.0mm 22713 sf7877 (P4B)

9536 Fragment. Split axially over whole length, surviving surface and edges worn smooth; incomplete axial perforation at top, not drilled through. As *9524*. L.37.0, W.10.0, T.5.0mm 22524 sf7912 (P4B) (*Fig.1209*)

9537 Fragment, both ends broken off, of triangular section. All surfaces somewhat fractured, long linear grooves worn (or possibly natural). As *9524*. L.109.0, W.18.0, T.11.0mm 22679 sf7939 (P4B)

9538 Fragment, both ends and one surface broken away. Remaining surface worn smooth. As *9524*. L.30.0, W.20.0, T.8.0mm 22748 sf7984 (P4B)

9539 Fragment, of rectangular section. Lower end broken away, top broken across axial perforation but new perforation drilled 7mm below. All surfaces worn smooth including where part of surface broken across. As *9524*. L.53.0, W.18.0, T.7.0mm 23936 sf8015 (P4B)

9540 Fragment broken away at both ends. Of triangular section, three surfaces worn smooth, the other broken away. As *9524*. L.39.0, W.13.0, T.15.0mm 24296 sf8220 (P4B)

9541 Square section. All surfaces worn smooth, diagonal striations on one surface and a thin shallow groove (possibly natural) along another. Sawn across bottom and then smoothed; smoothing on top gives faceted appearance to top surface. Axial perforations 8mm from top. As *9524*. L.77.0, W.7.0, T.7.0mm 25177 sf8281 (P4B) (*Fig.1209*)

9542 Fragment, of irregular section. Wear on one edge, rest is broken away. L.67.0, W.16.0, T.17.0mm 25177 sf8286 (P4B)

9543 Fragment. All surfaces, ends and edges broken away. As *9524*. L.36.0, W.16.0, T.7.0mm 25270 sf8326 (P4B)

9544 Fragments only. One worn surface survives, otherwise all surfaces and edges broken away. As *9524*. L.43.0, W.11.0, T.8.0mm 24028 sf8410 (P4B)

9545 Fragment. All surfaces, ends and edges broken away. As *9524*. L.34.0, W.17.0, T.9.0mm 24509 sf8532 (P4B)

9546 Rectangular section. Ends sawn then worn smooth, all other surfaces worn smooth, diagonal striations appear on two surfaces. As *9524*. L.80.0, W.8.0, T.5.0mm 25350 sf8543 (P4B) (*Fig.1209*)

9547 Fragment of rectangular section. Both ends broken away, all surfaces show signs of wear but not smooth. Four short striations at right-angles to main axis at one end. As *9524*. L.59.0, W.20.0, T.10.0mm 25350 sf8584 (P4B) (*Fig.1209*)

9548 Fragment. One end broken away, other end and one surface flaked off. Other surfaces worn smooth. As *9524*. L.48.0, W.17.0, T.5.0mm 25350 sf8907 (P4B)

9549 Rectangular section, one end broken, all four surfaces worn. As *9524*, but paler. L.87.0, W.15.0, T.11.0mm 26381 sf8946 (P4B)

9550 Fragment. One end sawn off, other end and one surface broken away. Remaining surface worn smooth and diagonal striations visible. As *9524*. L.63.0, W.21.0, T.7.0mm 26157 sf9006 (P4B)

9551 Fragment, of square section. Both ends broken away and one surface broken away. Two surfaces and remaining part of a third worn smooth. As *9524*, but paler. L.90.0, W.17.0, T.19.0mm 20747 sf9087 (P4B)

9552 Subrectangular section. All surfaces, including irregular bottom edge, worn smooth. Axial perforation 8mm from top. As *9524*. L.65.0, W.10.0, T.6.0mm 25598 sf9151 (P4B) (*Fig.1209*)

9553 One end sawn and then snapped, other end sawn. Saw marks very fresh and no indication of subsequent finishing or dressing. Only one surface shows any sign of wear; all other irregular surfaces undressed. As *9524*. L.40.0, W.27.0, T.15.0mm 25934 sf10078 (P4B) (*Fig.1209*)

9554 Fragment. Both ends and one surface broken away, remaining surface shows some signs of wear. Tool (possibly saw) marks at right-angles to axis on undressed surface. As *9524*. L.24.0, W.12.0, T.4.0mm 25934 sf10095 (P4B)

9555 Irregular shape and section. One end naturally rounded, the other sawn across. Some surfaces worn smooth, others roughly dressed. As *9524*. 25934 sf10104 (P4B)

9556 Rectangular section. All surfaces worn smooth; especially worn on surface below axial perforation. Lower end broken away where width of hone worn to 2mm. As *9524*. L.51.0, W.16.0, T.9.0mm 27892 sf11043 (P4B) (*Fig.1209*)

9557 Fragment. Part of one smooth surface survives, both ends and other surfaces broken away. As *9524*. L.24.0, W.14.0, T.3.0mm 31208 sf11185 (P4B)

9558 Irregular section, all surfaces broken away. As *9524*. L.8.03, W.21.0, T.9.0mm. 22574 sf11233 (P4B)

9559 Irregular section, all surfaces broken away. As *9524*. L.72.0, W.11.5, T.6.0mm 28904 sf12337 (P4B)

9560 Rectangular section. One end sawn and snapped, other end snapped. All surfaces show signs of wear. As *9524*. L.74.0, W.20.0, T.8.0mm 31476 sf12958 (P4B)

9561 Square section. Both ends partially sawn and then snapped. Other saw marks visible around top and bottom, possibly to take a thong or as part of the manufacturing process. All four surfaces worn, other cut marks visible on edges. As *9524*. L.98.0, W.12.0, T.14.0mm 34412 sf13005 (P4B) (*Fig.1209*)

9562 Fragment. Both ends and three surfaces broken away, remaining surface shows signs of wear. As *9524*. L.65.0, W.18.0, T.4.0mm 29835 sf13129 (P4B)

9563 Complete with square section, all four surfaces worn, both ends sawn. One end has several notches, 2–3 on each corner presumably to hold a thong or thread in place from which hone was suspended. As *9524*, but medium to dark grey, with sparse biotite. ?Purple-phyllite type. L.94.0, W.8.0, T.6.5mm 34725 sf13144 (P4B)

9564 Rectangular section. All surfaces worn smooth. Top end sawn straight across and axial perforation drilled from two sides, bottom end sawn to triangular point and beginnings of perforation visible on one surface. As *9524*. L.80.0, W.10.0, T.6.0mm 32589 sf13225 (P4B) (*Fig.1209*)

9565 Fragment. Both ends and most surfaces broken away. As *9524*. L.36.0, W.18.0, T.4.0mm 29925 sf13311 (P4B)

9566 Fragment. Both ends and most surfaces broken away. One surface and one edge worn smooth, other surfaces broken away. As *9524*. L.44.0, W.15.0, T.5.0mm 19714 sf13333 (P4B)

9567 Fragments (2), with sawn and broken edges, all surfaces broken away. As *9524*. L.67.0, W.15.0, T.7.0mm 35137 sf14201 (P4B)

9568 Fragment, of rectangular section. One end sawn, the other broken away; three surfaces worn, the fourth less so. As *9524*. L.40.0, W.15.0, T.8.0mm 2677 sf1172 (P5A)

9569 Fragment, of irregular section. One end sawn, the other broken away; one surface worn and scratched, the other surfaces irregularly worn or broken away. As *9524*. L.70.0, W.15.0, T.8.0mm 14940 sf6410 (P5A)

9570 Fragment, of irregular section. One surface worn, other surfaces and ends broken away. As *9524*. L.72.0, W.19.0, T.7.0mm 20143 sf7339 (P5A)

9571 Square section with slightly pointed end, worn on four surfaces. As *9524*, but brownish-grey, with very thin dark quartzitic layer. ?Purple-phyllite type. L.82.5, W.7.5, T.7.0mm 22340 sf7530 (P5A)

9572 Triangular section (probably originally square). Both ends partially sawn and then crudely broken across; part of one and all of another surface broken away; remaining surfaces are very worn. Beginning of a perforation drilled into the top of one surface. As *9524*. L.42.0, W.15.0, T.15.0mm 27679 sf12758 (P5A)

9573 Rectangular section, worn thin at one edge. One end sawn, the other broken away across a diagonal, three surfaces worn, saw marks across one edge. As *9524*, but with reddish-grey colour banding. Reddish colour possibly due to heat. L.93.0, W.21.0, T.7.0mm 8033 sf694 (P5B)

9574 Complete, rectangular section, worn on all four surfaces. Angled to form a point at the top with perforation worn by friction with thong or thread. Very fine example. As *9524*. L.17.5mm W.13.0, T.8.0mm. 7204 sf995 (P5B)

9575 Fragment, of triangular section. One end sawn across a diagonal, the other broken away; one surface and one edge worn, the other surface roughly dressed. As *9524*, but greenish-grey, with sparse pale green ?chlorite. L.48.0, W.16.0, T.8.0mm 7204 sf1015 (P5B) (*Fig.1209*)

9576 Fragment, of roughly rectangular section. One end sawn, the other broken away, three worn surfaces. As *9524*. L.51.0, W.10.0, T.15.0mm 5980 sf2244 (P5B)

9577 Fragment, of rectangular section. Ends broken away, four worn surfaces although one mostly flaked away. Pale to medium grey, very fine-grained, quartzitic, micaceous (mainly or all muscovite), with marked platy cleavage (giving slightly laminated appearance). L.40.0, W.27.0, T.14.0mm 13367 sf3349 (P5B)

9578 Fragment, of irregular section. Both ends broken away, all but one worn surface broken away. As *9524*, with more abundant quartz along one edge. L.75.0, W.28.0, T.12.0mm 13733 sf3598 (P5B)

9579 Roughly rectangular section. Perforation drilled into both sides at top, part subsequently flaked away. Both ends sawn, four worn surfaces. As *9524*, but paler, with minute ?gold smear near perforation (?used as touchstone). L.70.0, W.15.0, T.9.0mm 14184 sf3766 (P5B) (*Fig.1209*)

9580 Fragment, of roughly rectangular section. Both ends broken away, four worn but uneven surfaces. As *9524*. L.80.0, W.14.0, T.10.0mm 14595 sf4697 (P5B)

9581 Fragment, of square section; one end sawn, the other broken away, two surfaces worn, the other two broken away. As *9524*. L.50.0, W.6.0, T.6.0mm 14434 sf5469 (P5B)

9582 Fragment, of rectangular section; one edge and both ends broken away, three remaining surfaces worn As *9524*, but slightly coarser-grained in places (almost schist). ?Purple-phyllite type. L.32.0, W.29.0, T.8.0mm 6787 sf6166 (P5B)

9583 Sawn across both ends. Four worn surfaces, other end broken away, possibly across a perforation, although no sign

survives. As *9524*. L.79.0, W.8.0, T.8.0mm 14632 sf6499 (P5B)

9584 Fragment, of rectangular section; one end sawn and the other broken away; three worn surfaces; the other chipped away. As *9524*. L.68.0, W.20.0, T.8.0mm 6932 sf6986 (P5B)

9585 Fragment, of roughly triangular section. One end diagonally sawn, the other worn thin; three worn surfaces. As *9524*. L.63.0, W.19.0, T.9.0mm 20266 sf7105 (P5B)

9586 Fragment, of rectangular section. One edge is broken away, the other end sawn and then worn rounded. The fragment is worn thin towards the broken end suggesting this is the bottom of a hone, possibly suspended; four surfaces worn smooth. As *9524*. L.35.0, W.17.0, T.8.0mm 19360 sf8180 (P5B)

9587 Thin rectangular section. One end sawn, the other broken away; two slightly worn surfaces, possible original surfaces flaked off. As *9524*. L.50.0, W.20.0, T.3.0mm 21203 sf8263 (P5B)

9588 Fragment of rectangular section; broken away at both ends; four worn surfaces. As *9524*, but paler. L.57.0, W.30.0, T.15.0mm 21244 sf8292 (P5B)

9589 Triangular section; both ends sawn; three surfaces worn. As *9524*. L.64.0, W.11.0, T.13.0mm 20348 sf8433 (P5B)

9590 Rectangular section; perforation with worn hole at rounded top; other end sawn across and worn thin; scratched striations on surface. As *9524*. L.45.0, W.20.0, T.7.0mm 21382 sf8613 (P5B) (*Fig.1209*)

9591 Fragment, of rectangular section, one end broken away; perforation drilled from both sides at other end; shallow grooves run from top of perforation to top of hone on both sides and on both edges, and top is sawn across; a central shallow groove runs along the lower third of bottom of hone where it is broken. As *9524*. L.39.0, W.10.0, T.4.0mm 20170 sf8616 (P5B) (*Fig.1209*)

9592 Fragment, of roughly triangular section. One surface worn smooth, the other three show signs of wear. One end broken away, the other partially sawn and then snapped roughly across. As *9524*. L.70.0, W.18.0, T.10.0mm 21293 sf8719 (P5B)

9593 Approximately square section. One end sawn and then broken away, other end broken across partially drilled perforation which broke during the process (end was initially sawn). Two other lower perforations begun on the same surface but not completed. All four surfaces show signs of wear. As *9524*. L.55.0, W.7.0, T.5.0mm 21919 sf10125 (P5B) (*Fig.1209*)

9594 Fragment, of irregular section. Two worn surfaces, the others broken away. One end broken away, the other sawn, and a second line of sawing visible below. As *9524*, but slightly coarser-grained (almost schist). ?Purple-phyllite type. L.42.0, W.12.0, T.8.0mm 15192 sf11406 (P5B) (*Fig.1209*)

9595 Fragment. Part of one worn surface survives, other surfaces and ends broken away. As *9524*. L.50.0, W.18.0, T.10.0mm 21618 sf12248 (P5B)

9596 Fragment, broken away at one end and roughly dressed at the other. Signs of wear on all four surfaces. Medium grey, fine-grained with angular to subangular grains, well sorted and fairly well compacted, with some scattered muscovite; possibly fissile. Upper Carboniferous, probably Coal Measures. L.80.0, W.30.0, T.22.0mm 3521 sf3645 (P4/5)

9597 Fragment split axially and broken away at one end. Axial perforation drilled from two sides. As *9524*. L.30.0, W.7.0mm 3647 sf6716 (P4/5)

9598 Fragment, of rectangular section. Four worn surfaces, one end broken away. As *9524*, but slightly coarser-grained in places (almost schist). ?Purple-phyllite type. L.31.0, W.2.0, T.5.0mm 18744 sf6167 (P5Cr)

9599   Fragment, of rectangular section. Three worn surfaces, one surface and two ends broken away. As 9524, but slightly coarser-grained in places (almost schist). L.35.0, W.17.0, T.8.0mm 6781 sf6255 (P5Cr)

9600   Square section. Both ends sawn, two worn surfaces, the other surfaces broken away. As 9524. L.75.0, W.8.0, T.8.0mm 17742 sf6667 (P5Cr)

9601   Fragment, of rectangular section. One worn surface, other broken away. As 9524. L.35.0, W.20.0, T.10.0mm 6781 sf6996 (P5Cr)

9602   Fragment, of irregular section; all surfaces irregular. As 9524. L.52.0mm 21096 sf7038 (P5Cr)

9603   Fragment, of rectangular section. Axial perforation, broken off just below perforation which is worn, As 9524, but paler. L.22.0, W.9.0, T.4.0mm 15311 sf7424 (P5Cr)

9604   Fragment, of triangular section. Sawn diagonally across one end, broken across other; one worn surface with sawn 'nick' on one edge. As 9524. L.80.0, W.34.0, T.10.0mm 15311 sf7440 (P5Cr)

9605   Fragment, of irregular section. One worn surface, all other surfaces and ends broken away, saw marks across one end. As 9524. L.40.0, W.20.0, T.7.0mm 15311 sf7441 (P5Cr)

Possible touchstones

9606   Of rectangular section, all surfaces worn smooth, one end only is roughly dressed. Shallow linear depression worn into one surface Uncertain lithology. Dark grey to black, vaguely banded, very fine-grained rock with hardness exceeding 6 on Moh's Scale, and slight fissility along layering. Chert appearance, but chert unusual as a hone; it may have served as a touchstone, but is extremely rare in that capacity. Probably Lower Palaeozoic indurated quartzitic siltstone. Partly worn shape suggests broken erratic. L.84.0, W.42.0, T.22.0mm 32129 sf12678 (P4B) (Fig.1210)

9607   Rectangular section. Both ends sawn and one surface plus both ends subsequently chipped; all surfaces smoothed. Uncertain lithology. Black, very fine-grained rock with hardness exceeding 6 on Moh's Scale. Basaltic appearance. Probably tuff or Lower Palaeozoic indurated quartzitic siltstone or silty mudstone. L.35.0, W.23.0, T.14.0mm 22044 sf7087 (P5A) (Fig.1210)

9608   Worn on all surfaces, one especially polished; ends possibly sawn but now very polished, could be natural. Apparently drilled hole 2.5mm in diameter near centre. Uncertain lithology. Dark grey, very fine-grained rock with traces of grain-size layering or flow texture, and hardness exceeding 6 on Moh's Scale. Basaltic appearance. Probably tuff or Lower Palaeozoic indurated quartzitic siltstone or silty mudstone. L.120.0, W.37.0, T.26.0mm 15189 sf4102 (P5B) (Fig.1210)

Hone or possible pendant

9609   Complete, square section. Marked muted green, reddish-brown and brown stripes running diagonally across surface. Worn perforation at one end with copper alloy wire hoop still in place, ends joined by overlapping and twisting. Surfaces very smooth. Lithology uncertain, but probably either indurated silty mudstone/siltstone; pale to dark brown laminar banded with subsidiary medium green layers, containing very fine-grained quartz in the paler brown laminae. None of the four long surfaces exhibits evidence of hone usage. L.45.0, W.10.0, T.10.0mm 28493 sf11114 (P4B)

Rotary grindstones

All rotary grindstones are of Millstone Grit sandstone unless otherwise specified.

9610   Fragment, slightly sooted, worn grinding surface, ends roughly dressed. Tool marks visible. Pale to medium grey, mainly medium-grained with subangular to subrounded grains, moderately sorted and moderately compacted. Upper Carboniferous. D.360.0, T.110.0mm, perforation D.140.0mm 28408 sf10682 (P3)

9611   Complete, sooted, worn grinding surface; ends roughly dressed. Pale grey, medium- to coarse-grained with subangular to subrounded grains, moderately sorted and moderately compacted. D.70.0, H.65.0mm, perforation D.20.0mm 2452 sf1633 (P4B)

9612   Fragment, worn grinding surface, ends roughly dressed, broken in half along the perforation. Pale grey, medium- to coarse-grained with subangular to subrounded grains, moderately to poorly sorted and moderately compacted. D.80.0, H.90.0mm, perforation D.20.00mm 22656 sf7938 (P4B)

9613   Complete (in two pieces), worn grinding surface, ends roughly dressed. Pale grey, medium- to coarse-grained with subangular to subrounded grains, moderately sorted and moderately compacted. D.50.0, H.45.0mm, perforation D.20.0mm 22748 sf7979 (P4B) (Fig.1201)

9614   Complete, worn grinding surface, ends roughly dressed. As 9612. D.50.0, H.60.0mm, perforation D.20.0mm 22845 sf8035 (P4B)

9615   Fragment. Pale grey, medium-grained with subangular grains, fairly well sorted and fairly well compacted. Upper Carboniferous, probably Millstone Grit. D.300.0, L.85.0, T.65.0mm 22848 sf8054 (P4B)

9616   Complete, slightly sooted, worn grinding surface, ends roughly dressed. Pale grey, medium- to coarse-grained with subangular to subrounded grains, poorly sorted and poorly compacted. D.50.0, H.65.0mm, perforation D.25.0mm 23841 sf8185 (P4B)

9617   Complete, worn grinding surface, ends dressed smooth. Pale grey, medium-grained with angular to subangular grains, moderately sorted and moderately compacted, with sparse muscovite and traces of low-angle cross-bedding. Upper Carboniferous, probably Millstone Grit. D.70.0, H.20.0mm, perforation D.20.0mm 25350 sf8556 (P4B)

9618   Complete, sooted, worn grinding surface, ends dressed smooth. Pale brownish-grey, medium-grained with angular to subangular grains, moderately sorted and moderately compacted. Upper Carboniferous, probably Millstone Grit. D.50.0, H.35.0mm, perforation D.20.0mm 25718 sf9369 (P4B)

9619   Complete, worn grinding surface, ends cut to form facets tapering towards perforation. Medium- to coarse-grained with angular to subrounded grains, moderately sorted in grain size-differentiated cross-bedded layers, and moderately compacted. D.60.0, H.50.0mm, perforation D.20.0mm 25812 sf9770 (P4B) (Fig.1201)

9620   Fragment, worn grinding surface, one face has two cone-shaped depressions drilled into it. Slight sooting around these suggests possible use as a cresset lamp. Pale grey, fine-grained with angular to (mainly) subangular grains, well sorted and fairly well compacted, with some fissile laminae. Upper Carboniferous probably Coal Measures of Elland Flags type. D.240.0, H.55.0mm, perforation D.100.0mm 28933 sf12171(P4B) (Fig.1202)

9621   Complete, worn grinding surface, ends roughly dressed, slightly off-centre perforation. Pale grey, medium-grained with angular to subrounded grains, moderately sorted and moderately compacted. Upper Carboniferous, probably Millstone Grit. D.50.0, H.50.0mm, perforation D.20.0mm 34646 sf13126 (P4B)

9622 Fragment, worn grinding surface, central perforation. As *9612*. D.100.0, H.70.0mm, perforation D.30.0mm 8281 sf1126 (P5A)

9623 Fragment, incomplete, perforation partly drilled from both sides; one face broken away. As *9616*. D.80.0, H.50.0mm, perforation D.20.0mm 20105 sf5959 (P5A) *(Fig.1201)*

9624 Fragment, only part of worn edge and part of perforation surviving, some evidence of burning. Pale grey, medium- to (slightly) coarse-grained with mainly subangular grains, moderately sorted and moderately compacted, but with siliceous matrix in places. D.320.0, T.110.0mm, perforation D.100.0mm 22052 sf7120 (P5A)

9625 Complete, worn grinding surface. At one end, off-centre perforation. Pale grey, fine-grained with subangular grains, well sorted and fairly well compacted. Upper Carboniferous probably Coal Measures. D.78.0, H.45.0mm, perforation D.20.0mm 14965 sf7249 (P5A)

9626 Complete, worn grinding surface at one end, other end dressed smooth. Pale grey, fine- to coarse-grained (including a few 2–4mm wide grains) with subangular to subrounded grains, poorly sorted and moderately compacted. D.70.0, H.58.0mm, perforation D.20.0mm 22141 sf7348 (P5A) *(Fig.1201)*

9627 Fragment, worn grinding surface. Pale grey, medium-grained with subangular to subrounded grains, moderately sorted and moderately compacted. Upper Carboniferous, probably Millstone Grit. D.60.0, H.60.0mm, perforation D.15.0mm 26889 sf12224 (P5A)

9628 Complete, worn grinding surface and one end, other end roughly dressed, central perforation, pale grey, medium-grained with mainly subangular grains, moderately to fairly well compacted and well sorted. Upper Carboniferous probably Millstone Grit. D.70.0, H.35.0mm, perforation D.20.0mm 7348 sf1083 (P5B)

9629 Fragment, two holes drilled into upper surface comparable with *9620*. Pale grey, fine-grained with angular to subangular grains, well-sorted and well compacted, with appreciable muscovite, mainly concentrated on fissile laminae. Coal Measures of Elland Flags type. H.32, D.110mm 14184 sf3761 (P5B) *(Fig.1202)*

9630 Complete, slightly elliptical form, worn grinding surface. Pale grey with brown ferruginous staining, medium- to coarse-grained with angular to (mainly) subangular grains, moderately sorted and moderately compacted. D.140.0, H.95.0mm, perforation D.25.0mm 14184 sf3781 (P5B)

9631 Complete, worn grinding surface, ends roughly dressed, off-centre perforation. As *9630*. D.105.0, H.111.0mm, perforation D.45.0mm 14184 sf3782 (P5B)

9632 Fragment, worn grinding surface. Pale brownish-grey, coarse-grained with angular to subangular grains, moderately sorted and poorly compacted. D.180.0, H.30.0mm, perforation D.20.0mm 20277 sf6457 (P5B)

9633 Fragment, edge worn smooth, both surfaces dressed but not worn, part of central perforation. Pale brownish-grey with brown ferruginous mottling, fine-grained with angular to subangular grains, well sorted and fairly well compacted, with sparse muscovite, but not concentrated on slightly fissile bedding planes. Coal Measures. D.440.0, H.71.0mm 27513 sf10529 (P5B)

9634 Complete, worn grinding surface, ends dressed smooth. Pale grey, medium-grained with angular to subangular grains, moderately sorted and moderately compacted, with sparse muscovite. Upper Carboniferous, probably Millstone Grit. D.50.0, H.40.0mm, perforation D.20.0mm 27513 sf11004 (P5B)

9635 Fragment, edge and one surface used for grinding, other surface quite smooth. Pale grey, medium-grained with angular to subangular grains, fairly well sorted and fairly well compacted. Upper Carboniferous, probably Millstone Grit. D.140.0, H.56.0mm 6785 sf6181 (P5Cr)

9636 Complete, sooted exterior, worn grinding surface, off-centre perforation. Pale grey (passing to dark grey at surface), fine-grained with angular to (mainly) subangular grains, well sorted and fairly well compacted, with sparse muscovite. Upper Carboniferous, probably Coal Measures. D.70.0, H.35.0mm, perforation D.20.0mm 18331 sf5364 (B6a5, C6c3; early 12th century) (P6)

9637 Complete, worn grinding surface, ends dressed smooth. Pale grey. As *9636*. Upper Carboniferous, probably Coal Measures. D.75.0, H.40.0mm, perforation D.20.0mm 16612 sf6065 (D6a1; late 11th century) (P6)

9638 Fragment, worn grinding surface, ends roughly dressed. As *9613*. D.180.0, H.60.0mm, perforation D.20.0mm 16612 sf6718 (D6a1; late 11th century) (P6)

Chalk cores and burnishers

All cores and burnishers belong to the Chalk Group unless otherwise specified.

9639 Rod with broken top, round section. Base has pronounced 'foot' which is a little worn in places. Facets resulting from scraping clearly visible running the length of the rod. Very fine-grained. D.12.0, H.23.0mm 26419 sf8975 (P4A) *(Fig.1227)*

9640 Irregular cone with possibly sawn base and broken top. Cut and facets resulting from scraping visible on the surface. White, very fine-grained. L.24.0, W.15.5, T.13.5mm 26419 sf8976 (P4A)

9641 Fragment of a rod with sawn base and broken top. Flattened ovoid section. Facets from scraping clearly visible running the length of the surviving rod. White, very fine-grained. L.31.0, W.27.0, T.18.0mm 26419 sf8979 (P4A)

9642 Irregular block with groove worn into the top and an ovoid cavity with two points worn into the centre. Base is worn smooth from polishing or burnishing and other irregular surfaces show cuts and scraping marks. White, very fine-grained. L.50.0, H.36.0, W.44.0mm 23312 sf7506 (P4B) *(Fig.1227)*

9643 Rod with ovoid section, top broken off, irregular base with smoothed patches. Clear facets from scraping surface running the surviving length of the rod. White, fine-grained. Probably Ferriby Chalk Formation. L.31.0, W.16.0, T.13.0mm 20765 sf7636 (P4B)

9644 Rod fragment with broken top and end. One side broken away. Facets on the surviving side resulting from scraping the surface. White, very fine-grained, with a small flint nodule and a few forams. Chalk Group, Welton Chalk Formation or (less probably) Burnham Chalk Formation. D.20.0, H.35.0mm 24556 sf8918 (P4B)

9645 Irregular 'boat-shaped' block with worn base and edges resulting from use as a polisher or burnisher. A deep long groove has been worn into the upper surface by scraping with a point. White, very fine-grained. L.46.0, W.17.0, T.14.0mm 25931 sf9979 (P4B) *(Fig.1227)*

9646 Squared block with conical groove worn into centre of the top surface and a small point worn into the base. Edges of the block are rounded from wear as is the base. White, very fine-grained. L.32.0, W.30.0, T.29.0mm 21903 sf10457 (P4B) *(Fig.1227)*

9647 Tapering square block, broken at both ends, though the remains of the 'foot' are intact. Cuts and scraping marks visible on the four surfaces. One surface smooth, possibly used as a polisher or burnisher. Chalk, white, fine-grained. Probably Ferriby Chalk Formation. W.20.0, T.16.0, H.50.0mm 21903 sf10471 (P4B) (*Fig.1227*)

9648 Cone with slightly bevelled base and broken top. Clear facets around the body of the cone. Base smoothed, possibly as a result of wear. White, fine-grained. Probably Ferriby Chalk Formation. D.35.0, H.33.0mm 28820 sf11136 (P4B) (*Fig.1227*)

9649 Cone of triangular section. Top broken or sawn away and base angled as a result of wear. Facets from scraping the surface clearly visible running the length of the rod. White, very fine-grained. W.20.0, T.20.0, H.40.0mm 25598 sf12232 (P4B)

9650 Rod fragment with irregular round section. Perforation and irregular surface. White, fine-grained. Probably Ferriby Chalk Formation. Perforation may be natural, possibly part of belemnite mould. D.20.0, H.15.0mm, perforation D.5.0mm 28967 sf12435 (P4B)

9651 Fragment of rod with square section, ends sawn or broken. Clear wide facets where the sides have been scraped. Greyish-white, fine-grained. Probably Ferriby Chalk Formation. D.15.0, H.20.0mm 23881 sf12703 (P4B)

9652 Rod with round section and top broken or sawn away. Base is angled and worn on one side just above the base. Facets resulting from scraping the surface clearly visible running the length of the surviving rod. White, very fine-grained. D.20.0, H.57.0mm 18467 sf5733 (P5A) (*Fig.1227*)

9653 Roughly triangular in shape, one surface worn smooth from use as a polisher or burnisher. White, very fine-grained, with a few forams. L.39.0, W.27.0, T.7.0mm 14922 sf7100 (P5A)

9654 Flat, square form, perforation worn through from both sides. Worn edges and surfaces. White, very fine-grained. L.16.0, W.16.0, T.6.0mm 31300 sf11125 (P5A)

9655 Fragment with curved edge worn smooth, upper and lower surfaces rough or broken away. White, very fine-grained, with a few forams. D.60.0, T.15.0mm 15189 sf4151 (P5B)

9656 Square block with inverted conical hole drilled into one surface and scratch marks on base. Two surfaces roughly dressed. White, fine-grained, with a few forams. Probably Ferriby Chalk Formation. D.480.0, L.170.0, T.115.0mm, perforation D.120.0mm 29263 sf10862 (P5B)

9657 Cone, top broken off, clear facets down the side where surface has been scraped. Surface shattered on one side, possibly heat fractured. Creamy white, fine-grained, with a few small scattered quartz grains. Probably Ferriby Chalk Formation. Intense cracking implies heat. D.34.0, H.47.0mm 19090 sf5859 (P5Cr)

9658 Square block with holes drilled into centre of each face to form a hollow centre. Possible unusual bead or playing piece. White, very fine-grained. T.10, L.10, W.10mm 1502 sf1328 (C6e11, D6e3; mid 13th century) (P6)

9659 Possible bead, discoid. Greyish-white fine-grained. Probably Ferriby Chalk Formation. D.11.5, T.3.5mm, perforation D.6.5mm 15033 sf3729 (C6v1; late 11th/early 12th century) (P6)

9660 Fragment irregularly shaped, two faces smoothed, others roughly broken. Smooth concave groove, worn to hour-glass shape. White, very fine-grained. L.58.2, W.44.4, T.49.1mm 13532 sf3883 (A6n3, B6c1; late 12th/early 13th century) (P6)

Slick-stones

Note: Full catalogue entries for 6579–81 appear in *AY* 17/11. These are illustrated on Fig.827.

6579 Flat, almost round pebble. Area of artificial polish on one face. Sandstone. D.64–73.0, T.20.0mm 28239 sf10185 (P3)

6580 Fragment of naturally glossy black stone. Possibly indurated mudstone or siltstone, or volcanic rock. L.53.0, W.21.0, T.21.0mm 31072 sf11010 (P3)

6581 Possible slick-stone. Fragment of naturally glossy black stone, similar to 6580. L.56.0, W.43.0, T.20.0mm 31161 sf11072 (P4A)

Lamps

9661 Fragmentary oval block with shallow depression pecked into upper surface. Sooted on upper edges, half broken away. Limestone, pale grey to yellowish-brown mottle, microcellular, mainly dolomitic. Lower Magnesian Limestone. L.130.0, W.80.0, H.85.0mm 26783 sf9214 (P3) (*Fig.1243*)

9662 Fragmentary round block, approximately half surviving. Deep depression carved into upper surface, base is flat. External sooting and some tool marks visible. Limestone, pale yellowish-grey, microcellular, mainly dolomitic. Lower Magnesian Limestone. D.105.0, H.55.0mm 26721 sf12479 (P3) (*Fig.1243*)

9663 Incomplete, tall slender lamp with carinated plinth and flaring base and top; part of rim survives. Surfaces decorated with scratched star, criss-crosses and roundel patterns. Deep cone-shaped depression cut into upper surface. Limestone, greyish-white, well-sorted. Finely relict oolitic, appreciably dolomitic, with a few shell fragments. Lower Magnesian Limestone. Base D.53.0, H.115.0mm 25795 sf9594 (P4A) (*Fig.1244*)

9664 Large, crudely fashioned to cylindrical form, top sooted around central hollow. Sandstone, pale to medium grey, medium- to coarse-grained with angular to subrounded grains and a few small quartz pebbles, poorly sorted but with grain size-differentiated cross-bedded layers, and moderately compacted. Millstone Grit. H.220.0, D.180.0mm 20916 sf7288 (P4B)

9665 Complete, cylindrical shape. Surfaces roughly finished with visible tool marks, patches of burning. A depression at each end, one long and narrow, the other wider and shallow. Limestone, pale yellowish-grey to white, moderately sorted, fine to medium oolitic, with a few monoliths and small shell fragments. Middle or Upper Jurassic. D.145.0, D.85.0mm 22017 sf7774 (P4B)

9666 Rounded block, complete except for broken rim edge. Slight base collar or 'plinth', very sooted exterior. Wide shallow hollow cut into upper surface, tool marks visible. Chalk, white, fine-grained (i.e. slightly coarser than most chalk), with a few forams. Chalk Group, probably Ferriby Chalk Formation. D.75.0, H.68.0mm 22809 sf8131 (P4B) (*Fig.1243*)

9667 Complete, roughly square block (in 2 pieces). Hollow cut deep into upper surface, sooting on top and edge of hollow. Sandstone, medium grey, medium- to coarse-grained with subangular to subrounded grains, moderately sorted and moderately compacted. Millstone Grit. L.100.0, W.90.0, H.120.0mm 8499 sf1577 (P5A)

9668 Fragmentary block, approximately one-quarter survives. Shallow depression pecked into upper surface, external sooting, slightly tapered towards the base. Limestone, pale grey, well sorted, finely oolitic. Middle or Upper Jurassic. L.140.0, W.110.0, T.60.0mm 20808 sf7277 (P5A) (*Fig.1243*)

9669 Circular block, approximately three-quarters survives. Shallow depression pecked into both ends, one slightly deeper than the other. Little evidence of sooting. Limestone, pale grey, fine-grained, mainly dolomitic. Lower Magnesian Limestone. D.80.0, H.95.0mm 3588 sf8807 (P5Cr) (*Fig.1243*)

9670 Fragmentary block, approximately one-third survives. conical hollow pecked into upper surface. Exterior slightly faceted. Flat base with some sooting. Limestone, greyish-white, fine-grained, dolomitic. Lower Magnesian Limestone. D.100.0, H.97.0mm u/s sf320 (*Fig.1243*)

Vessels

9671 Bowl with flat-topped, squared rim. External sooting. Iron suspension loop attached through four holes which pierce the rim 15mm below top edge and are held in place at the top by smaller iron strips, of which one survives. External sooting. Steatite, pale silvery grey, medium- to coarse-grained. Probably Dalradian Supergroup. D.270.0, H.74.0, T.14.0mm 22306 sf7565, 22670 sf7792, 22574 sf7723 (P4B) (*Figs.1240, 1242*)

9672 Fragment. External sooting, smoothed surfaces. Steatite, pale silvery grey, medium-grained. Probably Dalradian Super-group. L.11.0, T.21.0, W.86.0mm 27639 sf10083 (P4B)

9673 Fragment. Schist, pale silvery grey, medium- to coarse-grained, talc; strongly schistose. Probably Dalradian Supergroup. L.64.0, T.25.0, W.35.0mm 29222 sf10409 (P4B)

9674 Fragment, worked, possibly part of a bowl. Schist, pale silvery grey, medium- to coarse-grained, talc; only moderate schistosity. Probably Dalradian Supergroup. L.75.0, W.22.0, T.18.0mm 29222 sf10474 (P4B)

9675 Fragment of possible vessel but form is unclear. There is one straight flat edge, the rest is broken away. All surfaces show signs of wear and a narrow V-profile groove has been cut into both flat surfaces. Sandstone, medium grey, fine-grained with angular to subrounded grains, fairly well sorted and well compacted, with sparse muscovite and dark minerals and/or rock fragments. Upper Carboniferous, probably Coal Measures. L.85.0, W.60.0, T.25.0mm 29193 sf11738 (P4B)

9676 Fragment, internal sooting, smoothed surfaces. Steatite, pale silvery grey, medium-grained; mainly talc with a few minute flakes of a chlorite-like mineral. Probably Dalradian Supergroup. L.85.0, D.15.0, W.55.0mm 20808 sf7256 (P5A)

9677 Fragment, external and internal sooting, smoothed surface. Steatite, pale silvery grey, medium- to coarse-grained, with a few minute flakes of a chlorite-like mineral. Probably Dalradian Supergroup. L.121.0, W.89.0, T.17.0mm 20808 sf7280 (P5A)

9678 Fragment, no signs of working, schist, white to pale silvery grey, medium-grained, talc. Probably Dalradian Supergroup. L.44.0, W.10.0, T.7.0mm 21478 sf9011 (P5B)

9679 Fragment. Schist, pale silvery grey, medium-grained, talc. Probably Dalradian Supergroup. L.36.0, W.17.0, T.7.0mm 21478 sf9027 (P5B)

9680 Fragment, blackened inside, smoothed surfaces, perforation 9mm diameter. Schist, pale silvery grey, medium-grained, talc; only slightly schistose. Probably Dalradian Supergroup. L.99.0, W.89.0, T.18.0mm 21554 sf9925 (P5B) (*Fig.1240*)

9681 Fragment. Schist, pale silvery grey, medium-grained, talc. Probably Dalradian Supergroup. L.110.0, H.45.0, T.24.0 D.c.300.0mm 21510 sf9326 (P5B)

9682 Bowl fragment with angled rim and single suspension hole drilled through 60mm below rim, smoothed surfaces. Sooting on exterior, tool marks visible on inside surface. Steatite, pale silvery grey, medium- to coarse-grained, with a few minute flakes of a chlorite-like mineral. Probably Dalradian Supergroup. D.c.380.0, T.16.5mm 21898 sf9935 (P5B)

9683 Fragments (10) unworked, and one bowl fragment. Schist, pale silvery grey, coarse-grained, talc. Probably Dalradian Supergroup. L.80.0, W.40.0, T.25.0mm 29263 sf10603 (P5B)

9684 Fragment, worked, possibly part of a bowl. Schist, pale silvery grey, coarse-grained, talc; strongly schistose. Prob-

ably Dalradian Supergroup. L.38.0, W.26.0, T.20.0mm 29263 sf10879 (P5B)

9685 Fragment, worked. Schist. As *9684*. Probably Dalradian Supergroup. L.38.0, W.30.0, T.20.0mm 29263 sf10880 (P5B)

9686 Fragment, unworked. Schist. As *9684*, with a chlorite-like mineral. Probably Dalradian Supergroup. L.50.0, W.40.0, T.24.0mm 29263 sf10882 (P5B)

9687 Fragments (4), unworked. Schist. As *9684*. Probably Dalradian Supergroup. L.40.0, W.25.0, T.20.0mm 29263 sf10883 (P5B)

9688 Fragments (7), unworked. Schist. As *9684*. Probably. Dalradian Supergroup. L.25.0, W.15.0, T.14.0mm 29263 sf10885 (P5B)

9689 Fragment, external sooting, rough surface. Steatite, pale to medium silvery grey, medium- to coarse-grained; with a few flakes of a chlorite-like mineral; slight trace of schistosity in places. Probably Dalradian Supergroup. L.14.0, T.20.0mm 9224 sf2300 (C6e9; mid 13th century) (P6)

9690 Fragment, unworked. Schist, pale silvery grey, medium-grained, talc, with a chlorite-like mineral and ?magnesite in small masses and lining fractures. Probably Dalradian Supergroup. L.42.0, W.24.0, T.15.0mm 3256 sf2434 (A6i2; 14th/15th century) (P6)

9691 Fragment, possibly base. Sandstone, pale grey, medium-grained (but including a few scattered coarse grains) with subangular to (mainly) subrounded grains, moderately sorted and uncompacted, slightly oolitic, strongly calcareous, with sparse minute fossil debris. Middle Jurassic, probably from north-eastern Yorkshire. D.152.0, H.20.0mm13527 sf3978 (B6c7; early 13th century) (P6)

9692 Bowl fragment with squared rim. Steatite, pale silvery grey, medium-grained; with a few minute flakes of a chlorite-like mineral. Probably Dalradian Supergroup. H.41.0, W.37.0, T.10.0mm 3453 sf15703 (A6c1, 12th century) (P6) (*Fig.1240*)

Querns

Sandstone

All sandstone querns are of Millstone Grit unless otherwise specified.

9693 Fragment of upper stone with part of edge socket surviving. Pale grey, mainly coarse-grained with subangular to subrounded grains and a few rounded coarse grains, fairly well sorted and moderately compacted, with sparse muscovite. D.460.0, T.70.0mm 28020 sf10032 (P3)

9694 Fragment of upper stone, part of central perforation surviving. Edges bevelled and upper surface dressed. Pale grey, medium- to coarse-grained with mainly subangular grains and a few subrounded coarse grains, moderately sorted and fairly well compacted. D.480.0, T.60.0mm, perforation D.30.0mm 27083 sf10183 (P3)

9695 Fragment. Pale to medium grey, medium- to coarse-grained (including some 2–4mm wide grains) with subangular to subrounded grains, a few rounded coarse grains and scattered small subrounded to rounded quartz and fine-grained sandstone pebbles, poorly sorted and poorly compacted, with one large and a few minute reddish-brown subrounded ferruginous nodules. L.90.0, W.70.0, T.60.0mm 27878 sf11005 (P3)

9696 Fragment, part of worn edge survives. Medium grey, medium- to coarse-grained (including some 2–4mm wide grains) with subangular to subrounded grains and a few small rounded quartz pebbles, moderately to fairly well sorted in grain size-differentiated layers, and moderately compacted, with sparse muscovite. D.420.0, T.80.0mm 30575 sf11787 (P3)

9697 Fragment of upper stone with edge and part of central perforation surviving and well-worn grinding surface. Possible secondary use as a grinding surface over whole face. Upper surface roughly dressed. Pale to medium grey, medium- to (slightly) coarse-grained with subangular to subrounded grains, moderately sorted and moderately compacted. D.420.0, T.80.0mm, perforation D.30.0mm 30615 sf11819 (P3)

9698 Fragment only, upper stone, socket close to the edge perforated through to other side, worn on grinding edge, part of central perforation survives. Pale grey, medium- to coarse-grained with subangular to subrounded grains and a few scattered subrounded quartz pebbles, poorly sorted except in some grain size-differentiated cross-bedded layers, and poorly compacted. D.460.0, T.38.0, perforation D.c.100.0mm 36155 sf13649 (P3) (*Fig.1249*)

9699 Fragment with edge surviving. Pale to medium grey, medium- to (mainly) coarse-grained with subangular to subrounded grains, moderately sorted in partly grain size-differentiated layers, and moderately compacted. D.380.0, T.70.0mm 22723 sf7905 (P4B)

9700 Half of upper stone with worn edge, part of perforation and shallow socket survive. Pale to medium grey, fine- to medium-grained with subangular to subrounded grains, moderately sorted and moderately compacted, with a few moulds of small wood fragments. Upper Carboniferous, probably Coal Measures. D.350.0, L.340.0, T.60.0mm, perforation D.75.0mm 23663 sf7962 (P4B) (*Fig.1249*)

9701 Fragment of upper stone, part of socket survives. Pale to medium grey, fine- to coarse (but mainly medium)-grained (including a few 2–4mm wide grains), with angular to subrounded grains, moderately sorted and moderately compacted. D.480.0, L.250.0, T.75.0mm 34730 sf13155 (P4B)

9702 Fragment, part of perforation survives. Pale grey, medium- to coarse-grained with angular to subrounded grains, poorly sorted and poorly to moderately compacted. L.150.0, W.90.0, T.60.0mm, perforation D.40.0mm 22723 sf18962 (P4B)

9703 Fragment of upper stone with central perforation. Pale grey with brown ferruginous staining along bedding layers, fine- to medium- and slightly coarse-grained with subangular to subrounded grains, moderately to well sorted in grain size-differentiated layers, and moderately compacted, with sparse muscovite. Upper Carboniferous, probably Millstone Grit. D.440.0, T.75.0mm, perforation D.80.0mm 22124 sf10873 (P5A)

9704 Fragment with part of perforation remaining. Pale to medium grey, medium- to coarse-grained with subangular to subrounded grains, moderately sorted and moderately compacted. L.180.0, T.90.0mm, perforation D.80.0mm 22053 sf13079 (P5A)

9705 Fragment with part of central perforation remaining. Pale brownish-grey, fine-grained with subangular to subrounded grains, well sorted and well compacted, with sparse muscovite mainly on slightly fissile laminae. Upper Carboniferous, probably Coal Measures, but alternatively could conceivably be Middle Jurassic. D.450.0, T.36.0mm, perforation D.80.0mm 13733 sf3609 (P5B)

9706 Fragment, probably of lower stone, edge survives. Dressing marks visible on lower face. Pale grey, fine- to coarse (but mainly medium)-grained with angular to subrounded grains, poorly sorted and moderately compacted. D.480.0, L.190.0, T.60.0mm 15368 sf4239 (P5B)

9707 Fragment, raised rim around perforation survives, pale to medium brownish and locally yellowish-grey, medium to coarse-grained with sub angular to subrounded grains

and a few coarse rounded grains, moderately sorted in partly grain size -differentiated layers, and poorly to moderately compacted. D.360.0, T.60.0mm 14887 sf6077 (P5B)

9708 Fragment of upper stone with part of perforation remaining. Pale to medium grey, medium- to coarse-grained with subangular to subrounded grains and a few rounded coarse grains, moderately sorted and moderately compacted, with sparse muscovite. D.540.0, L.36.0, T.90.0mm, perforation D.100.0mm 21845 sf9783 (P5B)

Lava

All lava querns are of Mayen type lava unless otherwise specified.

9709 Fragment. Medium to dark grey, vesicular with a few crystals of both white translucent and green minerals. L.80.0, T.4.0mm 25990 sf10794 (P3)

9710 Fragment part of grinding surface survives. Medium grey, vesicular. L.105.0, W.40.0, T.46.0mm 28750 sf11079 (P3)

9711 Fragment possibly of upper stone. As *9710*. L.120.0, T.50.0mm 28750 sf11102 (P3)

9712 Fragment. As *9710*. L.45.0, W.40.0, T.23.0mm 27819 sf11554 (P3)

9713 Fragment. Medium grey, vesicular, with a few crystals of a green mineral. L.105.0, W.100.0, T.75.0mm 30633 sf11814 (P3)

9714 Fragment, including part of socket. Pale to medium grey, otherwise as *9709*. L.60.0, W.50.0, T.20.0mm 30727 sf11883 (P3)

9715 Fragment. Medium grey, vesicular, with a few crystals of white translucent, green and black minerals. L.75.0, T.50.0mm 30922 sf12296 (P3)

9716 Fragment. As *9710*. L.50.0, W.30.0, T.45.0mm 32547 sf13550 (P3)

9717 Fragment. Medium to dark grey, vesicular with a few crystals of a white translucent mineral. L.63.0, W.28.0, T.20.0mm 31595 sf14547 (P3)

9718 Fragment. Medium grey, vesicular, with minute inclusions of ?detrital quartz grains. L.50.0mm 30954 sf14548 (P3)

9719 Fragment. As *9710*. L.82.0, W.28.0, T.12.0mm 22233 sf7651 (P4B)

9720 Fragment. As *9710*. L.95.0, W.55.0, T.25.0mm 25340 sf8460 (P4B)

9721 Fragment. Pale to medium grey, otherwise as *9715*. L.120.0, W.110.0, T.60.0mm 19390 sf10501 (P4B)

9722 Fragment. Medium to dark grey, otherwise as *9713*. L.210.0, W.110.0, T.85.0mm 27741 sf11108 (P4B)

9723 Fragment. As *9710*. L.75.0, W.40.0, T.22.0mm 28882 sf12112 (P4B)

9724 Fragment. As *9710*. L.90.0, W.80.0, T.27.0mm 19390 sf12679 (P4B)

9725 Fragment. Vesicular, with a few crystals of both white translucent and black minerals. L.60.0, W.50.0, T.35.0mm 32406 sf12983 (P4B)

9726 Fragment. As *9710*. L.50.0, W.50.0, T.32.0mm 22180 sf7448 (P5A)

9727 Fragment. As *9710* L.45.0, W.35.0, T.30.0mm 2695 sf383 (P5B)

9728 Fragment. Medium grey, otherwise as *9717*. L.80.0, W.65.0, T.55.0mm 14372 sf4005 (P5B)

9729 Fragment. Medium to dark grey, vesicular. L.40.0, W.30.0, T.20.0mm 15731 sf5164 (P5B)

9730 Fragment. Pale to medium grey, vesicular. L.70.0, W.45.0, T.40.0mm 15731 sf5203 (P5B)

9731 Fragment. As *9710*. L.30.0mm 15933 sf8436 (P5B)

9732 Fragment possibly of lower stone part of central perforation survives. As *9710*. L.125.0, W.83.0, T.36.0mm 28071 sf11779 (P5B)

Limestone

9733 Upper stone, incomplete, one edge sheered off and another damaged. Grinding surface well worn, tool marks visible on upper surface. Limestone, pale grey, fine-grained and moderately oolitic (with fine to medium moderately sorted and poorly compacted ooliths, sparse scattered pisoliths and oncoliths) and containing appreciable finely fragmented fossil debris and a few larger fossil fragments, notably of echinoid spines and bivalves, and sparse *Pentacrinites* ossicles. Upper Jurassic Corallian Group of north-eastern Yorkshire, probably Malton Oolite Member of Coralline Oolite Formation in Howardian Hills. D.374.0, T.111.0, perforation D.68.0mm 26471 sf8846 (P4A)

Counters and possible pot lids

9734 Counter?, both edges dressed to form rough disc. Sandstone, pale grey, fine-grained with subangular to subrounded grains, well sorted and fairly well compacted, with appreciable muscovite mainly concentrated on fissile laminae. Coal Measures of Elland Flags type. D.38.0, T.10.0mm 30922 sf14375 (P3)

9735 Counter. Sandstone, as *9734*. Coal Measures of Elland Flags type. D.55.0, T.15.0mm 26610 sf9200 (P4A) (*Fig.1261*)

9736 Pot lid?, edges shaped to form disc, both surfaces dressed. Sandstone, pale brownish-grey, otherwise as *9734*. Coal Measures of Elland Flags type. D.88.0, T.18.0mm 30134 sf11569 (P4A)

9737 Counter, edges dressed to form disc, surfaces dressed. Sandstone, pale brownish-grey, otherwise as *9734*. Coal Measures of Elland Flags type. D.20.0, T.4.0mm 18023 sf4781 (P4B)

9738 Pot lid? Sandstone, pale brownish-grey, otherwise as *9734*. Coal Measures of Elland Flags type. D.90.0, T.16.0mm 22418 sf7585 (P4B) (*Fig.1261*)

9739 Counter. Suboval form with domed top and flat base. Sandstone, medium brownish-grey with pale yellowish-brown ferruginous patches, medium-grained with subangular to subrounded grains, moderately sorted and fairly well compacted. Upper Carboniferous. D.27.0, H.25.0mm 22416 sf7607 (P4B)

9740 Counter. Roughly chipped disc with two flat surfaces. Sandstone, pale brownish-grey, otherwise as *9734*. Coal Measures of Elland Flags type. D.23.0, T.5.0mm 22415 sf7628 (P4B)

9741 Counter. Irregularly shaped, roughly discoid, two flat surfaces. Sandstone, medium grey, otherwise as *9734*. Coal Measures of Elland Flags type. D.23.0, T.5.0mm 22449 sf7707 (P4B)

9742 Pot lid. Edges dressed to form rough disc, both surfaces dressed. As *9734*. Coal Measures of Elland Flags type. D.86.0, T.20.0mm 19390 sf8917 (P4B)

9743 Counter. Sandstone, as *9734*. Coal Measures of Elland Flags type. D.24.0, T.3.0mm 32169 sf12609 (P4B) (*Fig.1261*)

9744 Counter. Roughly chopped disc with two flat surfaces. Sandstone, medium grey, otherwise as *9734*. Coal Measures of Elland Flags type. D.46.0, T.15.0mm 22122 sf7525 (P5A)

9745 Counter fragment, edges dressed to form rough disc. Sandstone, pale mottled brownish-grey, fine-grained with subangular to subrounded grains, well sorted and fairly well compacted, with scattered muscovite; probably fissile. Upper Carboniferous, probably Coal Measures. D.57.0, T.16.0mm 22368 sf7903 (P5A)

9746 Pot lid, edges dressed to form rough disc, both surfaces dressed. Sandstone, pale brownish-grey, otherwise as *9734*. Coal Measures of Elland Flags type. D.64.0, T.13.0mm 2800 sf473 (P5B)

9747 Counter fragment, surfaces not dressed. Sandstone, pale to medium grey, fine- to medium-grained with angular to subangular grains, moderately sorted and fairly well compacted, with sparse muscovite and dark minerals and/or rock fragments; fissile. Upper Carboniferous. Possibly natural fragment of pebble used as a counter. D.37.0, T.6.0mm 7005 sf583 (P5B)

9748 Counter?, edges dressed to form rough disc, surfaces not dressed. Sandstone, pale brownish-grey, otherwise as *9745*. Upper Carboniferous, probably Coal Measures. D.42.0, T.13.0mm 15494 sf4507 (P5B)

9749 Counter, highly polished on all surfaces, possibly used as a burnisher. Lithology uncertain. Dark grey, very fine-grained rock with hardness exceeding 6 on Moh's Scale. Probably Lower Palaeozoic indurated quartzitic siltstone or silty mudstone. D.22.0, T.4.0mm 14666 sf5475 (P5B)

9750 Pot lid, edges shaped to form disc, one surface dressed, the other flaked away. Sandstone, pale brownish-grey, otherwise as *9734*. Coal Measures of Elland Flags type. D.75.0, T.17.0mm 21925 sf11795 (P5B)

9751 Counter, subdiscoidal, faces smooth, edge ground smooth. Sandstone, as *9734*. Coal Measures of Elland Flags type. D.40.0, T.9.5mm u/s sf12026

Playing pieces

9752 Dome-headed *hnefatafl* piece. Chalk, white, very fine-grained. Chalk Group. D.20.0, H.18.0mm 22233 sf7630 (P4B) (*Fig.1263*)

9753 Dome-headed *hnefatafl* piece. Chalk, white, very fine-grained. Chalk Group. D.25.0, H.18.0mm 22421 sf7656 (P4B)

9754 Dome-headed *hnefatafl* piece. Chalk, white, very fine-grained. Chalk Group. D.22.0, H.17.0mm 22421 sf7667 (P4B)

9755 Pointed-headed *hnefatafl* piece. Chalk includes few forams and minute shell fragments. D.20.0, H.20.0mm 22421 sf7668 (P4B)

9756 Dome-headed *hnefatafl* piece. Chalk, white, very fine-grained. Chalk Group. Painted with thin red ochre. D.22.5, H.16.0mm 25725 sf9523 (P4B)

9757 Pointed-headed *hnefatafl* piece. Chalk, white, very fine-grained. Chalk Group. D.19.5, H.18.0mm 25808 sf9852 (P4B) (*Fig.1263*)

9758 Dome-headed *hnefatafl* piece. Chalk, white, very fine-grained. Chalk Group. Traces of red ochre patches; chalk includes few forams. D.23.0, H.18.5mm 21618 sf12231 (P5B)

9759 Dome-headed *hnefatafl* piece. Chalk includes few forams. D.20.0, H.20.0mm 21200 sf8234 (P5B)

Beads

9760 Steatite, with some ?chlorite. Probably Dalradian Supergroup. D.11.0, L.15.0mm, perforation D.5.0mm 18666 sf5434 (P4B) (*Fig.1291*)

9761 Tiny, discoid. Crinoid ossicle of calcite, with trace of worn radial structure. Carboniferous. D.4.0, T.2.0mm, perforation D.2.0mm 34201 sf14397 (P4B)

9762 Fragment, discoid. Uncertain lithology; greyish-white translucent material with scattered minute dark fan-shaped and lath-shaped inclusions; probably quartzitic rock in chalcedonic or similar form. Source unknown. D.12.0, T.1.0mm, perforation D.3.0mm 8524 sf1611 (P5B)

9763 Discoid. Marble, pale greyish-white, fine-grained, slightly translucent in places, containing appreciable white, convoluted, porphyroblastic (i.e. larger) calcite crystal clusters. Probably non-British. D.12.0, T.1.0mm, perforation D.3.0mm 13716 sf3540 (P5B)

9764 Discoid. Mudstone, dark grey, ?silty, ?fissile. Lower Palaeozoic, Carboniferous or Lower Jurassic. D.13.0, T.2.0mm, perforation D.4.0mm 15193 sf4194 (P5B)

9765 Discoid. Mudstone, black, very fine-grained, ?fissile, possibly slaty but no trace of cleavage. Lower Palaeozoic, Carboniferous or Lower Jurassic. D.12.0, T.1.0mm, perforation D.3.0mm 21076 sf8778 (P5B)

9766 Discoid. Mudstone, medium to dark grey, fissile. Lower Palaeozoic, Carboniferous or Lower Jurassic. D.9.0, T.1.0mm, perforation D.3.0mm 21033 sf9389 (P5B) (Fig.1291)

9767 Discoid. Marble, mottled greyish-white translucent, with yellowish-white inclusions. Probably non-British source. D.9.0, T.1.5mm, perforation D.2.0mm 21680 sf9484 (P5B)

9768 Discoid. D.18.0, T.1.0mm, perforation D.3.0mm 21680 sf9486 (P5B)

9769 Discoid. Mudstone, dark grey, silty, ?fissile. Lower Palaeozoic, Carboniferous or Lower Jurassic. D.14.0, T.1.0mm, perforation D.3.0mm 21680 sf9488 (P5B)

9770 Discoid. Mudstone as 9769. Lower Palaeozoic, Carboniferous or Lower Jurassic. D.12.0, T.1.0mm, perforation D.4.0mm 21680 sf9489 (P5B)

9771 Discoid. Mudstone, as 9769. Lower Palaeozoic, Carboniferous or Lower Jurassic. D.9.0, T.1.0mm, perforation D.4.0mm 21680 sf9491 (P5B)

9772 Discoid. Marble, as 9767, probably non-British source. D.9.0, T.1.0mm, perforation D.2.0mm 21680 sf9492 (P5B)

9773 Discoid. Marble, as 9767, probably non-British source. D.9.0, T.1.0mm, perforation D.2.0mm 21680 sf9494 (P5B)

9774 Discoid. Marble, as 9767, probably non-British source. D.9.0, T.1.3mm, perforation D.2.0mm 21680 sf9495 (P5B)

9775 Fragment of discoid bead. Mudstone, dark grey, silty slightly quartzitic. Lower Palaeozoic, Carboniferous or Lower Jurassic. D.9.0, Perforation D.9.0, T.2.0mm 21244 sf9719 (P5B)

9776 Discoid. As 9767. D.13.0, T.1.3mm, perforation D.3.0mm 2409 sf16256 (P5B) (Fig.1291)

9777 Discoid. Siltsone, pale grey, medium- to coarse-grained, slightly quartzitic. Lower Palaeozoic or Carboniferous. D.11.0, T.1.3mm, perforation D.3.4mm 7257 sf19527 (P5B)

9778 Discoid Mudstone, medium grey, slightly fissile. Lower Palaeozoic, Carboniferous or Lower Jurassic. D.18.0, T.1.0mm, perforation D.3.0mm 20205 sf6398 (P5Cr)

9779 Discoid. Mudstone, medium to dark grey, ?fissile. Lower Palaeozoic, Carboniferous or Lower Jurassic. D.12.0, T.1.0mm, perforation D.4.0mm 12869 sf3706 (D6a19–21; late 12th/early 13th century) (P6)

9780 Discoid. Mudstone, dark grey, ?fissile, slightly calcareous on ?laminae. Probably Lower Jurassic , but could be Carboniferous. D.11.0, T.1.0mm, perforation D.3.0mm u/s sf4662

9781 Discoid. Mudstone, as 9765. Lower Palaeozoic, Carboniferous or Lower Jurassic. D.11.0, T.1.0mm, perforation D.2.0mm u/s sf8790

Fossils

Identified by Dr G.D. Gaunt with the following exceptions: Mr C.J. Wood identified 9788 and 9807; Mr M. Mitchell identified 9783, 9800, 9804 and 9810; Dr H.C. Ivimey-Cook identified 9797.

9782 Bivalve of calcite, Gryphaea arcuata. Lias Group. 26647 sf9007 (P3)

9783 Coral, simple, of calcite. Dibunophyllum bipartitum. Carboniferous Limestone. Worn shape suggests erratic. 11674 sf30220 (P3)

9784 Crinoid ossicle, of calcite. Carboniferous Limestone. Yoredale sequence or Harrogate Roadstone. 14139 sf30808 (P3)

9785 As 9784. 14384 sf30841 (P3)

9786 Consists of five items. Two are crinoid ossicles (possibly used as beads), of calcite. Carboniferous Limestone. Yoredale sequence or Harrogate Roadstone. Two more are matching fragments of a small (2.5mm diameter) calcareous convexo-concave disc. Uncertain lithology; possibly a foram or part of a crinoid cup or an echinoid. Carboniferous Limestone.Yoredale sequence or lower part of Millstone Grit. The other is a small (3mm diameter) non-calcareous convexo-concave disc with fluted edge, texture like very fine-grained sand in a brown gelatinous matrix, and abundant minute pores. Uncertain lithology; possibly a silicified form or part of a crinoid cup or an echinoid. Carboniferous Limestone.Yoredale sequence or lower part of Millstone Grit. 14383 sf30922 (P3)

9787 Echinoid (part) of pale grey flint, slightly reddish in places. Micraster sp. Chalk Group. Reddish colour indicates heat. 11368 sf31230 (P3)

9788 As 9782. 12819 sf32296 (P3)

9789 Two items. Both are limestone, pale to medium grey, fine-grained bioclastic; one item includes crinoid ossicles. Carboniferous Limestone.Yoredale sequence or Harrogate Roadstone. 14379 sf33094 (P3)

9790 Chert mottled grey with abundant casts and moulds, and also some residual calcitic, crinoid ossicles. Yoredale sequence. Worn shape suggests erratic. 25252 sf8520 (P4A)

9791 Unknown lithology. Pale brownish-cream (with darker brown spots) heavy material, with hardness exceeding 6 on Moh's Scale, slight response to dilute HCl implying some finely dispersed calcite or other $CaCO_3$ compound, pits and scoring on some surfaces suggesting bone structure, but without any indication from its shape of an organic origin. Conceivably an unusual form of silicified bone fragment, but otherwise unlike any rock, mineral or fossil. 30132 sf11558 (P4A)

9792 Ammonite of calcite. Amaltheus margaritatus. Cleveland Ironstone Formation of Lias Group. 20918 sf7292 (P4B)

9793 Bivalve of calcite. Inoceramus sp. with very fine-grained chalk infilling. Chalk Group. 22233 sf7689 (P4B)

9794 Chert, black, containing abundant minute fossil fragments of residual calcite and mould of large crinoid ossicle. Yoredale sequence. 24386 sf8225 (P4B)

9795 Limestone, medium grey, medium-grained, bioclastic, with large crushed bivalves including ?Gryphaea arcuta. Jurassic, probably Lias Group. 24668 sf8342 (P4B)

9796 Sandstone, pale grey, fine- to medium-grained with subangular to subrounded grains, well sorted and fairly well compacted, with carbonaceous-lined parallel grooves and ridges; probably cast of wood fragment. Upper Carboniferous, probably Coal Measures. 25285 sf8358 (P4B)

9797 Limestone, pale grey, fine-grained (part of large flattish concretion), with layers of crushed bivalves, possibly including cf. Protocardia and cf. Pleuromia. Jurassic, probably Lias Group. 21479 sf9367 (P4B)

9798 Limestone, pale grey, fine- to medium-grained, bioclastic, with moulds of bivalves including Gryphaea bilobata. Middle Jurassic. 28920 sf11328 (P4B)

9799 Crinoid ossicles, pale grey with reddened surface of calcite. Carboniferous Limestone.Yoredale sequence or Harrogate Roadstone. 35059 sf13810 (P4B)

9800 Consists of two items. The longer is coral, compound of calcite. Lithostrotion junceum. Carboniferous Limestone.

The round item is crinoid ossicle of calcite. Carboniferous Limestone. Yoredale sequence or Harrogate Roadstone. 14378 sf27371 (P4B)

9801 Limestone, medium grey to brownish-grey, fine-grained, silty, with casts of moulds of bivalves possibly ptermyaiids and modiolids. Jurassic, probably Lias Group. 20400 sf7122 (P5A)

9802 Limestone, pale, mottled reddish-grey, largely silicified, with brachiopod *Productus SS sp.* other brachiopods, some crinoid ossicles. ?Burrow fills and abundant spicule casts. Yoredale sequence or lower part of Millstone Grit. Partly worn shape suggests erratic. 20143 sf7142 (P5A)

9803 Chert, pale grey, containing crinoid ossicle of residual calcite. Yoredale sequence. 22016 sf7171 (P5A)

9804 Chert, pale grey, containing some residual calcite with part of Brachipod, possibly *Avonia sp.* Yoredale sequence. 22104 sf7336 (P5A)

9805 Crinoid ossicles (four joined together) of calcite. Carboniferous Limestone, Yoredale sequence or Harrogate Roadstone. 26953 sf14380 (P5A)

9806 Sea urchin? fragment. 1611 sf369 (P5B)

9807 Oechinoid of flint with off-white patina. *Conulus sp. or Galerites sp.,* probably the latter. Welton Formation or Burnham Formation of Chalk Group. Worn and battered condition suggests erratic. 1473 sf434 (P5B)

9808 Trilobite? fish tooth. 1473 sf466 (P5B)

9809 Trilobite? fish tooth. 2789 sf479 (P5B)

9810 Brachipod of calcite. *Productus productus?* Carboniferous Limestone. Partly worn condition suggests erratic. 18485 sf5009 (P5B)

9811 Limestone, variably grey silicified, with abundant crinoid ossicles, some in lengths of intact stems. Yoredale sequence or Harrogate Roadstone. 18827 sf5440 (P5B)

9812 Chalk, white to pale yellow, very fine-grained with casts and moulds of crushed inoceramid and ostreaid bivalve fragments. Chalk Group. 14843 sf7097 (P5B)

9813 Limestone, pale to medium grey, medium- to coarse-grained, partly bioclastic, with bivalve *cf. Liostrea* and other bivalve fragments. Jurassic, probably Lias Group. 15366 sf7428 (P5B)

9814 Crinoid ossicle (split) or calcite. Carboniferous Limestone, Yoredale sequence or Harrogate Roadstone. 15779 sf15726 (P5B)

9815 Sandstone, pale grey, fine- to medium-grained with subangular to subrounded grains, moderately sorted and fairly well compacted, with casts and moulds of a productid brachiopod, other brachiopods and ?bivalves. Lower part of Millstone Grit. 6785 sf6204 (5Cr)

Net weight

9816 Small Norwegian Ragstone pebble in which a perforation has been drilled, possibly for use as a small weight or sinker. D.9.5, T.3.3mm sf6240 6789 (5Cr) (*Fig.1237*)

Porphry slabs

9817 Fragment of polished slab. Rectangular shape with slightly domed top, sides still have parts of their original surfaces but both ends are broken away. Andesite or basalt, very fine-grained, porphyritic, with pale greyish-green large (up to 15mm long) single, inter penetration-twinned and compound phenocrysts of feldspar, probably plagioclase. Similar to Eycott Hill lavas in north-eastern Lake District. L.34.0, W.19.0, T.11.0mm 24829 sf8435 (P3)

9818 Triangular-shaped polished slab, all surfaces survive and all are highly polished. Black, very fine-grained rock with hardness exceeding 6 on Moh's Scale. Possibly basalt, or chert, or indurated quartzitic mudstone or siltstone. L.36.0, T.5.0, W.29.0mm. 20341 sf7106 (P4B)

9819 Tiny fragment of polished slab, one original surface survives. As *9817.* L.9.0, W.7.0, T.5.0mm 29263 sf10888 (P5B)

9820 Fragment of polished slab, three original surfaces survive, one is unpolished. Andesite or basalt, dark grey, very fine-grained porphyritic, with pale greyish-brown (but wide green bordered) angular to subrounded large (up to 13mm long) single phenocrysts of feldspar, probably plagioclase, and a few small angular to subrounded black masses around which the interfaces with the groundmass have been deeply eroded, probably by polishing. Similar to Eycott Hill lavas in north-eastern Lake District. L.28.0, W.18.0, T.11.0mm 19120 sf6073 (P5Cr)

9821 Fragment of polished slab with upper and lower surfaces surviving, the rest is broken away. Upper surface is highly polished. Andesite or basalt, dark grey, very fine-grained, porphyritic, with pale greyish-brown phenocrysts, mainly single but at least one twinned, of feldspar, probably plagioclase, and a few small rounded quartz masses, possibly filling vesicles. Similar to Eycott Hill lavas in north-eastern Lake District. L 53.0, T.12.0, W.26.0mm 16612 sf6069 (D6a1; late 11th century) (P6)

Miscellaneous

9822 Fragment of roughly ovoid section. Three surfaces worn smooth, the fourth and the ends are broken away. A worn depression appears on one surface. Uncertain lithology. Pale greenish-grey, very fine-grained rock with subconchoidal fracture and hardness exceeding 6 on Moh's Scale. Probably tuff or rhyolitic-andesitic lava or Lower Palaeozoic indurated quartzitic silty mudstone. Shape suggests fragment of Neolithic/Early Bronze Age stone axe, and general appearance similar to Group VI axes of epidotised tuff from Great Langdale, Cumbria. L.28.0, W.35.0, T.21.0mm 20747 sf9093 (P4B)

Fragments

9823 Ironstone fragment with faceted sides. L.20.0, W.12.0, T.19.0mm 26890 sf9273 (P3)

9824 Large lump of limestone with two parallel grooves in it, whose purpose is uncertain but may be related to some form of structure. L.185.0, W.95.0, T.55.0mm 22528 sf7665 (P4B)

9825 Joining fragments of worked sandstone. Two worked surfaces form a right-angle, rest broken away. L.55.0, W.30.0, T.30.0mm 22745 sf8014, 22848 sf8055 (P4B)

9826 Small ovoid pebble of Norwegian Ragstone schist, used as a burnisher or polisher, one worn surface. D.50.0, T.15.0mm 22883 sf8094 (P4B)

9827 Rectangular limestone fragment with one worked surface. L.24.0, W.20.0, T.20.0mm 29193 sf10442 (P4B)

9828 Schist fragment possibly from a hone. L.27.0, W.5.0, T.4.0mm 34290 sf14555 (P4B)

9829 Sandstone fragment with a glaze from metal or glass working. L.25.0, W.18.0, T.19.0mm 35675 sf15704 (P4B)

9830 Norwegian Ragstone pebbles with naturally occurring holes. Possibly collected as amulets. L.47.0, W.38.0, T.12.0mm 25294 sf8343, 22179 sf7384 (P5A)

Jet, jet-like material and shale

Manufacturing evidence

9831 Roughout, disc-shaped, incomplete perforation begun on both surfaces, random scratches on both surfaces. D.33.0, T.5.0mm 31072 sf11040 (P3)

9832 Fragment, worked. Offcut or roughout, roughly rectangular, possibly intended for a pendant, edges worn smooth, one or two slight chips. L.54.0, W.18.0, T.10.0mm 25205 sf8267 (P4A)

9833 Fragment, unworked. Irregular lump of unworked jet with naturally smoothed edges and surfaces. L.69.0, T.38.0, W.48.0mm 22713 sf7907 (P4B)

9834 Roughout, finger-ring. Approximately discoid with rough edges, cone-shaped central perforation begun on one surface, slight trace on other surface. D.34.0, T.12.0mm 25624 sf9181 (P4B) (Fig.1217)

9835 Fragment, unworked. Angular lump, irregular shape. L.21.0, W.20.0, T.10.0mm 19634 sf9314 (P4B)

9836 Fragment, unworked. Small pebble, irregular shape. L.21.0, W.20.0, T.10.0mm 28904 sf12511 (P4B)

9837 Fragment, approximately square with natural or possibly cut surfaces. L.42.0, W.37.0, T.20.0mm 29263 sf10943 (P5B)

Counters and playing pieces

9838 *Hnefatafl* piece. Approximately two-thirds survives. Exterior faceted with narrow shallow grooves cut vertically along the facets. Surface smooth from polishing, possibly the result of handling. Base D.18.0, H.34.0mm 20893 sf12711 (P3) (Fig.1263)

9839 Counter fragment. Approximately half of a flat, lathe-turned disc with polished, bevelled edge (possibly re-used Roman object). D.48.0, T.6.5mm 28005 sf9889 (P5B) (Fig.1263)

9840 *Hnefatafl* piece, rounded top, cut base, faceted body, worn smooth through use. H.19.0, D.15.0mm18366 sf4941 (B6a5; 11th/12th century) (P6) (Fig.1263)

Finger-rings

9841 Fragment. D-profile, highly polished. D.20.0, H.1.0. T.2.0mm 32668 sf13414 (P3)

9842 Fragment. D-profile, surface polished, signs of wear. D.20.5, H.8.0, T.2.5mm 22560 sf7853 (P4B) (Fig.1281)

9843 Fragment. D.27.0, T.4.5mm 25350 sf8594 (P4B) (Fig.1281)

9844 Fragment. D-profile, highly polished. D.21.0, T.2.5, H.8.0mm 25748 sf9437 (P4B)

9845 Fragment. D-profile, highly polished. D.20.0, T.2.0, H.10.0mm 34227 sf12842 (P4B)

9846 Complete. D-profile, irregularly carved rather than lathe-turned, worn. D.30.0, T.4.0, H.7.0mm 34412 sf13007 (P4B) (Fig.1281)

9847 Fragment. D-profile, surface polished, signs of wear. D.20.0, T.2.0, H.10.0mm 2680 sf483 (P5B)

9848 Fragment. D-profile, surface polished, signs of wear. D.19.0, T.3.0, H.9.0mm 5426 sf1619 (P5B)

9849 Fragment. D-profile, surface polished, signs of wear. L.18.0, W.12.0, T.3.0mm 8666 sf1821 (P5B)

9850 Fragment. D-profile, surface polished, signs of wear. D.20.0, T.3.0, H.9.0mm 14849 sf5988 (P5B)

9851 Fragment. D-profile, surface polished, signs of wear. D.21.5, T.1.5, H.9.0mm 19307 sf7410 (P5B)

9852 Fragment. Shale. D.34.0, T.3.5mm 24395 sf8396 (P5B) (Fig.1281)

9853 Fragment, possibly from a ring. Polished. L.5.0, W.3.0, T.2.0mm 21381 sf11266 (P5B)

9854 Fragment. Oval profile, highly polished. D.24.0, T.4.0, H.7.0mm 3463 sf4810 (P5Cr) (Fig.1281)

Bracelets

9855 Fragment only, plain. Part of D-profile. Shale, flaking surface. Diameter unmeasurable, W.7.5 (broken), T.3.0mm (broken) 31067 sf10705 (P3)

9856 Fragment of thin bracelet. Oval profile. Shale. D.60.0, W.4.0, T.3.0mm 30132 sf10608 (P4A)

9857 Four fragments of thick D-profile bracelet. Jet-like material but not jet. D.84.0, T.12.0, W.20.0mm 27621 sfs10893 and 10791 (P4A) (Fig.1293)

9858 Fragment, plain and highly polished. D-profile. Jet. D.61.0, W.18.0, T.5.0mm 26949 sf9443 (P4B)

9859 Fragment of D-profile. Jet-like material, not jet. D.80.0, T.8.0, W.14.0mm 25350 sf8561 (P4B)

9860 Fragment of bracelet with oval profile. Shale. D.40.0, W.8.0, T.5.0mm 2456 sf1049 (P5A) (Fig.1293)

9861 Fragment plain. Part of D-profile, shows signs of wear. Jet-like material, not jet. D.c.80.0, T.10.0, W.18.0mm 3607 sf5462 (P4/5)

Pendants

9862 Equal-armed cross, of rectangular section, central ring-and-dot motif, smaller single ring-and-dot motifs on each arm, all filled with unidentified inlay, possibly orpiment. L.11.8, W.11.4, T.4.4mm 2841 sf500 (A6z2; late 12th century) (P6) (Figs.1282, 1284)

9863 Cross with integral projection for suspension, ends of arms rounded, single ring-and-dot motif in centre and on each arm, all inlaid with orpiment. L.33.7, W.5.1mm 3536 sf3763 (A6c3; 12th century) (P6) (Figs.1282, 1284)

Amber

Beads

Blanks and roughouts

9864 Roughout, knife marks, cloudy and translucent in patches. D.23.0, perforation D.4.0, H.15.0mm, Wt.1.79g 36048 sf13505 (P3) (Fig.1292)

9865 Blank or core from lathe-turning, both surfaces unfinished, with tool marks. D.20.0, T.6.0mm, Wt.0.57g 8232 sf1087 (P4B)

9866 Roughout, central perforation started, tool marks visible. D.24.0mm, Wt.3.54g 25350 sf8428 (P4B)

9867 Roughout, cloudy with surface crust, possible lathe-turning striations, possibly striations in perforation. T.15.0, D.25.0, perforation D.5.0mm, Wt.3.77g 21903 sf10536 (P4B) (Fig.1292)

9868 Roughout with pitted translucent surface. D.12.0mm, Wt.0.67g 29919 sf13073 (P4B)

9869 Unpolished or roughout, opaque with pitted surface. D.10.0, perforation D.5.0mm, Wt.0.25g 32573 sf13724 (P4B) (Fig.1292)

9870 Blank or core, osseous. Surfaces unfinished, off-centre perforation beginning on both sides. D.17.0, T.8.0mm, Wt.0.69g 26953 sf9363 (P5A) (Fig.1292)

9871 Roughout, no perforation, translucent with tool marks, surfaces cut but not smoothed. D.15.0, T.6.0mm, Wt.0.55g 15473 sf4413 (P5B)

9872 Roughout, broken when perforation drilled from one side and hit flaw in amber, surfaces cut roughly, translucent with tool marks. D.19.0, T.9.0mm, Wt.0.81g 6245 sf3313 (D6a6; late 11th/early 12th century) (P6)

9873 Roughout, surfaces cut but not smoothed, no perforation, translucent with tool marks. T.10.0, W.8.0mm, Wt.0.37g 13147 sf3512 (B6u1; late 11th–early 13th century) (P6)

9874 Roughout, broken across perforation, surfaces cut smooth but not polished, osseous with tool marks. D.14.0, T.9.0mm, Wt.0.49g 6258 sf5706 (C6c3, D6a5; 11th–12th century) (P6)

Unfinished

9875 Tiny, broken in production, translucent. D.8.0mm, Wt.0.05g 27621 sf10739 (P4A)

9876 Bead or ring, broken. D.30.0, T.8.0, H.13.0mm, Wt.1.19g 31161 sf11071 (P4A) (*Fig.1292*)

9877 Biconical; broken in production, osseous. D.14.0, H.10.0mm, perforation D.5.0mm, Wt.0.48g 30352 sf11551 (P4A)

9878 Fragments (2), broken when surface unfinished but after perforation drilled from both sides, osseous. Wt.0.45g 20667 sf7175 (P4B)

9879 Fragment, one side lathe-turned, other unfinished, broken after perforation drilled, bastard with tool marks, possibly lathe-turned. D.22.0, T.9.0mm, Wt.0.58g 8453 sf1465 (P5A) (*Fig.1292*)

9880 Unfinished, beginning of perforation on one side, surfaces cut smooth but unpolished, osseous. D.12.0, T.4.0mm, Wt.0.21g 21554 sf9942 (P5B)

Finished beads (including fragments)

9881 Biconical, with some signs of wear. D.16.0, perforation D.5.0, H.10.0mm, Wt.1.27g 26419 sf8978 (P4A) (*Fig.1292*)

9882 Opaque. Roughly shaped rectangular block, split across top over a fault in the amber, possibly intended for a pendant. L.24.0, W.21.0, T.15.0mm, Wt.6.57g 22958 sf8135 (P4B)

9883 Translucent, chipped around the perforation, drilled from both sides, tool marks. D.16.0, perforation D.6.0, H.6.5mm, Wt.1.12g 25748 sf9448 (P4B) (*Fig.1292*)

9884 Tiny fragment, translucent, wear on surface and from thong or thread. H.6.0, T.4.0, D.2.0, perforation. D.0.4mm, Wt.0.06g 32115 sf12533 (P4B)

9885 Broken in use, wear visible on surfaces and around perforation. D.15.5, perforation D.8.0mm, T.9.0mm, Wt.0.68g 29835 sf13038 (P4B) (*Fig.1292*)

9886 Tiny spherical, very crusty surfaces. D.7.0, H.5.0, perforation D.2.0mm, Wt.0.12g 25750 sf14518 (P4B) (*Fig.1292*)

9887 Osseous with tool marks. Wt.0.08g 8290 sf1304 (P5A)

9888 Irregular form, shows signs of surface wear and around perforation, despite misshapen appearance. Translucent. D.13.0mm, Wt.0.38g 8499 sf1515 (P5A)

9889 Fragment, broken in use, wear around perforation, osseous. D.20.0, T.8.0, H.12.0, perforation D.12.0mm, Wt.0.43g 26953 sf9824 (P5A)

9890 Tiny fragment, broken at perforation where it was drilled from two sides on different planes, tool marks visible, diameter unmeasurable, surviving length 5mm. Wt.0.09g 5775 sf1955 (P5B)

9891 Polished, translucent with wear around perforation. D.11.0, perforation D.4.0mm, Wt.0.53g 5714 sf2116 (P5B) (*Fig.1292*)

9892 Globular, complete, lathe-turned, well polished, nicked around the perforation, no evidence of wear. D.18.0, T.12.0, perforation D.6.0mm, Wt.2.39g 6179 sf2609 (P5B)

9893 Unpolished, pitted surface, drilled from both sides, cloudy/opaque. D.15.0, perforation D.4.0mm, Wt.0.95g 14541 sf4374 (P5B) (*Fig.1292*)

9894 Drilled from both sides. Subconical drilled from both sides. Perforation shows signs of wear. D.9.0, perforation D.5.0, H.5.0, T.3.0mm, Wt.0.24g 14973 sf6925

9895 Translucent. Knife trimming marks visible. D.14.0, perforation D.4.0mm, Wt.0.61g 21646 sf9857 (P5B) (*Fig.1292*)

9896 Polished, surface nicked, some wear around the perforation, no tool marks, translucent. T.9.0, D.15.0, perforation D.3.0mm, Wt.1.23g 10732 sf2638 (D6f7–13; late 15th–late 17th century) (P6) (*Fig.1292*)

9897 Complete, crust on surface, wear on perforation. D.18.0, perforation D.3.0mm, Wt.1.81g 13215 sf3668 (B6w1, C6z1; 14th–early 15th century) (P6) (*Fig.1292*)

Finger-rings
Blanks and roughouts

9898 Roughout, translucent, evidence for central core being taken out at lathe-turning stage. D.27.0, T.6.0mm, Wt.0.65g 15894 sf5787 (P4B) (*Fig.1280*)

9899 Roughout, fragment, surfaces unfinished, unmeasurable, translucent. Wt.0.32g 24066 sf8127 (P4B)

9900 Roughout, cloudy pitted surface with pits oblique to knife marks, inside carved out. D.32.0, T.6.5mm, perforation D.20.0mm, Wt.1.86g 35293 sf13862, 34467 sf12959 (P4B) (*Fig.1280*)

9901 Roughout, cloudy with knife-marks. D.23.0, perforation D.15.0, H.7.0mm, Wt.1.29g 34877 sf13401 (P3), 34765 sf13210 (P4B) (*Fig.1280*)

9902 Roughout? fragment, surfaces cut but not smoothed, translucent, possibly lathe-turned, unmeasurable. Wt.0.14g 2370 sf186 (P5B)

Unfinished rings

9903 Broken in production, surfaces unfinished, tool marks visible. D.30.0, H.10.0mm, Wt.1.19g 32696 sf13592 (P3)

Finished rings, including fragments

9904 Ring, translucent. D.25.0, H.10.0mm, Wt.0.82g 32696 sf13586, 34877 sf13388 (P3) (*Fig.1280*)

9905 Fragment, highly polished. D.25.0, H.8.0, T.4.5mm 23797 sf8053 (P4B) (*Fig.1280*)

9906 Fine ring or core following lathe-turning, surfaces flaked, translucent with tool marks. D.22.0, perforation D.16.0mm, Wt.0.09g 24918 sf8522 (P4B)

9907 Fragment, some signs of wear, complete or broken in production, translucent. D.30.0, H.7.0, T.4.0, Wt.0.14g 22523 sf11000 (P4B) (*Fig.1280*)

9908 Ring of irregular shape, osseous. D.25.0, T.10.0mm, perforation D.20.0, Wt.0.56g 27341 sf12371 (P4B)

9909 Fragment, broken in use, translucent. D.25.0, perforation D.20.0, T.9.0mm, Wt.0.26g 22144 sf7350 (P5A)

9910 Fragment, unpolished on interior and exterior, tool marks visible, osseous. W.10.0, T.6.0mm, Wt.0.46g 7361 sf1160 (P5B)

9911 Ring, diameter unmeasurable. T.10.0mm, Wt.0.57g 16881 sf8142 (P5B)

9912 Lathe-turned opaque, D-profile, worn through use. D.22.0, H.7.0, T.4.0mm, Wt.0.48g 6776 sf6896 (P5Cr), 5981 sf2182 (C6c3, D6a5; 11th–12th century) (P6) (*Fig. 1280*)

Pendants

Blanks and roughouts

9913 Blank, beginning of perforation on one side, tool marks, cloudy. L.21.0, W.15.0, T.8mm, Wt.2.01g 26902 sf9302 (P4B)

9914 Roughout, drilled perforation begun, tool marks, cloudy. L.9.0, W.10.0, T.8mm, Wt.0.68g 28087 sf10691 (P4B)

9915 Roughout, perforation drilled from both sides. Tool marks visible, translucent. L.18.0, W.14.0, T.8.0, perforation D.4.0mm, Wt.0.96g 29844 sf12955 (P4B)

9916 Roughout with crust on one side, cloudy with tool marks. L.32.0, W.16.0, T.6.0mm, Wt.3.64g 21592 sf9207 (P5B) (*Fig.1283*)

9917 Roughout, no perforation, surfaces cut smooth but not polished, bastard, with tool marks. H.27.0, W.9.0, T.7.0mm, Wt.0.72g 1469 sf302 (C6x2–6; late 12th–mid13th century) (P6)

Unfinished pendants

9918 Broken across initial perforation. Another perforation begun at opposite end, started from both sides but incomplete. L.15.0, W.10.0, T.7.0mm, perforation D.2.5mm, Wt.0.83g 34663 sf13117 (P4B)

9919 Fragments (2), broken in production, perforation drilled from one side only, surface unsmoothed, translucent with tool marks. T.7mm, Wt.0.35g 18594 sf5865 (P5A)

9920 Fragment, indeterminate form, perforation drilled partially on one side only, translucent with tool marks. T.6mm, Wt.0.13g 18594 sf5868 (P5A)

Finished pendants (including unpolished examples)

9921 Fragment of a tapering form, perforation drilled from both sides, otherwise osseous. T.7.0mm, Wt.0.03g 23251 sf7512 (P4B)

9922 Rectangular form, some wear from thong/thread through perforation, translucent with tool marks. Amber contains stress rings. L.19.0, W.12.0, T.9.0mm, perforation D.3.0mm, Wt.1.18g 22943 sf8130 (P4B)

9923 Fragment of tapering form, perforation drilled from both sides, but otherwise unmeasurable, osseous. T.7.0mm, Wt.0.53g 23881 sf8421 (P4B) (*Fig.1283*)

9924 Pitted surfaces, opaque with some translucent areas, possible thong marks around perforation. L.48.0, W.23.0, T.15.0mm, perforation D.4.5mm, Wt.11.90g 22802 sf8568 (P4B) (*Fig.1283*)

9925 Triangular, translucent with scratches and knife marks from wear or manufacture, faceted edges, possibly unpolished. L.25.0, W.12.0, T.5.0mm, perforation D.3mm, Wt.0.92g 8800 sf2160 (P5A) (*Fig.1283*)

9926 Broken at perforation which was drilled from two sides on different planes, surfaces smoothed but not finally polished, some tool marks visible. W.14.0, T.14.0, H.26.0mm, Wt.3.58g 2875 sf606 (P5B) (*Fig.1283*)

9927 Triangular, with scratches or knife marks, drilled from both sides, opaque. L.21.0, W.10.0, T.4.0mm, perforation D.5.0mm, Wt.0.68g 7480 sf1697 (P5B) (*Fig.1283*)

9928 Fragment, broken off below perforation, signs of wear, surface extensively burned. H.24.0, T.10.0, W.14.0mm, Wt.1.75g 9615 sf2126 (P5B)

9929 Fragment from above perforation which was drilled from two sides on different planes, tools marks visible, translucent. H.8.0, T.4.0mm, Wt.0.09g 5714 sf2345 (P5B) (*Fig.1283*)

9930 Some signs of wear but surface polishing appears incomplete. H.16.0, W.13.0, T.10.0mm, Wt.1.13g 13875 sf4201 (P5B) (*Fig.1283*)

9931 Opaque with translucent areas. L.18.0, W.10.0, T.8.0mm, perforation D.4.0mm, Wt.0.63g 21510 sf9113 (P5B) (*Fig.1283*)

9932 Fragment, indications of wear, perforation drilled from both sides, broken across perforation and across bottom, translucent. H.13.0, T.5.0, W.8.0mm, Wt.0.31g 21646 sf9846 (P5B) (*Fig.1283*)

9933 Broken across perforation, signs of wear on surfaces and in perforation, translucent. H.18.0, W.10.0, T.5.0mm, Wt.0.71g 21554 sf9990 (P5B) (*Fig.1283*)

9934 Fragment, broken at both ends, flat in section, both surfaces polished. L.13.0, W.11.0, T.5.0mm, Wt.0.44g 29156 sf10318 (P5B)

9935 Triangular, perforation begun on one side but incomplete, large air bubbles, faint knife marks, translucent. L.28.0, W.10.0, T.9.0mm, Wt.1.52g 3519 sf2918 (P5Cr) (*Fig.1283*)

9936 Burned base, triangular form, wear marks around the perforation, opaque. L.23.0, W.7.0, T.10.0, perforation D.2.5mm, Wt.1.28g 3224 sf893 (A6j1; 15th century) (P6)

9937 Translucent. L.20.0, W.15.0, T.9.0mm, Wt.1.24g 16465 sf4545 (D6a19; late 12th century) (P6)

9938 Complete pendant, drilled from one side, perforation very close to edge, cloudy. L.34.0, W.17.0, T.10.0mm, Wt.4.23g 17890 sf5599 (B6a1, C6a1; late 11th century) (P6) (*Fig.1283*)

9939 Broken across possible burned perforation, surfaces smoothed but not polished. H.20.0, W.10.0, T.10.0mm, Wt.1.27g u/s sf13222

Fragments from unidentifiable finished or part-made objects

9940 Fragments, unmeasurable. Wt.0.64g 29844 sf12981 (P4B)

9941 Partially polished flake off a bead, ring or pendant, unmeasurable, translucent. Wt.0.02g 8253 sf1198 (P5A)

9942 Flaked off fragment from partially lathe-turned bead or ring, translucent, unmeasurable. Wt.0.12g 27806 sf10273 (P5A)

9943 Fragment, unmeasurable. Wt.7.60g 8033 sf737 (P5B)

9944 Fragment, unmeasurable. Wt.2.82g 6054 sf2343 (P5B)

9945 Fragment, chip off object, translucent, unmeasurable. Wt.0.01g 14184 sf3747 (P5B)

9946 Fragment, unmeasurable. Wt.1.12g 14666 sf5224 (P5B)

9947 Bead or ring fragment, exterior and interior surfaces unpolished, translucent. H.15.0, T.4.0, D.20.0mm, Wt.0.51g 19294 sf6661 (P5B)

9948 Fragment (lost). 14973 sf6774 (P5B)

9949 Fragment from ?ring, broken across perforation, translucent, unmeasurable. Wt.0.16g 1390 sf1061 (C6x4–6; early–mid13th century) (P6)

9950 Degraded fragment, unmeasurable. Wt.0.34g 13206 sf3194 (B6e2; late 13th/early 14th century) (P6)

9951 Degraded fragments, unmeasurable. Wt.0.04g 17551 (C6c3; early 12th century) (P6)

Waste (small find numbers cited)

Period 1/3

11153 = 1

Period 3

9933 (2), 9041, 10757, 13266, 13349, 13903, 13300, 13398, 13408, 13466, 14515 = 12

Period 4A

8902, 9914, 10177, 10443, 11401, 30039, 30352 = 7

Period 4B

2022, 4668, 4687, 6614, 7282, 7386, 7473–6, 7478–81, 7482 (2), 7626, 7653, 7675, 7679–80, 7842, 7958, 7982, 8005–7, 8081, 8084, 8103, 8120, 8141, 8194, 8201, 8217, 8247, 8302, 8328, 8361, 8381, 8385, 8394, 8409, 8413, 8416, 8455–6, 8498, 8533, 8554, 8634, 8923, 8941, 9166, 9199, 9215, 9540, 9795, 10121, 10342, 10356–7, 10404, 11221, 11234, 11247, 11255 (2), 11278–81, 12308, 12383, 12426, 12569, 12586, 12850, 12893, 12913, 12924, 12943, 12980, 12984, 13024, 13051, 13077, 13108–9, 13116, 13120, 13167, 13187, 13196, 13204, 13217, 13242, 13308, 13332, 13336, 13350, 13356, 13385–6, 13419, 13510, 13618, 13701, 13855, 14027, 14156, 14357, 14360, 14362–7, 14369–70, 14373–4, 14514 = 124

Period 5A

1090, 1093, 1152, 1535, 1606, 2191, 2211, 2285, 2357, 4860, 5173, 5756, 5974, 6267, 6286–7, 6322, 6347, 6361, 6418, 6493, 6605, 6628, 6634, 7047, 7071, 7116, 7139, 7248, 7367, 7385, 9963, 10271, 11241, 11516, 11531, 12825–6, 12832, 13567, 13572, 14371, 16243 = 43

Period 5B

108, 157, 435, 683, 853, 876, 1258, 1449, 1451, 1645, 1718, 1793,1796, 1806, 1964, 2710, 2826, 3513, 3539, 3614, 3821, 3987, 4208, 4220, 4299, 4388, 4448, 4458, 4479, 4511, 4607 (2), 4643, 4953, 5245, 5256, 5275, 5290, 5301, 5415, 5531, 5819, 5968, 6173, 6338, 6527, 6567, 6597, 6647, 6687, 6693, 6697, 6740 (3), 6773, 6788, 6821, 6937, 7304, 8968, 9638, 9684, 9687, 10364, 10526, 10768, 10774, 10845, 10957, 11223, 11269, 11515, 11522, 11536, 12770, 14368, 14372, 15709, 15739 = 80

Period 4/5

5401, 14359 = 2

Period 5C

3547, 5905, 5953, 6023, 6057, 6115, 6224, 6536, 6553, 6556, 6561, 6756, 7426, 11528 (6),11530 (3), 16009 = 23

Period 6

299, 358, 1133, 1162,1419, 1676, 1716, 1868, 1993, 2189, 3112, 3373, 3386, 3391–2, 3395, 3434, 3629, 4716, 4805, 4939, 4945, 5989, 6054 = 24

Raw Amber (small find numbers cited)

Period 3

6976, 6982, 6989, 6990, 9322, 12712 = 6

Period 4A

9550 = 1

Period 4B

4669, 11169, 12412, 12800, 12911, 13207, 13293, 13322 = 8

Period 5A

7361, 10447 = 2

Period 5B

492, 851, 861, 2237, 3656, 4241, 4585, 6425, 6602, 6826, 6888, 7330, 9972, 11159 = 14

Period 4/5

4678 = 1

Period 5C

3482, 6481 = 2

Period 6

73, 300, 1972, 2672(4), 3249 (6), 3328, 3506, 3551, 3562, 4056 = 18

Unstratified

9464, 12824, 12939 = 3

Fired clay

Spindle whorl

Note: A full catalogue entry for *6582* appears in *AY* 17/11. It is illustrated on Fig.809.

6582   Irregular, shallow cylindrical; one face slightly rounded; undecorated. D.32.0, T.11.0, hole D.8.2mm, Wt.12.3g 21075 sf7025 (P5Cr)

Spindle whorls made from re-used pot sherds

Catalogue by P. Walton Rogers; fabrics identified by B. Hartley

All cut to disc shape and central hole cut or drilled.

9952   Fragment, including central hole. Sherd of samian ware, eroded and chipped. Central Gaulish, second half of 2nd century. L.37.6, T.6.0mm, Wt.3.6g. 31808 sf12361 (P3)

9953   Fragment, approximately half. Sherd of black-burnished ware, ?2nd or 3rd century. D.45.2, T.7.4, perforation D.6.6mm, Wt.12.7g. 32687 sf13436 (P3)

9954   Complete. Foot-ring and base from beaker of dark grey fabric; broken edges rubbed smooth. Mid 3rd century or later. D.46.0, T.9.3–10.8mm, perforation D.9.4, Wt.27.8g. 22560 sf7861 (P4B)

9955   Complete, but chipped. Charred sherd of samian. Place of manufacture not known; second half of 2nd century. D.37.4, T.7.2, perforation D.6.8mm, Wt.11.4g. 25630 sf9223 (P4B)

Loom weights

Note: Full catalogue entries for *6585–9* (all made from baked/ fired brick clay) appear in *AY* 17/11.

6585   Two fragments conjoining; bun-shaped, D-section. Central hole larger on one side than other. D.100.0, T.35.0, H.40.0mm, Wt. (larger fragment) 166.0g 20459 sfs7000, 7004 (P4B) (*Fig.1234*)

6586   Fragment, intermediate between bun-shaped and annular. D-section. L.90.0, T.36.0, H.48mm, Wt.154.0g 19644 sf12676 (P4B) (*Fig.1234*)

6587   Irregular bun-shaped; D-section. Hole off-centre. Worn groove from attachment cord. D.84.0–90.0, T.31.0–35.0, H.40.0–45.0mm, Wt.335g 24500 sf8291 (P4B) (*Fig.1234*)

8588   Almost complete, intermediate between bun-shaped and annular; rounded section. Four impressed circular marks on one face. D.110.0, T.39.0, H.30.0–37mm, Wt.287.0g 20387 sf6723 (P5B) (*Fig.1234*)

6589   Fragment, wedge-shaped cross-section with internal lip. Prick marks in form of angular B on one face. L.75.0, T.31.0, H.32.0mm, Wt.73.0g 9070 sf958 (D6e7; 13th/14th century) (P6) (*Fig.1234*)

Fragments

(small find numbers followed by context numbers in parentheses)

Period 3

11011 (31061), 12957 (19743), 13277 (32410), 14186 (34993), 14540 (19739)

Period 4A

8875 (20423)

Period 4B

7092 (20427), 7796 (23099), 8215 (24386), 10026 (25881), 12781–2 (19644), 13174 (32528), 14541 (19644)

Period 5A

4878 (2080), 7107 (14787)

Period 5B

4646 (15876), 6764 (20391), 6793 (20387), 6797 (19320), 7093 (21018), 7209 (19285), 8304 (21200), 10016 (21678), 11524 (29465), 6917 (19441)

Period 5Cr

14539 (6789)

Period 6

1905 (5398)

Counters

Roman pottery

9956   Subdiscoidal, made from samian ware sherd. D.30.0, T.4.0mm 31167 sf1117 (P3)

9957   Subdiscoidal made from samian sherd, on one face the red surface has been almost all abraded off, apparently deliberately. D.30.0, T.8.0mm 30963 sf12487 (P3)

9958   Subdiscoidal, made from Roman grey ware sherd. D.35.0, T.8.0mm 30404 sf12655 (P3)

9959   Subdiscoidal made from samian ware sherd. D.30.0, T.7.0mm 32772 sf13967 (P3)

9960   Subdiscoidal made from Roman grey ware. D.60.0, T.10.0mm 24520 sf8312 (P4B)

9961   Subdiscoidal made from samian sherd, possible lathe centering hole visible on both surfaces. D.22.0, T.12.0mm 27271 sf9591 (P4B)

9962   Subdiscoidal, made from Roman colour-coated ware. D.30.0, T.12mm 8696 sf702 (P5B)

Anglo-Scandinavian wares

9963   Subdiscoidal, made from a coarse sherd with splashes of glaze. D.50.0, T.6.0mm 9057 sf867 (P4B)

9964   Roughly discoidal, edges roughly chipped made from grey ware. D.22.0, T.8.0mm 8569 sf1766 (P5A)

9965   Subdiscoidal, made from a sherd of Torksey-type ware. D.21.0, T.4.0mm 6774 sf6241 (P5Cr)

Tile

9966   Subdiscoidal, chipped from plain tile. D.70.0, T.17.0mm 9450 sf2316 (P4B)

9967   Subdiscoidal, chipped from plain tile. D.60.0, T.19.0mm 5588 sf1770 (P5B)

Glass

Glassworking debris

9968   Black glass fragment. 27819 sf10643 (P3)

9969   Green glass fragment, melted. 27819 sf10863 (P3)

9970   Adhering to fired clay, colourless. 26732 sf11244 (P3)

9971   Black glass on fired clay. 30189 sf11650 (P3)

9972   Colourless, melted. 15688 sf4565 (P4B)

9973   Blue droplet. 24556 sf8635 (P4B)

9974   Blue fragment. 22797 sf11242 (P4B)

9975   Golden brown glass on fired clay. 27017 sf11710 (P4B)

9976   Colourless glass on fired clay sherd. 8023 sf1965 (P5A)

9977   Green lump. 16882 sf6466 (P5B)

9978   Blue glass on fired clay lump. 6284 sf6585 (P5B)

9979   Green glass waste on fired clay. 15311 sf5815 (P5Cr)

9980   Tessera, blue. 11886 sf3579 (B6f4; early 14th century) (P6)

9981   Colourless, melted. 18366 sf4921 (B6a5; 11th/12th century) (P6)

9982   Colourless glass on inside of fired clay sherd. 16612 sf5429 (D6a1; late 11th century) (P6)

9983   Iron rod coated in green glass, unfinished. 6774 sf5784 (P5Cr)

Textile working

Slick-stones

Note: Full catalogue entries for *6592–4* appear in *AY 17/11*.

6592   Fragment, one-quarter extant, bun-shaped, with curved side and concave back with part of manufacturing scar, pale transparent green with iridescent surfaces, opaque green/white impurities towards centre. L.58.0, W.43.0, T.41.0mm, original D.80.0–90.0mm 22789 sf7990 (P4B) (*Fig.1236*)

6593   Fragment, bun-shaped, black, original surface dull with criss-cross scratches, fracture surfaces highly reflective. L.59.0, W.43.0, T.26.0mm 34663 sf13121 (P4B) (*Fig.1236*)

6594   Fragment, approximately half, bun-shaped including curved side and flat back face with part of manufacturing scar, irregular front face, marbled brown/black. L.76.0, W.39.0, T.38.0mm, original D.80.0mm 22962 sf8177 (P4B) (*Fig.1236*)

9984   Fragment, including part of original outer surface, brown-black, semi-crystalline. L.22.0, W.19.0, T.9.0mm 30273 sf11035 (P4A)

9985   Fragment retaining part of upper surfaces. L.16.0, W.13.0, T.7.0mm 25922 sf13666 (P4A)

9986   Fragments (2), highly decayed, brown crystalline. L.20.0, W.20.0, T.19.0mm 20427 sf7040 (P4B)

9987 Fragment including side and part of concave back face. L.40.0, W.40.0, T.33.0mm 22911 sf8106 (P4B)

9988 Fragment including part of outer surface. L.46.0, W.35.0, T.29.0mm 19534 sf9310 (P4B)

9989 Fragment including almost flat front face and part of back surface. L.51.0, W.42.0, T.33.0mm 23234 sf12527 (P4B)

9990 Internal fragment. L.33.0, W.24.0, T.23.0mm 29844 sf12937 (P4B)

9991 Fragment including curved side and concave back face, brown/black. L.41.0, W.35.0, T.34.0mm 34424 sf12982 (P4B)

9992 Fragments (2), retaining part of some original surface. L.15.0, W.7.0, T.10.0mm 29528 sf13387 (P4B)

9993 Fragment retaining small part of original outer surface. L.26.0, W.22.0, T.17.0mm 36247 sf13851 (P4B)

9994 Internal fragment, fracture surfaces highly reflective black. L.26.0, W.14.0, T.13.0mm 14925 sf6360 (P5A)

9995 Fragment retaining curved side, reflective black with beginnings of blue/grey film on fracture surfaces. L.21.0, W.15.0, T.24.0mm 14787 sf6757 (P5A)

9996 Internal fragments (2). L.18.0, W.13.0, T.8.0mm 22384 sf7561 (P5A)

9997 Internal fragment, dark green with iridescent fracture surfaces. L.29.0, W.25.0, T.11.0mm 7500 sf1537 (P5B)

9998 Internal fragment, brown, semi-crystalline. L.35.0, W.24.0, T.13.0mm 5588 sf1787 (P5B)

9999 Internal fragment, pale, semi-crystalline. L.19.0, W.19.0, T.11.0mm 15457 sf4302 (P5B)

10000 Fragment retaining part of original outer surface, golden-brown, semi-crystalline. L.20.0, W.18.0, T.13.0mm 15550 sf4431 (P5B)

10001 Internal fragment, golden brown, semi-crystalline. L.20.0, W.17.0, T.12.0mm 15550 sf4434 (P5B)

10002 Fragments (9), including one curved side, one including front face, seven internal, mainly brown crystalline. L.19.0, W.18.0, T.11.0mm 14548 sf5116 (P5B)

10003 Fragment, including curved side, decayed brown/black. L.29.0, W.5.0, T.30.0mm 26802 sf9109 (P5B)

10004 Fragment retaining part of original outer surface. L.18.0, W.17.0, T.11.0mm 21245 sf15698 (P5B)

10005 Internal fragment, brown, crystalline. L.35.0, W.30.0, T.30.0mm 21204 sf16231 (P5B)

Vessel glass

Catalogue by Matthew Stiff

Rims

10006 Tall beaker fragment. Light green-blue. Fire-rounded and thickened rim sherd. Horizontally elongated bubbles. Good gloss and clarity. L.20.0, W.14.0, T.2.0mm 25990 sf10334 (P3) (*Fig.1239*)

10007 Vessel fragments. Dark opaque brown-grey. Severely devitrified and crumbling fire-rounded and thickened rim fragment, and at least nine other small fragments, including two sherds decorated with thick, unmarvered, self-coloured trails. Poor gloss and clarity. L.11.0, W.6.0, T.1.4mm 18601 sf5207 (P4B)

10008 Squat jar fragment. Dark blue. Outsplayed, fire-rounded and thickened rim sherd. No evidence of folding. Horizontally elongated bubbles. Good gloss and clarity. L.20.0, W.18.0, T.2.2mm 27637 sf10653 (P4B) (*Fig.1239*)

10009 Funnel beaker fragment. Very light blue-green. Fire-rounded and thickened rim. Tiny, horizontally elongated bubbles, good gloss and clarity. H.10.0, W.10.0, T.1.2mm 34521 sf13041 (P4B) (*Fig.1239*)

10010 Squat jar fragment. Black. Inward folded rim sherd. Colour appears black in reflected light (possibly very dark red). Decorated with opaque yellow horizontal marvered trails around outside edge of rim and neck. Light iridescent weathering layer. Poor gloss and clarity. L.20.0, W.9.0, T.1.3mm, original rim D.c.80mm 34983 sf13465 (P4B) (*Fig.1238*)

10011 Squat jar fragment. Light blue-green. Fire-rounded and thickened rim sherd with possible inward fold. Decorated with opaque yellow, horizontal marvered trails around outer edge of rim and neck. Tiny bubbles, good gloss and clarity. H.8.0, W.11.0, T.1.5mm 22053 sf13033 (P5A) (*Fig.1239*)

10012 Vessel fragments. Opaque brown-grey. Five fragments of devitrified glass from out-turned rim of vessel. Fire-rounded and thickened. Possibly from jar or small beaker. Poor gloss and clarity. L.13.0, W.9.0, T.1.6mm 5714 sf1873 (P5B)

10013 Vessel fragment. Dark opaque brown-grey. Devitrified rim sherd. Heat distorted with weathered fabric. Fair gloss, poor clarity. L.18.0, W.13.5, T.2.5mm 5673 sf1997 (P5B)

10014 Funnel beaker fragment. Light green-blue. Fire-rounded and thickened rim. Outsplayed. Dull, weathered surface. Tiny bubbles, good gloss and clarity. L.19.0, W.8.0, T.1.6mm 24899 sf9596 (P5B) (*Fig.1239*)

10015 Vessel fragments. Dark opaque brown-grey. Five sherds of devitrified glass from vessel with fire-rounded and thickened rim of vessel. Outsplayed. Possibly from beaker or jar. Fair gloss, poor clarity. L.30.0, W.15.0, T.1.1mm, original rim D.c.95.0mm 6570 sf5731 (P5Cr)

10016 Fragments. Opaque brown-grey. Five severely devitrified glass fragments, one with fire-rounded edge. Sherds are flattened suggesting that they have been distorted by heat or that they are from a piece of window glass. Poor gloss and clarity. L.19.0, W.17.0, T.3.0mm 19255 sf11544 (P5Cr)

10017 Funnel beaker or squat jar fragment. Very light green-blue. Sherd from just below edge of outsplayed rim (probably inward folded and fire-rounded). Decorated with fine opaque yellow marvered trails. Rim is outsplayed (diameter indeterminable). Tiny, elongated bubbles, good gloss and clarity. L.11.0, W.6.0, T.1.5mm 5415 sf1912 (C6c6, D6a7; 11th–12th century) (P6)

Bases

10018 Vessel fragment. Very dark opaque brown-grey. Devitrified sherd from vessel with broad kicked base, possibly jar. Thick weathering layer. Edge of annular pontil scar visible. Fair gloss, poor clarity. L.27.0, W.22.0, T.3.2mm 30352 sf11540 (P4A)

10019 Squat jar fragment. Very dark grey-green/black. Fragment from edge of jar with kicked base. Decorated with horizontal opaque yellow marvered trails. Horizontally elongated bubbles. Light weathering layer. Poor gloss and clarity. L.20.0, W.18.0, T.2.2mm 19390 sf8904 (P4B) (*Fig.1238*)

10020 Tall palm cup fragment. Light green-blue base fragment with vertical optic-blown ribbing. Indications of moulded bosses, probably placed both on and between the arms of a base cross. Only one cross arm visible. Tiny bubbles in fabric, slightly horizontally elongated. Good gloss and clarity. L.28.0, W.18.0, T.2.9mm 29459 sf12876 (P4B) (*Fig.1239*)

10021 Jar or bottle fragment. Opaque brown/grey. Devitrified sherd from domed part of kicked vessel base. Pontil wad visible on lower surface. Metal is mottled, probably due to weathering and degradation of glass. Poor gloss and clarity. L.20.0, W.15.0, T.1.4mm 22110 sf7345 (P5A)

10022　Vessel fragment. Dark opaque brown-grey. Devitrified sherd from flattened base of vessel. Poor gloss and clarity. L.23.0, W.18.0, T.1.7mm 6347 sf5327 (P5B)

Body fragments

10023　Vessel sherd coated with thick, opaque grey-green weathering layer. Dark green. Poor gloss and clarity. L.13.0, W.16.0, T.3.0mm 20893 sf8473 (P3)

10024　Thick vessel sherd coated with creamy weathering layer. Black. Slight lamination. Colour impossible to determine. Poor gloss and clarity. L.13.0, W.8.0, T.2.9mm 26977 sf10143 (P3)

10025　Thick fragment. Dark blue. Probably blown, but may have been re-used as a tessera. Light iridescent weathering layer. Tiny bubbles, fair gloss and clarity. L.13.0, W.12.0, T.0.5mm 27819 sf10808 (P3)

10026　Vessel fragment. Brown-yellow. Possible evidence of optic-blown ribbing. Tiny bubbles, good gloss and clarity. L.10.0, W.9.0, T.0.9mm 32549 sf13409 (P3)

10027　Vessel fragment. Dark grey-green. Possibly decorated with optic-blown ribbing. Iridescent weathering layer on interior surface. Poor gloss, fair clarity. L.13.0, W.8.0, T.0.5mm 36049 sf13587 (P3)

10028　Two glass sherds with matt weathering layer. Light yellow. Tiny bubbles, poor gloss, fair clarity. L.6.0, W.5.0, T.0.8mm 30969 sf14312 (P3)

10029　Devitrified vessel sherd and several smaller fragments. Dark opaque brown-grey. Fair gloss, poor clarity. L.11.0, W.7.0, T.0.6mm 22348 sf7573 (P4B)

10030　Blue thick sherd with iridescent weathering layer. Probably from towards base. Tiny bubbles, fair gloss and clarity. L.12.0, W.7.0, T.2.0mm 23649 sf7831 (P4B)

10031　Devitrified sherd. Light opaque brown. Colour is due to thick weathering layer (original colour impossible to determine). Decorated with thick self-coloured trailing. Poor gloss and clarity. L.14.0, W.14.0, T.1.3mm 24872 sf8499 (P4B)

10032　Very light green vessel sherd from spherical or hemispherical form. Coated with white, iridescent weathering layer. Poor gloss and clarity. L.15.0, W.12.0, T.1.7mm 20411 sf8766 (P4B)

10033　Five very small crumbling and devitrified sherds. Opaque brown. Poor gloss and clarity. L.3.0, W.2.0, T.0.6mm 25934 sf10046 (P4B)

10034　Eight devitrified fragments, possibly from vessel. Dark opaque brown-grey. Original colour possibly light green. Poor gloss and clarity. L.9.0, W.7.0mm 25934 sf10094 (P4B)

10035　Chip of thick glass, possibly from vessel. Very dark grey-green. Coated with thick, iridescent weathering layer. Poor gloss and clarity. L.14.0, W.10.0mm 28492 sf10961 (P4B)

10036　At least ten small fragments of crumbling devitrified glass, probably from vessel. Opaque brown-grey. Poor gloss and clarity. L.7.0, W.6.0, T.2.1mm 29528 sf13403 (P4B)

10037　Vessel fragment. Dark brown-green. Decorated with horizontal self-coloured trail. Possibly from neck of small jar. Tiny bubbles, good gloss and clarity. L.12.0, W.8.0, T.1mm 8056 sf1354 (P5A)

10038　Sherd with possible optic-blown ribbing. Turquoise blue. Tiny, elongated bubbles (possibly vertically), good gloss and clarity. L.7.0cm, W.6.0, T.1.2mm 18600 sf5552 (P5A)

10039　Opaque white. Thick sherd coated on exterior face with dark opaque brown-grey, laminating surface weathering layer. No similar layer on interior face. Fair gloss (interior), poor clarity. L.21.0, W.8.0, T.2.2mm 14883 sf6172 (P5A)

10040　Vessel fragment. Grey-green. Light, iridescent weathering layer. Evidence of two, horizontal trails (now missing), probably executed in opaque white or opaque yellow glass. Tiny bubbles, fair gloss and clarity. L.16.0, W.13.0, T.0.5mm 20131 sf6472 (P5A)

10041　Vessel fragment. Very light yellow-green/colourless. Sherd decorated with two, horizontal, lightly marvered opaque orange-red trails. Tiny bubbles, good gloss and clarity. L.8.0, W.6.0, T.0.7mm 20880 sf7222 (P5A)

10042　Five dark devitrified glass sherds. Dark opaque brown-grey. Poor gloss and clarity. L.13.0, W.9.0, T.1.7mm 22110 sf7358 (P5A)

10043　Sherd with optic-blown corrugations, probably from vessel with spherical or hemispherical form. Light green-blue. Decorated with curving trail of heavily marvered transparent yellow glass. Very light iridescence. Tiny elongated bubbles, good gloss and clarity. L.29.0, W.21.0, T.1.7mm 1473 sf430 (P5B)

10044　Vessel fragment. Light green-blue. Decorated with horizontal, opaque yellow marvered trail. Tiny bubbles, good gloss and clarity. L.19.0, W.17.0, T.1.9mm 2875 sf659 (P5B)

10045　Vessel fragment. Light brown-yellow. Decorated with vertical self-coloured trail. Tiny, vertically elongated bubbles, good gloss and clarity. L.18.0, W.11.0, T.0.8mm 7480 sf1708 (P5B)

10046　Four severely devitrified sherds. Very dark opaque grey. Decorated with self-coloured trail. Original colour impossible to determine. Three fragments conjoin. Poor gloss and clarity. L.12.0, W.8.0, T.1.7mm 5673 sf2018 (P5B)

10047　Blue chip, possibly from base of vessel. Tiny bubbles, slightly elongated, good gloss and clarity. L.12.0, W.10.0, T.6.3mm 5848 sf2019 (P5B)

10048　Dark opaque brown-grey body sherd. Iridescent weathering layer. Poor gloss and clarity. L.1.5, W.1.1, T.1.6mm 6119 sf2365 (P5B)

10049　Two devitrified glass chips, probably from vessel. Opaque grey-brown. Poor gloss and clarity. L.10.0, W.8.0mm 21769 sf3681 (P5B)

10050　Vessel fragments. Dark opaque brown-grey. Four fragments of devitrified vessel glass. Poor gloss and clarity. L.10.0, W.7.0, T.1.2mm 15659 sf4586 (P5B)

10051　Vessel sherd encrusted with surface layer on exterior, possibly caused by exposure to intense heat. Turquoise blue. Tiny bubbles, fair gloss and clarity. L.13.0, W.10.0, T.2.1mm 6276 sf5341 (P5B)

10052　Four devitrified vessel sherds. Dark opaque brown-grey. Poor gloss and clarity. L.1.0, W.6.0, T.1.7mm 14878 sf6024 (P5B)

10053　Blue flake, possibly from vessel. Tiny bubbles, good gloss and clarity. L.8.0, W.5.0mm 6833 sf6152 (P5B)

10054　Vessel fragment. Grey-green. Light surface iridescence. Fair gloss and clarity. L.9.0, W.8.0, T.0.8mm 14973 sf6741 (P5B)

10055　Turquoise blue sherd with thick opaque brown weathering layer. Tiny bubbles, fair gloss and clarity. L.27mm, W.12mm, T.2.2mm 20345 sf6836 (P5B)

10056　Blue sherd with shallow internal curvature. Slightly elongated bubbles. Exterior surface more dull, worn and scratched than interior. Good gloss and clarity. L.22.0, W.9.0, T.1.6mm 18949 sf9673 (P5B)

10057　Several crumbling devitrified vessel sherds. Light opaque brown. Poor gloss and clarity. L.4.0, W.3.0, T.0.3mm 27513 sf10491 (P5B)

10058　Four crumbling, devitrified sherds. Light opaque yellow-brown. Poor gloss and clarity. L.6.0, W.5.0, T.1mm 29467 sf10867 (P5B)

10059　Vessel sherd with light surface iridescence. Light green-grey. Tiny bubbles, fair gloss and clarity. L.11.0, W.9.0, T.1.1mm 29457 sf11138 (P5B)

10060 Three small fragments of devitrified, laminating glass, probably from vessel. Dark opaque brown-grey. Poor gloss and clarity. L.3.0, W.2.0, T.0.7mm 19271 sf6509 (P5Cr)

10061 Vessel fragment. Light green-yellow. Decorated with opaque red streaked trail (unmarvered). Light surface iridescence. Tiny bubbles, fair gloss and clarity. L.8.0, W.6.0, T.0.5mm u/s sf2989

Finger-rings

10062 Fragment, of irregular plano-convex section, thinning to one end, very dark appearing black. D.19.4, H.4.0mm, internal D.13.8mm 7252 sf1574 (P5B) (*Fig.1280*)

10063 Fragment, of plano-convex section, very dark appearing black. D.18.7, T.3.8, internal D.13.3mm 15470 sf4410 (P5B)

10064 Incomplete, subcircular, of plano-convex section, yellow. D.23.4, T.4.9, internal D.15.5mm 11125 sf5070 (P5B)

10065 Fragment, of plano-convex section, dark green/black. D.25.5, T.5.0, internal D.19.1mm 1331 sf295 (C6x2–6; 11th–13th century) (P6)

10066 Fragment, of plano-convex section, dark green. D.21.8, T.5.0, internal D.14.9mm 20110 sf6151 (B6c8; early 13th century) (P6)

Glass beads

Monochrome

Type 1: Annular

10067 Pale blue-green. D.19.2, H.9.6mm 32923 sf13807 (P3)

10068 Fragment, pale green. L.19.9, H.10.9mm 23634 sf7918 (P4B)

10069 Fragment, opaque yellow-brown. D.18.5, H.9.1mm 27503 sf10328 (P4B)

10070 Yellow. D.8.3, H.4.0mm 1473 sf464 (P5B) (*Fig.1228*)

10071 Yellow, with tapering perforation. D.7.2, H.3.6mm 18489 sf5047 (P5B) (*Fig.1228*)

10072 Fragment, yellow. L.10.4, H.5.9mm 6773 sf5374 (P5B)

10073 Off-centre tapering perforation, yellow. D.9.0, H.4.3mm 6871 sf6387 (P5B)

10074 Fragment, irregular, yellow. D.13.0, H.5.9mm 6433 sf6916 (P5B)

10075 Fragment, yellow. L.8.6, H.4.6mm 20301 sf8170 (P5B)

10076 Fragment, very dark appearing black. D.11.4, H.5.7mm 21309 sf8384 (P5B)

10077 Fragment, subannular, yellow. D.12.0, H.6.0mm 24870 sf8465 (P5B)

10078 Fragment, green. D.13.5, H.4.2mm 20170 sf8700 (P5B)

10079 Fragment, yellow. D.11.2, H.5.3mm 21437 sf8888 (P5B)

10080 Opaque yellow. D.10.1, H.3.9mm 21033 sf9387 (P5B)

10081 Yellow. D.11.1, H.5.1mm 3543 sf3333 (P5Cr) (*Fig.1228*)

10082 Yellow. D.11.2, H.4.5mm 6304 sf5013 (P5Cr)

10083 Two halves, pale yellow. D.11.6, H.5.2mm 19090 sf5938 (P5Cr)

10084 Off-centre perforation, very dark appearing black. D.10.3, H.5.0mm 18744 sf6058 (P5Cr)

10085 Yellow. D.9.0, H.4.1mm 6774 sf6541 (P5Cr)

10086 Fragment, green. D.10.5, H.3.7mm 1005 sf189 (D6y1; late 12th–13th century) (P6)

10087 Fragment, green. L.11.1, H.5.4mm 1359 sf366 (D6y1; late 12th–13th century) (P6)

10088 Fragment, blue. L.10.7, H.5.3mm 1568 sf1641 (D6y1; late 12th–13th century) (P6)

10089 Incomplete, green. D.8.0, H.3.2mm 3345 sf2374 (A6j2; 15th century) (P6)

10090 Fragment, blue. D.6.4, H.3.0mm 5906 sf2425 (C6c3, D6a5; 11th–12th century) (P6)

10091 Yellow. D.7.6, H.3.8mm 7782 sf3132 (D6y1; late 12th–13th century) (P6)

10092 In two adjoining fragments, green. D.11.8, H.5.2mm 5668 sf3206 (C6e6; early 13th century) (P6)

10093 Yellow. D.10.9, H.3.8mm 13908 sf3684 (B6w1; 14th–early 15th century) (P6) (*Fig.1285*)

10094 Yellow. D.8.0, H.3.5mm 15592 sf4673 (B6a3, C6c1; 11th–12th century) (P6)

10095 Fragment, yellow. L.10.0, H.4.0mm 6291 sf5069 (C6c1, D6a3; late 11th–early 12th century) (P6)

10096 Fragment, blue. L.7.1, H.6.8mm 17787 sf5183 (C6c1; early 12th century) (P6)

10097 Fragment, yellow. L.11.2, H.5.0mm 17890 sf5542 (B6a1, C6a1; late 11th century) (P6)

10098 Fragment, yellow. L.8.8, H.4.6mm 17129 sf7446 (D6a2; late 11th century) (P6)

10099 Yellow. D.12.5, H.5.9mm u/s sf7036

Type 2: Globular

10100 Fragment, opaque yellow with grey striations. D.9.4, H.5.9mm 36361 sf13931 (P3)

10101 Subglobular, tapering perforation, yellow. D.5.5, H.3.7mm 26016 sf14396 (P3)

10102 Subglobular, pale blue-green. D.11.0, H.8.5mm 22714 sf7894 (P4B)

10103 Pale blue-green. D.12.0, H.7.5mm 22714 sf7933 (P4B)

10104 Tapering perforation, green. D.3.6, H.3.0mm 20462 sf8123 (P4B)

10105 Fragment, opaque yellow. D.4.3, H.3.1mm 20462 sf8171 (P4B)

10106 Subglobular, opaque pale brown. D.5.5, H.4.2mm 25340 sf8441 (P4B)

10107 Colourless. D.13.0, H.12.6mm 25667 sf9296 (P4B)

10108 Fragment, green. D.4.2, H.4.1mm 22714 sf11219 (P4B)

10109 Two adjoining fragments, subglobular, blue. D.9.4, H.5.3mm 19643 sf12721 (P4B)

10110 Subglobular, opaque cream-yellow. D.7.7, H.4.5mm 34622 sf13262 (P4B)

10111 Red. D.2.3, H.1.9mm 35448 sf14033 (P4B)

10112 Subglobular, opaque pale brown. D.8.6, H.5.1mm 35519 sf14389 (P4B)

10113 Two fragments, one green, one opaque brown D.2.6, H.1.9mm 27368 sf15949 (P4B)

10114 Tapering perforation, opaque brown-black. D.8.2, H.7.4mm 2325 sf147 (P5A)

10115 Very dark appearing black. D.3.0, H.1.8mm 8844 sf2408 (P5A)

10116 Blue. D.4.0, H.2.6mm 20105 sf5986 (P5A)

10117 Off-centre perforation, blue-green. D.8.3, H.4.3mm 14925 sf6417 (P5A)

10118 Subglobular, very pale blue-white. D.8.4, H.5.5mm 14922 sf7081 (P5A)

10119 Yellow-white. D.11.6, H.8.9mm 20143 sf7088 (P5A)

10120 Subglobular, yellow. D.8.6, H.5.3mm 2767 sf381 (P5B)

10121 Fragment, green. L.9.8, H.6.6mm 1473 sf427 (P5B)

10122 Irregularly globular with tapering perforation, green. D.5.2, H.4.1mm 1611 sf1040 (P5B)

10123 Fragment, green. L.3.0, H.3.4mm 7257 sf1110 (P5B)

10124 Subglobular, dark green. D.3.8, H.2.0mm 7553 sf2415 (P5B)

10125 Dark appearing black. D.10.0, H.5.5mm 14184 sf3827 (P5B)

10126 Irregularly globular, very dark appearing black. D.8.5, H.5.6mm 14300 sf3876 (P5B)

10127 Fragment, irregular perforation, green. D.6.5, H.5.7mm 15402 sf4231 (P5B)

10128 Fragment, very dark appearing black. L.5.9, H.4.4mm 15382 sf4235 (P5B)

10129 Fragment, very dark appearing black. L.4.6, H.5.4mm 15382 sf4244 (P5B)

10130 Fragment, very dark appearing black. D.7.5, H.4.3mm 15192 sf4271 (P5B)

10131 Subglobular, green. D.3.9, H.3.3mm 15457 sf4300 (P5B)

10132 Fragment, orange. D.7.6, H.4.8mm 15432 sf4361 (P5B)

10133 Blue. D.11.8, H.8.4mm 15550 sf4441 (P5B)

10134 Fragment, yellow. D.7.4, H.7.2mm 6440 sf5457 (P5B)

10135 Fragment, tapering perforation, green. D.11.2, H.5.6mm 6433 sf5871 (P5B)

10136 Very dark appearing black. D.5.7, H.3.6mm 6433 sf5961 (P5B) (*Fig.1285*)

10137 Subglobular, yellow, irregularly shaped perforation. D.6.8, H.3.6mm 19293 sf6637 (P5B)

10138 Fragment, subglobular, black. D.11.2, H.5.9mm 6927 sf6949 (P5B) (*Fig.1228*)

10139 Irregularly globular, irregular tapering perforation, yellow. D.8.4, H.4.2mm 21244 sf8297 (P5B)

10140 Subglobular, yellow. D.6.5, H.4.1mm 20170 sf8605 (P5B)

10141 Fragment, yellow. D.7.2, H.4.6mm 26888 sf9295 (P5B)

10142 Very dark appearing black. D.8.6, H.5.6mm 29263 sf10889 (P5B)

10143 Subglobular, very dark appearing black. D.9.2, H.6.6mm 29263 sf10915 (P5B)

10144 Opaque yellow-brown. D.8.8, H.5.5mm 21880 sf12751 (P5B)

10145 Dark green. D.2.9, H.1.9mm 3661 sf14398 (P4/5)

10146 Very dark appearing black. D.7.8, H.4.9mm 7866 sf3501 (P5Cf)

10147 Fragment, green. L.7.3, H.7.1mm 18744 sf5792 (P5Cr)

10148 Fragment, tapering perforation, yellow. D.7.5, H.5.0mm 18931 sf5853 (P5Cr)

10149 Blue. D.10.1, H.6.6mm 19244 sf6422 (P5Cr) (*Fig.1285*)

10150 Unfinished, subglobular, yellow, tapering hole which does not fully perforate. D.6.5, H.3.7mm 16733 sf6463 (P5Cr)

10151 Irregular, very dark appearing black. D.4.0, H.3.2mm 15311 sf11519 (P5Cr)

10152 Fragment, dark green. L.4.0, H.3.4mm 15311 sf11529 (P5Cr)

10153 Fragment, yellow. D.5.2, H.4.0mm 16887 sf14403 (P5Cr)

10154 Green. D.2.6, H.1.6mm 16877 sf16239 (P5Cr)

10155 Fragment, yellow, opaque. L.6.0, H.4.9mm 1028 sf91 (C6i1; late 17th century) (P6)

10156 Fragment, green. L.10.4, H.7.3mm 1455 sf353 (C6x2–6; 11th–13th century) (P6)

10157 Fragment, green. L.8.8, H.5.6mm 4402 sf586 (C6f1; late 13th century) (P6)

10158 Fragment, pale blue-green. L.20.0, H.12.9mm 5021 sf1038 (C6e10–11; mid–13th century) (P6)

10159 Fragment, yellow. D.11.0, H.6.5mm 5241 sf1179 (D6d3; 13th century) (P6)

10160 Tapering perforation, very dark appearing black. D.3.6, H.2.1mm 4620 sf1209 (C6e9; mid–13th century) (P6)

10161 Fragment, olive green. D.9.9, H.5.4mm 5484 sf1748 (C6e1, D6a16; 12th–13th century) (P6)

10162 Green. D.9.4, H.8.0mm 1404 sf1951 (D6y1; late 12th–13th century) (P6)

10163 Malformed, yellow. D.7.9, H.5.0mm 5348 sf2000 (C6e1, D6a16; 12th–13th century) (P6)

10164 Subglobular, olive green. D.9.9, H.5.7mm 5348 sf2055 (C6e1, D6a16; 12th–13th century) (P6)

10165 Yellow. D.5.2, H.3.4mm 1404 sf2106 (D6y1; late 12th–13th century) (P6)

10166 Tapering perforation, yellow. D.6.1, H.3.6mm 1404 sf2119 (D6y1; late 12th–13th century) (P6)

10167 Fragment, very dark appearing black. D.9.0, H.6.8mm 5981 sf2138 (C6c3, D6a5; 11th–12th century) (P6)

10168 Fragment, subglobular, yellow. D.7.5, H.5.6mm 3256 sf2364 (A6i2; 14th/15th century) (P6)

10169 Fragment, yellow. D.5.5, H.3.8mm 12561 sf2510 (D6a3–25; late 11th–13th century) (P6)

10170 Fragment, green. D.11.0, H.6.9mm 12412 sf3156 (C6e5; early 13th century) (P6)

10171 Green. D.7.4, H.4.2mm 9801 sf3299 (D6y1; late 12th–13th century) (P6)

10172 Fragment, opaque yellow. D.6.1, H.3.9mm 12635 sf4106 (D6a18; late 12th century) (P6)

10173 Fragment, yellow. L.7.0, H.5.3mm 16734 sf4457 (C6a1, D6a1; late 11th century) (P6)

10174 Fragment, royal blue. D.7.6, H.6.2mm 17457 sf4797 (B6a5; 11th/12th century) (P6)

10175 Green, tapering perforation. D.6.7, H.4.9mm 6344 sf5085 (D6a1; late 11th century) (P6)

10176 Irregularly globular, opaque blue. D.8.0, H.5.1mm 17699 sf5342 (C6c1; early 12th century) (P6)

10177 Subglobular, yellow. D.6.5, H.3.8mm 6281 sf5354 (D6a4; late 11th century) (P6)

10178 Fragment, green. L.2.8, H.2.8mm 18256 sf5481 (B6a7; early 12th century) (P6)

10179 Fragment, very dark appearing black. L.5.0, H.4.0mm 18256 sf5483 (B6a7; early 12th century) (P6)

10180 Fragment, green. L.7.0, H.5.5mm 17890 sf5518 (B6a1, C6a1; late 11th century) (P6)

10181 Yellow. D.10.0, H.5.7mm 17890 sf5544 (B6a1, C6a1; late 11th century) (P6)

10182 Fragment, tapering perforation, yellow. D.7.3, H.4.0mm 16612 sf5973 (D6a1; late 11th century) (P6)

10183 Fragment, yellow. L.7.4, H.5.5mm 18194 sf11408 (B6c2; 12th/13th century) (P6)

10184 Two adjoining fragments, subglobular, yellow. D.4.9, H.3.1mm 13212 sf14268 (B6w1; 14th–early 15th century) (P6)

10185 Irregular, very dark appearing black. D.6.3, H.5.4mm 5981 sf18969 (C6c3, D6a5; 11th–12th century) (P6)

10186 Fragment, irregular, yellow. D.9.3, H.6.5mm 20331 u/s sf6547

10187 Subglobular, pale blue-green, tapering perforation. D.11.7, H.8.1mm 32440 u/s sf13047

Type 3: Cylindrical

10188 Fragment, subcylindrical, pale blue. W.6.0, H.9.2mm 31061 sf10954 (P3)

10189 Green. D.3.0, H.3.1mm 26016 sf14516 (P3)

10190 Two adjoining fragments, squat cylinder, very dark appearing black. D.10.4, H.6.3mm 24402 sf8244 (P4B)

10191 Short cylinder, very dark appearing black. D.3.0, H.2.3mm 25340 sf11001 (P4B)

10192 Green. D.4.0, H.2.7mm 31424 sf14266 (P4B)

10193 Tapering perforation, green. D.2.9, H.2.8mm 21441 sf14400 (P4B)

10194 Irregular, tapering perforation, green. D.2.5, H.2.7mm 32243 sf14401 (P4B)

10195 Incomplete, green. D.3.0, H.2.5mm 27299 sf15744 (P4B)

10196 Irregular, tapering perforation, green. D.2.5, H.2.0mm 26992 sf15930 (P4B)

10197 Tapering cylinder, irregularly wound, green. D.2.8, H.4.5mm 26992 sf16233 (P4B)

10198 Green. D.2.9, H.3.1mm 8800 sf2185 (P5A)

10199 Disc, cylinder, green, opaque. D.7.3, H.3.6mm 14787 sf6584 (P5A)

10200 Opaque yellow. D.3.4, H.2.2mm 15086 sf11458 (P5A)

10201 Tapering cylinder, dark appearing black. D.3.3, H.3.2mm 2170 sf29 (P5B)

10202 Fragment, green. L.2.9, H.4.8mm 5711 sf1846 (P5B)

10203 Green. D.3.7, H.2.1mm 7553 sf2427 (P5B)

10204 Tapering perforation, dark appearing black. D.3.2, H.3.0mm 5848 sf2460 (P5B)

10205 Irregularly wound, green. D.2.9, H.5.3mm 16883 sf6452 (P5B) (*Fig.1285*)

10206 Six fragments, one incomplete, three green, three blue-green. D.2.9, H.3.0mm 6434 sf7419 (P5B)

10207 Malformed, irregularly wound, very dark appearing black. D.3.4, H.6.0mm 29263 sf10939 (P5B)

10208 Tapering cylinder, dark green. D.3.3, H.4.5mm 21381 sf11094 (P5B)

10209 Irregular, tapering perforation, green. D.3.5, H.3.0mm 26015 sf11235 (P5B)

10210 Irregular, tapering perforation, very dark appearing black. D.3.0, H.1.9mm 20234 sf11538 (P5B)

10211 Fragments (2), both malformed, one green, one very dark appearing black. D.5.1, H.4.8mm 21680 sf14395 (P5B)

10212 Irregular, tapering perforation, green. D.3.0, H.4.6mm 16733 sf4438 (P5Cr)

10213 Opaque yellow. D.3.1, H.2.0mm 16887 sf19052 (P5Cr)

10214 Fragment, red. D.2.6, H.1.3mm 16877 sf19053 (P5Cr)

10215 Incomplete, half only, short cylinder, orange with gold foil. D.9.0, H.6.3mm 1229 sf289 (C6z1; late 14th–early 15th century) (P6) (*Fig.1286*)

10216 Fragment, tapering cylinder, green. W.6.6, H.8.6mm 4125 sf307 (C6z1; late 14th–early 15th century) (P6)

10217 Tapering cylinder, green. D.3.7, H.4.2mm 5981 sf2243 (C6c3, D6a5; 11th–12th century) (P6)

10218 Tapering perforation, green. D.3.2, H.2.9mm 3419 sf2355 (A6c1; 12th century) (P6)

10219 Irregularly wound, dark green. D.3.0, H.4.0mm 3419 sf2356 (A6c1; 12th century) (P6)

10220 Fragment, very dark appearing black. D.3.6, H.3.8mm 9570 sf2410 (D6a9; early 12th century) (P6)

10221 Subcylindrical, tapering perforation, yellow. D.3.3, H.2.6mm 5981 sf2416 (C6c3, D6a5; 11th–12th century) (P6)

10222 Irregular, dark green. D.4.2, H.3.9mm 5331 sf2419 (D6a17; late 12th century) (P6)

10223 Irregular, yellow-green. D.2.2, H.2.6mm 8304 sf2421 (A6z4; 13th century) (P6)

10224 Tapering perforation, green. D.3.3, H.4.2mm 5906 sf2424 (C6c3, D6a5; 11th–12th century) (P6)

10225 Irregular, very dark appearing black. D.4.6, H.4.4mm 1404 sf2426 (D6y1; late 12th–13th century) (P6)

10226 Irregular, very dark appearing black. D.3.9, H.3.2mm 1404 sf2461 (D6y1; late 12th–13th century) (P6)

10227 Fragment, green. L.2.8, H.2.6mm 7837 sf3294 (C6x6; mid 13th century) (P6)

10228 Irregular, yellow. D.6.0, H.8.1mm 13147 sf3511 (B6u1; late 11th–early 13th century) (P6)

10229 Green. D.1.8, H.1.7mm 6258 sf5056 (C6c3, D6a5; 11th–12th century) (P6)

10230 Tapering cylinder, green. D.3.7, H.4.5mm 6281 sf5274 (D6a4; late 11th century) (P6)

10231 Irregular tapering cylinder, opaque yellow. D.4.3, H.3.8mm 18668 sf5454 (C6d6; mid 12th century) (P6)

10232 Irregular, opaque yellow. D.3.5, H.3.5mm 17551 sf11457 (C6c3; early 12th century) (P6)

10233 Two fragments, irregular, tapering perforations, green. D.3.8, H.5.0mm 13212 sf14267 (B6w1; 14th–early 15th century) (P6)

Type 4: *Gadrooned/dimpled*

10234 Fragment, very dark appearing black. L.6.8, H.8.4mm 15192 sf4195 (P5B)

10235 Fragment, irregular, very dark appearing black. L.5.4, H.7.6mm 15193 sf4203 (P5B)

10236 In three adjoining fragments, irregular, very dark appearing black. D.9.2, H.7.2mm 15382 sf4240 (P5B)

10237 Fragment, very dark appearing black. L.9.6, H.6.5mm 15192 sf4266 (P5B)

10238 Tapering perforation, dark green. D.9.4, H.6.2mm 15316 sf4279 (P5B) (*Fig.1285*)

10239 Fragment, blue. L.13.6, H.8.1mm 18489 sf5058 (P5B)

10240 Fragment, pear-shaped, dimpled, very dark appearing black. D.8.1, H.6.5mm 6866 sf11484 (P5B) (*Fig.1228*)

10241 Irregular, green. D.8.3, H.6.3mm 7953 sf3345 (P5Cf)

10242 Irregular, blue. D.12.4, H.5.6mm 16865 sf4467 (P5Cr)

10243 Fragment, irregular truncated cone, green. D.10.0, H.6.3mm 20205 sf6450 (P5Cr)

10244 Fragment, blue. L.4.4, H.4.3mm 19255 sf11409 (P5Cr)

10245 Fragment, blue. L.9.0, H.6.7mm 15311 sf11450 (P5Cr)

10246 Irregularly shaped, green. D.9.5, H.6.0mm 1096 sf227 (C6z1; late 14th–early 15th century) (P6)

10247 Fragment, green. W.6.2, H.6.4mm 1096 sf274 (C6z1; late 14th–early 15th century) (P6))

10248 Fragment, green. L.9.2, H.6.8mm 1455 sf354 (C6x2–6; 11th–13th century) (P6)

10249 Blue. D.13.2, H.6.2mm 5145 sf1734 (D6e3; 13th/14th century) (P6)

10250 Fragment, blue. D.9.8, H.4.5mm 1565 sf1788 (D6e8; early 14th century) (P6)

10251 Irregular, blue. D.10.7, H.6.8mm 5981 sf2168 (C6c3, D6a5; 11th–12th century) (P6)

10252 Blue. D.13.2, H.5.1mm 5981 sf2215 (C6c3, D6a5; 11th–12th century) (P6)

10253 Fragment, blue. L.7.4, H.5.2mm 5978 sf2230 (D6a6; 11th/12th century) (P6)

10254 Fragment, blue. L.6.5, H.5.9mm 5981 sf2235 (C6c3, D6a5; 11th–12th century) (P6)

10255 Blue. D.10.4, H.5.8mm 11000 sf2840 (B6c7; early 13th century) (P6)

10256 Fragment, green. L.5.7, H.6.6mm 3549 sf2973 (A6c1; 12th century) (P6)

10257 Fragment, dimpled, green. L.6.6, H.5.6mm 7782 sf3131 (D6y1; late 12th–13th century) (P6)

10258 Blue. D.12.0, H.4.9mm 3493 sf3483 (A6c1; 12th century) (P6)

10259 Fragment, blue. L.5.8, H.6.9mm 13465 sf3639 (B6c1; 12th/13th century) (P6)

10260 Fragment, green. D.8.0, H.7.4mm 17699 sf4571 (C6c1; early 12th century) (P6) (Fig.1228)

10261 Fragment, green. D.9.6, H.8.1mm 6258 sf5016 (C6c3, D6a5; 11th–12th century) (P6)

10262 Fragment, green. L.7.6, H.7.2mm 16612 sf6154 (D6a1; late 11th century) (P6)

10263 Fragment, blue. L.8.1, H.5.8mm u/s sf4408

Type 5: Barrel-shaped

10264 Opaque orange. D.9.1, H.6.5mm 31389 sf11345 (P3)

10265 Irregular, tapering perforation, opaque red. D.10.0, H.6.5mm 25350 sf8550 (P4B)

10266 Irregular, opaque yellow. D.10.1, H.7.7mm 29193 sf10285 (P4B)

10267 Fragment, opaque red. L.9.0, H.9.9mm 34730 sf13154 (P4B)

10268 Opaque cream and orange. D.8.0, H.6.5mm 14963 sf6540 (P5A)

10269 Opaque orange. D.11.5, H.7.7mm 5848 sf1866 (P5B) (Fig.1285)

10270 Fragment, opaque orange. L.7.8, H.6.6mm 18541 sf5099 (P5B)

10271 Fragment, opaque orange. L.6.7, H.6.3mm 20269 sf6404 (P5B)

10272 Fragment, opaque orange. L.8.9, H.6.1mm 18838 sf10353 (P5B)

10273 Fragment, opaque orange. L.9.3, H.6.1mm 18744 sf5670 (P5Cr)

10274 Fragment, opaque orange. L.7.5, H.7.6mm 18931 sf5898 (P5Cr)

10275 Opaque orange-brown. D.9.0, H.8.9mm 6789 sf6127 (P5Cr)

10276 Irregular, opaque orange. D.10.0, H.7.2mm 4535 sf686 (C6e11; mid 13th century) (P6)

10277 Opaque orange-brown. D.9.4, H.10.2mm 5906 sf2098 (C6c3, D6a5; 11th–12th century) (P6)

10278 Irregular, opaque orange. D.11.0, H.8.1mm 5981 sf2133 (C6c3, D6a5; 11th–12th century) (P6)

10279 Fragment, opaque orange. L.10.1, H.7.3mm 5981 sf2223 (C6c3, D6a5; 11th–12th century) (P6)

10280 Fragment, opaque orange. D.10.5, H.8.3mm 12671 sf3477 (D6a16; mid 12th century) (P6)

10281 Opaque orange-brown. D.10.3, H.6.4mm 6258 sf5023 (C6c3, D6a5; 11th–12th century) (P6)

Type 6: Biconical

10282 Colourless. D.6.1, H.3.5mm 26016 sf14517 (P3) (Fig.1285)

10283 Malformed, blue. D.4.0, H.2.4mm 30973 sf15932 (P3)

10284 Irregular, blue. D.3.3, H.1.6mm 26636 sf11095 (P4B)

10285 Irregular, tapering perforation, blue. D.5.0, H.2.8mm 18988 sf11107 (P4B)

10286 Light blue, decayed. D.12.2, H.9.3mm 8101 sf895 (P5A)

10287 Fragment, blue. L.8.8, H.7.8mm 20052 sf6247 (P5B)

10288 Fragment, blue. D.10.3, H.6.1mm 18744 sf6130 (P5Cr)

10289 Fragment, turquoise blue. D.9.5, H.7.4mm 2096 sf42 (B6u1, C6v1; late 11th–early 13th century) (P6)

10290 Fragment, short biconical, blue. D.11.7, H.5.2mm 1283 sf284 (C6z1; late 14th–early 15th century) (P6)

10291 Fragment, half only, orange with gold foil. D.10.8, H.8.2mm 1283 sf308 (C6z1; late 14th–early 15th century) (P6) (Fig.1286)

10292 Fragment, blue. D.11.2, H.4.9mm 9274 sf1284 (D6a5–24; 11th/13th century) (P6)

10293 Opaque orange. D.8.9, H.9.6mm 5230 sf1320 (D6a7; 11th/12th century) (P6)

10294 Blue. D.16.7, H.7.8mm 5246 sf1545 (C6e5; early 13th century) (P6)

10295 Incomplete, blue. D.11.0, H.5.6mm 9302 sf1563 (D6a26; 12th/13th century) (P6)

10296 Fragment, blue. D.11.3, H.9.0mm 5655 sf1939 (D6a17–23; 12th/13th century) (P6)

10297 Opaque orange. D.5.2, H.4.6mm 12662 sf3452 (D6a26–d1; 12th/13th century) (P6)

10298 Fragment, blue. D.5.7, H.3.9mm 6296 sf4998 (D6a5; 11th/12th century) (P6)

10299 Very pale blue. D.12.4, H.9.2mm 2286 sf5072 (C6v2; 12th century) (P6) (Fig.1285)

10300 Irregular, blue. D.12.4, H.4.9mm 16612 sf6044 (D6a1; late 11th century) (P6)

Type 7: Segmented

10301 Single-segment, colourless. D.7.5, H.6.2mm 32687 sf13751 (P3)

10302 Double-segmented, colourless. D.5.0, H.9.6mm 25759 sf9683 (P4A)

10303 Double-segmented, blue. D.5.9, H.9.4mm 15897 sf7415 (P4B)

10304 Single-segment, broken at one end, blue. D.7.2, H.5.8mm 25176 sf8232 (P4B)

10305 Single-segment, colourless but retaining traces of opaque white diagonal line decoration under covering layer of glass. D.7.2, H.6.0mm 24787 sf8889 (P4B)

10306 Double-segmented, blue-green. D.5.5, H.11.1mm 24787 sf8914 (P4B)

10307 Double-segmented, opaque yellow. D.5.1, H.7.9mm 31201 sf11098 (P4B)

10308 Single-segment, yellow. D.5.7, H.6.2mm 31275 sf11156 (P4B)

10309 Quadruple-segmented, pale yellow-white. D.3.6, H.15.7mm 22713 sf11329 (P4B) (Fig.1285)

10310 Double-segmented, opaque yellow-white. D.5.8, H.10.0mm 32115 sf12535 (P4B)

10311 Incomplete, single-segment, opaque cream-yellow. D.5.7, H.6.3mm 25303 sf13650 (P4B)

10312 Double-segmented, blue. D.6.1, H.9.5mm 24064 sf14388 (P4B) (Fig.1285)

10313 Single-segment, colourless. D.6.7, H.5.3mm 34289 sf14390 (P4B) (Fig.1285)

10314 Double-segmented, olive green. D.4.9, H.9.6mm 29528 sf14392 (P4B)

10315 Triple-segmented, colourless containing gold-coloured foil layer. D.5.5, H.14.3mm 2458 sf1431 (P5A)

10316 Triple-segmented, yellow-white, opaque. D.6.2, L.14.9mm 18286 sf4995 (P5A)

10317 Single-segment, colourless with fragment of coloured layer over one end. D.10.2, H.9.7mm 20185 sf7010 (P5A)

10318 Two segments, one incomplete, blue. D.5.3, H.9.0mm 20740 sf7239 (P5A)

10319 Double-segmented, yellow. D.4.6, H.7.8mm 27118 sf9961 (P5A) (*Fig.1285*)

10320 Single-segment, yellow-white. D.4.7, H.5.9mm 15657 sf4558 (P5B)

10321 Triple-segmented, royal blue. D.5.4, H.13.2mm 3633 sf8252 (P4/5)

10322 Single-segment, colourless with internal gold-coloured metal layer. D.7.1, H.5.0mm 18931 sf5963 (P5Cr)

Unidentifiable

10323 Fragments, very dark appearing black. L.5.6, W.5.2, T.3.2mm 30001 sf10309 (P4B)

10324 Fragment, very dark appearing black. L.3.6, W.2.4, T.2.0mm 22523 sf11002 (P4B)

10325 Fragments (2), opaque grey. L.3.5, W.2.8, T.1.4mm 22259 sf11270 (P4B)

10326 Fragments (7), opaque brown. 22808 sf11283 (P4B)

10327 Fragments (2), brown. L.4.2, W.3.6, T.1.6mm 29222 sf14265 (P4B)

10328 Fragments (5), opaque brown. L.5.1, W.3.7, T.1.6mm 14787 sf6489 (P5A)

10329 Fragment, yellow. L.6.0, H.3.1mm 20746 sf7411 (P5A)

10330 Fragments, white. L.2.4, W.2.2mm 7553 sf2411 (P5B)

10331 Malformed, opaque brown. D.25.0, H.9.8mm 14549 sf5139 (P5B)

10332 Fragment, green. L.4.3, W.2.4, T.2.3mm 6287 sf5276 (P5B)

10333 Malformed, blue-green. L.11.8, H.7.9mm 20269 sf6415 (P5B)

10334 Fragment, blue. L.6.5, W.6.4, T.6.0mm 19545 sf6978 (P5B)

10335 Fragment, green. L.11.5, H.14.1mm 16733 sf4420 (P5Cr)

10336 Fragment, misshapen, opaque orange. L.16.2, H.6.0mm 1346 sf294 (C6z1; late 14th–early 15th century) (P6)

10337 Fragment, blue. L.4.3, H.4.6mm 6026 sf2242 (D6a6; 11th/12th century) (P6)

10338 Malformed, of irregular section, light green. D.12.1, H.3.5mm 3414 sf2305 (A6e1; early 13th century) (P6)

Roman form

10339 Hexagonal section, green, irregular perforation. W.7.9, H.8.3mm 30385 sf12683 (P3)

Polychrome

Type 1: Annular

10340 Opaque brown with applied marvered white wave. D.13.6, H.6.8mm 2137 sf27 (P5B) (*Fig.1289*)

10341 Half, blue with applied marvered opaque yellow crossed waves. D.22.5, H.10.8mm 14069 sf3586 (P5Cf) (*Fig.1289*)

10342 Fragment, turquoise with marvered yellow cable decoration. L.13.2, H.8.0mm 3463 sf3631 (P5Cr) (*Fig.1289*)

10343 Subannular, blue with marvered opaque yellow spirals. D.11.0, H.4.5mm 6344 sf5091 (D6a1; late 11th century) (P6)

10344 Blue with applied opaque marvered white spiral. D.15.4, H.4.3mm 6258 sf5284 (C6c3, D6a5; 11th–12th century) (P6)

Type 2: Globular

10345 Opaque pale brown with light brown concentric circle decoration. D.15.5, H.9.4mm 25785 sf9599 (P4B)

10346 Tapering perforation, opaque brown with applied marvered opaque cream blobs, some blobs lost. D.17.6, H.11.1mm 21887 sf9956 (P4B) (*Fig.1289*)

10347 Subglobular, with malformed perforation, darkly coloured with applied cream-white concentric trail. D.15.1, H.13.0mm 26953 sf9809 (P5A) (*Figs.1289–90*)

10348 Irregular, blue-white with wave trail and blobs on sides. D.22.0, H.11.0mm 6444 sf7414 (P5B) (*Fig.1289*)

10349 Black with opaque marvered white wave design. D.15.5, H.9.7mm 17890 sf5537 (B6a1, C6a1; late 11th century) (P6) (*Fig.1289*)

Type 5: Barrel-shaped

10350 Very dark appearing black, decorated with applied and marvered green blobs each surrounded by a green circle with yellow lines through. D.14.5, H.12.6mm 34687 sf13728 (P4B) (*Fig.1289*)

Type 6: Biconical

10351 Fragment, very dark appearing black with applied marvered cream-white concentric circles around perforation and irregular waves. D.9.6, H.6.0mm 30842 sf15957 (P3) (*Fig.1288–9*)

10352 Dark appearing brown-black, decorated with white double crossed waves, irregularly applied, with yellow blobs between. D.14.1, H.8.2mm 4189 sf393 (C6z1; late 14th–early 15th century) (P6) (*Fig.1288–9*)

10353 Fragment, blue with applied opaque cream crossed double waves. L.7.9, H.5.6mm u/s sf11 (*Fig.1289*)

Unidentifiable

10354 Fragment, irregularly shaped, blue with opaque applied marvered yellow eyes and crossed waves. L.28.0, W.18.4, T.9.8mm 35011 sf13345 (P4B) (*Fig.1289*)

Roman form

10355 Subsquare section, rounded corners, blue, each facet decorated with a marvered lozenge or sublozenge shaped motif, all originally white. W.9.8, H.8.8mm 1473 sf426 (P5B)

Iron

Weights

10356 Globular, top and bottom flattened, with copper alloy coating split at both ends, which are decorated with triskele motif within circle of dots. D.19.0mm, Wt.21.90g 32549 sf15879 (P3) (*Fig.1259–60*)

10357 Globular, top and bottom flattened, with copper alloy coating split at one end, both ends decorated with stamped circle of dots with four linked dots within. D.21.0mm, Wt.26.97g 32694 sf15880 (P3) (*Fig.1259–60*)

10358 Barrel-shaped with copper alloy coating around circumference. D.30.5mm, Wt.97.20g 25934 sf10059 (P4B) (*Fig.1259*)

10359 Lead coating, subglobular. D.20.8, H.12.3mm, Wt.25.00g 25466 sf11330 (P4B) (*Fig.1259*)

10360 Globular, coated in copper alloy, coating split. D.19.2mm, Wt.18.50g 7863 sf3312 (P5Cf)

Copper alloy

Needles

Note: Full catalogue entries for 6623–5 appear in *AY* 17/11. These are illustrated on Fig.830.

6623   A bayonet point, with shank of subcircular section, upper end flattened to rectangular section, top cut square with perforation below, lower two-thirds of shank flattened and expanded then tapering to spatulate end at right-angles to perforation and slightly bent up. L.90.6, W.5.7, T.3.7mm, shank section D.3.0mm 30352 sf11553 (P4A)

6624   Incomplete, head broken through oval eye, shank of subcircular section. D.1.7, L.40.7mm 19390 sf8751 (P4B)

6625   Shank of subcircular section, tapering to tip, subcircular eye. D.1.7, L.54.3mm 24119 sf8119 (P4B) (*Fig.1235*)

10361   Subcircular section, tapering to tip, head incomplete, broken through oval eye, lower half of shank bent up. D.1.6, L.58.4mm 27621 sf10521 (P4A)

10362   Subcircular section, head incomplete, broken across oval eye. D.1.9, L.60.3mm 23311 sf7489 (P4B)

10363   Subcircular section, tapering to blunt point, top of head broken off across circular eye which has V-shaped depression below. D.2.2, L.49.2mm 26171 sf8829 (P4B) (*Fig.1235*)

10364   Circular section, with oval eye through flattened end, shank tapering to point, upper end bent up at right-angles. D.2.1, L.59.2mm 19353 sf6898 (P5B) (*Fig.1235*)

Household equipment

10365   Spoon with tapering stem of suboval section, one end pointed, long narrow upturned bowl. L.50.2, W.4.9mm, stem W.2.7, T.1.6mm 22819 sf8027 (P4B) (*Fig.1245*)

10366   Spoon double-ended, one end with virtually flat broad oval bowl, incised line along each edge, spirally twisted stem of rectangular section, second bowl a flat narrow oval with pointed tip, curved up, also with incised line along edges. L.154.2, T.4.1mm, broad bowl, L.34.3, W.26.5, T.1.1mm, narrow bowl, L.33.6, W.17.6, T.0.9mm u/s sf3805 (*Fig.1245*)

Fittings and furnishings
Stapled hasp

10367   Subrectangular, of rectangular section, perforated at upper end, tapering to lower end which is rolled up with perforated lug just above this on reverse face, upper end curved. The front is decorated with punched dots and an incised saltire within two pairs of transverse parallel lines just above the lug. L.106.3, W.8.6, T.2.6mm, lug W.6.5, T.2.9mm 29575 sf11127 (P5B) (*Fig.1250*)

Hinge fittings

10368   Incomplete. Sheet, perforated at upper end which is rounded and has incomplete looped eye, also perforated at lower end which is subcircular with decoratively toothed terminal. There are traces of an incised circle around the lower perforation on the reverse face, and smaller perforations, one incompletely punched, just above the perforation. L.53.5, W.16.6, T.0.7mm 27819 sf10837 (P3) (*Fig.1250*)

10369   Fragment, tongue-shaped, broken at one end, central rivet hole, tapering to other end with expanded oval terminal with surviving iron rivet, several other possible rivet holes. L.62.5, W.23.9, T.3.7mm 32668 sf13752 (P3) (*Fig.1250*)

Strip fittings

10370   Strip fitting or hinge, a folded strip, subrectangular, with trapezoidal terminal with two perforated bosses, and axial row of bosses along one half of strip. There are the remains of three rivets on the plain half strip, part of an iron ring within the loop and fragments of wood between the strips. L.72.3, W.14.8, T.8.6mm, sheet T.0.5mm 23278 sf7389 (P4B) (*Fig.1250*)

10371   Two adjoining fragments, attached to wood, subrectangular, tapering from one broken end, decorated with axial row of bosses, copper alloy rivets through some of the bosses. L.127.2, W.15.2, T.1.8mm 22590 sf7736 (P4B) (*Fig.1250*)

10372   Incomplete, subrectangular, broken at both ends, decorated with axial row of bosses, three rivet holes punched through bosses. L.80.4, W.11.1, T.0.7mm 22590 sf7737 (P4B)

10373   Fragment, subrectangular, both ends broken, decorated with stamped ring, centrally perforated. L.15.2, W.14.0, T.1.2mm 18025 sf7971 (P4B)

10374   Possible strip fitting fragments (2), adjoining, tapering to one end, other end broken, decorated with axial row of dots. L.38.7, W.6.0, T.0.9mm 24618 sf8295 (P4B)

10375   Fragment, of plano-convex section, both ends broken, one across incomplete backplate which follows curve of strip on one side, extends out on inner side. The strip is decorated with incised diagonal lines, with axial rivet holes, one subsquare and torn through one edge, another perforates strip and backplate fragment. L.48.1, W.10.3, T.2.0mm, strip W.6.9, T.1.6mm 19390 sf9072 (P4B)

10376   One end broken across perforation, other end rounded and folded under, perforations through both thicknesses, upper face of strip decorated with incised lines along each edge, with Z-shaped motifs between. L.53.2, W.8.1, T.0.7mm 21903 sf10577 (P4B)

10377   Terminal, trapezoidal, one end broken, decorated with three bosses. L.19.6, W.15.5, T.0.5mm 31013 sf10890 (P4B)

10378   Fragment subsemicircular, of irregular section, broken at straight edge. L.21.1, W.12.4, T.4.0mm 34412 sf13004 (P4B)

10379   Fragment, subrectangular, one end broken, with incised line along each edge on one face, and two axial perforations. L.55.6, W.11.3, T.0.9mm 2080 sf4891 (P5A)

10380   Fragment of sheet, one curved edge with ragged rim, other edges roughly broken. L.52.7, W.23.6, T.2.1mm 22010 sf13482 (P5A)

10381   Fragment, U-shaped section, one end broken across perforation, bent towards centre. There is an axial row of perforations and one on one edge close to broken end. L.53.1, W.9.0, T.1.8mm 8122 sf1039 (P5B) (*Fig.1250*)

10382   Fragment, irregularly shaped with five bosses, two of which have been perforated. L.20.1, W.14.8, T.0.5mm 9726 sf3035 (P5B) (*Fig.1250*)

10383   Fragment, one edge and one end torn, other end with trapezoidal projections, axial perforations, torn end bent up. L.38.1, W.11.5, T.0.8mm 3533 sf4771 (P4/5)

Possible fittings

10384   Trapezoidal plate with off-centre perforation containing loop of subcircular section, broken at scarf joint. L.32.7, W.15.0, T.1.0mm, loop D.11.4, T.3.4mm 26438 sf8780 (P3) (*Fig.1250*)

10385   Clip made of sheet, subrectangular with two axial perforations, tapering to points at both ends which are hooked up. L.55.0, W.8.8, T.1.0mm 19120 sf6063 (P5Cr) (*Fig.1250*)

Mounts

10386   Fragment of sheet, subtrapezoidal, tapering from one end which is broken to other which has small perforation, decorated with perforated ring-and-dot motif. L.13.3, W.5.6, T.0.4mm 31013 sf10874 (P4B)

10387 Sheet, tongue-shaped, tapering slightly from one end with grooved decoration and rivet hole below, other end broken, upper face perforated by punched ring-and-dot motifs in cross arrangement. L.42.0, W.12.5, T.0.5mm 36058 sf13576 (P4B)

10388 Subovoid, domed, with projection at each end on reverse for attachment. L.24.3, W.10.8, T.2.3mm, projection L.6.3mm 14297 sf3853 (P5B)

10389 Made of sheet, subcrescent-shaped, with two perforations, decorated with ring-and-dot motifs and rocked-tracer ornament. L.45.7, W.11.5, T.0.7mm 16881 sf9082 (P5B) (Fig.1254)

10390 Made of sheet, subtrapezoidal, both long edges incomplete, tapering to one end which is incomplete and slightly curved under, other end with tiny perforation, second perforation on one edge. The whole is decorated with incised herring-bone hatching. L.30.0, W.14.0, T.0.9mm 6570 sf5736 (P5Cr) (Fig.1254)

Binding fragment

10391 Semi-circular strip folded transversely, broken at both ends across perforations, one side of subsquare section, thinning out to flat sheet on other side. L.31.1, W.5.8, T.3.4mm 15311 sf5572 (P5Cr) (Fig.1254)

Rings

10392 Lozenge-shaped section. D.17.2, T.2.7mm 27369 sf10300 (P3)

10393 Circular section, broken. D.18.0mm, section D.2.9mm 30920 sf12990 (P3) (Fig.1254)

10394 Incomplete, with hoop of square section, tapering slightly to broken tip, other end flattened and perforated, at right-angles to tip, whole curved. L.34.8, W.4.2, T.2.0mm 26147 sf8653 (P4B) (Fig.1254)

10395 Fragment, with hoop of circular section, one end flattened and broken across a perforation, tapering to other end which is curved up. D.4.6, L.38.2mm, shank D.2.4mm 14704 sf5640 (P5B)

10396 Subcircular section, gilded. D.32.9mm, section D.6.0mm 3726 sf10247 (P4/5) (Fig.1254)

Double-spiked loop

10397 Upper end subcircular and folded over, both sides with narrow projection tapering to tip, the front projection being the longer and bent, both with extreme tips broken off. L.35.7, W.9.3, T.1.7mm 14467 sf4124 (P5B) (Fig.1254)

Perforated strip

10398 Fragment, rectangular, one end broken across rivet, other end thickened and ragged, strip bent up. L.45.7, W.12.3, T.6.5mm, unbent length L.93.7mm 18744 sf5753 (P5Cr)

Miscellaneous fittings

10399 Tube made from rolled up sheet, butted seam, one end broken. D.4.1, L.36.1mm 25922 sf15854 (P4A)

10400 Tube fragment, flattened into plano-convex section at one end, with edges overlapped, edges broken towards other end. L.68.2, W.9.3, T.6.8mm, sheet T.0.6mm 32758 sf13691 (P4B)

10401 Sheet fragment, irregularly shaped, with the remains of two perforations on one broken edge. L.28.6, W.4.1, T.0.8mm 19268 sf11446 (P5Cr)

Horse harness

10402 Strap distributor fragment, of rectangular section, curved and tapering from one end which is broken to the other which terminates in a stylised animal head. There are two loops to one side, and one larger loop to other, and the central strip is decorated with red enamelled geometric motifs. L.34.5, W.28.9, T.2.6mm 30286 sf11180 (P4A) (Fig.1256)

10403 Strap distributor fragment, with trilobate terminal, each lobe circular and perforated, with incomplete double-pronged extension developing from it, rivet hole between lobes. L.45.6, W.33.9, T.6.5mm, lobe D.14.7, T.4.1mm 8568 sf1701 (P5A) (Fig.1256)

10404 Harness mount of rectangular section, central roundel, with three projections at cardinal points, fourth broken away. Terminals of all projections incomplete, stems rectangular. Traces of gilding. D. (roundel) 16.6, T.2.9mm, projection L.23.2, W.9.4, T.2.7mm 21746 sf10333 (P5B) (Fig.1256)

Trade and exchange

10405 Balance beam with folding arms of circular section, tapering to moulded ends which are perforated for suspension of scale pans, arms hinged on rivets at each end of the beam, which has remains of central pointer. L.29.8, W.5.6, T.4.9mm, arm D.4.4, L.70.3mm 22323 sf7576 (P4B) (Fig.1258)

10406 Balance arm from folding balance, of circular section, with flat perforated lug at one end for suspension of scale pan, moulded below, pivotal end of plano-convex section. Also small ring of square section, incomplete. D.1.9, L.48.7mm, lug D.3.0mm, ring D.5.7, T.1.0mm 22690 sf7848 (P4B) (Fig.1258)

10407 Balance stirrup, incomplete, of rectangular section at one end which is curved up into incomplete hook, broadening and flattening out to other end which is perforated. L.44.9, W.3.2, T.1.6mm 19390 sf8908 (P4B)

10408 Weight, discoidal. D.8.3, H.4.0mm, Wt.1.50g 19390 sf8929 (P4B) (Fig.1259)

10409 Balance beam and two scale pans, the beam of circular section tapering to moulded ends, perforated and containing loops. A triangular pointer rises from the centre of the beam between the two arms of the suspension fork from which the beam is suspended, and which at upper end has a ring through the lug on the cross-bar. Both scale pans are circular and dished with three perforations. L.87.9mm, beam section D.2.7mm, fork L.31.0, W.3.8, T.5.1mm, scale pan D.32.2, T.0.9mm 22802 sf9512 (P4B) (Fig.1258)

10410 Balance arm from folding balance, of circular section, perforated at one end for suspension of scale pan, pivotal end of square section. D.4.6, L.37.3mm 31089 sf11178 (P4B)

10411 Balance arm fragment, of square section with moulding at one end which is incomplete, remainder of circular section, tapering to other end which is also broken. D.4.0, L.43.2mm 20181 sf7052 (P5A) (Fig.1258)

10412 Balance arm fragment, from folding balance, broken at both ends, of oval section at pivotal end. Below is a cuboidal swelling decorated with stamped ring-and-dot motifs, with arm of circular section continuing and tapering slightly to the other end, also broken. D.3.8,

L.35.3mm, swelling W.6.4, T.5.5mm 15177 sf4034 (P5B) (*Fig.1258*)

10413 Balance suspension bracket, with three arms of polygonal section, projecting from discoidal centre with suspension loop, one arm incomplete, other two with expanded discoidal terminals with suspension loop below, upper face decorated with ring-and-dot motif. D.9.1, T.4.0mm, arm L.34.9, W.6.5mm, central loop W.8.3, T.3.1mm 20351 sf8372 (P5B) (*Fig.1257*)

10414 Balance chain, formed from eleven S-shaped links with one oval link. L.107.0mm, section D.1.7mm 19328 sf6801 (P5Cr) (*Fig.1257*)

10415 Balance beam with arms of circular section, bent up on each side, tapering towards ends which are perforated and each contain suspension loops for chains. From middle of beam is attached via transverse perforation a triangular pointer perforated at base to take suspension mechanism, which is perforated at the upper end and contains a loop, shaped terminal, decorated on both faces with incised saltire and a triangular notch on each edge. D.5.0, L.135.6mm, suspension mechanism L.38.9, W.12.2, T.0.9mm, pointer L.23.0, W.4.6, T.1.2mm, loops D.6.2mm, loop section D.1.3mm 12863 sf3716 (C6e4; 12th–13th century) (P6) (*Fig.1258*)

10416 Balance stirrup, incomplete, broken at one end, other end flattened with perforation, rectangular, of plano-convex section, decorated with two pairs of mouldings with chevrons, and third moulding just below perforation. L.81.6, W.4.1, T.1.2mm 1283 sf425 (C6z1; late 14th–early 15th century) (P6) (*Fig.1257*)

Dress accessories

Buckles

10417 D-shaped frame, of subtriangular section, flat rectangular pin, perforating fragment of strap attachment plate. L.18.4, W.13.0, T.2.4mm, plate L.17.5, W.12.4, T.0.4mm, pin L.15.7, W.3.3, T.0.9mm 30352 sf12759 (P4A) (*Fig.1264*)

10418 Buckle loop, oval, of subtriangular section, pin lost, part of attachment plate remains looped around frame. L.42.2, W.24.2, T.6.4mm, section W.6.9mm 2078 sf4868 (P5A) (*Fig.1264*)

10419 Incomplete oval hoop, of rectangular section, pin of rectangular section, slightly bent. L.29.0, W.21.0mm, section W.3.2, T.1.2mm, pin L.28.9, W.4.1, T.1.9mm 19620 sf8951 (P5B)

Strap-guide or belt loop

10420 Made of sheet, sublozenge-shaped, ends tapered and folded under, decorated on upper face with ring-and-dot motifs and incised lateral line along each edge. L.20.0, W.7.1, T.0.8mm 18025 sf7940 (P4B) (*Fig.1264*)

Strap-ends

10421 In the form of an openwork conventionalised vine scroll, developing from subrectangular upper end split for strap attachment with iron rivets, decorated with ring-and-dot motifs at upper end and over openwork. L.58.0, W.26.7, T.3.0mm 22268 sf7501 (P4B) (*Fig.1265*)

10422 Broad tongue shape with four iron rivets at broader upper end, body stepped up from this end and decorated in relief with acanthus leaf surrounding a central rosette motif. L.51.0, W.31.0mm 27098 sf11100 (P4B) (*Fig.1265*)

10423 Split at upper end for attachment, tapering slightly to animal head terminal with squared snout and dot eyes,

and decorated with Borre-style ring-chain ornament in main field. L.47.5, W.12.6, T.2.0mm 20131 sf5976 (P5A) (*Fig.1265*)

10424 One end split and retaining rivet, tapering down to a stylised zoomorphic terminal, with pair of ears in relief on both faces, tapering slightly again to incised eyes, waisted below with ring-and-dot for nostrils, tapering to elongated rounded snout. L.39.0, W.8.8, T.6.8mm 5395 sf1898 (C6c6, D6a7; 11th–12th century) (P6) (*Fig.1265*)

Brooches

10425 Penannular brooch fragment comprising terminal and fragment of hoop, terminal essentially square with cusped sides, decorated with equal-armed cross with central setting originally with blue glass stud of which a small fragment survives. There is a boss in each of the angles of the cross encircled with interlace, the cross arms are also filled with interlace. The broken hoop of plano-convex section develops from one corner of the terminal. L.60.6, W.40.2, T.4.6mm, hoop W.11.7, T.3.7mm 20809 sf7159 (P3) (*Fig.1266*)

10426 Equal-armed bow brooch of the 'caterpillar' type, with a subrectangular bow with unexpanded subsquare terminals with indented edges. The catch-plate, attachment plate and part of the pin survive on the reverse. The upper faces of the terminals are decorated with incised lines, and the bow with mouldings. L.55.1, W.14.1, T.4.2mm 22449 sf7706 (P4B) (*Fig.1266*)

10427 Equal-armed bow brooch of the 'caterpillar' type, with head and foot tapering slightly from the bow, and separated from it by pairs of transverse mouldings. In the middle of the bow is a group of three transverse mouldings. The catch and part of the hinge plate survive, but the pin is lost. L.41.2, W.7.6, T.2.9mm 24808 sf9209 (P4B) (*Fig.1266*)

10428 Disc brooch, cast, with a border of radial grooves enclosing a backward-looking quadruped in relief. There is a suboval perforation through the animal's front leg, and on the reverse only the catch plate survives. D.24.0, T.1.6mm 26495 sf8803 (P4B) (*Fig.1267*)

10429 Disc brooch, cast backing, with disc on front attached by folding over the edge, disc with *repoussé* decoration of two circumferential circles of beading enclosing backward-looking animal. The pin attachment and clasp plate have been broken away. D.32.4, T.2.4mm 34569 sf13106 (P4B) (*Fig.1267*)

10430 Disc brooch, cast backing, with disc attached to front by folding over edge, backing and disc torn on one side, disc with *repoussé* decoration of a beaded border, and beaded frame around backward-looking animal. The backing carries the remains of attachment for pin and catch. D.31.2, T.1.7mm 35519 sf14116 (P4B) (*Fig.1267*)

10431 Cross brooch, equal-armed with expanded arms, with slightly raised triangular field on each arm, a boss in the centre and a smaller boss at each corner at ends of arms, pin and attachment lost, catch-plate survives. L.35.0, W.33.6, T.4.1mm 22560 sf7808 (P4B) (*Fig.1270*)

10432 Brooch pin of subsquare section, with remains of silver hinge fitting; brooch pin and hinge perforated by brass hinge pin. L.29.0, W.8.3, T.6.2mm, pin section W.2.3, T.2.0mm 22090 sf15767 (P5A) (*Fig.1272*)

10433 Brooch pin of rectangular section, tapering to point at one end, incomplete loop at other. L.52.8, W.2.8, T.1.6mm 13733 sf3594 (P5B)

10434 Brooch pin shank of subrectangular section, tapering to a point at one end, loop at upper end. L.38.0, W.2.2, T.1.8mm, loop D.4.2mm 19120 sf6751 (P5Cr) (*Fig.1272*)

Hooked tags

10435 Subtriangular plate with perforated subrectangular extensions, triangular cut-outs between the perforations at broad end, hook of rectangular section tapering and turned under at other, decorated with ring-and-dot motifs on one face. L.30.3, W.15.3, T.1.6mm 32836 sf13760 (P3) (*Fig.1273*)

10436 Subtriangular plate with perforated subcircular extensions, both with upper edge bent over, with triangular cut-outs between, decorated with an off-centre punched single boss, tapering to hook turned under at lower end. L.27.5, W.15.6, T.0.7mm 22103 sf11212 (P5B) (*Fig.1273*)

10437 Discoidal plate with tapering projection hooked up at lower end, and two perforations at upper end. One face of the plate is decorated with incised wave and scrolls within a circular field. L.20.5mm, head D.16.0, T.0.9mm 16612 sf5176 (D6a1; late 11th century) (P6) (*Fig.1273*)

Dress pins

Type 1: Globular head

10438 Subglobular head, with single collar, with shank of circular section, tapering to tip, lower half bent up. D.2.1, L.71.6mm, head D.6.7mm 26937 sf10113 (P3) (*Fig.1274*)

10439 Single collar, shank of circular section, hipped towards tip where section changes to square. D.1.7, L.47.2mm, head D.5.4mm 27819 sf10706 (P3)

10440 Shank of circular section, with swelling towards tip which is bent up. D.1.6, L.40.3mm, head D.3.6mm 31643 sf11843 (P3)

10441 Fragment, shank broken off. L.7.7mm, head D.3.7mm 30841 sf14411 (P3)

10442 Fragment, head with ridged decoration, majority of shank broken off. L.9.7mm, head D.6.4mm 30936 sf14480 (P3) (*Fig.1274*)

10443 Single collar, shank of circular section, with central swelling, tapering to tip, upper end of pin bent up. D.2.4, L.69.5mm, head D.7.3mm 27623 sf10042 (P4A)

10444 Shank of circular section, tapering to tip, lower half of shank bent up. D.2.2, L.55.8mm, head D.3.8mm 30132 sf10558 (P4A)

10445 Corroded, traces of single collar, shank of uncertain section. D.1.4, L.48.5mm, head D.3.0mm 15311 sf4209 (P5Cr)

10446 Incomplete, most of shank broken away, subglobular head with slight collar beneath, shank of oval section. D.2.0, L.16.0mm, head D.7.0mm 6789 sf6139 (P5Cr)

10447 Single collar, shank of circular section, swelling with incised spiral motif towards tip. D.1.7, L.55.5mm, head D.7.0mm u/s sf11310

Type 2: Polyhedral head

10448 Polyhedral head of rectangular section, with lozenge- and triangular-shaped facets, stamped with ring-and-dot motifs, shank of subcircular section. D.2.4, L.68.4mm, head L.7.4, W.5.6, T.5.1mm 27429 sf10175 (P1/3)

10449 Polyhedral head, with lozenge-shaped and triangular facets on top and sides, all decorated with punched dots, shank of circular section, swelling towards tip. D.2.4, L.54.8mm, head L.8.4, W.6.9, T.5.6mm 20819 sf7177 (P4B) (*Fig.1274*)

10450 Polyhedral head, lozenge-shaped facets on top of head, also on sides which are decorated with punched ring-and-dot motifs, single collar, shank of circular section, tapering to tip. D.2.2, L.59.0mm, head L.7.6, W.6.5, T.5.9mm 26171 sf8815 (P4B) (*Fig.1274*)

10451 Complete apart from tip, polyhedral head of square section, lozenge-shaped facets on sides of head, each with punched dot, shank of circular section with swelling towards tip. D.2.4, L.57.6mm, head L.7.3, W.3.4mm 2570 sf322 (P5B)

10452 Polyhedral head of square section with lozenge-shaped facets on sides and top, decorated with ring-and-dot motifs, subtriangular facets on corners, shank of circular section, lower third bent. D.2.2, L.79.0mm, head W.4.3, T.4.0mm 17699 sf5197 (C6c1; early 12th century) (P6)

Type 3: Baluster head

10453 Baluster head of square section, with lozenge-shaped and triangular facets, the former with punched dot decoration, and top of head cut into lozenge. Shank of circular section with swelling towards tip. D.2.2, L.54.0mm, head L.7.2, W.2.3mm 31359 sf11290 (P3) (*Fig.1274*)

10454 Baluster head, of square section, lozenge-shaped top, sides faceted and with punched dots, shank of circular section tapering to tip, lower two-thirds of shank bent up at swelling. D.2.0, L.62.4mm, head L.8.3 W.2.2, T.1.9mm 30735 sf12407 (P3) (*Fig.1274*)

10455 Baluster head of square section, top lozenge-shaped, collar beneath, shank of circular section tapering to tip. D.2.1, L.57.6mm, head L.7.1, W.2.3, T.2.0mm 26254 sf9178 (P4B)

Type 4: Biconical head

10456 Irregularly biconical head, ring collar, shank of circular section, tapering to tip. D.2.0, L.61.6mm, head D.4.3mm 3697 sf9040 (P3) (*Fig.1274*)

10457 Faceted biconical head of circular section, flattened top, ring collar, shank of circular section, slight swelling towards tip. D.2.0, L.63.1mm, head D.6.6mm 36532 sf14148 (P3)

10458 Incomplete, tip broken off, biconical head, shank too corroded to identify. L.32.0mm, head D.3.6mm 26423 sf12686 (P4A)

10459 Incomplete, part of shank broken off, faceted biconical head with collar, shank of subcircular section. D.2.1, L.41.0mm, head D.9.5mm 19633 sf9276 (P5B) (*Fig.1274*)

Type 5: Spiral head

10460 Shank fragment, upper end broken, shank of square section, split into two at upper end. L.38.5, W.1.9mm 31061 sf10942 (P3)

10461 Incomplete, with inwardly spiralled head, shank of rounded polygonal section, with incised rings at top of shank. D.2.2, L.54.0mm 31225 sf11362 (P3)

10462 Spiral head formed by splitting top of shank axially, flattening and inwardly spiralling each side. The shank is of circular section with swelling towards tip. D.2.2, L.55.9mm, head W.7.1, T.1.4mm 20375 sf6638 (P4B) (*Fig.1274*)

10463 Incomplete inwardly spiralled head, shank of oval section. D.1.7, L.53.0mm 20411 sf8890 (P4B)

10464 Spiral head formed by splitting top of shank axially, flattening and inwardly spiralling each side, shank of circular section, tip broken off. D.2.0, L.54.7mm, head W.9.3mm 7296 sf1600 (P5B)

Type 6: Inverted plano-convex head

10465 Head of hexagonal section, shank of square section tapering to tip. L.52.4, W.1.9mm, head L.4.9, W.6.0mm 30623 sf11809 (P3)

10466 Head of circular section, shank of circular section, slight swelling towards tip which is broken off. D.3.0, L.50.0mm, head D.5.2mm 30840 sf12072 (P3)

10467 Inverted conical head of circular section, decorated with incised spiral grooves on side, incised saltire on flat top, single collar, upper two-thirds of shank of circular section, hipped towards tip where shank changes to lozenge-shaped section. D.2.2, L.62.3mm, head D.7.3mm, hip W.3.0mm 7849 sf3530 (C6x2; 11th–13th century) (P6) (*Fig.1274*)

Type 7: Linked pin

10468 Flat subcircular head perforated and retaining two links of chain, shank of circular section tapering to tip which is broken off. D.1.8, L.47.4mm, chain link D.3.6mm 26996 sf9708 (P4B) (*Fig.1274*)

Type 8: Flat oval head

10469 Incomplete flat head, with ring-and-dot motifs on both faces, shank of oval section. D.1.8, L.62.5mm, head W.5.0mm 25759 sf9742 (P4A)

10470 Incomplete, top half of head broken off, decorated on both faces with incised ring-and-dot, shank of circular section, expanded near tip. D.2.9, L.52.0mm, estimated head size D.5.0mm 6054 sf2339 (P5B) (*Fig.1274*)

Type 9: Flat trapezoidal head

10471 Flat inverted trapezoidal head, decorated on both faces with ring-and-dot motifs, shank of circular section with slight swelling, lower third of shank tapering to tip. D.2.0, L.58.0mm, head L.7.4, W.6.0, T.2.3mm 6950 sf6789 (P5B) (*Fig.1274*)

Type 10: Flat, sub-figure-of-eight-shaped head

10472 Head of rectangular section, with two perforations, each surrounded with punched ring-and-dot decoration on both faces. Two subcircular perforated extensions at top of head each contain single wire ring, shank of oval section. D.2.6, L.92.3mm, head L.11.6, W.6.4, T.1.3mm, ring D.4.7, T.1.4mm 17890 sf5632 (B6a1, C6a1; late 11th century) (P6) (*Fig.1274*)

Type 11: Flat polygonal head

10473 Lozenge-shaped head of rectangular section, with angular projections on three corners, decorated on both faces along each side with rocked-tracer ornament, shank of circular section, tapering to point. D.2.9, L.53.0mm, head W.10.5, T.1.5mm 20178 sf6294 (P5Cr) (*Fig.1274*)

Type 12: Ringed pins

10474 Ringed pin shank of loop-headed type, shank of circular section, tapering to point at lower end, upper end flattened and turned over to form loop for ring. L.65.7, D.1.8mm 22524 sf7872 (P4B)

10475 Rolled up hollow shank, tip left open, with rolled up loop attachment at right-angles to shank. D.3.2, L.81.0mm, loop D.5.4, L.10.9mm 16612 sf4399 (D6a1; late 11th century) (P6) (*Fig.1275*)

10476 Ringed pin with baluster head of square section, with lozenge- and triangular-shaped facets, decorated with punched dots, shank of circular section, lower half flattening into rectangular section and tapering to tip, ring of lozenge-shaped section. D.2.9, L.140.3mm, head W.3.8, T.3.7mm, ring D.12.8mm, ring section W.2.2mm 2677 sf774 (P5A) (*Fig.1275*)

10477 Ringed pin with baluster head of square section with faceted corners, decorated with punched dots, shank of circular section tapering to tip, ring of lozenge-shaped section. D.3.8, L.141.6mm, head W.4.5, T.4.0mm, ring D.14.3mm, ring section W.1.9mm 22180 sf7388 (P5A) (*Fig.1275*)

10478 Ringed pin with baluster head of square section, notched on each corner close to top, decorated with incised saltires and transverse lines. The shank is of circular section, flattening from halfway down to rectangular section and tapering to tip, with incised transverse and lateral lines. The ring is subcircular, of lozenge-shaped section. D.3.8, L.149.7mm, head L.11.8, W.4.1mm, ring D.18.6mm, ring section W.2.9, T.3.0mm u/s sf13149 (*Fig.1275*)

10479 Ringed pin with trapezoidal head of square section, with lozenge-shaped corner facets, faces decorated with punched dots, shank of oval section, tapering to tip, ring of square section. D.2.0, L.49.4mm, ring D.18.6mm, ring section W.1.9, T.2.0mm 5698 sf1822 (P5B)

10480 Ringed pin with square head of rectangular section with lozenge- and triangular-shaped facets, shank of subcircular section, tapering and flattening into rectangular section from halfway down, ring oval and of subcircular section. D.4.1, L.180.0mm, head W.7.5, T.7.5mm, ring D.18.2mm, ring section D.4.0mm 32440 u/s sf13035 (*Fig.1275*)

10481 Ringed pin ring, suboval, of lozenge-shaped section, one end broken, remains of hinge on other end. L.31.9, W.28.2mm, section W.4.8, T.4.4mm 19701 sf12738 (P3)

10482 Ringed pin ring, suboval, of circular section, ends flattened, one end broken. L.22.0, W.17.1mm, section D.2.9mm 25630 sf9245 (P4B) (*Fig.1275*)

10483 Ringed pin ring, oval, of subcircular section, wire projection from hinge at one end. L.18.6, W.16.2mm, section D.3.6mm 3607 sf8368 (P4/5) (*Fig.1275*)

Miscellaneous pins

10484 Shank of circular section, swelling towards tip, head cut square. L.55.8mm, section D.2.2mm 19390 sf8759 (P4B)

10485 Shank, of circular section, cut square at upper end. D.1.6, L.54.7mm 5261 sf1247 (D6c1; mid 13th century) (P6)

10486 Shank fragment, both ends broken, of circular section, swelling on lower third of shank. D.2.3mm 30863 sf12151 (P3)

10487 Shank fragment, upper end broken, circular section. D.1.9, L.51.0mm 30936 sf12346 (P3)

10488 Shank fragment, of circular section, with swelling, tapering to tip which is bent up, upper end broken. L.52.7mm, section D.2.3mm 19390 sf8931 (P4B)

10489 Shank fragment, of subcircular section, both ends broken. D.1.7, L.26.3mm 24814 sf10064 (P4B)

10490 Shank fragment, broken at both ends, of circular section. D.1.6, L.33.3mm 28120 sf10131 (P4B)

10491 Shank, broken at both ends, circular section. D.0.8, L.36.5mm 2600 sf2600 (P5B)

10492 Shank, of oval section, point formed by filed or hammered facets, raised ridge on part of shank. D.1.5, L.40.0mm 14297 sf3887 (P5B)

10493 Shank fragment, upper end broken off, subcircular section, incised spiral three-fifths of way down shank. D.2.0, L.59.0mm 19285 sf6615 (P5B)

10494 Shank fragment, roughly broken at upper end, of subsquare section. L.41.0, W.2.1mm 6932 sf6749 (P5B)

10495 Shank fragment, upper end broken, of circular section. D.1.1, L.32.0mm 18744 sf5667 (P5Cr)

10496 Shank fragment, upper end broken, circular section, faceted point. D.1.8, L.41.0mm 6789 sf6107 (P5Cr)

10497 Shank fragment, broken at upper end, circular section. D.2.0, L.33.5mm 20162 sf6543 (P5Cr)

Personal ornament

Twisted wire rings

10498 Made of twisted double-strand wire, ends twisted around hoop to form ring. D.13.6, T.2.2mm 26022 sf9445 (P3)

10499 Circular, of subcircular section, tapering to the ends which are twisted around to form join. D.22.7mm, section D.2.0mm 22560 sf7806 (P4B) (Fig.1277)

10500 Subcircular, with wire core, single-strand wire wound tightly around, ends hooked, now separated. D.22.2mm, section D.2.0mm, wire D.1.0mm 29919 sf13195 (P4B) (Fig.1277)

10501 Made of wire tapering to ends which are twisted around to form hoop. D.15.9mm, wire D.1.1mm 22154 sf7516 (P5A)

10502 Circular section, ends originally twisted around hoop. D.18.0mm, wire D.1.4mm 22309 sf7537 (P5A)

10503 Wire core, single-strand wire wound tightly around, ends now separated. D.16.7, T.1.6mm, wire D.0.6mm 14928 sf14500 (P5A) (Fig.1277)

10504 Rectangular section, formed by twisting tapered ends around hoop. D.15.0, W.2.0, T.1.0mm 15361 sf4232 (P5B) (Fig.1277)

10505 Circular, made of wire of circular section, tapering to ends twisted together to form join. D.21.8mm, wire section D.1.2mm 15314 sf4613 (P5B)

10506 Distorted to oval shape, made of wire of circular section, ends twisted around to form join. L.17.0, W.12.6mm, section D.1.0mm 13964A sf6145 (B6c8; early 13th century) (P6)

Large twisted wire rings

10507 Incomplete, made of two strands of wire spirally twisted, wire of rectangular section, both ends broken. W.3.6, T.4.0mm, original D.46.0mm 19686 sf12739 (P3)

10508 Made of two wires twisted together and tapering to the ends which have separated. D.37.1mm, wire D.1.3mm 36514 sf14154 (P4B) (Fig.1227)

Finger-rings

10509 Rectangular section, ends overlapped, decorated with small angled nicks along each edge. D.19.6mm, section W.5.6, T.1.5mm 30751 sf11997 (P3) (Fig.1279)

10510 Triangular section, each facet decorated with punched dots. D.22.5mm, section W.4.0, T.1.7mm 20667 sf7253 (P4B)

10511 Made of tightly coiled wire, broken apart at one point, possible traces of solder where ends of ring joined. D.20.8, section D.1.8mm 23184 sf7366 (P4B) (Fig.1279)

10512 Triangular section, decorated circumferentially on each facet with pair of interlacing strands, now very worn. D.24.9mm, section W.5.5, T.2.6mm 23339 sf7590 (P4B) (Fig.1279)

10513 Hexagonal hoop, each side an ovoid facet. D.21.0, W.5.2, T.2.3mm 22670 sf7797 (P4B) (Fig.1279)

10514 Triangular section, each facet decorated with row of widely spaced punched dots. D.22.4, T.3.5mm 22713 sf7890 (P4B) (Fig.1279)

10515 Made of sheet, tapering to overlapping ends, lozenge-shaped bezel decorated with ring-and-dot motifs. L.19.4, W.17.0mm, section W.6.9, T.1.0mm 22816 sf8118 (P4B) (Fig.1279)

10516 Subcircular, of suboval section. D.23.1mm, section W.3.0, T.1.7mm 32217 sf13036 (P4B) (Fig.1279)

10517 Made of sheet, tapering to ends originally twisted together, with single incised line along each edge, bezel decorated with ring-and-dot motifs. D.19.5mm, section W.7.0, T.0.9mm 32470 sf13093 (P4B) (Fig.1279)

10518 Twisted double-strand wire, wrapped around at join. D.23.2, T.2.8mm 8023 sf1916 (P5A)

10519 Plano-convex section, hoop worn thin on one side. D.16.3, W.2.5, T.1.4mm 20132 sf6670 (P5A)

10520 Made of twisted double-strand wire. D.24.1, T.1.6mm 22053 sf7119 (P5A) (Fig.1279)

10521 Made of sheet, distorted into suboval shape, decorated with incised hatching either side of a plain mid-line. L.23.8, W.2.7, T.1.2mm 22340 sf7536 (P5A) (Fig.1279)

10522 Made of sheet, distorted, with lozenge-shaped bezel with incised lines around edge, tapering to ends of ring which have parted. L.22.5, W.5.0, T.0.5mm 14750 sf5657 (P5B) (Fig.1279)

10523 Made of sheet, circular. D.20.5, W.5.6, T.1.1mm 14722 sf7153 (P5B)

10524 Finger-ring or ear-ring, penannular, made from wire of subcircular section, tapering to ends. D.20.9mm, section D.3.1mm 5975 sf3220 (C6c6; mid 12th century) (P6)

Pendants

10525 Pendant or amulet, of sheet, tongue-shaped, with loop at upper end at right-angles, decorated on one face with pseudo-runic marks. L.63.7, W.13.0, T.1.3mm, loop L.9.8, W.5.3, T.2.7mm 29904 sf13043 (P4B) (Fig.1282)

10526 Discoidal, with perforation. D.16.9, T.1.6mm 29835 sf13089 (P4B) (Fig.1282)

Bead

10527 Globular, made of copper sheet. D.10.9, T.1.0mm 30922 sf14425 (P3) (Fig.1291)

Other personal items

Bell

10528 Incomplete, hexagonal with incomplete loop, edges ragged, originally scalloped. L.25.9, W.17.9, T.2.5, H.28.1mm 20062 sf5791 (P5A) (Fig.1294)

Tweezers

10529 Slide, penannular, of rectangular section. D.10.8mm, section W.6.3, T.1.9mm 28815 sf12526 (P4B)

10530 Made from narrow strip bent in half lengthways, ends inturned, incomplete slide towards upper end, and twisted wire ring, ends separated, through loop. Both faces are decorated with ring-and-dot motifs, now worn. L.50.0, W.5.9, T.3.5mm, ring section D.1.1mm 22215 sf7463 (P5A) (Fig.1295)

10531 Formed from strip folded in half lengthways, both sides with ring-and-dot decoration, twisted wire ring with opaque white glass globular bead through loop. L.40.8, W.6.2, T.0.7mm, ring D.4.9, H.4.3mm 20543 sf6956 (P5B) (Fig.1295)

10532 Made from single strip bent in half, ends turned inwards to form grip, part of slide remains on one side, both faces decorated with incised line along each edge, knotted suspension ring of circular section through loop. L.49.1, W.5.8, T.0.7mm, ring D.18.8mm, ring section D.1.2mm 3599 sf6901 (P4/5) (*Fig.1295*)

Toilet instruments

10533 Narrow stem of rectangular section at upper end which has perforation for suspension. At the lower end the stem has been flattened at right-angles and expanded to one side into subrectangular blade, one edge serrated. L.50.1, W.3.0, T.2.5mm, blade L.11.5, W.5.8, T.0.9mm 22348 sf7572 (P4B) (*Fig.1295*)

10534 Stem of rectangular section, flattened convex upper end with perforation, stem tapering and thickening centrally. Below this, the stem flattens and expands, one edge serrated, decorated with axial row of ring-and-dot motifs, tip with irregular lobed extension to one side. L.47.7, W.10.6, T.1.9mm 25630 sf9234 (P4B) (*Fig.1295*)

Gold

10535 Fragment, possibly of a panel from a kite brooch, comprising pierced filigree foil on backplate, two-strand simple pattern interlace motif delineated by three-strand band filigree consisting of central beaded wire flanked by finer spiral-beaded wire on each edge. Gold alloy, containing 20–30% silver and traces of copper. L.11.4, W.7.1, T.1.2mm 28036 sf09878 (P3) (*Figs.1270–1*)

10536 Stud or boss, with central squat squarish dome which is damaged, flattened rim with punched dot decoration. D.10.0, H.4.1mm, rim T.0.9mm 30286 sf11182 (P4A) (*Figs.1251, 1253*)

10537 Twisted wire ring now distorted, made of wire of circular section, tapering to ends which were originally twisted around. Gold alloy, containing 20–30% silver and traces of copper. D.1.5, L.47.0mm 15124 sf4103 (C6a1; late eleventh century) (P6) (*Fig.1277*)

Silver

10538 Wire fragment, twisted double-strand, both ends broken. L.63.0, T.1.2mm 32693 sf13461 (P3)

10539 Finger-ring, a subcircular band of sheet, parts of edges ragged. D.21.4mm, band W.6.0, T.1.3mm 22845 sf8038 (P4B)

10540 Finger-ring fragment, of twisted double-strand wire, one end broken at twisted-over join. D.16.5, T.1.9mm 6836 sf6445 (P5B)

10541 Stud, circular, with a blue glass setting within band, encircled by filigree wire, two prongs on reverse face. Mercury gilded with debased silver gilt. D.13.9, H.8.6mm, stud D.10.9mm, prong L.5.3mm 19320 sf6861 (P5B) (*Figs.1251–2*)

10542 Mount or fitting, incomplete, broken at one end, of rectangular section, with tongue-shaped terminal with foliate decoration projecting from expanded perforation encircled by punched dots. This in turn projects from an elongated oval strip, now bent up, decorated with an axial elongated saltire and punched dots along both edges, which broadens out slightly at other end into a rectangular strip decorated with axial row of chevrons containing punched dots. L.75.0, W.5.0, T.2.3mm, perforation D.5.5mm 18744 sf5885 (P5Cr) (*Fig.1250*)

10543 Finger-ring of rectangular section with flat, circular bezel, engraved with a backward-biting beast with lolling tongue within a roundel, incised grooves to each side of bezel. D.22.8, T.8.0mm, section W.2.8, T.1.6mm, bezel D.8.0mm u/s sf9212 (*Fig.1279*)

Lead alloy

Non-ferrous metalworking

Note: Full catalogue entries for *4147–9* and *4277–8* appear in *AY* 17/7.

4147 Rectangular bow brooch with beaded edge and three axial bosses each surrounded with a beaded collar. The flash lines are still visible. L.50.0, W.17.0, T.10.0mm 22867 sf8062 (P4B) (*Fig.1197*)

4148 Pendant with sprue and casting flash still attached. It is perforated for suspension and is decorated with a pseudo-runic inscription surrounding a central boss. L.27.0, W.19.5, T.6.0mm 24647 sf8323 (P4B) (*Fig.1197*)

4149 Failed casting of circular pendant with sprue still attached. The metal has failed to fill the mould completely, producing two accidental perforations in the disc. L.21.5, W.12.5, T.4.0mm 18988 sf9449 (P4B) (*Fig.1197*)

4277 Circular badge with a beaded border and a plain zone surrounding a raised central area with an openwork design of two concentric circles and superimposed radiating lines, four meeting at the centre and the others stopping at the second ring. The metal has incompletely filled the mould, producing breaks in the design, so this is technically a failed casting. The flash which partly fills the openwork has not been removed. The point of attachment of the runner can seen on the rim, midway between the two U-shaped attachment loops. L.43.0, W.33.0, T.6.0mm 9248 sf1071 (D6c1; mid 13th century) (P6) (*Fig.1197*)

4278 Circular openwork badge with loops to either side, similar to *4277*. D.37.0, T.5.0mm 13902 sf4950 (B6c3; 12th/13th century) (P6) (*Fig.1197*)

10544 Cross matrix made of sheet, with four extended plano-convex lobes separated from the central field by transverse lines, and with U-shaped devices in the angles. L.44.0, W.42.7, T.2.3mm 9360 sf1897 (P5B) (*Fig.1198*)

Spindle whorls

Note: Full catalogue entries for *6635–9* appear in *AY* 17/11. Spindle whorls are ordered according to form.

6635 Tapering hemispherical with concave upper face, with vertical and horizontal scratches on sides, cast with former for spindle hole. Form A1. D.24.9, T.14.0mm, Wt.39.50g, hole D.8.4mm 22523 sf7762 (P4B) (*Fig.1233*)

6636 Conical. Cast, with former for spindle hole. Spindle hole faceted and tapering. Form A1. D.20.6, T.15, hole D.5.6–6.8mm, Wt.27.0g 28236 sf10847 (P4B)

6637 Failed casting, irregular flattened hemispherical shape, spindle hole does not penetrate fully. Form A1. D.21.2, T.7.9mm, Wt.14.90g u/s sf9052

6638 Cylindrical with rounded sides, cast with former for spindle hole. Form B. D.24.5, T.10.6mm, Wt.42.10g, hole D.8.8mm 35137 sf13738 (P4B) (*Fig.1233*)

6639 Discoidal or shallowly cylindrical, cast with former for spindle hole. Form B. D.27.9, H.18.6mm, Wt.44.72g, hole D.8.0mm, cleaned Wt.44.62g 22867 sf8070 (P4B) (*Fig.1233*)

6640 Disc-shaped. Cast, spindle hole gouged. Form ?B. D.16.6–17.3, T.3.6, hole D.5.5mm, Wt.6.2g 23557 sf7687 (P4B)

10545 Hemispherical, roughly cast with former for spindle hole, then crudely cut to shape. Perforation incomplete. Form

A1. D.20.5, H.13.6mm, Wt.31.59g, hole D.6.1mm, cleaned Wt.31.55g 22728 sf7873 (P4B)

10546 Flattened hemispherical, cast with former for spindle hole, then trimmed. There are scratches down the hole. Form A1. D.26.0, H.9.5mm, Wt.33.85g, hole D.10.3mm, cleaned Wt.33.75g 22806 sf8048 (P4B)

10547 Discoidal with one slightly convex face, cast with former for spindle hole, one face shaved flat. Form A1. D.29.0, H.6.8mm, Wt.37.34g, hole D.7.7mm 22816 sf8485 (P4B)

10548 Flattened hemispherical, round face filed, cast with former for spindle hole. Form A2. D.24.9, T.8.4mm, Wt.27.30g, hole D.7.5mm 25793 sf10516 (P4A)

10549 Rounded conical, cast with former for spindle hole which has scratches down it. Form A2. D.18.5, H.14.7mm, Wt.23.30g, hole D.8.8mm, cleaned Wt.23.29g 30511 sf11742 (P4A)

10550 Shallow truncated cone, cast and then cut down. Form A2. D.21.2, T.6.4mm, Wt.18.19g, hole D.8.3mm 25085 sf8406 (P4B)

10551 Discoidal with rounded sides. Form B. D.25.0, H.8.6mm, Wt.31.02g, hole D.9.1mm 25350 sf8585 (P4B)

10552 Subdiscoidal, cast with former for spindle hole, knife-trimmed. Form B. D.26.9, T.5.2mm, Wt.22.65g, hole D.7.3mm, cleaned Wt.22.52g 16628 u/s sf6017

Net sinkers

10553 Cylindrical, with axial perforation. D.9.0, L.18.0mm 26636 sf11306 (P4B) (*Fig.1237*)

10554 Cylindrical, flat overlapped seam. D.13.0, L.31.1mm 14704 sf5645 (P5B) (*Fig.1237*)

Fittings and furnishings
Studs

10555 Domed head, decorated with stamped rings close to circumference, shank of circular section. D.12.7, L.11.3mm, shank D.4.4mm 30835 sf15777 (P3) (*Fig.1251*)

10556 Domed boss surrounded by a beaded false-filigree collar, short shank. D.6.5, L.4.0mm 25084 sf11218 (P4B) (*Fig.1251*)

Rings

10557 Penannular, made from wire of subcircular section, tapering towards each end. D.14.8mm, wire D.2.2mm 22416 sf7602 (P4B)

10558 Square section, distorted. L.32.6, W.16.3mm, wire W.2.8mm 22841 sf8032 (P4B)

10559 Made from strip of rectangular section, ends overlapped, one end rounded, other cut square. D.16.9mm, wire W.3.5, T.2.5mm 8023 sf1932 (P5A)

Nails

10560 Shank of subsquare section, tip cut square, rectangular head at oblique angle. L.36.9, W.11.5, T.10.3mm 22593 sf7765 (P4B)

10561 Shank of circular section tapering to a point, subcuboid head. D.6.7, L.40.1mm, head L.11.3, W.10.3, T.10.9mm 2078 sf4869 (P5A) (*Fig.1255*)

10562 Head, incomplete, originally subcircular, shank of square section, majority broken away. D.13.7, L.10.1, W.6.7, T.6.6mm 18922 sf5925 (P5A)

10563 Head, subcircular, majority of shank broken away. D.20.8, L.7.2mm 22127 sf13563 (P5A)

10564 Shank of subcircular section, square head of rectangular section. D.6.3, L.35.8mm, head W.10.3, T.6.9mm 14434 sf5046 (P5B)

10565 Subcircular head, shank of subcircular section, tip broken off. D.8.0, L.35.1mm, head D.19.4mm 7483 sf15886 (P5B)

Clench bolts

10566 Clench bolt or stud, shank of subcircular section, with a subcircular head and plate. D.7.5, L.21.9mm, head D.16.3mm, plate D.12.4mm 25253 sf8296 (P4B) (*Fig.1255*)

10567 Incomplete, with subcircular head, shank of circular section, part of head and shank cut away. D.8.4, L.15.9mm, head D.18.2mm 25257 sf8319 (P4B)

10568 Clench bolt or stud, squat, shank of circular section, subcircular head and plate. D.9.8, L.14.0mm, head D.17.1mm, plate D.16.7mm 36009 sf13447 (P4B)

10569 Suboval head, plate incomplete, shank of subcircular section. D.10.5, L.22.9mm, head L.23.4, W.14.5mm 2457 sf1456 (P5A)

10570 Shank of circular section, plate lozenge-shaped, the head partially cut away. A curved strip partially encompasses the shank. D.10.0, L.20.4mm, plate L.20.2, W.18.0, T.4.2mm, strip L.15.2, W.6.9, T.1.2mm 8800 sf2187 (P5A)

10571 Sublozenge-shaped head and plate, shank of subcircular section. D.8.4, L.19.1mm, head L.21.7, W.16.5mm, plate L.20.0, W.15.5mm 21925 sf10346 (P5B)

10572 Shank of subcircular section, circular head and plate. D.8.8, L.21.2mm, head D.21.9mm, plate D.19.2mm 29156 sf11784 (P5B)

10573 Flattened irregular head and lozenge-shaped plate, driven through perforations in the end of a folded rectangular strip. L.38.5mm, Shank D.7.5mm, strip L.41.5 W.32.2mm 3599 sf4717 (P4/5) (*Fig.1255*)

10574 Lozenge-shaped plate with majority of shank and head broken away. L.24.6, W.23.2mm 3519 sf3007 (P5Cr)

10575 Circular head curled up, with a shank of circular section, the plate broken away. L.29.6mm, head, D.21.4mm 3543 sf3338 (P5Cr)

10576 Incomplete head, circular rove. D.9.0, L.38.4mm, head D.24.5mm 9229 sf2940 (C6e9; mid 13th century) (P6)

10577 Head or plate, the shank and opposing end cut away. D.24.6mm 17740 sf5132 (C6c3; early 12th century) (P6)

10578 Shank of circular section with subcircular head and plate. D.10.4, L.30.5mm, head D.18.5mm 16612 sf6348 (D6a1; late 11th century) (P6)

Perforated strips

10579 One end rounded, punched perforation close to this end, other end broken and folded over. L.37.2, W.21.0, T.4.7mm 20484 sf6828 (P5B)

10580 Cut square at one end, perforated close to other end which is broken and folded. L.31.8, W.31.6, T.5.9mm 16887 sf6973 (P5Cr)

Window cames

10581 Fragment of H-shaped section, roughly broken at either end and folded in two. L.50.0mm, section W.6.9, T.8.1mm 20229 sf08966 (P5B)

10582 Fragment of H-shaped section, crushed. L.59.8, W.9.0, T.4.1mm 19353 sf14506 (P5B)

Weights

10583 Weight or pendant in the shape of a ship with a central mast, of rectangular section, upper end of mast torn through perforation for suspension, main body of mast incised with crude representations of furled sails. At the lower end, the hull is incised with apparent waves at the front and wake at the rear, with one or possibly two stick crewmen with oars. Two notches have been cut into the base. L.55.3, W.58.0mm, Wt.26.37g, section W.9.4, T.3.8mm 23102 sf7606 (P4B) (*Fig.1259*)

10584 Cylindrical, both faces flat. D.22.7, H.13.8mm, Wt.53.10g, cleaned Wt.53.09g 22659 sf8012 (P4B) (*Fig.1259*)

10585 Truncated cone, of square section, upper and lower faces cut square. W.16.7, T.15.9, H.14.2mm, Wt.27.24g 25085 sf8411 (P4B)

10586 Inverted truncated conical, of subcircular section, incomplete axial perforation. D.22.9, H.20.0mm, Wt.58.70g, cleaned Wt.58.60g 25340 sf8475 (P4B) (*Fig.1259*)

10587 Spherical, axially perforated. D.17.4mm, Wt.28.08g 21143 sf8658 (P4B) (*Fig.1259*)

10588 Disc, subcircular, centrally perforated, one edge folded up. D.31.1, T.0.9mm, Wt.4.84g 25598 sf9157 (P4B) (*Fig.1259*)

10589 Cylindrical, faces flat. D.15.9, H.7.0mm, Wt.12.03g 34988 sf13450 (P4B)

10590 Disc, suboval, perforated close to one edge, part of this edge torn and folded over. L.41.2, W.29.7, T.2.1mm, Wt.14.91g 8800 sf2161 (P5A)

10591 Disc, circular, faces uneven. D.19.2, T.2.5mm, Wt.4.60g 18467 sf5566 (P5A)

10592 Spherical, with flattened top and bottom where lead alloy is visible, coated with copper alloy. D.22.1mm, Wt.35.65g 1473 sf444 (P5B)

10593 Disc, subcircular, slightly twisted, marked with lightly incised lines on both faces. D.20.9, T.1.1mm, Wt.2.79g 18962 sf6179 (P5B) (*Fig.1259*)

10594 Disc, subcircular. D.21.3, T.1.3mm, Wt.11.02g 4620 sf1210 (C6e9; mid 13th century) (P6)

10595 Disc, circular. D.18.9, T.0.7mm, Wt.1.30g 5484 sf1853 (C6e1, D6a16; 12th/13th century) (P6)

10596 Disc, subcircular. D.15.7, T.0.7mm, Wt.0.79g 9572 sf2362 (D6a9; early 12th century) (P6)

10597 Disc, circular. D.19.6, T.1.3mm, Wt.2.67g 16612 sf6013 (D6a1; late 11th century) (P6)

10598 Disc, subcircular. D.19.0, T.0.8mm, Wt.1.43g u/s sf4765

Dress accessories

Strap-end

10599 Upper end incomplete but originally split for attachment, body tapering to moulded animal head terminal with prominent eyes and well-rounded ears, main field with ribbon interlace in low relief between plain borders. L.48.9, W.12.6, T.3.0mm 20978 sf7306 (P5A) (*Fig.1265*)

Disc brooches

10600 Fragment missing from circumference, pin and attachment point broken off, catch-plate survives. The upper face is decorated with a circumferential beaded frame containing zig-zag ornament, and central circular field filled with central boss surrounded by six equally spaced bosses, each boss encircled by a beaded collar, groups of three dots between the bosses. D.40.0, T.3.3mm, catch-plate L.5.2, W.7.5, T.1.8mm 22172 sf7989 (P4B) (*Fig.1268*)

10601 Decorated with eleven false-filigree rings encircling a field with foliate ornament arranged in a cross around a central boss, parts of catch and pin attachment plates sur-

viving on reverse. D.70.0, T.3.3mm, catch-plate, W.7.2mm 34373 sf12888 (P4B) (*Figs.1191, 1268*)

10602 Composed of six concentric plain mouldings surrounding a circular field divided into quadrants each containing a pinched up boss, with larger central dome-like boss. On the reverse face are the hinge attachments and catch-plate, the pin now lost. D.38.1, T.3.7mm, catch-plate L.7.7, W.6.7, T.1.5mm 22358 sf7548 (P5A) (*Fig.1268*)

10603 Cast, with plain border with incomplete circumferential line of beading on inside, enclosing a stylised foliate design in imitation filigree. The cross-shaped pattern has a quatrefoil at the centre, and a ring between each arm. The catch-plate and pin attachment survive on the reverse. D.30.6, T.1.9mm, catch-plate L.6.5, W.5.1, T.2.3mm 7296 sf1520 (P5B)

10604 Complete apart from attachment and catch-plates, with a single billeted frame encircling a backward-looking two-toed animal which has open jaws and an elongated tongue interlacing the body and passing behind its rear leg. The contoured body of the beast is decorated with cross-hatching. D.27.5, T.2.2mm 21904 sf9964 (P5B) (*Fig.1267*)

Pin

10605 Shank of circular section, assuming a rectangular section towards the point, curved, upper end incomplete and bent over. L.38.1mm, shank D.3.3mm, shank tip, W.3.4, T.2.6mm 27296 sf9856 (P5A)

Personal ornament

Twisted wire rings

10606 Subcircular, made from wire of square section, join formed by ends twisted around hoop. D.18.7mm, wire W.1.7, T.2.0mm 25630 sf9317 (P4B)

10607 Made from wire of square section, ends originally wound round each other. D.16.4mm, wire W.1.8, T.1.6mm 27428 sf9726 (P5A)

Arm-rings

10608 Made of rod of circular section, subcircular, tapering towards the ends which are twisted around to form hoop. D.45.8mm, rod D.4.0mm 24787 sf8502 (P4B) (*Fig.1278*)

10609 Irregularly shaped hoop, of subcircular section, tapering towards the ends which are twisted around each other. L.68.1, W.53.0mm, section D.5.6mm 26902 sf9366 (P4B) (*Fig.1278*)

Penannular ring

10610 Subcircular, made from wire of subcircular section, tapering towards each end. D.14.8mm, wire D.2.2mm 22416 sf7602 (P4B)

Finger-rings

10611 Incomplete, cast, decorated around the circumference with three parallel rows of beading. D.22.9mm, ring section W.4.9, T.1.9mm 25391 sf8500 (P4B)

10612 Subcircular hoop of sheet, ends tapering to join, with raised axial band, decorated with transverse grooves, as are the bands along each edge. D.20.0mm, hoop W.5.0, T.1.9mm 2458 sf1404 (P5A) (*Fig.1279*)

10613 Made of double-strand twisted wire of subcircular section, hoop broken. D.21.6, T.4.2mm wire, D.2.4mm 14466 sf4958 (P5A)

10614 Made up of three pieces of double-strand wire of circular section, plaited together, with flat bezel. D.21.7, T.3.7mm 15471 sf4331 (P5B) (*Fig.1279*)

Pendants

10615 Circular, wedge-shaped suspension loop, beaded frame, central boss surrounded by 4 outward-facing crescents, separated by plain moulding from border decorated with bosses alternating with outward-facing crescents. D.21.0mm, loop L.6.3, W.6.0, T.3.1mm 8023 sf2213 (P5A) (*Fig.1283*)

10616 Subdiscoidal, with subrectangular lug with perforation for suspension. D.14.3, T.1.7mm, lug L.6.5, W.5.1mm 22309 sf7523 (P5A) (*Fig.1283*)

Tin

10617 Twisted wire ring, circular, with the ends overlapped, with an applied pellet opposite the join. D.14.2mm, wire D.1.0mm 18949 sf9280 (P5B)

10618 Arm-ring made from a single twisted rod tapering to flattened ends twisted around to form oval hoop. L.59.5, W.54.1, T.4.4mm 35519 sf14115 (P4B) (*Fig.1278*)

10619 Ring, incomplete, made from wire of circular section. D.12.0mm, wire D.2.2mm 29128 sf10242 (P5B)

10620 Pendant, circular with incomplete suspension loop, and perforated below this. One face is decorated with a relief circle, divided into quadrants, with a boss in each quadrant and in the centre, the field between the circle and circumference divided by relief lines into eight. The decoration is slightly offside to the pendant's central axis. D.14.4, L.20.6, T.2.1mm, loop T.3.9mm 27338 sf9728 (P4B)

Shell

10621 Four flat discoidal shell beads. D.12.0, T.1.5mm 2409 sf172a (P5B)

10622 Two flat discoidal shell beads. D.12.5, T.1.8mm 2409 sf211 (P5B)

Uncertain material

10623 Three flat discoidal beads. These have been examined by S. O'Connor and G.D. Gaunt, and neither has been able to identify the material with conviction. Analysis would be totally destructive (i) D.10.0, T.1.0mm, perforation D.4.0mm; (ii) D.10.0, T.1.1mm perforation D.3.0mm; (iii) D.11.0, T.1.0mm, perforation D.4.0mm 2409 sf172b (P5B) (*Fig.1291*)

Finds from the Coppergate Watching Brief (1982.22)

Stone

10624   Spindle whorl, flat profile with worn edges. Complete (in two pieces), cracked possibly as a result of burning. D.47.0, T.8.0, perforation D.14mm 1546 sf83

10625   Possible hone or burnisher, elongated oval shape with oval profile, smooth on all surfaces, one end particularly worn. L.140.0, W.48.0, T.40.0mm 1777 sf165

Amber

10626   Finger-ring, unfinished, approximately half survives. No evidence for lathe-turning, probably carved. Square profile. D.27.0, T.6.5, perforation D.15.0mm 1247 sf34

10627   Minute polished fragment from a ring or a bead. L.3.0, W.2.0, T.1.0mm 1481 sf355

Glass

10628   Bead, irregularly shaped, subcylindrical, blue. D.8.1, H.5.0mm 1247 sf38

Lead alloy

10629   Disc brooch complete apart from some damage at catch-plate, shallow dome at centre, decorated with three circumferential concentric circles, the central circle with raised dots, the other two billeted, enclosing a field decorated with an eight-pointed star, outlined by a billeted border, four bosses in centre of star, outlined by double circles containing parallel lines and central dome. D.53.8, T.2.2mm 1247 sf14 (*Fig.1269*)

Finds from 22 Piccadilly (1987.21)

Stone

Mould

10630   Roughly triangular-shaped re-used block of limestone. Two incomplete parallel grooves cut into one surface, one at a slightly lower level than the other. Grooves are c.120.0mm long, 5.0mm deep and 9.5mm wide. Block: L.170.0, H.66.0, W.140.0mm 2168 sf478 (P4)

Hones

10631   Fragment, subrectangular, broken at one end across slight waist, section thinning towards broken end. All surfaces smooth, broad sharpening groove on one side. Purple-phyllite, medium to dark grey, quartz-muscovite. L53.2, W.18.4, T.9.4mm 2089 sf213 (P4)

10632   Fragment, part of one face and one edge surviving, both smooth. Purple-phyllite, medium grey, quartz-muscovite. L64.3, W.21.4, T.16.0mm 2146 sf538 (P4)

10633   Fragment. Purple-phyllite, medium grey, quartz-muscovite. L.29.0, W.9.0, T.2.0mm 2291 sf760 (P4)

10634   Fragment. Schist, pale silvery grey, fine- to medium-grained, quartz-muscovite, Norwegian Ragstone. L.66.0, W.25.0, T.20.0mm 2162 sf804 (P4)

Querns

10635   Fragment. Sandstone, pale to medium grey, medium- to coarse-grained, poorly sorted, poorly compacted, Millstone Grit. L.182.0, W.125.0, T.118.0mm 2255 sf692 (P4)

Minerals

10636   Haematite fragment, pale red, of reddle type. L.25.0, W.18.0, T.7.0mm 4004 sf834 (P5)

Fired clay

Loom weight

10637   Fragment. L.99.0, W.85.0, T.34mm u/s sf190

Glass

Glassworking debris

10638   Manufacturing debris chip, and two ?rod ends with pincer marks. 2162 sf380 (P4/1) (*Fig.1229*)

10639   Droplet waste or trail with pincer marks. L.18.0, W.5.0, T.1.0mm 2162 sf614 (P4/1) (*Fig.1229*)

10640   Droplet fragments (2), from crucible. L.5.0, W.4.0, T.2.0mm 2162 sf871 (P4/1)

10641   Manufacturing debris fragments. 2187 sf1261 (P4/1)

10642   Manufacturing debris chunks (6) with ceramic/stone inclusions. 2042 sf294 (P6) (*Fig.1229*)

Vessel glass

Catalogue by Matthew Stiff

Base fragment

10643   Tall palm cup fragment with optic-blown decoration. Light blue-green. Base cross with quincuncial bosses between cross arms. Tiny bubbles, good gloss and clarity. L.22.0, W.18.0, T.1.7mm 1003 sf660 (P4/2) (*Fig.1239*)

Body fragments

10644   Light green-blue. Light surface iridescence. Scratched surface. Tiny bubbles, fair gloss and clarity. L.18.0, W.8.0, T.1.4mm 1060 sf387 (P1)

10645 Light green-blue. Light surface iridescence. Tiny bubbles, good gloss and clarity. L.12.0, W.9.0, T.0.7mm 2311 sf800 (P1)

10646 Very light green-yellow. Decorated with self-coloured trail. Tiny bubbles, good gloss and clarity. L.14.0, W.8.0, T.0.4mm 1060 sf1307 (P1)

10647 Light yellow-green. Light surface iridescence. Tiny bubbles, good gloss and clarity. L.10.0, W.7.0, T.1.1mm 1058 sf355 (P2)

10648 Light green-blue. Light surface iridescence. Tiny bubbles, good gloss and clarity. L.15.0, W.11.0, T.1.0mm 3118 sf577 (P4/1)

Glass beads

Monochrome

Type 1: Annular

10649 Malformed, blue. D.8.3, H.2.9mm 2162 sf376 (P4/1)

10650 Fragment, green. D.11.1, H.3.7mm 2291 sf823 (P4/1)

10651 Blue. D.11.3, H.3.0mm 3035 sf317 (P4/3) (Fig.1232)

10652 Malformed, pale blue. D.7.3, H.2.6mm 2042 sf269 (P6)

Type 2: Globular

10653 Fragment, blue. D.11.3, H.7.0mm 2186 sf439 (P4/1)

Type 4: Gadrooned

10654 Complete (2), and fragments (2), all malformed, blue. D.10.2, H.2.8mm 2162 sf381 (P4/1) (Fig.1231)

10655 Fragments (7), blue, some malformed. D.12.5, H.4.8mm 2162 sf382 (P4/1) (Figs.1231–2)

10656 Fragment, blue. L.5.0, W.4.6, T.3.5mm 2186 sf504 (P4/1)

10657 Fragment, blue. D.9.4, H.4.3mm 2187 sf555 (P4/1)

10658 Fragment, blue. D.10.6, H.4.6mm 2089 sf187 (P4/2)

10659 Fragment, very dark appearing black. L.6.3, W.6.3, T.3.7mm 2083 sf223 (P6)

10660 Fragmentary, opaque pink-white. L.10.0, W.9.9, T.6.0mm 2042 sf923 (P6)

Type 5: Barrel-shaped

10661 Opaque orange-brown. D.9.0, H.8.4mm 2186 sf485 (P4/1)

10662 Opaque dark brown. D.8.4, H.9.2mm 2169 sf644 (P4/1) (Fig.1287)

10663 Opaque orange-brown. D.12.2, H.7.8mm 2166 sf653 (P4/1) (Fig.1287)

10664 Fragment, opaque orange. L.7.5, W.7.7, T.2.6mm 2113 sf241 (P4/2)

10665 Fragment, opaque red. L.8.1, W.7.0mm 2042 sf262 (P6)

10666 Opaque orange. D.9.6, H.8.3mm 2042 sf291 (P6)

Type 6: Biconical

10667 Fragment, blue. D.11.9, H.5.9mm 2089 sf194 (P4/1)

10668 Fragment, blue. D.13.6, H.13.1mm 2089 sf239 (P4/1)

10669 Malformed, blue. L.12.8, W.10.5, H.4.1mm 2162 sf375 (P4/1) (Fig.1231)

10670 Complete (2), fragments (4), blue. D.14.8, H.7.5mm 2162 sf400 (P4/1)

10671 Opaque orange. D.11.6, H.8.4mm 2187 sf554 (P4/1)

10672 Fragment, blue. D.10.6, H.5.3mm 2243 sf645 (P4/1)

10673 Fragment, blue. D.12.6, H.4.3mm 2254 sf698 (P4/1)

10674 Fragment, blue, malformed. D.10.5, H.5.9mm 2112 sf257 (P4/2) (Fig.1231)

10675 Complete (2), larger biconical, smaller irregular barrel-shaped, both opaque orange-brown. D.11.5, H.12 2042 sf299 (P6) (Fig.1287)

10676 Half, blue, perforation containing fragment of carbonised wood rod. D.13.1, H.6.0mm 2042 sf937 (P6)

Unidentifiable

10677 Fragment, opaque orange-brown. L.7.8, W.6.2, T.2.9mm 2042 sf205 (P6)

Amber

10678 Raw unworked. L.23.0, W.20.0, T.8.0mm, Wt.3.88g 3080 sf417 (P4)

10679 Raw unworked. L.28.0, W.24.0, T.9.0mm, Wt.5.40g 3080 sf520 (P4)

10680 Raw unworked. L.34.0, W.16.0, T.12.0mm, Wt.4.24g 2162 sf557 (P4)

Copper alloy

Furnishings and fittings

10681 Patch of sheet metal, irregularly rectangular with folded sheet rivets, strip folded up to four thicknesses. L.37.0, W.28.4, T.5.1mm 1058 sf361 (P2) (Fig.1254)

10682 Stud head, or boss, domed, centrally perforated, with gilding on upper face. Traces of pewter on underside. D.13.5, H.4.6mm 2293 sf787 (P3) (Fig.1251)

10683 Perforated strip, folded, subrectangular, ends broken off, one rivet through both faces close to folded end. L.17.5, W.9.1mm, sheet T.0.4mm, rivet L.3.3mm 3080 sf1263 (P4/1)

Dress accessories

10684 Hooked tag fragment, made of sheet, subtrapezoidal, broken at lower end, two perforations at upper end, decorated with rocked-tracer engraving. L.12.7, W.11.0, T.0.7mm 3080 sf469 (P4/1) (Fig.1273)

10685 Dress pin with inverted plano-convex head, shank of polygonal section, tapering to tip which is broken away. L.50.0, W.3.1, T.2.8mm 1043 sf320 (P3) (Fig.1274)

10686 Dress pin, incomplete, part of flat head broken off, shank of subrectangular section, tapering to square section at tip, remaining part of head decorated with ring-and-dot motif around a perforation. L.85.0, W.2.6, T.1.7mm, head W.6.9, T.0.9mm 2186 sf501 (P4/1) (Fig.1274)

Personal ornament

10687 Twisted wire ring, distorted, suboval, ends untwisted. L.16.9, W.14.0mm, section D.1.6mm 3080 sf468 (P4/1)

10688 Ring, oval, of plano-convex section, tapering and thinning to ends originally joined by scarf joint now sprung apart. L.20.1, W.17.2mm, section W.3.1, T.2.4mm 3080 sf467 (P4/1)

10689 Penannular ring tapering to ends, of subsquare section. D.21.8, W.2.6, T.2.4mm 2042 sf286 (P6)

Other personal items

10690 Tweezers made from folded rectangular strip, ends slightly bowed out, with slide. L.37.5, W.5.2, T.4.0mm, sheet T.0.7mm 3080 sf466 (P4/1)

Balances

10691 Chain link, of circular section, S-shaped. D.1.3, L.19.0mm 2293 sf791 (P3)

Lead alloy

10692 Sheet fragment, irregularly shaped and twisted up. L.34.6, W.9.2, T.5.2mm 1041 sf339 (P2)

10693 Sheet fragment, irregularly shaped and folded up. L.18.5, W.16.7, T.4.5mm 1058 sf373 (P2)

10694 Spillage fragments (2). L.24.4, W.20.1, T.7.7mm 2293 sf796 (P3)

10695 Sheet fragment, irregularly shaped. L.15.9, W.13.0, T.1.2mm 2186 sf502 (P4/1)

10696 Strip fragment, ends folded up and the whole curled up into distorted ring. L.14.8, W.9.8, T.10.0mm, sheet T.0.9mm 2216 sf773 (P4/1)

10697 Strip fragments, both ends broken. L.29.8, W.7.3, T.2.3mm 2291 sf822 (P4/1)

Finds from the College of Vicars Choral at Bedern

Finds from the following sites are grouped below: Bedern long trench, 1973–5.13.III/IV; Bedern north-east 1979–80.14.IV

Jet

10698 Bracelet fragment of plano-convex section, roughly broken at each end, polished. L.24.6, W.9.5, T.4.9mm 4084 sf476 (P8) (1979–80.14.IV)

Glass beads

Monochrome

Type 1: Annular

10699 Irregular, opaque bright yellow. D.3.9, H.1.8mm 7609 sf2844 (P2) (1973–5.13.III/IV)

10700 Irregular, light green. D.8.3, H.2.5mm 5410 sf2277 (P7) (1973–5.13.III/IV)

Type 2: Globular

10701 Yellow. D.6.6, H.4.4mm 1142 sf883 (P1A) (1973–5.13.III/IV)

10702 Blue. D.5.0, H.3.6mm, 1504 sf591 (P9) (1973–5.13.III/IV)

Type 3: Cylindrical

10703 Half, green. D.6.4, H.4.6mm 7020C sf2949 (P7) (1973–5.13.III/IV)

10704 Blue. D.4.0, H.2.9mm 6201 sf2932 (P9) (1973–5.13.III/IV)

Type 5: Barrel-shaped

10705 Dark orange-brown. D.12.6mm 1131 sf840 (P1A) (1973–5.13.III/IV)

Type 6: Biconical

10706 Irregular, blue. D.12.0mm 1590 sf743 (P6) (1973–5.13.III/IV)

Polychrome

10707 Incomplete, dark appearing black with yellow marvered blobs. L.8.7, H.9.3mm 7561 sf2808 (P5) (1973–5.13.III/IV)

Copper alloy

Furnishings and fittings

10708 Mount fragment, of subrectangular section and irregular thickness, openwork, gilded on front face, back corroded, with two rivet holes. L.46.0, W.29.5, T.3.1mm 1054 sf165 (P9) (1979–80.14.IV) (*Fig.1254*)

Dress pins

10709 Rectangular head of rectangular section, perforated close to upper end, perforation containing an incomplete ring. The head has been decorated with punched dots on all faces and sides and top, the shank tapers towards missing tip, shank bent up. D.2.2, L.87.0mm, head L.8.7, W.5.2, T.2.6mm, ring section D.1.2mm 1640 sf776 (P1) (1973–5.13.III/IV) (*Fig.1276*)

10710 Lozenge-shaped head, with corner projections, head centrally perforated. D.3.1, L.87.1mm, head L.13, W.12, T.2mm 7449 sf2764 (P6) (1973–5.13.III/IV)

Amber from Clifford Street

Raw Amber

10711 YORYM: C 599b 7.54g, YORYM: C 599g 6.51g, YORYM:
C 599i 5.48g, YORYM: C 599a 7.43g, YORYM: C 599c
6.79g, YORYM: C 599k 4.53g, YORYM: C 599m 3.73g,
YORYM: C 599d 6.85g, YORYM: C 599n 3.85g, YORYM:
C 599l 3.98g, YORYM: C 599j 7.01g, YORYM: C 599h
5.05g, YORYM: C 599e 7.28g, YORYM: C 600b 3.89g,
YORYM: C 599f 4.48g

Raw amber with one or more cut or worked surface

10712 One possible flaked surface. L.20.0, W.14.0, T.10.0mm,
Wt.1.52g YORYM: C 599o

10713 One flaked surface. L.22.0, W.19.0, T.10mm, Wt.2.18g
YORYM: C 600q

10714 One flaked surface. L.32.0, W.22.0, T.10.0mm, Wt.6.72g
YORYM: C 616a

10715 One flaked surface. L.24.0, W.13.0, T.12.0mm, Wt.1.83g
YORYM: C 620k

10716 One flaked surface. L.22.0, W.18.0, T.9.0mm, Wt.2.31g
YORYM: C 600e

10717 Cut and flaked surfaces. L.20.0, W.12.0, T.11.0mm,
Wt.1.64g YORYM: C 600g

10718 Cut and flaked surfaces. L.21.0, W.18.0, T.9.0mm, Wt.0.99g
YORYM: C 600u

10719 One flaked surface. L.13.0, W.12.0, T.7mm, Wt.0.61g
YORYM: C 600r

10720 Cut and flaked surfaces. L.19.0, W.12.0, T.9.0mm, Wt.1.58g
YORYM: C 600f

10721 One flaked surface. L.18.0, W.16.0, T.5.0mm, Wt.0.73g
YORYM: C 600w

10722 One flaked surface. L.22.0, W.15.0, T.7.0mm, Wt.0.98g
YORYM: C 600j

10723 Flaked surfaces. L.20.0, W.12.0, T.17.0mm, Wt.1.69g
YORYM: C 600o

10724 Two flaked surfaces. L.16.0, W.10.0, T.10.0mm, Wt.0.89g
YORYM: C 600k

10725 Three flaked surfaces. L.17.0, W.12.0, T.5.0mm, Wt.0.96g
YORYM: C 600y

10726 One flaked surface. L.30.0, W.13.0, T.8.0mm, Wt.2.16g
YORYM: C 600d

10727 One flaked surface. L.17.0, W.12.0, T. 9.0mm, Wt.0.78g
YORYM: C 600g

Approximately formed

10728 Roughly shaped pebble. D.25.0, T.15.0mm, Wt.6.89g
YORYM: C600a (Fig.1219)

10729 Roughly shaped cube. L.12.0, W.9.0, T.8.0mm, Wt.0.79g
YORYM: C 600c

10730 Roughly square. L.17.0, W.15.0, T.7.0mm, Wt.1.53g
YORYM: C 600l

10731 Roughly square. L.17.0, W.12.0, T.7.0mm, Wt.1.17g
YORYM: C 600m

10732 Elongated chipped flake. L.23.0, W.14.0, T.6.0mm,
Wt.1.00g YORYM: C 600n

Beads

Stage 1

10733 Roughly shaped, no finishing or polishing. T.13.0,
D.20.0mm, Wt.2.00g YORYM: C 617d (Fig.1219)

10734 Roughly shaped, bevelled edges, no finishing or polishing. T.13.0, D.21.0mm, Wt.3.38g YORYM: C 617j

Stage 2

10735 Natural pebble fragment, split across perforation.
T.8.0mm, D.22.0mm, Wt.1.47g YORYM: C 616c

10736 Roughly shaped flat disc, perforation most of the way
through. T.6.0, D.19.0mm, Wt.1.02g YORYM: C 617b
(Fig.1219)

10737 Roughout fragment with part drilled perforation. T.15.0,
D.18.0mm, Wt.c.1.71g YORYM: C 619b

10738 Roughout fragment broken across perforation. T.9.0,
D.24.0mm YORYM: C 622d

Stage 3

10739 Roughly shaped square disc, perforation drilled through.
T.8.0mm, D.24.0, Wt.1.66g YORYM: C 616e

10740 Roughly shaped disc, drilled from one side. T.7.0,
D.17.0mm, perforation D.5.0mm, Wt.1.08g YORYM: C
618b

10741 Roughly shaped disc, perforation drilled through. T.8.0,
D.20.0, perforation D.5.0mm, Wt.2.23g YORYM: C 618c
(Fig.1219)

Stage 4

10742 Fragment of roughout, perforation drilled through. T.8.0,
D.c.21.0mm, perforation D.3.1mm, Wt.1.04g YORYM: C
620i (Fig.1219)

10743 Fragment of roughout, perforation drilled from both sides.
T.12.0, D.19.0mm, perforation D.4.0mm, Wt.1.21g
YORYM: C 620j

10744 Roughout fragment, perforation drilled from both sides.
T.11.0, D.13.0mm, perforation D.3.0mm, Wt.0.93g
YORYM: C 620o

10745 Roughout fragment, perforation drilled from one side.
T.10.0, D.25.0mm, perforation D.5.0mm, Wt.1.93g
YORYM: C 620c

10746 Roughout fragment, perforation drilled from both sides.
T.9.0, D.19.0, perforation D.4.0, Wt.0.87g YORYM: C 620l

10747 Roughout fragment, perforation drilled from one side.
T.9.0, D.21.0mm, perforation D.3.0mm, Wt.1.14g YORYM:
C 621h

10748 Roughout fragment, drilled from one side. T.14.0,
D.25.0mm, perforation D.3.0mm, Wt.1.56g YORYM: C
621i (Fig.1219)

10749 Roughout fragment, perforation drilled from one side.
T.9.0, D.14.0, perforation D.6, Wt.1.73g YORYM: C 621e

10750 Roughout fragment, perforation drilled from one side.
T.6.0, D.18.0mm, perforation D.4.0, Wt.1.24g YORYM: C
620e

10751 Roughout fragment, perforation drilled from one side.
T.10.0, D.19.0mm, perforation D.6.0, Wt.1.21g YORYM:
C 620b (ii)

10752 Roughout fragment, perforation drilled from one side. T.11.0, D.22.0mm, perforation D.4.0mm, Wt.1.14g YORYM: C 621d

10753 Roughout fragment, perforation drilled from one side. T.8.0, D.22.0, perforation D.4.0mm, Wt.0.97g YORYM: C 621k

10754 Roughout fragment, bevelled edges, perforation drilled from one side. T.10.0, D.22.0, perforation D.5.0mm, Wt.1.70g YORYM: C 621g

10755 Roughout fragment, perforation drilled from one side. T.10.0, D.18.0mm, perforation D.5.0mm, Wt.1.04g YORYM: C 621b (Fig.1219)

10756 Large roughout fragment. Drilled from two sides. T.20.0, D.28.0mm, perforation D.6.0mm 5.76g YORYM: C 620f (Fig.1219)

10757 Roughout fragment, perforation drilled from two side. T.14.0, D.25.0mm, perforation D.3.0mm, Wt.2.72g YORYM: C 621c

10758 Two fragments forming complete roughout, drilled from one side. T.14.0, D.20.0mm, perforation D.5, Wt.3.75g YORYM: C 622a, YORYM: C 622e

10759 Roughout fragment, perforation drilled from one side. T.8.0, D.14.0mm, perforation D.4.0mm, Wt.0.66g YORYM: C 620m

10760 Roughout fragment, perforation drilled from one side. T.10.0, D.25.0mm, perforation D.5.0mm, Wt.1.4g YORYM: C 620q (Fig.1219)

10761 Roughout fragment, perforation drilled from one side. T.13.0, D.21.0mm, perforation D.6.0mm, Wt.2.19g YORYM: C 620a

10762 Roughout fragment, perforation drilled from both sides. T.10.0, D.22.0mm, perforation D.5.0mm, Wt.1.86g YORYM: C 622c

10763 Roughout fragment, lathe-turned on one side, drilled from one side. T.12.0, D.28.0mm, perforation D.6.0mm, Wt.2.86g YORYM: C 623j

10764 Roughout fragment, perforation drilled from one side. T.10.0, D.10.0mm, perforation D.6.0mm, Wt.0.91g YORYM: C 620b

10765 Roughout fragment, one bevelled edge, drilled from both sides. T.15.0, D.18.0mm, perforation D.5.0mm, Wt.1.98g YORYM: C 622b

10766 Roughout fragment, lathe-turned on one side. T.11.0, D.25.0mm, perforation D.5.0mm, Wt.1.73g YORYM: C 623g

10767 Roughout fragment, drilled from two sides, lathe-turned on one side. T.13.0, D.26.0mm, perforation D.6.0mm, Wt.3.05g YORYM: C 623k

10768 Roughout fragment, lathe turned on one side, drilled from one side. T.7.0, D.22.0mm, perforation D.4.0mm, Wt.1.23g YORYM: C 623c

10769 Roughout fragment, drilled from both sides. T.9.0, D.29.0mm, perforation D.5.0mm, Wt.2.21g YORYM: C 621f

10770 Roughout fragment, drilled from both sides. T.10.0, D.26.0mm, perforation D.5, Wt. 2.11g YORYM: C 620h

10771 Roughout fragment, drilled from both sides. T.9.0, D.27.0mm, perforation D.7.0mm, Wt.1.91g YORYM: C 620n

10772 Roughout fragment, drilled from one side, lathe-turned on one side. T.10.0, D.28.0mm, perforation D.5.0, Wt.3.01g YORYM: C 623a

10773 Roughout fragment, drilled from one side. T.17.0, D.27.0mm, perforation D.6.0mm, Wt.3.62g YORYM: C 620g

10774 Roughout fragment, drilled from one side. T.10.0, D.24.0, perforation D.6.0mm, Wt.1.96g YORYM: C 620p

Stage 5

10775 Roughout fragment, lathe-turned on both sides, drilled from one side. T.12.0, D.17.0mm, perforation D.6.0mm, Wt.1.10g YORYM: C 624c

10776 Roughout fragment, lathe-turned, drilled from one side. T.10.0, D.18.0mm, perforation D.5.0mm, Wt.1.07g YORYM: C 624d

10777 Roughout fragment, lathe-turned on two sides, drilled from one side. T.8.0, D 21.0mm, perforation D.6, Wt.1.1.3g YORYM: C 624b

10778 Roughout fragment, lathe-turned on both sides, drilled from one side. T.7.0, D.24.0mm, perforation D.6.0mm, Wt.1.08g YORYM: C 623n (Fig.1219)

10779 Roughout fragment, lathe-turned on both sides, drilled from one side. T.11.0, D.27.0mm, perforation D.7.0mm, Wt.2.70g YORYM: C 626a

Stage 6

10780 Complete, unpolished, drilled from both sides. T.12.0, D.21.0mm, perforation D.4.0mm, Wt 3.02g YORYM: C 618d (Fig.1219)

10781 Complete, some polishing, drilled from one side, lathe-turned. T.6.0, D.20.0mm, perforation D.6.0mm, Wt.1.14g YORYM: C 625a (Fig.1219)

10782 Complete, highly polished, worn around perforation. T.8.0, D.17.0mm, perforation D.6.0mm, Wt.1.38g YORYM: C 625b (Fig.1219)

Finger-rings

Stage 1

10783 Ring blank, discoidal with rough surfaces. T.6.0, D.34.0mm, Wt.5.69g YORYM: C 617a (Fig.1220)

Stage 2

10784 Ring blank, discoidal with rough surfaces, perforation part-drilled through. T.10.0, D.32.0mm, Wt.4.0g YORYM: C 619a (Fig.1220)

Stage 3

10785 Ring roughout, surfaces rough, central hole drilled for lathe-turning. T.14.0, D.34.0mm, perforation D.5.0mm, Wt.8.70g YORYM: C 618a (Fig.1220)

Stage 4A

10786 Ring roughout fragment, lathe-turned on one side, core begun to be cut away on one side. T.8.0, D.30.0mm, perforation D.3.0mm, Wt.1.96g YORYM: C 626e

10787 Ring roughout fragment, lathe-turned on both side, core begun to be cut away from one side. T.10.0, D.24.0mm, perforation D.6.0, Wt.1.57g YORYM: C 626b (Fig.1220)

Stage 4B

10788 Ring roughout fragment, lathe-turned on both sides, core begun to be cut away on both sides. T.10.0, D.25.0mm, perforation D.6.0mm, Wt.1.88g YORYM: C 626d (Fig.1220)

10789 Ring roughout fragment, lathe-turned on both sides, core begun to be cut away on one side. T.11.0, D.27.0mm, perforation D.7.0mm, Wt.0.71g YORYM: C 626c

10790 Ring roughout fragment, lathe-turned on both sides with core attached. T.7.0, D.30.0mm, perforation D.6.0mm, Wt.1.92g YORYM: C 626i

Stage 4C

10791 Ring roughout fragment, lathe-turned on both sides with core still attached but deeply cut. T.11.0, D.30.0mm, perforation D.5.0mm, Wt.2.75g YORYM: C 626f (*Fig.1220*)

10792 Ring roughout fragment, lathe-turned on both sides with core still attached but deeply cut. T.10.0, D.25.0mm, perforation D.8.0mm, Wt.1.62g YORYM: C 626g

Cores

10793 Core resulting from lathe-turning finger-ring. T.13.0, D.12.0mm, perforation D.6.0mm, Wt.1.26g YORYM: C 626l (*Fig.1220*)

10794 Core resulting from lathe-turning finger-ring. T.8.0, D.11.0mm, perforation D.8.0mm, Wt.0.56g YORYM: C 626k (*Fig.1220*)

Stage 5

10795 Completed ring fragment, lathe-turned, surface polished. T.10.0, D.28.0mm, perforation D.10.0mm, Wt.0.52g YORYM: C 626h (*Fig.1220*)

10796 Ring fragment with rough surfaces, carved not lathe-turned. T.12.0, D.25.0mm, perforation D.8.0mm, Wt.2.25g YORYM: C 626j (*Fig.1220*)

Pendants

Stage 1

10797 Pendant blank, worked on two surfaces from a naturally triangular shaped flake. L.27.0. W.13.0, T.7.0mm, Wt.1.42g YORYM: C 601b (*Fig.1221*)

10798 Pendant blank, knife cut to form shape. L.22.0. W.7.0, T.10.0mm, Wt.2.04g YORYM: C 601c (i)

10799 Pendant roughout?, rectangle worked on two surfaces, broken across top. L.21.0, W.11.0, T.7.0mm, Wt.1.02g YORYM: C 601c

10800 Pendant blank, tapering rectangle, shaped but not polished. L.24.0, W10.0, T.10.0mm, Wt.2.00g YORYM: C 601h (*Fig.1221*)

10801 Pendant blank, shaped from natural flake, knife marks visible. L.22.0, W.8.0, T.6.0mm, Wt.0.70g YORYM: C 601d

10802 Pendant blank, flat triangle with bevelled shoulders and bevelled edges, no perforation, surfaces shaped but not polished. L.20.0, W.13.0, T.5.0mm, W.0.74g YORYM: C 601q (*Fig.1221*)

Stage 2

10803 Pendant roughout, surfaces shaped but not polished, perforation begun from one side but incomplete. L.22.0, W.17.0, T.12.0mm, Wt.2.65g YORYM: C 601e (*Fig.1221*)

10804 Pendant roughout fragment, rectangular, three surfaces weathered, one freshly broken, beginnings of a perforation on one side.L.16.0, W.4.0, T.3.0, W.0.35g YORYM: C 600v (*Fig.1221*)

Stage 3

10805 Pendant roughout fragment, tapering rectangle, surfaces shaped but not polished, broken across part drilled per-

foration. L.22.0, W.13.0, T.12.0mm, Wt.2.88g YORYM: C 601f

10806 Pendant roughout fragment tapering rectangle broken across natural fissure. L.22.0, W.10.0, T.5.0mm, T.0.67g YORYM: C 601p

10807 Pendant roughout, faceted edges shaped but not polished, broken across perforation. L.18.0, T.11.0, W.11.0mm, Wt.1.10g YORYM: C 601j

10808 Pendant roughout, shaped but not polished, broken across perforation. L.26.0, W.16.0, T.10.0mm, Wt.2.89g YORYM: C 601m (*Fig.1221*)

10809 Pendant roughout, shaped roughly formed by knife. L.21.0, W.11.0, T.7.0mm YORYM: C 601c (i)

10810 Pendant roughout, flat tapering rectangle with bevelled edges, surfaces shaped but not polished, broken across perforation. L.18.0, W.14.0, T.17.0mm, Wt.0.89g YORYM: C 601r

10811 Pendant roughout, tapering rectangle with bevelled edges, broken across perforation. L.19.0, W.8.0, T.8.0mm, Wt.0.80g YORYM: C 601i

10812 Pendant roughout, tapering rectangle broken across perforation, surfaces shaped but unpolished. L.20.0, W.10.0, T.11.0mm, Wt.1.69g YORYM: C 601n

10813 Pendant roughout, tapering rectangle with bevelled edges, surfaces shaped but not polished, broken across perforation, perforation drilled form both sides. L.20.0, T.13.0mm, Wt.1.79g YORYM: C 601o

10814 Pendant roughout, tapering rectangle broken across perforation, surfaces shaped but unpolished. L.20.0, W.10.0, T.8.0mm, Wt.1.13g YORYM: C 601k (*Fig.1221*)

Stage 4

10815 Pendant roughout, perforation drilled from both sides, surfaces roughly finished, top broken away above perforation. L.25.0, W.12.0, T.9.0mm, Wt.1.35g YORYM: C 602d

10816 Pendant roughout, triangular shaped, perforation drilled from both sides, bell-shaped base. L.16.0, W.10.0, T.11.0mm, perforation D.4.0mm, Wt.0.96g YORYM: C 602f (*Fig.1221*)

10817 Small pendant (or bead) roughout, possible cut down from longer broken original, perforation at top, side and top bevelled, surfaces smoothed but unpolished, perforation drilled from one side. L.14.0, W. 11.0, T.8.0mm, perforation D.4.0mm, Wt.0.82g YORYM: C 602e

10818 Pendant, triangular shaped with bell-shaped base. Perforation drilled from both sides, surface unpolished (or weathered). L.15.0, W.9.0, T. 9.0, W.0.96g YORYM: C 602f

10819 Tapering rectangle with bevelled edges and shoulders, perforation drilled through tapering end. Surfaces smoothed but not polished. L.25.0, W.13.0, T.9.0mm, perforation D.4.0, Wt.1.41g YORYM: C 602c (*Fig.1221*)

10820 Tapering rectangular pendant with perforation through top or rounded tapering end. Perforation worn. Polish, probably from natural wear, on surface. Stress rings visible in amber. L.27.0, W.13.0, T.11.0mm, Wt.3.32g YORYM: C 602a (*Fig.1221*)

10821 Tapering rectangular pendant with perforation drilled through top of rounded, tapering end. Drilled through both sides, surfaces smoothed, edges bevelled but not polished. Bottom end square cut with flake missing. L.42.0, W.10.0, T.10.0mm, Wt.3.81g YORYM: C 602b (*Fig.1221*)

10822 Pendant fragment broken across perforation through wear. L.13.5, W.11.5, T.10.0mm, Wt.1.29g YORYM: C 601i (*Fig.1221*)

Unprovenanced items, probably from York, in the Yorkshire Museum

10823 Amber pendant, triangular, perforation drilled from both sides, notch chipped roughly into the lower edge, diagonal scratches. L.32.0, W.15.0, T.8mm YORYM: 734.48 (*Fig.1283*)

10824 Amber pendant, triangular, perforation drilled from both sides, notch chipped roughly into the lower edge, vertical scratches. L.27.5, W.16.0, T.5.5mm YORYM: 735.48 (*Fig.1283*)

Sculpted stone from 16–22 Coppergate

10825 Probable cross fragments, fine-grained oolitic limestone. 9450 sf2163; 23648 sf7922 (P4B); 22052 sfs7111–12; 22083 sf7181; 22073 sfs7187, 7189; 22077 sf7193; 22085 sfs7206, 7210–11, 7238; 22087 sfs7257–8; 22098 sfs7270, 7272; 22081 sfs7273–5; 22089 sfs7283, 7287; 22087 sfs7285, 7319–20; 22148 sf7392 (P5A)

10826 Fragments of a grave-cover, Magnesian Limestone. L.230.0, W.223.0, T.115.0mm 7553 sf2115 (P5B) (*Figs.1296–7*)

10827 Part of a small grave-marker, limestone. H.330.0, W.227.0, T.107.0mm 20553 sf7101 (P5B) (*Fig.1298*)

10828 Fragment of a grave-cover, Millstone Grit. L.180.0, W.168.0, T.84.0mm 29128 sf10264 (P5B) (*Fig.1298*)

Stolen

As a result of theft of the site van in 1982 the following items, all from 16–22 Coppergate, have now been lost.

Fragment of Mayen lava quern. 7362 sf1277 (P5B)

Fragment of roughout for amber finger-ring. 8874 sf2271 (P5A)

Fragment of roughout for amber finger-ring. 22412 sf7584 (P5A)

Fragment of unidentified amber object. 23339 sf7591 (P4B)

Fragment of unidentified amber object. 22346 sf7593 (P4B)

Fragment of jet ring. 23488 sf7596 (P4B)

Fragment of jet ring. 23586 sf7632 (P4B)

Fragment of jet ring. 22415 sf7681 (P4B)

Hone. 23538 sf7714 (P4B)

Fragment of jet ring. 23497 sf7724 (P5A)

Jet bead. 14787 sf6607 (P5A)

Fragment of unidentified amber object. u/s sf7741

Provenances

Finds were recovered from contexts on the sites as follows; context numbers are given in Roman type, catalogue numbers in italics.

16–22 Coppergate

1005: *10086*; 1028: *10155*; 1092: *6562*; 1096: *10246–7*; 1106: *6551*; 1229: *10215*; 1283: *10290–1, 10416*; 1331: *10065*; 1346: *10336*; 1359: *10087*; 1390: *9949*; 1404: *10162, 10165–6, 10225–6*; 1455: *10156, 10248*; 1469: *9917*; 1473: *9462, 9807–8, 10043, 10070, 10121, 10355, 10592*; 1502: *9658*; 1565: *10250*; 1568: *10088*; 1595: *9294*; 1611: *9806, 10122*; 2078: *9442, 10418, 10561*; 2080: *10379*; 2096: *10289*; 2137: *10340*; 2170: *10201*; 2286: *10299*; 2325: *10114*; 2370: *9902*; 2409: *9776, 10621–3*; 2452: *9611*; 2456: *9860*; 2457: *10569*; 2458: *10315, 10612*; 2570: *10451*; 2600: *10491*; 2677: *9568, 10476*; 2680: *9847*; 2695: *9727*; 2767: *10120*; 2789: *9809*; 2800: *9746*; 2801: *9463*; 2841: *9862*; 2875: *9353, 9464–5, 9926, 10044*; 2901: *6564*; 3224: *9936*; 3256: *9690, 10168*; 3345: *10089*; 3414: *10338*; 3419: *10218–9*; 3445: *9515*; 3453: *9692*; 3463: *9854, 10342*; 3493: *10258*; 3519: *9935, 10574*; 3521: *9596*; 3533: *10383*; 3536: *9863*; 3537: *6550*; 3543: *6567, 10081, 10575*; 3549: *10256*; 3577: *9516*; 3588: *9669*; 3599: *10532, 10573*; 3607: *9861, 10483*; 3633: *10321*; 3647: *9597*; 3661: *10145*; 3697: *10456*; 3726: *10396*; 3729: *3990*; 4125: *10216*; 4189: *10352*; 4402: *10157*; 4535: *10276*; 4620: *10160, 10594*; 4793: *9325*; 5021: *10158*; 5145: *10249*; 5230: *10293*; 5241: *10159*; 5246: *10294*; 5261: *10485*; 5321: *9473*; 5331: *10222*; 5348: *10163–4*; 5395: *10424*; 5415: *10017*; 5426: *9848*; 5484: *10161, 10595*; 5588: *9967, 9998*; 5655: *10296*; 5668: *10092*; 5673: *10013, 10046*; 5698: *10479*; 5711: *10202*; 5714: *9891, 9929, 10012*; 5759: *9248*; 5775: *9890*; 5848: *10047, 10204, 10269*; 5906: *10090, 10224, 10277*; 5975: *10524*; 5978: *10253*; 5980: *9576*; 5981: *9912, 10167, 10185, 10217, 10221, 10251–2, 10254, 10278–9*; 6026: *10337*; 6054: *9944, 10470*; 6119: *10048*; 6179: *9892*; 6245: *9872*; 6258: *9874, 10229, 10261, 10281, 10344*; 6276: *10051*; 6281: *10177, 10230*; 6284: *9978*; 6287: *10332*; 6291: *10095*; 6296: *10298*; 6304: *10082*; 6344: *10175, 10343*; 6347: *10022*; 6425: *9358*; 6429: *9298*; 6433: *9299, 10074, 10135, 10136*; 6434: *10206*; 6440: *10134*; 6444: *10348*; 6570: *10015, 10390*; 6773: *10072*; 6774: *9965, 9983, 10085*; 6776: *9912*; 6781: *9519, 9599, 9601*; 6785: *9635, 9815*; 6787: *9484, 9582*; 6789: *9816, 10275, 10446, 10496*; 6833: *10053*; 6836: *10540*; 6866: *10240*; 6870: *9487*; 6871: *10073*; 6925: *9485*; 6927: *10138*; 6932: *9584, 10494*; 6933: *9486*; 6950: *10471*; 7005: *9747*; 7123: *9466*; 7204: *9293, 9467–8, 9574–5*; 7232: *6549*; 7252: *10062*; 7257: *9777, 10123*; 7296: *10464, 10603*; 7348: *9628*; 7361: *9910*; 7377: *9470*; 7473: *9295*; 7480: *9927, 10045*; 7483: *10565*; 7500: *9471, 9997*; 7553: *10124, 10203, 10330, 10826*; 7782: *10091, 10257*; 7837: *10227*; 7849: *10467*; 7863: *10360*; 7866: *10146*; 7953: *10241*; 8011: *9292*; 8023: *9976, 10518, 10559, 10615*; 8033: *9573, 9943*; 8051: *9469*; 8056: *10037*; 8101: *10286*; 8122: *10381*; 8232: *9865*; 8251: *9438*; 8253: *9941*; 8281: *9622*; 8290: *9887*; 8304: *10223*; 8367: *9440*; 8453: *9879*; 8491: *9439*; 8499: *9667, 9888*; 8524: *9762*; 8568: *10403*; 8569: *9964*; 8666: *9849*; 8696: *9962*; 8800: *9925, 10198, 10570, 10590*; 8844: *10115*; 9057: *9963*; 9070: *6589*; 9224: *9689*; 9229: *10576*; 9248: *4277*; 9274: *10292*; 9302: *10295*; 9360: *9472, 10544*; 9450: *9371, 9966, 10825*; 9487: *9324*; 9570: *10220*; 9572: *6544, 10596*; 9615: *9928*; 9722: *9354–5*; 9726: *9296, 10382*; 9797: *9513, 9524*; 9801: *10171*; 9802: *4001*; 10624: *4409*; 10732: *9896*;

11000: *10255*; 11125: *10064*; 11368: *9787*; 11674: *9783*; 11886: *9980*; 12412: *10170*; 12561: *10169*; 12635: *10172*; 12662: *10297*; 12671: *10280*; 12819: *9788*; 12863: *10415*; 12869: *9779*; 13147: *9873, 10228*; 13206: *9950*; 13212: *10184, 10233*; 13215: *9897*; 13367: *9577*; 13465: *10259*; 13527: *9691*; 13532: *9660*; 13716: *9474–5, 9763*; 13733: *9578, 9705, 10433*; 13875: *9930*; 13902: *4278*; 13908: *10093*; 13964: *10506*; 14005: *9297*; 14069: *10341*; 14139: *9784*; 14179: *9514*; 14184: *9579, 9629–31, 9945, 10125*; 14297: *10388, 10492*; 14300: *10126*; 14372: *9728*; 14378: *9800*; 14379: *9789*; 14383: *9786*; 14384: *9785*; 14403: *9476*; 14434: *9581, 10564*; 14466: *10613*; 14467: *10397*; 14515: *9498–9*; 14532: *10132*; 14541: *9893*; 14548: *10002*; 14549: *10331*; 14595: *9580*; 14625: *3998*; 14632: *9583*; 14633: *9360*; 14666: *9749, 9946*; 14704: *10395, 10554*; 14722: *10523*; 14750: *10522*; 14787: *9995, 10199, 10328*; 14843: *9812*; 14849: *9850*; 14851: *9482*; 14874: *9444*; 14878: *10052*; 14883: *10039*; 14887: *9483, 9707*; 14922: *6561, 9653, 10118*; 14925: *9994, 10117*; 14928: *10503*; 14940: *9569*; 14963: *10268*; 14965: *9625*; 14973: *9361, 9894, 9948, 10054*; 14974: *9345*; 15033: *9659*; 15086: *10200*; 15124: *10537*; 15173: *6557*; 15177: *10412*; 15189: *9608, 9655*; 15192: *9477, 9594, 10130, 10234, 10237*; 15193: *9764, 10235*; 15311: *9603–5, 9979, 10151–2, 10245, 10391, 10445*; 15314: *10505*; 15316: *10238*; 15361: *10504*; 15366: *9813*; 15368: *9706*; 15371: *9356*; 15382: *10128–9, 10236*; 15402: *10127*; 15457: *9999, 10131*; 15470: *10063*; 15471: *10614*; 15473: *9871*; 15494: *9748*; 15550: *10000–1, 10133*; 15587: *9478*; 15592: *10094*; 15608: *9480*; 15645: *9481*; 15657: *10320*; 15659: *10050*; 15663: *6563*; 15685: *9372*; 15688: *9972*; 15731: *9729–30*; 15779: *9814*; 15870: *9357*; 15894: *9898*; 15897: *10303*; 15933: *9731*; 15999: *9359*; 16465: *9937*; 16612: *9637–8, 9821, 9982, 10182, 10262, 10300, 10437, 10475, 10578, 10597*; 16628: *10552*; 16733: *10150, 10212, 10335*; 16734: *10173*; 16763: *9517*; 16865: *10242*; 16877: *10154, 10214*; 16881: *9911, 10389*; 16882: *9479, 9977*; 16883: *10205, 10213, 10580*; 16887: *10153*; 17129: *10098*; 17457: *10174*; 17551: *9951, 10232*; 17699: *10176, 10260, 10452*; 17740: *10577*; 17742: *9600*; 17787: *10096*; 17890: *9938, 10097, 10180–1, 10349, 10472*; 18023: *9737*; 18025: *10373, 10420*; 18194: *10183*; 18256: *10178–9*; 18286: *9441, 10316*; 18331: *9636*; 18366: *9840, 9981*; 18467: *9652, 10591*; 18485: *9810*; 18489: *10071, 10239*; 18536: *6558–9*; 18541: *10270*; 18571: *9450*; 18594: *9919–20*; 18600: *10038*; 18601: *10007*; 18666: *9760*; 18668: *10231*; 18744: *9518, 9598, 10084, 10147, 10273, 10288, 10398, 10495, 10542*; 18827: *9811*; 18838: *10272*; 18922: *10562*; 18931: *9520, 10148, 10274, 10322*; 18949: *10056, 10617*; 18962: *10593*; 18988: *4149, 10285*; 19090: *9657, 10083*; 19120: *9820, 10385, 10434*; 19190: *9523*; 19244: *10149*; 19255: *10016, 10244*; 19268: *10401*; 19271: *10060*; 19285: *9301, 9489, 10493*; 19293: *10137*; 19294: *9947*; 19307: *9851*; 19320: *9302, 10541*; 19328: *10414*; 19353: *10364, 10582*; 19360: *9586*; 19390: *6542, 6552–3, 6624, 9278, 9721, 9724, 9742, 10019, 10375, 10407–8, 10484, 10488*; 19460: *9303*; 19534: *9988*; 19545: *10334*; 19620: *10419*; 19632: *3999*; 19633: *10459*; 19634: *9331, 9835*; 19643: *9341, 10109*; 19644: *6586*; 19686: *10507*; 19701: *10481*; 19714: *9566*; 19719:

9343; 20052: *9300, 10287;* 20062: *10528;* 20105: *9443, 9445, 9623, 10116;* 20110: *10066;* 20131: *10040, 10423;* 20132: *10519;* 20143: *9447, 9570, 9802, 10119;* 20162: *10497;* 20170: *9591, 10078, 10140;* 20178: *10473;* 20181: *6560, 10411;* 20185: *9346, 10317;* 20205: *9363, 9778, 10243;* 20229: *10581;* 20234: *10210;* 20266: *9585;* 20269: *10271, 10333;* 20277: *9632;* 20301: *10075;* 20341: *9818;* 20345: *10055;* 20348: *9589;* 20351: *10413;* 20375: *10462;* 20387: *8588;* 20400: *9801;* 20411: *10032, 10463;* 20427: *6537, 9262, 9986;* 20459: *6585;* 20462: *10104–5;* 20484: *10579;* 20543: *10531;* 20553: *10827;* 20604: *9446;* 20667: *9263, 9878, 10510;* 20718: *9448;* 20719: *9347;* 20740: *10318;* 20746: *10329;* 20747: *9340, 9551, 9822;* 20749: *9373;* 20765: *9643;* 20808: *9668, 9676–7;* 20809: *10425;* 20819: *10449;* 20880: *10041;* 20893: *9319, 9838, 10023;* 20916: *9664;* 20918: *9792;* 20978: *10599;* 21033: *9766, 10080;* 21044: *9521;* 21075: *6582;* 21076: *9765;* 21096: *9602;* 21107: *9522;* 21143: *10587;* 21200: *9759;* 21203: *9587;* 21204: *10005;* 21244: *9588, 9775, 10139;* 21245: *9490–2, 10004;* 21293: *9592;* 21309: *10076;* 21381: *9853, 10208;* 21382: *9304, 9590;* 21437: *10079;* 21441: *10193;* 21478: *9494, 9678–9;* 21479: *9797;* 21510: *9681, 9931;* 21512: *9495–6;* 21543: *9497;* 21554: *9509, 9680, 9880, 9933;* 21592: *9916;* 21597: *9306;* 21618: *9595, 9758;* 21646: *9895, 9932;* 21660: *9500;* 21678: *9511;* 21680: *9767–74, 10211;* 21746: *10404;* 21769: *9507, 10049;* 21845: *9708;* 21880: *10144;* 21887: *10346;* 21898: *9682;* 21903: *9646–7, 9867, 10376;* 21904: *10604;* 21919: *9362, 9502, 9593;* 21925: *9750, 10571;* 21961: *4000;* 22010: *10380;* 22016: *9803;* 22017: *9665;* 22044: *9607;* 22050: *9348;* 22052: *9624, 10825;* 22053: *9704, 10011, 10520;* 22073: *10825;* 22077: *10825;* 22081: *10825;* 22083: *10825;* 22084: *9449;* 22085: *10825;* 22087: *10825;* 22090: *3997, 9452, 10432;* 22087: *10825;* 22089: *10825;* 22098: *10825;* 22103: *10436;* 22104: *9804;* 22110: *10021, 10042;* 22122: *9454, 9744;* 22124: *9459, 9703;* 22127: *10563;* 22128: *9351;* 22141: *9626;* 22144: *9909;* 22148: *10825;* 22154: *10501;* 22166: *9350, 9453;* 22172: *10600;* 22179: *9830;* 22180: *9726, 10477;* 22192: *9349;* 22215: *10530;* 22233: *9719, 9752, 9793;* 22238: *9530;* 22259: *10325;* 22268: *10421;* 22306: *9326, 9671;* 22309: *6548, 9290, 9455, 10502, 10616;* 22323: *9529, 10405;* 22340: *9571, 10521;* 22348: *10029, 10533;* 22358: *10602;* 22368: *9745;* 22384: *9996;* 22415: *6556, 9376, 9531, 9740;* 22416: *9375, 9739, 10557, 10610;* 22418: *9738;* 22421: *9247, 9753–5;* 22449: *9741, 10426;* 22523: *6635, 9377, 9907, 10324;* 22524: *9536, 10474;* 22528: *9824;* 22560: *9266, 9533, 9534, 9842, 9954, 10431, 10499,* 22574: *9532, 9558, 9671;* 22590: *9265, 9272, 10371–2;* 22593: *10560;* 22631: *9379–80;* 22656: *9612;* 22659: *10584;* 22670: *9671, 10513;* 22679: *6538, 9267–9, 9383–4, 9537;* 22690: *10406;* 22713: *6546–7, 9381, 9535, 9833, 10309, 10514;* 22714: *10102–3, 10108;* 22723: *9699, 9702;* 22728: *10545;* 22745: *9386;* 22747: *9385;* 22748: *9387–90, 9538, 9613;* 22789: *6592;* 22797: *9974;* 22800: *6540;* 22802: *9924, 10409;* 22806: *10546;* 22808: *10326;* 22809: *9666;* 22815: *6541, 9391;* 22816: *9393, 10515, 10547;* 22819: *10365;* 22841: *10558;* 22845: *6545, 9271, 9392, 9614, 10539;* 22848: *9615, 9825;* 22867: *4147, 6639;* 22883: *9826;* 22911: *6539, 9987;* 22943: *9922;* 22958: *9882;* 22962: *6594;* 23000: *9451;* 23102: *10583;* 23125: *9374;* 23184: *10511;* 23234: *9989;* 23251: *9921;* 23278: *10370;* 23311: *10362;* 23312: *9642;* 23339: *10512;* 23531: *9264;* 23634: *10068;* 23658: *10825;* 23649: *10030;* 23663: *9700;* 23669: *9378;* 23700: *6555;* 23788: *9382;* 23794: *9270;* 23797: *9905;* 23841: *9616;* 23881: *9651, 9923;* 23936: *9539;* 24003: *9394;* 24028: *9544;* 24064: *10312;* 24066: *9899;* 24119: *6625;* 24241: *9274;* 24296: *9540;* 24341: *3995;* 24386: *9794;* 24395: *9852;* 24402: *10190;* 24500: *6587;* 24509: *9545;* 24520: *9960;* 24556: *9400, 9644, 9973;* 24618: *10374;* 24647: *4148;* 24668: *9795;* 24766: *9366;* 24770: *9525;*

24787: *9275, 10305–6, 10608;* 24808: *9404, 9423, 10427;* 24814: *10489;* 24829: *9817;* 24870: *10077;* 24872: *10031;* 24899: *9512, 10014;* 24918: *9906;* 24946: *9310;* 25084: *10556;* 25085: *9397, 10550, 10585;* 25176: *10304;* 25177: *9541–2;* 25205: *9832;* 25252: *9790;* 25253: *10566;* 25257: *9273, 10567;* 25270: *9543;* 25285: *9395–6, 9796;* 25294: *9830;* 25303: *10311;* 25330: *9327;* 25340: *9720, 10106, 10191, 10586;* 25341: *3253;* 25350: *6554, 9276, 9546–8, 9617, 9843, 9859, 9866, 10265, 10551;* 25380: *9398–9, 9427;* 25391: *10611;* 25450: *9277;* 25466: *10359;* 25593: *9320;* 25598: *9552, 9649, 10588;* 25622: *9330;* 25624: *9834;* 25630: *9955, 10482, 10534, 10606;* 25667: *10107;* 25698: *9401;* 25718: *9618;* 25725: *9280–1, 9756;* 25748: *9844, 9883;* 25750: *9886;* 25759: *9527, 10302, 10469;* 25780: *9282;* 25785: *10345;* 25793: *10548;* 25795: *9663;* 25808: *9757;* 25812: *9619;* 25860: *9283;* 25922: *9985;* 25931: *9645;* 25934: *9333–8, 9344, 9402–3, 9406–14, 9416–20, 9553–5, 10033–4, 10358;* 25987: *9323, 9369;* 25990: *9315, 9709, 10006;* 25992: *10399;* 25994: *9528;* 26015: *9493, 10209;* 26016: *10101, 10189, 10282;* 26022: *10498;* 26059: *9365;* 26147: *10394;* 26157: *9550;* 26171: *9328, 10363, 10450;* 26181: *9249, 9307, 9364;* 26200: *9250;* 26202: *9311;* 26245: *9305;* 26247: *9424;* 26254: *9279, 10455;* 26381: *9549;* 26419: *9639–41, 9881;* 26423: *10458;* 26427: *9256;* 26438: *10384;* 26471: *9733;* 26491: *9329;* 26495: *10428;* 26496: *9456;* 26610: *9735;* 26616: *6565, 9257;* 26631: *9312;* 26636: *10284;* 26636: *10553;* 26647: *9782;* 26721: *9662;* 26732: *9970;* 26748: *9405;* 26783: *9661;* 26792: *9352;* 26802: *10003;* 26868: *9291;* 26871: *9461;* 26888: *10141;* 26889: *9627;* 26890: *9823;* 26902: *9913, 10609;* 26937: *10438;* 26949: *9858;* 26953: *9457, 9805, 9870, 9889, 10347;* 26960: *9332;* 26977: *10024;* 26992: *10196, 10197;* 26996: *10468;* 27017: *9975;* 27083: *9694;* 27098: *10422;* 27118: *9458, 10319;* 27271: *9961;* 27296: *10605;* 27299: *10195;* 27338: *10620;* 27341: *9287, 9908;* 27368: *10113;* 27369: *10392;* 27413: *9367,* 27422: *6536, 9258;* 27428: *10607;* 27429: *10448;* 27440: *9321;* 27485: *9322;* 27503: *10069;* 27504: *3992, 9285;* 27509: *9284, 9422;* 27513: *9633–4, 10057;* 27621: *9857, 9875, 10361;* 27623: *10443;* 27637: *10008;* 27639: *9672;* 27679: *9572;* 27741: *9722;* 27804: *9460;* 27806: *9942;* 27819: *9314, 9712, 9968–9, 10025, 10368, 10439;* 27878: *9695;* 27892: *9556;* 28005: *9839;* 28020: *9693;* 28036: *10535;* 28066: *9313;* 28071: *9732;* 28087: *9914;* 28120: *10490;* 28236: *6636;* 28239: *6579, 9526;* 28356: *9286;* 28408: *9610;* 28492: *10035;* 28493: *9609;* 28750: *9710–1;* 28808: *9421;* 28815: *10529;* 28820: *9648;* 28882: *9723;* 28904: *9339, 9426, 9559, 9836;* 28920: *9798;* 28933: *9620;* 28967: *9425, 9650;* 29045: *9501;* 29128: *10619, 10828;* 29156: *9934, 10572;* 29193: *9675, 9827, 10266;* 29222: *9673–4, 10327;* 29263: *9503–6, 9508, 9510, 9656, 9683–8, 9819, 9837, 10142–3, 10207;* 29457: *10059;* 29459: *10020;* 29467: *10058;* 29528: *9992, 10036, 10314;* 29575: *10367;* 29835: *9562;* 29835: *9885, 10526;* 29844: *9915, 9940, 9990;* 29904: *10525;* 29919: *9868, 10500;* 29925: *9565;* 30001: *10323;* 30132: *9259, 9791, 9856, 10444;* 30134: *9736;* 30189: *9971;* 30273: *9370, 9984;* 30274: *9260;* 30286: *10402, 10536;* 30352: *6623, 9261, 9877, 10018, 10417;* 30385: *10339;* 30404: *9958;* 30511: *10549;* 30575: *9696;* 30585: *9309, 9317, 10615;* 30615: *9697;* 30623: *10465;* 30633: *9713;* 30713: *6543, 9251;* 30727: *9714;* 30735: *10454;* 30751: *10509;* 30835: *10555;* 30840: *10466;* 30841: *10441;* 30842: *10351;* 30863: *10486;* 30920: *10393;* 30922: *9715, 9734, 10527;* 30936: *10442, 10487;* 30954: *9718;* 30963: *9957;* 30969: *10028;* 30973: *10283;* 31013: *10377, 10386;* 31061: *9316, 10188, 10460;* 31067: *9855;* 31072: *6580, 9831;* 31089: *10410;* 31161: *6581, 9876;* 31167: *9956;* 31201: *10307;* 31208: *9557;* 31225: *10461;* 31275: *10308;* 31300: *9654;* 31359: *10453;* 31389: *10264;* 31424: *10192;* 31476: *9428–9, 9560;* 31478: *9342;* 31595: *9717;* 31643: *10440;* 31808:

9952; 32115: *9884, 10310*; 32129: *9606*; 32169: *9743*; 32217: *9430, 10516*; 32243: *10194*; 32406: *9725*; 32440: *10480*; 32465: *9433*; 32470: *10517*; 32547: *9716*; 32549: *9253*; 32549: *10026, 10356*; 32573: *9869*; 32589: *9564*; 32668: *9841, 10369*; 32687: *9953, 10301*; 32693: *10538*; 32694: *10357*; 32696: *9903–4*; 32702: *9368*; 32755: *9308*; 32758: *10400*; 32772: *9959*; 32836: *10435*; 32923: *10067*; 32969: *9255*; 32993: *9435*; 33017: *9318*; 33072: *9252*; 34201: *9761*; 34207: *3994*; 34227: *9845*; 34244: *9254*; 34289: *10313*; 34290: *9828*; 34373: *10601*; 34412: *9432, 9561, 9846, 10378*; 34424: *9991*; 34467: *9900*; 34492: *9437*; 34521: *10009*; 34569: *10429*; 34622: *10110*; 34646: *9621*; 34663: *6593, 9918*; 34670: *9431*; 34687: *10350*; 34725: *9563*; 34730: *9701, 10267*; 34765: *9901*; 34877: *9901, 9904*; 34983: *10010*; 34988: *10589*; 35011: *10354*; 35059: *9799*; 35137: *6638, 9567*; 35147: *9434*; 35293: *9900*; 35448: *10111*; 35451: *9288*; 35483: *9289*; 35519: *10112, 10430, 10618*; 35675: *9829*; 36009: *10568*; 36048: *9864*; 36049: *10027*; 36058: *10387*; 36155: *9698*; 36247: *9993*; 36361: *10100*; 36434: *9436*; 36514: *10508*; 36532: *10457*

Unprovenanced: *6566, 6637, 9415, 9488, 9670, 9751, 9780–1, 9939, 10061, 10099, 10186–7, 10263, 10353, 10366, 10447, 10478, 10543, 10598*

Watching Brief

1247: *10628–9*; 1546: *10624*; 1777: *10625*

22 Piccadilly

1003: *10643*; 1041: *10692*; 1043: *10685*; 1058: *10647, 10681, 10693*; 1060: *10644, 10646*; 2042: *10642, 10652, 10660, 10665–6, 10675–7, 10689*; 2083: *10659*; 2089: *10631, 10658, 10667–8*; 2112: *10674*; 2113: *10664*; 2146: *10632*; 2162: *10634, 10638–40, 10649, 10654–5, 10669–70, 10680*; 2166: *10663*; 2168: *10630*; 2169: *10662*; 2186: *10653, 10656, 10661, 10686, 10695*; 2187: *10641, 10657, 10671*; 2216: *10696*; 2243: *10672*; 2254: *10673*; 2255: *10635*; 2291: *10633, 10650, 10697*; 2293: *10682, 10691, 10694*; 2311: *10645*; 3035: *10651*; 3080: *10678–9, 10683–4, 10687–8, 10690*; 3118: *10648*; 4004: *10636*

Unprovenanced: *10637*

College of The Bedern Vicars Choral

1054: *10708*; 1131: *10705*; 1142: *10701*; 1504: *10702*; 1590: *10706*; 1640: *10709*; 4084: *10698*; 5410: *10700*; 6201: *10704*; 7020: *10703*; 7449: *10710*; 7561: *10707*; 7609: *10699*

Acknowledgements

York Archaeological Trust and the authors wish to express their thanks to all those who have helped in the preparation of this fascicule.

The excavation at 16–22 Coppergate was directed by R.A. Hall, with supervision by D.T. Evans (1976–81), S. Power (1976–8), M. Humphreys (1976–7) and I. Lawton (1978–81). Post-excavation work is under the overall direction of R.A. Hall. The excavation was made possible through the generous co-operation of York City Council, the site owners, and the financial support of the then Department of the Environment and a number of generous benefactors and donors.

The excavation at 22 Piccadilly was directed by N.F. Pearson, assisted by R. Finlayson who undertook post-excavation analysis. The project was financed by Wimpey Property Holdings Limited.

The Bedern excavations were initially directed for York Archaeological Trust by B.Whitwell, then by M.J. Daniells, and finally M. Stockwell. For Beden southwest and Bedern north-east, initial post-excavation analysis and production of the archive reports was undertaken by A. Clarke and M. Stockwell. York Archaeological Trust is most grateful to the original owner of the site, York City Council, and the subsequent owner, Simons of York, and also the Dean and Chapter of York Minster who own the Chapel, for making the land available for excavation, and for giving every assistance during the work. The excavations were supported by grants from the Department of the Environment, now English Heritage. Many of the excavation assistants were employed on a STEP scheme administered by the Manpower Services Commission, whilst the supervisory staff were financed directly by the Department of the Environment. From 1976–8 the excavation was staffed with DOE-funded excavation assistants and supervisors who were supplemented by Manpower Services Commission Job Creation Programme staff from 1978–9. Later all employees were replaced with MSC Special Temporary Employment Programme personnel although the DOE continued to provide funding for supervision. Until 1979 additional summer help was provided by many hard-working volunteers, students from the University of Pennsylvania and the College of Ripon and York St John, and inmates from HM Open Prison at Askham Bryan.

The project has been managed at the Trust by D. Petts and Dr P. Wilson for English Heritage.

Thanks are expressed to the staff, students and volunteers of the YAT Conservation Department, both past and present; to C. McDonnell and the Trust Finds Department staff, especially B. Shaw, who supervised the transport of artefacts for study and illustration; to Ailsa Mainman and Sylvia Bowen for work on the list of provenances, and to the Yorkshire Museum for the loan of the collection of amber from Clifford Street for research. The authors are also grateful to all of the following for support and advice: L. Allason-Jones, M. Baldwin, M. Barnes, J. Bayley, L. Blackmore, C. Bourke, C. Caple, H.E.M. Cool, R. Doonan, G. Egan, G.D. Gaunt, H. Geake, J. Graham-Campbell, E. Hartley, P. Harvey de Terra, M. Hutchinson, P. Judkins, A.-C. Larsen, K. Leahy, R. Ó Floinn, R. Page, P. Rahtz, C. Richardson, J. Stevenson, M. Stiff, G. Thomas, D. Tweddle, P.F. Wallace, P. Walton Rogers, N. Whitfield and S. Youngs.

The majority of the object illustrations are by Paula Chew, with others by Charlotte Bentley, Glenys Boyles, Terry Finnemore, Sheena Howarth and Eddie Moth. The maps, plans, diagrams and distribution plots were produced by Paula Chew and Terry Finnemore. All the illustrations were prepared for publication by Charlotte Bentley and Paula Chew, with the assistance of Mike Andrews.

The photographs are by S.I. Hill, FRPS (Scirebröc), except for Fig.1252 which is reproduced by courtesy of M. Hutchinson and Figs.1228–32 which are reproduced by courtesy of the Ancient Monuments Laboratory.

The summary was translated into French by C. Sheil-Small and into German by Mrs K. Aberg. This fascicule was edited by D. Petts, who also prepared the text for publication. The project has been funded and the fascicule published with the assistance of a generous subvention by English Heritage.

Summary

This report presents the evidence for artefacts produced from stone, glass, fired clay, jet, amber and non-ferrous metalwork of Anglo-Scandinavian date (c.850–late 11th century) from York. Most of this evidence derives from sites in the Piccadilly/Coppergate area of the city, the majority being recovered from excavations of well-preserved structures and associated features at 16–22 Coppergate. In addition, an important collection of amber found in the late 19th century at Clifford Street, near Coppergate, is published here for comparison with the amber from the other sites.

The report includes a brief description of the sites from which the material was recovered. This is followed by a discussion of the conservation techniques, and the results of a study of the provenance of the amber.

The rest of the report presents the material in two main sections. The first section, 'Craft and Industry', describes and evaluates the evidence for the production of objects. This includes evidence relating to ferrous and non-ferrous metalworking (in the form of stone moulds, hones, grindstones and failed castings), glass working, jet and amber working, and textile production. The mode of production for these crafts seems to cover the full range from professional (in the case of the metalworking) to domestic (in the case of the textiles). As is the case with material published in earlier parts of Volume 17, the distribution of the evidence makes it possible in some cases to suggest which structures might have served as particular workshops at different times.

The second section, 'Everyday Life', presents a wide range of artefacts, some of which might have been made on site and others which were produced elsewhere. Some relate to the structures on site, their fixtures and fittings, while others relate to activities within the buildings. These include a range of items of a domestic character as well as objects associated with trade. There are a wide range of personal ornaments and dress accessories produced in different materials. These artefacts, together with those previously published, give a vivid account of the activities and daily life of York's inhabitants in the Anglo-Scandinavian period. There is also a brief account of stone sculptural fragments.

The final discussion aims to synthesise this wide range of new material and to examine the information it provides concerning trade, cultural influences and the character of Viking Age York. A catalogue of all the material recovered from the sites and a concordance of provenances completes this report.

Resumé

Ce rapport présente la documentation sur les objets fabriqués produits à partir de pierre, verre, argile cuite, jais, ambre et métal non ferreux de date anglo-scandinave (d'environ 850 à la fin du 11ème siècle), découverts à York. La plupart de ces indices proviennent de sites dans la zone Piccadilly/Coppergate de la ville, la majorité d'entre eux ayant étés découverts lors de fouilles de structures bien conservées et d'attributs s'y rapportant au 16–22 Coppergate. En outre, une importante collection d'ambre découverte à la fin du 19ème siècle à Clifford Street, près de Coppergate, est publiée ici pour permettre de faire une comparaison avec l'ambre en provenance des autres sites.

Le rapport comprend une brève description des sites où le matériel a été découvert. Cette description est suivie d'une discussion des techniques de conservation et des résultats d'une étude sur la provenance de cet ambre.

Le reste du rapport présente le matériel en deux parties principales. La première section, 'Artisanat et Industrie', décrit et évalue les indices de production d'objets. Ceci comprend les indices se rapportant au travail des métaux ferreux et non ferreux (sous la forme de moules en pierre, de pierres à aiguiser, de meules, et de moulages manqués), à la manufacture du verre, au travail du jais et de l'ambre et à la production des textiles. Le mode de production pour ces artisanats semble englober toute la gamme allant de la production professionnelle (dans le cas du travail des métaux) à la production domestique (dans le cas des textiles). Comme avec la publication du matériel dans les premières parties du Volume 17, la répartition des indices donne la possibilité, dans certains cas, de suggérer quelles structures pourraient avoir servi d'ateliers précis à différentes périodes.

La deuxième section, 'La vie quotidienne', présente une grande variété d'objets fabriqués, dont certains auraient pu être fabriqués sur place alors que d'autres avaient été fabriqués ailleurs. Certains objets ont un rapport avec les structures du site, leurs installations, alors que d'autres se rapportent à des activités à l'intérieur des bâtiments. Ceux-ci comprenaient une gamme d'articles à caractère domestique ainsi que des objets associés au commerce. Il y a une grande variété d'ornements personnels et d'accessoires vestimentaires produits dans différentes matières. Ces objets fabriqués, ainsi que ceux ayant déjà fait l'objet d'une publication, fournissent un récit vivant de la vie quotidienne des habitants d'York pendant la période anglo-scandinave. Il y a également un bref compte-rendu à propos de fragments de pierre sculptée.

La discussion finale vise à faire une synthèse de cette grande gamme de nouveau matériel et à examiner les informations que ce matériel fournit concernant le commerce, les influences culturelles et le caractère de York pendant l'âge des Vikings. Un catalogue de tout le matériel découvert dans les sites et une concordance des provenances complètent ce rapport.

Zusammenfassung

Dieser Bericht legt den Befund für die aus Stein, Glas, gebranntem Ton, Bernstein und Nichteisenmetallen gefertigten Artefakten aus der anglo-skandinavischen Zeit Yorks (c.850–bis zum ausgehenden 11.Jahrhundert) vor. Dieser Befund stammt hauptsächlich aus den Grabungsstellen in der Piccadilly/Coppergate Gegend der Stadt; der größte Teil wurde aus Ausgrabungen guterhalterner Bauten und aus benachbarten Anlagen auf dem Areal 16–22 Coppergate geborgen. Hinzu kommt eine bedeutende Sammlung von Bernstein, die im ausgehenden 19.Jahrhundert in der Clifford Street, nahe der Coppergate gefunden wurde und die hier zum Vergleich mit den Bernsteinfunden aus den anderen Fundstellen veröffentlicht wird. Der Bericht schließt eine kurze Beschreibung der Fundstellen, aus denen das Material stammt, ein. Daran schließt sich eine Diskussion der Konservierungstechniken an, weiterhin diskutiert werden die Ergebnisse der Untersuchungen über die Provenienz des Bernsteins.

Der verbleibende Teil des Berichtes legt das Material unter zwei Hauptthemen vor. Der erste Teil 'Handwerk und Industrie' beschreibt und bewertet den Befund im Bezug auf Eisen- und Nichteisenverarbeitung (in der Form von steinernen Gußformen, Wetz- und Schleifsteinen und Fehlgüssen), Glasverarbeitung, Jet- und Bernsteinverarbeitung und Textilherstellung. Die Ebene der Herstellung in diesen Handwerken reicht von der gewerblichen (im Fall der Metallverarbeitung) zur häuslichen (im Fall der Textilien) Produktion. Wie im Bezug auf das Fundmaterial, das in den früheren Teilen des Bandes 17 veröffentlicht wurde, läßt auch hier die Verteilung des Fundmaterials in einigen Fällen erschliessen, welche der Bauten zu verschiedenen Zeitpunkten als jeweilige Werkstätten gedient haben könnten.

Der zweite Teil 'Tägliches Leben' präsentiert eine große Auswahl an Artefakten, von denen einige an Ort und Stelle, andere jedoch auswärts hergestellt worden waren. Einige von ihnen standen mit den Bauten in Verband, wie etwa bewegliches und unbewegliches Zubehör, andere hingegen weisen auf Aktivitäten innerhalb der Gebäude hin. Zu diesen gehört eine weite Auswahl an Gegenständen mit häußlichem Charakter, sowie Gegenstände, die mit Handel in Verbindung stehen. Weiterhin gibt es eine große Auswahl von persönlichen Schmuckgegenständen und Kleiderzubehör, die aus den verschiedensten Materialien hergestellt waren. Diese Artefakte geben im Zusammenhang mit dem bisher veröffentlichten Material einen lebhaften Einblick in die Aktivitäten und das tägliche Leben der Einwohner von York in anglo-skandinavischer Zeit. Weiterhin beigefügt ist eine kurze Beschreibung von Fragmenten steinerner Skulpturen.

Die abschließende Diskussion strebt eine Synthese dieses weitreichenden neuen Materials an, zusammen mit einer Erörterung der Information, die sich daraus im Bezug auf Handel, kulturelle Einflüsse und den Charakter der Wikingerzeit in York ergibt. Ein Katalog des gesamten Materials, das aus den Grabungsstellen geborgen wurde, sowie eine Konkordanz der Provenienzen vervollständigt den Bericht.

Note

1 Pieces of a bright yellow material (sfs15519 and 15520 from contexts 22714 and 26636) were identified by the Ancient Monuments Laboratory as the pigment orpiment (Gettens and Stout 1966, 135). Further possible examples were recovered from contexts 32443, 32591 and 22714 (sfs15516–18) but these have yet to be analysed.

Bibliography

Allason-Jones, L., 1989. *Ear-Rings in Roman Britain*, British Archaeol. Rep., Brit. Ser. **201** (Oxford)

—— 1996. *Roman Jet in the Yorkshire Museum* (York)

Andrews, D.D. and Milne, G., 1979. *Wharram. A Study of Settlement on the Yorkshire Wolds 1. Domestic Settlement, 1: Areas 10 and 6* (London)

Arbman, H., 1935–7. 'Vikingatidsgravar vid Ulunda vad', *Upplands fornminnesförenings tidskrift* **XLV**:3, 261–75

—— 1940. *Birka 1 Die Gräber: Tafeln* (Stockholm)

—— 1943. *Birka 1 Die Gräber: Text* (Uppsala)

Armstrong, E.C.R., 1922. 'Irish Bronze Pins of the Christian Period', *Archaeologia* **72**, 71–86

Armstrong, P., Tomlinson, D. and Evans, D.H. (eds.), 1991. *Excavations at Lurk Lane, Beverley, 1979–82* (Sheffield)

Arthurton, R.S., Johnson, E.W. and Mundy, D.J.C., 1988. *Geology of the country around Settle. Memoir of the British Geological Survey, Sheet* **60**, HMSO (London)

Arwidsson, G. (ed.), 1989. *Birka 2/3. Systematische Analysen der Gräberfunde* (Stockholm)

Askrup, E.E. and Andersen, A.G., 1987. 'A study of metal-foiled glass beads from the Viking Period' *Acta Archaeologia* **58**, 222–8

AY. Addyman, P.V. (ed.). *The Archaeology of York* (London)

1 D.W. Rollason, D. Gore and G. Fellows-Jensen, 1998. *Sources for York History to AD 1100*

3 *The Legionary Fortress:*

    3 P. Ottaway, 1996. *Excavations and Observations on the Defences and Adjacent Sites, 1971–90*

6 *Roman Extra-mural Settlement and Roads:*

    2 P.J. Ottaway, in prep. *Coppergate, Blossom Street and Other Extra-mural Sites in York Excavated 1986–2000*

7 *Anglian York (AD 410–876):*

    1 R.L. Kemp, 1996. *Anglian Settlement at 46–54 Fishergate*

    2 D. Tweddle, J. Moulden and E. Logan, 1999. *Anglian York: A Survey of the Evidence*

8 *Anglo-Scandinavian York (AD 876–1066):*

    2 L.P. Wenham, R.A. Hall, C.M. Briden and D.A. Stocker, 1987. *St Mary Bishophill Junior and St Mary Castlegate*

    4 R.A. Hall in prep. Anglo-Scandinavian Structures from 16–22 Coppergate

10 *The Medieval Walled City north-east of the Ouse:*

    3 J.D. Richards, 1993. *The Bedern Foundry*

    4 D.A. Stocker, 1999. *The College of the Vicars Choral of York Minster at Bedern: Architectural Fragments*

    5 J.D. Richards, forthcoming. *The Vicars Choral of York Minster: The College in The Bedern*

14 *The Past Environment of York:*

    7 H.K. Kenward and A.R. Hall, *Biological Evidence from 16–22 Coppergate*

15 *The Animal Bones:*

    3 T.P. O'Connor, 1996. *Bones from Anglo-Scandinavian Levels at 16–22 Coppergate*

16 *The Pottery:*

    3 C.M. Brooks, 1987. *Medieval and Later Pottery from Aldwark and Other Sites*

    5 A.J. Mainman, 1990. *Anglo-Scandinavian Pottery from 16–22 Coppergate*

    6 A.J. Mainman, 1993. *The Pottery from 46–54 Fishergate*

17 *The Small Finds:*

    3 A. MacGregor, 1982. *Anglo-Scandinavian Finds from Lloyds Bank, Pavement and Other Sites*

    4 D. Tweddle, 1986. *Finds from Parliament Street and Other Sites in the City Centre*

    5 P. Walton, 1989. *Textiles, Cordage and Raw Fibre from 16–22 Coppergate*

    6 P.J. Ottaway, 1992. *Anglo-Scandinavian Ironwork from 16–22 Coppergate*

    7 J. Bayley, 1992. *Non-ferrous Metalworking from 16–22 Coppergate*

    8 D. Tweddle, 1992. *The Anglian Helmet from 16–22 Coppergate*

    9 N.S.H. Rogers, 1993. *Anglian Finds from 46–54 Fishergate*

    10 H.E.M. Cool, G. Lloyd-Morgan and A.D. Hooley, 1995. Finds from the Fortress

    11 P. Walton Rogers, 1997. *Textile Production at 16–22 Coppergate*

    12 A. MacGregor, A.J. Mainman and N.S.H. Rogers, 1999. *Craft, Industry and Everyday Life: Bone, Antler, Ivory and Horn from Anglo-Scandinavian York*

    13 C.A. Morris, 2000. *Craft, Industry and Everyday Life: Wood and Woodworking in Anglo-Scandinavian and Medieval York*

    – P.J. Ottaway and N.S.H. Rogers, in prep. *Craft, Industry and Everyday Life: Medieval Finds from York*

    – I. Carlisle, Q. Mould and E. Cameron, in prep. *Craft, Industry and Everyday Life: Leather and Leather-working in Anglo-Scandinavian and Medieval York*

18 *The Coins:*

    1 E. Pirie, 1986. *Post-Roman Coins from York Excavations 1971–81*

Barrow, G., Hinxman, L.W. and Craig, E.H.C., 1913. *The Geology of Upper Strathspey, Gaick and the Forest of Atholl. Memoirs of the Geological Survey, Scotland* (Edinburgh)

Batey, C., 1988. 'A Viking-Age Bell from Freswick Links, Caithness', *Medieval Archaeol.* **32**, 213–16

Baumgartner, E. and Kreuger, I., 1988. *Phoenix aus Sand und Asche: Glas des Mittelalters* (Munich)

Bayley, J., 1979. 'The glassworking residues' in C.M. Heighway et al., 'Excavations at 1 Westgate Street, Gloucester, 1975', *Medieval Archaeol.* **23**, 201–4

—— 1985. 'Comment: the glass beads and ring' in R. Shoesmith, *Hereford City Excavations Volume 3: The Finds*, Counc. Brit. Archaeol. Res. Rep. **56** (London), 24

—— forthcoming. 'Glassworking in Saxon England', in J. Price (ed.), *Glass in Britain and Ireland AD 350–1100*, Brit. Mus. Occ. Paper (London)

Bayley, J. and Doonan, R., 1999. *The high-lead glass from 16–22 Coppergate* AM Lab. Rep. 74/99

Bellamy, V., 1965. 'Excavations at Pontefract Priory 1957–1961', *Publications of the the Thoresby Society* **49**, 1–39

Beresford, G., 1987. *Goltho: The Development of an Early Medieval Manor c.850–1150* (London)

Bersu, G. and Wilson, D.M., 1966. *Three Viking Graves in the Isle of Man*, Soc. for Medieval Archaeol. Monogr. Series **1** (London)

Biddle, M. (ed.), 1990a. *Object and Economy in Medieval Winchester*, Winchester Studies **7** (2 vols) (Oxford)

—— 1990b. 'Tweezers' in Biddle 1990a, ii, 690–2

—— 1990c. 'Weights and Measures' in Biddle 1990a, ii, 908–28

Beck, C. and Shennan, S., 1991. *Amber in Prehistoric Britain*, Oxbow Monogr. **8** (Oxford)

Botfeldt, K. and Brinch Madsen, H., 1991. 'The Amber' in M. Bencard, L. Bender Jorgensen and H. Brinch Madsen (eds.) 1991, *Ribe Excavations 1970–76*, **3** (Esbjerg)

Bu'lock, J.D., 1960. 'The Celtic, Saxon and Scandinavian settlement at Meols in the Wirral', *Trans. Hist. Soc. of Lancashire and Cheshire* **112**, 1–28

—— 1972. *Pre-Conquest Cheshire 383–1066* (Chester)

Callmer, J., 1977. *Trade Beads and Bead Trade in Scandinavia c.800–1000 AD*, Acta Archaeologica Lundensia Ser. **40**/!1 (Malmö)

—— 1989. 'Gegossene Schmuckanhänger mit nordischer Ornamentik' in Arwidsson 1989, 19–42

Capelle, T., 1976. *Die frühgeschichtlichen Metallfunde von Domburg auf Walcheren 2*, Nederlandse Oudheden **5** (Amersfoort)

Charleston, R.J., 1990. 'Glass rings' in Biddle 1990a, ii, 652–3

Christensen, A.E., 1970. 'Klåstad skipet', *Nicolay* **8**, 21–4

Clarke C.H.M., 1976. 'Notes for the Guidance of Excavation Supervisors and Finds Supervisors', YAT (unpublished)

Craig, G.Y. (ed.), 1991. *Geology of Scotland* (London).

Cramp, R., 1969. 'Excavations at the Saxon monastic sites of Wearmouth and Jarrow, Co. Durham: an interim report', *Medieval Archaeol.* **13**, 21–66

Crosby, D.D.B. and Mitchell, J.G., 1987. 'A survey of British metamorphic hone stones of the 9th to 15th centuries AD in the light of potassium-argon and natural remanent magnetization studies', *J. Archaeol. Sci.* **14**, 483–506

Crummy, N., 1983. *The Roman Small Finds from Excavations in Colchester 1971–9*, Colchester Archaeol. Rep. **2** (Colchester)

Curle, C., 1982. *Pictish and Norse Finds from the Brough of Birsay 1934–74*, Soc. Antiq. Scotland Monogr. Ser. **1** (Edinburgh)

Daniels, R., 1990. 'The development of medieval Hartlepool: excavations at Church Close, 1984–85', *Archaeol. J.* **147**, 337–410

Davis, M., 1993. 'The Identification of Various Jet and Jet-like Materials Used in the Early Bronze Age in Scotland', *The Conservator* **17**, 11–18

Dekówna, M., 1990. 'Unterschungen an Glasfunden aus Haithabu', *Berichte über die Ausgrabungen in Haithabu* **27**, 9–63

Dickinson, T.M., 1973. 'Hooked tags' in A.C.C. Brodribb, D.R. Hands and A.R. Walker (eds.), *Excavations at Shakenoak Farm, near Wilcote, Oxfordshire: Part IV, Site C* (Oxford), 116–17

Dolley, M., 1971. 'The nummular brooch from Sulgrave' in P. Clemoes and K. Hughes (eds.), 1971. *England before the Conquest* (Cambridge), 333–49

Drinkall, R. and Stevenson, J., 1996. 'Weighing it all up', *London Archaeologist* **8/1**, 3–9

Duncan, S. and Ganiaris, H., 1987. 'Some sulphide corrosion products on copper alloys and lead alloys from London waterfront sites' in J. Black (ed.), *Recent Advances in the Conservation and Analysis of Artefacts*, 109–118 (London)

Durham, B., 1977. 'Archaeological investigations in St Aldate's, Oxford', *Oxoniensia* **42**, 83–203

Earwood, C., 1993. *Domestic Wooden Artefacts in Britain and Ireland from Neolithic to Viking Times* (Exeter)

Egan, G. and Pritchard, F., 1991. *Dress Accessories c.1150–c.1450; Medieval Finds from Excavations in London* **3** (London)

Ellis, S.E., 1969. 'The petrography and provenance of Anglo-Saxon and medieval English hone stones, with notes on some other hones', *Bull. Brit. Mus. Nat. Hist. (Mineralogy Series)* **2/3**, 9–187

Fanning, T., 1983a. 'The Hiberno-Norse pins from the Isle of Man' in C. Fell, P. Foote, J. Graham-Campbell and R. Thomson (eds.), *The Viking Age in the Isle of Man, Select Papers from the Ninth Viking Congress* (London), 27–36

—— 1983b. 'Some aspects of the bronze ringed-pin in Scotland' in A. O'Connor and D. Clarke (eds.), *From the Stone Age to the 'Forty-five* (Edinburgh), 324–42

—— 1994. *Viking Age Ringed-Pins from Dublin* (Dublin)

Follet, T., 1985. 'Amber in Goldworking', *Archaeology* **38/2**, 64–5

Foreman, M., 1991a. 'The Lead and Lead Alloy' in Armstrong et al. 1991, 155–63

—— 1991. 'Stone objects' in Armstrong et al. 1991, 122–32

Fraenkel-Schoorl, N., 1978. 'Carolingian Jewellery with Plant Ornament', *Berichten van de Rijksdienst voor het Oudheidkundig Bodemonderzoek* **28**, 346–97

Frandsen, L.B. and Jensen, S., 1987. 'Pre-Viking and Early Viking Age Ribe. Excavations at Nicoljgade 8, 1985–86', *J. Danish Archaeol.* **6**, 175–89

Fraquet, H., 1987. *Amber* (London)

Gettens, R.J. and Stout, G.L., 1966. *Painting Materials: A Short Encyclopaedia* (Dover)

Gilmour, L.A., 1988. *Early Medieval Pottery from Flaxengate, Lincoln*, Archaeol. Lincoln **17/2** (London)

Goodall, A., 1984. 'Non-ferrous metal objects' in Rogerson and Dallas 1984, 68–75

Goodall, I.H., 1990. 'Bridle-bits and associated strap-fittings' in Biddle 1990a, ii, 1043–6

—— 1991. 'The Iron' in Armstrong et al. 1991, 131–46

Graham-Campbell, J., 1980a. *Viking Artefacts* (London)

—— 1980b. *The Viking World* (London)

—— 1986. 'A late Celtic enamelled mount from Galson, Isle of Lewis', *Proc. Soc. Antiq. Scot.* **116**, 281–4

Graham-Campbell, J. and Okasha, E., 1991. 'A pair of inscribed Anglo-Saxon hooked tags from the Rome (Forum) 1883 hoard', *Anglo-Saxon England* **20**, 221–9

Grieg, S., 1940. 'Viking Antiquities in Scotland' in H. Shetelig (ed.), *Viking Antiquities in Great Britain and Ireland* **2** (Oslo)

Guido, M., 1978. *The Glass Beads of the Prehistoric and Roman Periods in Britain and Ireland*, Rep. Res. Comm. Soc. Antiq. **35** (London)

Haldenby, D., 1990. 'An Anglian Site on the Yorkshire Wolds', *Yorks. Archaeol. J.* **62**, 51–63

—— 1992. 'An Anglian Site on the Yorkshire Wolds — Continued', *Yorks. Archaeol. J.* **66**, 25–39

—— 1994. 'Further Saxon Finds from the Yorkshire Wolds', *Yorks. Archaeol. J.* **68**, 51–8

Hall, R.A.H., 1984. *The Viking Dig* (London)

—— 1994. *Viking Age York* (London)

Hamerow, H., 1993. *Excavations at Mucking 2: The Anglo-Saxon Settlement*, English Heritage Archaeol. Rep. **21** (London)

Hamilton, J.R.C., 1956. *Excavations at Jarlshof, Shetland*, Ministry of Works Archaeol. Rep. **1** (Edinburgh)

Harden, D.B., 1956. 'Glass Vessels in Britain, A.D. 400–1000' in D.B. Harden (ed.), *Dark Age Britain* (London), 132–67

Hattatt, R., 1987. *Brooches of Antiquity. A Third Selection from the Author's Collection* (Oxford)

Henderson, J., 1991. 'The Glass' in Armstrong et al. 1991, 124–30

Heslop, D.H., 1995. 'Excavation within the church at the Augustinian Priory of Guisborough, Cleveland, 1985–6', *Yorkshire Archaeol. J.* **67**, 51–126

Hinton, D.A., 1990a. 'Relief-decorated strap-ends' in Biddle 1990a, ii, 494–500

—— 1990b. 'Hooked tags' in Biddle 1990a, ii, 548–52

—— 1996. *The Gold, Silver and other Non-Ferrous Alloy Objects from Hamwic, and the Non-Ferrous Metalworking Evidence*, Southampton Finds **2** (Southampton)

Holdsworth, P., 1987. *Excavations in Medieval Perth 1979–1981*, Soc. Antiq. Scot. Monogr. Series **5** (Edinburgh)

Holgate, B., 1987. *Pagan Lady of Peel* (Isle of Man)

Hunter, F.C., McDonnell, J.G., Pollard, A.M., Morris, C.R. and Rowlands, C.C., 1993. 'The Scientific Identification of Archaeological Jet-Like Artefacts', *Archaeometry* **35/1**

Hunter K.P.M., 1980. (unpublished) *A Study to Determine the Possibility of Testing Archaeological Soils for Factors Influencing the Preservation of Artefacts*, Ph.D. thesis, University of Durham

Jackson, S., 1988. 'Copper alloy objects' in R. Daniels, 'The Anglo-Saxon monastery at Church Close, Hartlepool, Cleveland', *Archaeol. J.* **145**, 182

Johnstone, G.S. and Mykura, W., 1989. *The Northern Highlands of Scotland. British Regional Geology* (London)

Kisch, B., 1959. 'Weights and Scales in Medieval Scandinavia', *J. of the History of Medicine and Allied Sciences* **14**, 160–8

—— 1965. *Scales and Weights. A Historical Outline*, Yale Studies in the History of Science and Medicine **1** (Yale)

Kruse, S.E., 1992. 'Late Saxon Balances and Weights from England', *Medieval Archaeol.* **36**, 67–95

Lang, J., 1991. *A Corpus of Anglo-Saxon Sculpture 3: York and Eastern Yorkshire* (London)

Leahy, K., 1982. 'Two Late Saxon disc-brooches from South Humberside', *Archaeology in Lincolnshire and South Humberside* **18**, 107–8

Leeds, E.T., 1936. *Early Anglo-Saxon Art and Archaeology* (Oxford)

Lund, L., 1993. (unpublished) *Hulglas på markedspladsen Ribe, år 700 til 850*, Aarhus University

Lundström, A., 1976. 'Bead Making in Scandinavia in the Early Middle Ages', *Kungl. Vitterhets Historie och Antikvitets Akademien: Antikvarisk Arkiv* **61** (Stockholm)

—— 1981. 'Survey of the glass from Helgö' in A. Lundström and H. Clarke (eds.), *Excavations at Helgö* **7** (Stockholm), 1–38

Lynn, C.J., 1984. 'Some fragments of exotic porphyry found in Ireland', *J. Irish Archaeol* **2**, 19–32

MacGregor, A., 1978. 'Industry and commerce in Anglo-Scandinavian York' in R.A. Hall (ed.), *Viking Age York and the North*, Couc. Brit. Archaeol. Res. Rep. **27**, 37–57

Mann, J.E., 1982. *Early Medieval Finds from Flaxengate 1: Objects of Antler, Bone, Stone, Horn, Ivory, Amber and Jet*, The Archaeology of Lincoln **17/1**

Margeson, S., 1993. *Norwich Households: The Medieval and Post-Medieval Finds from Norwich Survey Excavations 1971–8*, E. Anglian Archaeol. Rep. **58** (Norwich)

—— 1995. 'The Non-Ferrous Metal Objects' in A. Rogerson, *A Late Neolithic, Saxon and Medieval Site at Middle*

Harling, Norfolk, E. Anglian Archaeol. Rep. **74** (Gressenhall), 53–68

—— 1996. 'Viking Settlement in Norfolk: a Study of New Evidence' in S. Margeson, B. Ayers and S. Heywood (eds.), *A Festival of Norfolk Archaeology* (Gressenhall), 47–57

—— 1997. *The Vikings in Norfolk*, Norfolk Museums Service (Norwich)

Meaney, A.L., 1970. 'The Winnall II cemetery: grave-goods (A)' in Meaney and Hawkes 1970, 33–9

Meaney, A.L. and Hawkes, S.C., 1970. *Two Anglo-Saxon Cemeteries at Winnall, Winchester, Hampshire*, Soc. Medieval Archaeol. Monogr. Ser. **4** (London)

Merrifield, M.P., 1967. *Original Treatises on the Arts of Painting* (New York)

Mitchell, J.G., Askvik, H. and Resi, H.G., 1984. 'Potassium-argon ages of schist honestones from the Viking age sites at Kaupang (Norway), Aggersborg (Denmark), Hedeby (West Germany) and Wolin (Poland), and their archaeological implications', *J. Archaeol. Sci.* **11**, 171–6

Molander, M., 1976. 'Redskap för handel' in A.W. Mårtensson (ed.), *Uppgrävt förflutet för Pkbanken i(n) Lund*, Archaeol. Lundensia **7**, 187–98

Moore, D.T., 1978. 'The petrography and archaeology of English honestones', *J. Archaeol. Sci.* **5**, 61–73

—— 1983. 'Petrological aspects of some sharpening stones, touchstones, and milling stones' in D.R.C Kempe and A.P. Harvey, *The Petrology of Archaeological Artefacts* (Oxford), 277–300

Mortimer, C., 1995. 'Glass linen smoothers from 16–22 Coppergate, York', *Ancient Monuments Laboratory Report* **22/95**

Muller, H., 1987. *Jet* (London)

Müller-Wille, M., 1973. 'Eisengeräte aus Haithabu (Ausgrabung 1963–64)' in Schietzel 1973, 23–38

Murdoch, T., 1991. *Treasures and Trinkets: Jewellery in London from pre-Roman Times to the 1930s* (London)

Newton, R. and Davison, S., 1989. *Conservation of Glass* (London)

Oakley, G.E. and Hall, A.D., 1979. 'The spindle whorls' in J.H. Williams, *St Peter's Street Northampton: Excavations 1973–1976* (Northampton), 286–9

Ó Floinn, R., 1989. 'Secular metalwork in the eighth and ninth centuries' in Youngs 1989, 72–124

O'Kelly, M., 1965. 'The Belt-Shrine from Moylough, Sligo', *J. Royal Soc. of Antiq. Irel.* **95**, 149–88

Parkhouse, J., 1976. ' The Dorestad quernstones', *Berichten van de Rijksdienst voor het Oudheidkundig Bodemonderzoek* **26**, 181–6

Peers, C. and Radford, C.A.R., 1943. 'The Saxon Monastery at Whitby', *Archaeologia* **89**, 27–88

Petersen, J., 1928. *Vikingetidens Smykker* (Stavanger)

—— 1951. *Vikingtidens redskaper, Skrifter utgitt av Det Norske Vitenskapsakademi ì Oslo*, Hist. Fil. Kl. **1951/4** (Oslo)

Pliny the Younger (trans. W.H.S. Johnson, 1951), *Natural History* (Cambridge)

Pritchard, F., 1991. 'Small Finds' in A. Vince (ed.), *Aspects of Saxo-Norman London 2: Finds and Environmental Evidence*, London and Middlesex Archaeol. Soc. Spec. Pap. **12**, 143–278

—— 1984. 'Late Saxon textiles from the city of London', *Medieval Archaeol.* **28**, 46–76

Radley, J., 1971. 'Economic aspects of Anglo-Danish York', *Medieval Archaeol.* **15**, 37–58

Richards, J., 1991. *Viking Age England* (London)

Richardson, C., 1993. (unpublished) *The Borre Style in the British Isles and Ireland: A Re-assessment*, M.Litt. thesis, University of Newcastle

Roes, A., 1963. *Bone and Antler Objects from the Frisian Terp-Mounds* (Haarlem)

Roes, A., 1965. *Vondsten van Dorestad*, Archaeologica Traiectina **7** (Groningen)

Roesdahl, E., Graham-Campbell, J., Connor, P. and Pearson, K. (eds.), 1981. *The Vikings in England and in their Danish Homeland* (London)

Roesdahl, E. and Wilson, D. (eds.), 1992. *From Viking to Crusader. The Scandinavians and Europe 800–1200* (London)

Rogerson, A. and Dallas, C., 1984. *Excavations in Thetford, 1948–59 and 1973–80*, E. Anglian Archaeol. Rep. **22** (Gressenhall)

Rogers, NS.H., forthcoming. 'Metal Finds' in C. Loveluck (ed.), *Flixborough: A HIgh-Status Middle to Late Saxon Settlement in North Lincolnshire AD 600–1000*

Ryan, M., 1989. 'Church metalwork in the eighth and ninth centuries' in Youngs 1989, 125–69

Sanderson, D.C.W. and Hutchings, J.B., 1987. 'The origins and measurement of colour in archaeological glasses', *Glass Technology* **28**, 99–105

Scull, C., 1990. 'Scales and Weights in Early Anglo-Saxon England', *Archaeol. J.* **147**, 183–215

Schietzel, K. (ed.), 1973. *Das archäologische Fundmaterial II der Ausgrabung Haithabu*, Berichte über die Ausgrabungen in Haithabu **6** (Neumünster)

Smedley, N. and Owles, E., 1965. 'Some Anglo-Saxon "Animal"-Brooches', *Proc. Suffolk Instit. for Archaeol.* **30**, 166–74

Spriggs, J.A., 1980. 'The Recovery and Storage of Materials from Waterlogged Deposits at York' *The Conservator* **4**, 19–24

Stiff, M.J.H., 1996. (unpublished) 'Through a glass darkly': 7th–9th Century Vessel Glass from 'Wics' and 'Emporia' in North Western Europe, D.Phil. thesis, University of Oxford

—— forthcoming. *Glass finds from the Royal Opera House Site*, Mus. of London Archaeol. Service

Taylor, D.B., 1982. 'Excavation of a promontory fort, broch and souterrain at Hurly Hawkin, Angus', *Proc. Soc. Antiq. Scot.* **112**, 215–53

Theophilus (trans. J.G. Hawthorne and C.S. Smith 1979). *On Divers Arts* (New York)

Thomas, G., forthcoming. *Late Anglo-Saxon Strap-ends*, Ph.D. thesis, Institute of Archaeology, London

Trewin, N.H., 1982. 'Stone objects' in J.C. Murray, *Excavations in the Medieval Burgh of Aberdeen 1973–81*, Soc. Antiq. Scot. Monogr. Series **2**, 184–5

Tweddle, D., 1983. 'The Weight of the Evidence', *Interim: Archaeology in York* **9/2**, 24–5

—— 1991. 'Brooches' in Armstrong et al.1991, 155–6

Tyson, R., 1996. *Medieval High-lead Glass Table Vessels*, Finds Research Group Datasheet **21**

Ullrich, D.G., 1989. 'Halbedelstein und Glasfunde' in A. von Müller and K. von Müller-Muci, *Ausgrabungen, Funde und Naturwissenschaftliche untersuchungen auf der Burgwall in Berlin-Spandau*, Berliner Beiträge zur Vor- und Frühgeschichte **6**, 57–99

Wallace, P.F., 1987. 'The Economy and Commerce of Viking Age Dublin', in K. Dirvel et al. (eds.), *Unterschungen zu Handel und Verkehr der Vor-und Frühgeschichtlichen* **4** (Gottingen), 200–45

—— 1998. 'Line Fishing in Viking Dublin: A Contemporary Explanation for archaeological evidence' in C. Manning (ed.), *Dublin and Beyond the Pale: Studies in Honour of Patrick Healey* (Co. Wicklow), 3–15

Wamers, E., 1985. *Insularer Metallschmuck in wikingerzeitlichen Gräbern Nordeuropas* (Neumünster)

—— 1994. *Die Frühmittelalterlichen Lesefunde Aus Der Löhrstrasse (Baustelle Hilton II) in Mainz* (Mainz)

Waterman, D., 1959. 'Late Saxon, Viking and Early Medieval finds from York', *Archaeologia* **97**, 59–105

Way, A., 1847. *Catalogue of Antiquities, Coins, Pictures and Miscellaneous Curiosities, in the possession of the Society of Antiquaries of London* (London)

Webster, L., 1984. 'Metalwork and Sculpture' in J. Backhouse, D.H. Turner and L. Webster (eds.), *The Golden Age of Anglo-Saxon Art 966–1066* (London), 89–112

Webster, L. and Backhouse, J., 1991. *The Making of England. Anglo-Saxon Art and Culture 600–900* (London)

Welander, R.D.E, Batey, C. and Cowie, T.G., 1987. 'A Viking Burial from Kneep, Uig, Isle of Lewis', *Proc. Soc. Antiq. Scot.* **117**, 149–74

Whitfield, N., 1997a. 'Filigree Animal Ornament from Ireland and Scotland of the Late Seventh to Ninth centuries' in C.E. Karkov, M. Ryan and R.T. Farrell (eds.), *The Insular Tradition* (New York), 211–43

—— 1997b. 'The Waterford kite-brooch and its place in Irish metalwork' in M.F. Hurley and O.M.B. Scully, *Late Viking Age and Medieval Waterford: Excavations 1982–92* (Dublin), 490–517

—— forthcoming. 'A gold filigree panel from an Irish crannog at Alnwick Castle, Northumberland' in M. Timorey (ed.), *A Celebration of Sligo*

Williams, V., 1994. 'Non-Ferrous Metal Objects' in B.S. Ayers, *Excavations at Fishergate, Norwich, 1985*, E. Anglian Archaeol. Rep. **68**, 14

Wilson, D.M. and Blunt, C.E., 1961. 'The Trewhiddle hoard', *Archaeologia* **98**, 75–122

Wilson, D.M., 1964. *Anglo-Saxon Ornamental Metalwork 700–1100 in the British Museum* (London)

—— 1973. 'The treasure' in A. Small, C. Thomas and D.M. Wilson, *St Ninian's Isle and its Treasure* (2 vols.), Aberdeen University Studies **152** (Oxford), 45–148

Winfield-Smith, R., 1957. 'New finds of ancient glass in North Africa', *Ars Orientalis* **2**, 91–117

Woodland, M., 1990. 'Spindle whorls' in Biddle 1990a, i, 216–25

Youngs, S. (ed.), 1989. *The Work of Angels. Masterpieces of Celtic Metalwork, 6th–9th Centuries A.D.* (London)

Ypey, J., 1964. 'Die Funde aus dem frühmittelalterlichen Gräberfeld Huinerveld bei Putten im useum Nairac in Barneveld', *Berichten van de rijkdienst voor het oudheidkundig bodemonderzoek*, 12–13, 99–151

Index

By Susanne Atkin

Page numbers in *italics* refer to illustrations. Street locations are in York (see map on p.2606).